Never before has an outsider had such access to record the remarkable history of the provisional IRA and Sinn Fein, the 'Provos', from their dramatic beginnings to the critical juncture they have reached today – on the brink of becoming part of the cabinet in the new government of Northern Ireland. It is an astonishing story.

Thirty years ago, the Irish Republican Army was a fading historical memory. It had dumped its guns and embraced extreme left-wing politics. The result was that when sectarian violence erupted in 1969 and nationalist areas came under loyalist attack, only a handful of IRA veterans were on hand to defend them. Taunting graffiti read 'IRA – I ran away'. The consequences were momentous. The IRA split and the Provisional IRA was born to become the most formidable organisation of its kind in the Western world. For more than a quarter of a century the Provisionals have fought a bloody campaign, in which over 3,000 lives have been lost, to force the British government to disengage from Northern Ireland and re-unify Ireland.

Today their leaders, once branded as 'terrorists', have been feted at the White House and become regular visitors to Downing Street. Gerry Adams and Martin McGuinness are now Westminister Members of Parliament, steering the 'Provos' to acceptance of the historic Good Friday peace Agreement which they believe will be the stepping stone to the United Ireland they and their followers have fought and died for. In a series of remarkable, first-hand interviews with the Provisionals who fought on the military and political fronts and the British who countered them, *Provos* tells the extraordinary story of the evolution of the Provisional IRA and Sinn Fein over 30 bloody years, from gunmen and bombers to potential statesmen. With IRA and loyalist ceasefires and the Good Friday Agreement in place, are we now about to see the final resolution of one of the world's most ancient conflicts?

PROVOS

The IRA and Sinn Fein

Peter Taylor

BLOOMSBURY

To Susan, Ben, Sam
Emmeline and Bob

First Published 1997
This paperback edition published 1998

Bloomsbury Publishing Plc
38 Soho Square
London, W1V 5DF

Copyright © by Peter Taylor 1997

The moral right of the author has been asserted

A copy of the CIP entry for this book
is available from the British Library

ISBN 0 7475 3818 2

10 9 8 7

Typeset by Hewer Text Ltd, Edinburgh
Printed in Great Britain by
Clays Ltd, St Ives plc

Contents

Acknowledgements

Provos has been a long journey. It began more than twenty-five years ago in 1972 when I went to Northern Ireland for the first time on 'Bloody Sunday'. I was shocked by what happened, and concerned to understand the historical forces that drove the various parties to the conflict to act as they did. As we stand on the brink of the implementation of the Good Friday Agreement, there is now the real possibility of peace finally coming to Ireland and most of the guns falling silent. How and why the 'Provos' have reached this stage – accepting historic compromises whilst not setting aside their goal of a united Ireland – is the theme of this remarkable and tragic story.

I could not have written this book without the considerable assistance given to me by Sinn Fein. I am grateful to all those in Sinn Fein who made it possible and all those party members and former prisoners who agreed to be interviewed – including other republicans too. I hope these interviews will contribute to greater understanding, which is the purpose of this book and the BBC television series on which it is based. I must thank too all those on the British and Irish sides – and in America – who gave me interviews and the benefit of their experience. There are many, too, who spoke to me off the record about critical events and their role in them. They know who they are and I am grateful to them.

Special thanks must go to all those who worked with me on the BBC series: to my producer, Andrew Williams, who toiled away in a sunless cutting room putting the series together whilst I worked away at a laptop; to Steve Hewlett who executive produced the programme and Mark Damazer who steered them through – all three were generously understanding of the time needed to write the book and make the series; to Pat Loughrey, Controller BBC Northern Ireland, Keith Baker and their colleagues for their unfailing support and guidance and to June Gamble who produced endless, vital newspaper cuttings.; and to Judy Groves and Julia Hannis and all those in the office who were always prepared to go the extra mile.

I could not have wished for a better and more supportive publisher than Bloomsbury. Alan Wherry, who commissioned *Provos*, was tirelessly enthusiastic in his support; Kate Morris was a meticulous editor of the manuscript and incredibly patient of my ever-slipping deadline; Kate Bouverie was a brilliant and speedy copy editor; and Ben Evans was a diligent pursuer of pictures. Thanks also to Peter Denton, a former colleague on *This Week*, for 'surfing the Net'. I am enormously grateful to them all.

Above all, thanks to my family, Sue, Ben and Sam, for all their love, support and advice during a testing period: for reminding me of my priorities and for putting up with my late arrival on holiday. I hope they and all those who helped make *Provos* possible, feel it has been worth it.

I have written two additional chapters for this paperback that cover the dramatic events from Sinn Fein's admission to all party talks in September 1997 to the historic votes in the North/South referenda that gave overwhelming support for the Good Friday Agreement. It is a critical period for the Republican Movement that saw a challenge to its leadership from a splinter group claiming to be the 'true' IRA and an astonishing constitutional change by Sinn Fein (authorised by the IRA), permitting its members to take seats in the new, partitionist Northern Ireland Assembly. The political and military currents moved at such dizzying speed that they often seemed unreal. Although the months were marked with continuing bloodshed as both republican and loyalist splinter groups carried on killing in the hope of destroying the peace process, it is a period that ends in hope. Nevertheless, I doubt whether this is the end of the story.

Prologue

America

In 1981, following the slow and agonizing deaths of ten men during the IRA hunger strike at the Maze prison in Belfast, recruits flocked to the 'Provos', determined to strike back at the government of the British Prime Minister, Margaret Thatcher, whom they accused of murdering their comrades. Now more than ever, the IRA needed not only guns to arm the hundreds of new Volunteers but also heavy weaponry to upgrade its capability and take on the British army. It was to America that the IRA's General Headquarters' Staff (GHQ) – the people who run the IRA's 'war' – turned for help. Across the Atlantic, the IRA's arms-buying network was overhauled and streamlined. A senior IRA figure came over from Ireland and told veteran arms supplier, George Harrison, that he was being stood down. Harrison had been diligent in his job. Throughout the seventies, he had shipped over 2,500 weapons and a million rounds of ammunition to Ireland. The US Federal Bureau of Investigation (FBI) believe that this figure is a 'conservative estimate'.

Harrison was telephoned and told, to his dismay, that 'Skinny Legs' would be taking over. 'Skinny Legs' was Gabriel Megahey, a Belfast republican who had joined the IRA after the upheavals of August 1969 and had later gone to England and taken a job in Southampton. He was now being sent to America to put George Harrison out of business. I met Megahey in New York, where he is currently fighting deportation, and asked him what his role had been. 'The Federal Government would deem me to have been the Officer Commanding (OC) of America and Canada.' I asked him if this was true but he would not elaborate. 'That's what they have on record.'

My job at that time was to do something to save the hunger strikers. We had men dying and I felt it was a moral duty to do something about it. Specifically, I knew Brendan Hughes very well. [Hughes was on hunger strike for fifty-three days.] I'd been a good friend of his for many years and it hurt me deeply that Brendan was lying on a death bed.

What Megahey did not know was that the FBI knew he was coming. In the wake of the IRA's assassination of Lord Mountbatten and the killing of eighteen British soldiers at Warrenpoint on the same day in 1979, the FBI had reorganized to combat the growing threat from the IRA's arms procurement operations in America. The British were delighted that at long last the United States Government, now under President Reagan, had grasped the fact that much of the blood being spilled on Irish soil was the result of American arms and money. In May 1980, an FBI 'PIRA Squad' (Provisional IRA) was set up in New York under Agent Lou Stephens, a veteran of anti-IRA operations in the seventies. At its height, Lou Stephens' 'PIRA Squad' was running around half a dozen wire taps on key IRA suspects. One of them was on George Harrison's phone.

At first the FBI did not know who 'Skinny Legs' was. It was only some time later, whilst carrying out surveillance on another IRA suspect's house on a hot summer's day that they saw the suspect talking to a man on the veranda in shorts, who had 'very thin legs'. Stephens and his unit put two and two together, got in touch with their British counterparts, and found that Gabriel Megahey emerged from the files. Megahey was placed under FBI surveillance. To Stephens and his team, he became known as 'Panicky' because he was clearly so surveillance conscious. Another suspect, Gerry McGeough, then appeared in the frame. McGeough came from County Tyrone, had joined the Provisional IRA in 1975, been active during the hunger strike and then gone on the run following an alleged murder attempt on an off-duty part-time soldier who was working as a postman. It was decided that McGeough's considerable talents as an IRA Volunteer would best be used in America so he was sent over to join Megahey's arms procurement operation. 'The hunger strike had the effect of re-awakening an Irish American giant,' he told me. 'An Anglophobic one.'

> Irish America fulfilled certain functions. They supplied guns, weapons, war material and financial and moral support. It was obvious to me personally that if we were going to prosecute a war, we would have to have the right weaponry with which to do it and I saw my role as helping to get that in place.

McGeough started work in Florida, travelling the state with a young American woman whose driving licence was used to buy dozens of sophisticated assault rifles from gun shops and arms dealers. Buying weapons across the counter in America posed no problem as all citizens have the constitutional right to bear arms and McGeough had the ready cash to pay for them. They were smuggled on board a Greyhound bus and driven to the North-Eastern seaboard for shipment to Ireland by IRA sympathizers who worked in the docks and elsewhere. I asked McGeough what sort of quantities he was assembling. He said the last consignment consisted of 'somewhere in the region of maybe forty or fifty weapons, that's Armalite AR 15 assault rifles, Heckler and Koch HK 91s'. McGeough ensured that the arsenal reached New York docks. Impressed by McGeough's cool efficiency, Megahey asked him to supervise the most important arms procurement operation ever undertaken by the IRA in America. Word had come from a senior IRA figure at GHQ, who today is believed to be one of the most uncompromising members of the IRA's ruling Army Council, that the men on the ground, in particular in operational areas like South Armagh, needed missiles to shoot down British army helicopters and deny the enemy their dominance of the skies. Megahey needed to be told no more.

> We felt that if we could nullify the helicopter, we would be well on the way to winning the war. A surface to air missile (SAM) or a Red-Eye missile will zero in on the heat of the helicopter motor and bring it down and you don't need too much knowledge to know how to use it. Gerry McGeough's role was to acquire the missiles, do the negotiations and basically to oversee with me the whole operation in America.

McGeough was enthusiastic.

> Taking out British army helicopters would have worked wonders for morale and boosted our ability to prosecute the war on a wider level. It would also have had a corresponding effect on the British, not just operationally but in terms of undermining their morale and weakening their resolve.

Megahey and McGeough were no strangers to the shady world of arms dealing. The missiles they sought were there to be had if they made the right contacts. At the time, with wars raging in Nicaragua and Honduras in Central America, some of which were financed and supported by America's Central Intelligence Agency (CIA), any weapon could be had with no questions asked if the buyers were prepared to pay the right price.

Megahey says he had $80,000 on hand to finance the missile deal. Neither man was surprised to be told that negotiations had to be conducted in New Orleans, a jumping-off point for the arms supply route to Latin

America. Megahey told McGeough to check that missiles were on offer. The rendezvous was a shabby office on the upper floor of a waterfront warehouse in New Orleans. Megahey had told McGeough to observe, say nothing and let the man who went with him do all the talking. In the room were a group of men, some obviously Latinos, others 'regular Americans'. The two IRA men were asked who they were and what they wanted. 'D'ye ever hear tell of the Provisionals?' asked McGeough's accomplice. 'Well, that's who we are. What we want are SAM missiles.' Did they have the money? Yes. How many did they want? Five. At $10,000 each that would be $50,000 altogether. The deal was agreed and another meeting arranged for two weeks later at a New York hotel, when details were to be finalized. McGeough then reported back to Megahey.

> Gerry felt that it was 'a go' and that it was what it seemed to be. We just had to come up with the money.

Megahey decided to go to the meeting himself to make sure the IRA was not being ripped off and there were no hitches. The meeting was held in a room at the St Regis hotel. This time, only one arms dealer was present, whom Megahey assumed to be the arms' network's 'Mr Big'. Megahey introduced himself as the IRA's 'Number One man in the USA' and was surprised to find that before business began, he was given an intensive interrogation by the arms supplier. 'Panicky's suspicions were aroused when the man said delivery of the missiles would be handled by the dealers. Megahey would have none of it. 'You're gone. The truck's hit. Money's gone. Missiles gone. I'm gone. The only one to lose is us.' Megahey suggested that they both offer themselves as hostages to secure the deal. 'I myself will personally go as the hostage,' he said. 'Wherever you want. I'll sit with whoever you want me to sit with. If I'm going to gaol, somebody's going down the hole. I know one thing for sure, if any of my men get nicked, you're dead!' But Megahey also offered a sweetener. 'What we're dealing with here moneywise is chicken shit,' he said. 'If this goes OK, then we're prepared to come in with a lotta big money.' It seemed the missiles were almost home and dry and Megahey and McGeough had pulled off the most sensational arms deal in the IRA's history.

Gabriel Megahey left home at ten o'clock on the morning of 21 June 1982 to begin work on a construction site in Manhattan where he worked as a crane and elevator operator. As he walked off the site, the FBI swooped. 'Federal agents threw me over a car with a barrage of guns in my ears and took me down to the FBI's Central Headquarters.' It was the culmination of the PIRA Units' 'Operation Hit and Win'. The arms consignment at

New York docks that Gerry McGeough had helped put together was also hit to reveal around sixty high velocity rifles and dozens of timer devices destined for the IRA's bombs, which enabled them to be triggered up to a mile away. 'It was better than sex,' remembers Agent Lou Stephens. 'Three times better. We really saved a lot of lives.' Megahey was sentenced to seven years. The evidence was incontrovertible. The FBI had secretly videoed the meetings in New Orleans and New York. The arms dealers were FBI agents posing as gun runners. Stephens had even ordered the missiles from the US Marine Corps who had said 'hell, yes' to the proposition and sent the missiles to the Brooklyn Navy Yard. He made the request with strict orders to de-activate them first. But Gerry McGeough escaped the FBI's net, and went on the run in America before returning to Ireland and the 'war'. He was due to return to Northern Ireland when it was decided that his talents, proven even more in America, would be better employed in Europe where the IRA was about to reopen the Third Front in its campaign. On 31 August 1988, McGeough was arrested on the Dutch–German border in a car in which two AK 47 assault rifles and three handguns were found. It was to be almost four years before his case was resolved, not by the German courts but by the American authorities who sought his extradition to stand trial for his gun-running activities. The German authorities suspended the case before a verdict was reached and agreed to hand him over. On return to the United States McGeough stood trial in Louisiana and was sentenced to three years. He was released in 1996 and returned to Ireland. I asked him if he had any regrets. He said he had none and had only fulfilled what he considered to be his 'patriotic duty'.

Chapter One

Origins

What drove intelligent young men like Gerry McGeough, who in any normal society would have become doctors, lawyers and teachers, to take up arms and be prepared to kill for the 'Provos'? There is no simple answer. Young men and women were driven by a variety of forces, from the history that set the framework of the state in which they lived, to the circumstances that conditioned the way they felt, thought and acted. These powerful forces exploded in a conflict that has lasted almost thirty years, claimed almost 3,300 lives and taxed the political skills of successive British, Irish and, more recently, American governments.

For Gerry McGeough it began on his grandmother's farm in 1966 when he was eight years old. It was a historic year for Ireland, the fiftieth anniversary of the 1916 Easter Rising in Dublin, an event commemorated by the Irish television network, RTE, with a powerful drama series, 'Insurrection'. It was emotional stuff, showing noble Irish patriots defying the might of the British Empire by seizing the GPO in Dublin, proclaiming the Irish Republic, free from British rule, and being executed by the British for their treason. Watching the film in his grandmother's border farmhouse, the young Gerry McGeough was mesmerized.

> Each evening we would be sitting riveted to granny's television watching what was going on. Then we were straight out the following morning and, instead of playing Cowboys and Indians or Cops and Robbers, we would immediately engage in our own version of Easter Week, which entailed storming our grandmother's hay shed and taking it over. It represented the GPO and here we were, a glorious little band of Irish rebels, holding out against the British Imperial hoards, armed with stick rifles and tin-can grenades.

From the age of eight, Gerry McGeough's ambition was to join the Irish Republican Army, the IRA. The events of the next decade made him even more determined to do so, as they did countless others who had no need of the influence of 'Insurrection'. The events themselves were powerful enough.

Whether we are British or Irish, nationalist or unionist, we are all prisoners of the history of our two islands. History teaches us lessons about what is and is not possible as well as having an uncanny habit of repeating itself. The past holds the key to our understanding of the present and illuminates what is realistic in any settlement and what is not. Difficult though it may be to believe given the endless spilling of blood, events of the past decade have slowly been moving towards a resolution of the conflict. This book is an endeavour to explain how and why that has happened and, critically, what the role of the 'Provos' has been in it.

There is, of course, a fundamental difference in narrating past and present. The body of this book consists of interviews with prime sources, those who have driven the Republican Movement, the term I use for convenience as the umbrella name for the IRA and Sinn Fein, through the past thirty turbulent years and those who have fought it on both the military and political fronts.[1] But there is a point at which prime sources run out. A few IRA veterans are still alive who fought through the forties, fifties and sixties and who went on to found the Provisional IRA at the end of 1969. But beyond them we have to rely on the writings, speeches and actions of their predecessors whose names and deeds are the lifeblood of republican history on which the 'Provos' still feed.

Where to begin? History has to start somewhere, in particular when there are still hopes – fuelled by the remarkable Good Friday Agreement (see Chapter 26) – that the conflict may be approaching its end. Does it begin in 1970 when the old IRA split and the 'Provos' were born? Or in 1969 when British troops marched into Belfast and Derry to prevent the slaughter of nationalists by loyalist mobs?[2] Or in 1968 when civil-rights marches first shook the state of Northern Ireland? Or with the Treaty in 1921 that partitioned Ireland? Or with Patrick Pearse's heroic stand at the GPO in Dublin in 1916? Or with the plantation of Ulster in the seventeenth century when Protestants first settled in the North-East corner of Ireland? Or, if you really want to go back to square one, in the twelfth century when King Henry II first set foot in Ireland and began the process of England's conquest and subjugation? Generally, the media has little time for background and context. Violence and confrontation are what it feeds off. Sound bites are easier to digest than analysis explaining why and how things happen. Peace only gets a look in when it breaks out or breaks up. Yet it is history that makes sense of it all. To understand the 'Provos', you have to look at where they came from and why.

I decided to start with 1916. British rule extended over all thirty-two counties of Ireland as it had done since the Act of Union of 1801. The Great War was at its height and the slaughter of the Somme was only months away. On Easter Monday, 24 April 1916, a handful of rebels seized the GPO in Dublin and proclaimed themselves to be the Provisional Government of the Irish Republic. They were led by Patrick Pearse, a nationalist schoolteacher, writer and poet, romantically obsessed by the notion of 'bloodshed as a sacrificing and cleansing thing' and James Connolly, a socialist revolutionary who had formed a 'Citizens Army'.

Dubliners that Easter must have been bemused to see a man in military uniform, whom they had never seen or heard of before, proclaim the 'Irish Republic' in front of the Post Office in O'Connell Street with the declaration that 'a sovereign, independent, Irish State [was] now in the course of being established by Irishmen in arms.' Above the Post Office flew the green and gold flag of the Irish Republic.[3] The small band that Pearse led was known as the 'Irish Volunteers' but their political philosophy was that of 'Sinn Fein' ('We Ourselves'), a separatist organization committed to Irish political and economic independence founded in 1905 by the Dublin journalist, Arthur Griffith. But by 1916 Sinn Fein was seen as an organization that had had its day, being practically confined to one branch in Dublin. Newspapers of the time disparagingly referred to the Easter Rising as the 'Sinn Fein Revolt'. Historically, Sinn Fein preceded the IRA and initially did not support the use of force – 'armed struggle' in contemporary jargon – to compel political change. But that was long ago.

Initially, the rebels were spat upon by Dubliners as they watched British troops reduce the Post Office and their city centre to rubble. Their reaction was not surprising since many of their sons had joined the British army to fight the Kaiser. But the planned countrywide insurrection never materialized. The leaders of the 'Sinn Fein Revolt' were arrested and stood trial before three judges of a British army court-martial. Their fate was never in any doubt. The rebels were believed to have had the active support of Germany, encouraged by the ancient adage that 'England's difficulty is Ireland's opportunity'. Their action was treason. In his speech from the dock, Pearse echoed the declarations of Wolfe Tone and Robert Emmet, Irish revolutionaries who had faced execution following their failed rebellions at the turn of the previous century.

'If you strike us down now, we shall rise again and renew the fight,' Pearse declared. 'You cannot conquer Ireland. You cannot extinguish the passion for Irish freedom. If our deed has not been sufficient to win freedom, then our children will win it by a better deed.'[4] Pearse's words were as prophetic as those of Tone and Emmett. Pearse, Connolly and thirteen of their colleagues were sentenced to death. Seven had been signatories to Pearse's Proclamation. That evening, at dinner, the President of the court-martial, General Blackadder, told his hostess, 'I have just done one of the hardest tasks I have ever had to do. I have had to condemn to death of one the finest characters I have ever come across. There must be something very wrong in the state of things that makes a man like that a Rebel.'[5] Pearse, Connolly and most of the ringleaders of the Rising faced a firing squad in the yard of Kilmainham Gaol. The executions, carried out over a period of two weeks, bestowed martyrdom upon the rebels and inspired Yeats' poem, 'Easter 1916', in which he famously declared that the Rising gave birth to 'a terrible beauty'. Seizing the Post Office had been a dramatic gesture that Pearse hoped would rekindle the spirit of Irish nationalism which had lain dormant for so long. He believed that the 'blood sacrifice' of a few would regenerate the national consciousness and lead, by force of Irish arms, to the eventual withdrawal of Britain from Ireland. Three years before the Rising, Pearse had written about 'The Coming Revolution':

> We must accustom ourselves to the thought of arms, to the sight of arms, to the use of arms . . . bloodshed is a cleansing and sanctifying thing, and the nation which regards it as the final horror has lost its manhood. There are many things more horrible than bloodshed; and slavery is one of them.[6]

The British Government, confronted by what it saw as a treacherous stab in the back in the midst of the titanic struggle against Germany, had no alternative other than to act as it did. But that action, as Pearse had willed and predicted, transformed Sinn Fein's fortunes and with them those of the embryo IRA. When war broke out in 1914, Sinn Fein was hardly a name on anyone's lips. The Easter Rising and the execution of its leaders changed all that. In the British general election of December 1918, a month after the end of the Great War, Sinn Fein swept to a stunning victory across Ireland. Of the 105 Irish seats that constituted the country's political representation at Westminster, Sinn Fein won seventy-three, legitimizing its claim that it now represented the majority of people on the island of Ireland. Unionists won twenty-six seats, all of them, bar three, in the northern, nine-county province of Ulster. The seeds of partition were sown. The newly elected Sinn Fein MPs refused to take their seats at Westminster, a 'foreign' parliament they did not recognize, and gathered in the Mansion House in Dublin. Here they declared themselves to be the 'Assembly of Ireland' – 'Dail Eireann' – and swore allegiance to the Irish Republic proclaimed at the GPO by Patrick Pearse barely two years before. Eamon de Valera, one of the leaders of the Rising who, along with Michael Collins, had survived, was elected President of what was now claimed to be the legitimate government of Ireland and its only lawful authority.

In 1919, the Irish Volunteers were officially constituted as the Irish Republican Army – the IRA. British forces in Ireland were now seen as an occupying army against whom the IRA was to wage war. Michael Collins, the IRA's Adjutant General, became its effective commander with the title of Director of Organization and Intelligence. Because Collins was also Minister of Finance in Dail Eireann, he was also the IRA's paymaster.

The first shots in what became known as the Anglo-Irish War were fired on 21 January 1919, the day Dail Eireann first met and officially declared an independent Irish Republic. Only twenty-six of the newly elected members were present. The rest were in British gaols, on the run or deported.[7] That day, an IRA unit shot dead two constables of the Royal Irish Constabulary (RIC), who were escorting a cart of explosives near a quarry at Soloheadbeg in County Tipperary. The RIC was the British-controlled police force who kept order throughout Ireland.[8] The attack provided the model for the IRA's 'flying columns' which under legendary commanders like Tom Barry from West Cork harassed the RIC and the 'Auxiliaries', a band of former British soldiers recruited in England and sent over to Ireland to help.

For almost two bloody years, from 1919 to 1921, Collins and the IRA waged a guerilla war against what were now regarded as the British forces of occupation. The British government of the day did not regard the conflict as a 'war' but as a criminal conspiracy to be countered by the police – in many ways reflecting what for years was the official attitude towards the current period of conflict. In the face of increasing IRA attacks and plummeting morale, many police officers left the RIC, leaving it depleted and vulnerable. In response, the government of the British Prime Minister, David Lloyd George, recruited a force that became known as the 'Black and Tans' to assist the beleaguered RIC whose stations in the south and west came under sustained IRA attack – a tactic replicated by the modern IRA in the North in the mid-1980s. The 'Tans', as they became notoriously known, were unemployed veterans of the Great War who took their name from their police/army uniforms of dark green, black and khaki. The force was raised in such a hurry that there was not time to provide them with proper uniforms. In March 1920 Lloyd George sent the 'Tans' to Ireland to make it 'a hell for rebels to live in'. This succeeded as they proceeded to 'terrorize the terrorists'. On one occasion, a party of 'Tans' captured a handful of the enemy at Kerry Pike near Cork, cut off the tongue of one, the nose of another, cut out the heart of a third and smashed the skull of a fourth.[9] To intimidate local populations who gave support to the IRA, they set fire to villages and torched Cork city centre in reprisal for an ambush in which seventeen Auxiliaries had been killed. But far from denying the IRA their popular base and isolating them from the population, the excesses of the 'Tans' only increased support for the IRA. Some security force actions in the current conflict have had the same effect. The atrocities the 'Tans' committed also shocked British public opinion and caused grave political embarrassment to Lloyd George's government. The emotional tide, which had already begun to flow the insurgents' way, turned into a flood when Terence MacSwiney, the Lord Mayor of Cork who had been arrested at an IRA conference, died in Brixton gaol on 24 October 1920 after a hunger strike lasting seventy-three days. MacSwiney took his place in history not just because of his sacrifice but because of his portentous words. 'It is not those who can inflict the most,' he warned, 'but those who can suffer the most who will conquer.' His words became the epigram of the 1981 hunger strike. Lloyd George, like Mrs Thatcher sixty years later, refused to give in. On both occasions, the political consequences were momentous.

The British media at the time regarded the IRA and its leaders in much the same way as the British media of today regards the IRA and Sinn Fein. Michael Collins was the archetypal 'terrorist'. On the morning of Sunday, 21 November 1920, his gunmen wiped out fourteen of what Collins called 'the Dublin Castle murder gang' in a series of surprise attacks throughout the city. Their victims were members of the British secret service in Dublin. Nine were shot dead whilst still in their pyjamas. Only a few days before Collins' bloody onslaught, Lloyd George had boasted that he had 'murder by the throat' and the Chief Secretary to Ireland, Sir Hamar Greenwood, had told an anxious House of Commons that 'things are very much better in Ireland'.[10] The reprisal for the dramatic killings that Sunday morning was swift. The same afternoon, a mixed force of RIC, military and 'Black and Tans' opened fire on 15,000 spectators watching a Gaelic football match between Dublin and Tipperary at Croke Park. The unit was said to be looking for Collins' men who had been responsible for the massacre that morning. The troops opened fire, killing twelve civilians. The day became known as 'Bloody Sunday'. The official British account was that their troops had been fired on by members of Sinn Fein, and had been forced to retaliate in self-defence. The British account of the eponymous 'Bloody Sunday' in Derry on 30 January 1972 has haunting parallels (see chapter nine).

The Anglo-Irish or 'Tan' war descended into savagery as both government and public became increasingly uncomfortable with its conduct and the losses sustained. Asquith, the former Liberal leader who had been Prime Minister at the time of the Easter Rising and who had expressed reservations about the executions, did not mince his words, declaring that 'Things are being done in Ireland which would disgrace the blackest annals of the lowest despotisms in Europe.'[11] In the eighteen months during which the war raged, over 500 soldiers and policemen and over 700 IRA volunteers were killed. Over 700 civilians died.[12] By the spring of 1921, both sides recognized that the other could not be defeated. A similar recognition was made in the current conflict in the late 1980s (see chapter twenty-one). The IRA for its part was stretched and exhausted as well as being short of men and munitions. Collins is reported to have subsequently said, 'You had us dead beat. We could not have lasted another three weeks.'[13] In July 1921, a truce was agreed as a prelude to negotiations between the British Prime Minister, David Lloyd George, and the Irish team led by Michael Collins of the IRA and Arthur Griffith of Sinn Fein, both acting as plenipotentiaries for the as yet unrecognized Irish government in Dublin.

But the problem of Ireland was not – and is not – solely about British withdrawal. It is historically complicated by the presence of around a million Protestants in the six counties of the North who regard themselves as British subjects and who owe their allegiance to the Crown. This problem lies at the heart of the Irish question and the inability of successive British governments to find a successful resolution to the conflict. The Protestant community is concentrated in the three north-eastern counties of Antrim, Down and Armagh where it constitutes a heavy majority. There are Protestants, too, although in smaller numbers, in the other three counties of Londonderry, Fermanagh and Tyrone as well as in the border counties of the Irish Republic of Donegal, Cavan and Monaghan that originally made up the ancient Irish province of Ulster. Many of these Protestants, especially those in the North-East, are the descendants of the 'plantation' of Ulster at the beginning of the seventeenth century when King James I encouraged the settlement of loyal Protestants in that corner of Ireland as a bulwark against his repeatedly rebellious Roman Catholic subjects.

The question of 'Ulster' was, and remains, explosive because of the threat of armed revolt that traditionally accompanies any attempt to coerce Northern Protestants into any form of United Ireland. History shows the threat to have been real. When the pre-war Prime Minister, Henry Asquith, finally steered Home Rule for Ireland through the House of Commons in 1912, granting the country semi-independence with its own parliament and powers, Protestants armed themselves, regarding Home Rule as the first step in the severance of the Union. In Belfast, the unionist leader, Sir Edward Carson MP, led nearly half a million Protestants in signing the Ulster Covenant on 28 September 1912 which declared their determination to defend their position in the United Kingdom by any means necessary.

By 1913, Protestants had formed the 'Ulster Volunteers' and had begun assembling and openly practising drills with wooden rifles throughout the North. The 'Irish Volunteers' who fought with Patrick Pearse in 1916 had originally been set up in response to them. But by 1914, the Ulster Volunteers had no need of wooden rifles. They had the real thing, 20,000 of them and three million rounds of ammunition smuggled into the ports of Larne and Bangor from Germany on 25 April 1914.[14] This Protestant citizens' army became known as the 'Ulster Volunteer Force' (UVF). Eighty years ago, the forerunners of the modern IRA and UVF were first ranged against each other. The showdown was postponed by the outbreak of the Great War on 4 August 1914, the year the Home Rule legislation received the royal assent. But the problem was still there when the Great War was over, despite the Treaty of Versailles designed to determine the future of small nations.

In 1921 as the Treaty negotiations began, the question high on the agenda of both negotiating teams was what was to happen to 'Ulster'. The Irish were demanding independence for the whole island of Ireland as proclaimed by Patrick Pearse, whilst the British were conscious of the need to accommodate the Protestants in the North and their unionist representatives at Westminster. Lloyd George thought he had already found the answer the previous year when the Government had passed the Government of Ireland Act of 1920 which finally introduced Home Rule, but not along the lines of Asquith's legislation of 1912. Under the new Act, the island was partitioned to create two separate states. But the new state of Northern Ireland was gerrymandered under unionist pressure despite the Cabinet's reluctance. The boundary was *not* drawn along the border of the historic nine-county province of Ulster, which included the counties of Donegal, Cavan and Monaghan, because this natural entity would not have provided Protestants with the inbuilt majority upon which they insisted. So the boundary of 'Northern Ireland' was drawn around six of the nine counties – Antrim, Down, Armagh, Tyrone, Fermanagh and Londonderry/Derry – thus guaranteeing what seemed at the time to be a permanent Protestant majority.[15] Put bluntly, it was the maximum area that unionists could hold. Dublin and Belfast, the capitals of the now divided island, were each given their own Home Rule parliaments. Northern Ireland's parliament was based at Stormont, just outside Belfast, and was to govern the province for the next fifty years.

But the Government of Ireland Act did not end there. The partition of Ireland was never intended to be permanent, but was seen as a temporary solution that would, it was hoped, lead to a final resolution of the Irish question. The legislation contained a clause that foresaw 'as soon as may be after the appointed day' the establishment of a Council of Ireland to harmonize and ultimately unify the island under 'a parliament for the whole of Ireland'.[16] It was a clever but eventually disastrous balancing act wherein the origins of the present conflict lie.

Ten days after the signing of the Truce that ended the Anglo-Irish war, de Valera went to London as President of Dail Eireann for exploratory talks with Lloyd George about the settlement that should follow the ending of hostilities. He came away convinced that the Republic was not on offer and any settlement would institutionalize partition since the British Government was not prepared to confront the unionists in the North. Michael Collins and Arthur Griffith were sent to London to get the best deal possible. The settlement was to be on Collins' head and not de Valera's. Collins did not want to go, arguing that he was a soldier and not a politician, but in the end he reluctantly agreed. On 6 December 1921, after three months of intensive negotiations and under threat of renewed war 'in three days' by Lloyd George, Collins, with heavy heart, signed the Treaty. Troops were to be withdrawn, partition was formalized and the twenty-six counties of the South were to become known as the 'Irish Free State' – Eire – with Dominion status like that of Canada, Australia and New Zealand. The Republic it was not, a fact underlined by the obligation on all members of the new Free State parliament to swear that they would be 'faithful to HM King George V, his heirs and successors'. Collins knew that Pearse would have turned in his grave at the oath, despite the compromise he had negotiated. Ironically it was the oath of allegiance and not partition that had proved the most controversial aspect of the negotiations for the Irish delegation.

Eight months earlier, Lloyd George had likened the prospect of meeting Collins to that of meeting a murderer and had described the IRA as 'a small body of assassins, a real murder gang, dominating the country and terrorizing it'. Now he described its commander as 'one of the most courageous leaders ever produced by a valiant race'.[17] It was not the first or last time that government attitudes towards 'terrorists' and their leaders changed. Seventy-two years later, the British Prime Minister, John Major, told the House of Commons that it would 'turn his stomach' to sit down and talk with 'Mr Adams and the Provisional IRA'.[18] A year later, the Government was talking to the Provisionals' leadership and it was not long before Gerry Adams and Martin McGuinness became regular visitors to Bill Clinton's White House and Tony Blair's Downing Street. In 1921, as Michael Collins left Downing Street to walk London's streets, 'cold and dank in the night air', he reflected prophetically:

> . . . what have I got for Ireland? Something which she has wanted these past seven hundred years? Will anyone be satisfied at the bargain? Will anyone? I tell you this – early this morning I signed my death warrant. I thought at the time, how odd, how ridiculous – a bullet may just as well have done the job five years ago.[19]

Collins knew the settlement was unsatisfactory but that the alternative, a return to war, would have been disastrous, with the IRA short of arms, men and energy after being stood down for almost six months. As we will see, the IRA was similarly weakened after prolonged inactivity during the bilateral truce of 1975 (see chapter thirteen). Collins had pinned his hopes on a 'get-out' clause in the Treaty that a Boundary Commission would finally determine the borders of Northern Ireland 'in accordance with the wishes of the inhabitants' and 'so far as may be compatible with economic and geographic conditions'.[20] Collins calculated that the new boundary would be drawn around the three predominantly Protestant counties, Antrim, Down and Armagh, to produce a political unit which would be economically unviable. The result, he calculated, would be the amalgamation of the Stormont and Dublin parliaments as originally envisaged in the Government of Ireland Act, thus bringing about the final integration of the two parts of the island.

Lloyd George was jubilant, convinced he had finally solved the Irish question. In reality he had essentially left it unresolved, although it is difficult to see what other option was realistically available at the time. The British Government felt obliged to remain true to their loyal subjects in the North who had sacrificed so much at the Somme, whilst Collins, who proved to be a political as well as a military realist, recognized that, at that time, the Irish Republic was simply not on.

Collins knew what the reaction would be when he returned to Ireland. The man who had brought the war to the British and forced them to the negotiating table was denounced as a traitor who had sold out the Republic. Dail Eireann debated the Treaty for a stormy four weeks with old comrades-in-arms unleashing their fury on each other. De Valera, who had skilfully remained aloof from the negotiations in London by staying away, rejected the Treaty out of hand. He said it had been signed 'at the point of a pistol' and under the threat of 'immediate war'. He declared that the Treaty 'makes the British authority our masters in Ireland'.

Collins passionately defended his decision to sign the Treaty with his famous argument that it gave Ireland the opportunity to achieve freedom:

In my opinion it gives us freedom, not the ultimate freedom that all nations desire and develop to, but the freedom to achieve it . . . The Treaty has made an effort . . . to deal with it [the Protestant North] on lines that will lead very rapidly to goodwill and the entry of the North-East under the Irish parliament.[21]

Collins' recognition of the political realities of Northern unionism and the dire consequences of coercion are recurring themes of the current conflict as the North-East did not, as Collins had fervently hoped, enter the Irish parliament. As far as the unionists were concerned, partition was permanent. After decades of rejecting the notion, the IRA and Sinn Fein of today finally recognize that their fellow Irishmen and women of unionist persuasion have to be accommodated in any new political structure and not forced into it. This has always been the view of the British Government and latterly of the Irish Government in Dublin. For the Republican Movement to accept it represents a major departure in its thinking.

The Treaty was finally ratified by the Dail by the narrow margin of sixty-four to fifty-seven. On 16 January 1922, Dublin Castle, the seat of British rule, was handed over to Collins and the Provisional Government of the new Irish Free State was formed. British soldiers left Ireland with their former enemies fatally divided. The animosities and divisions the Treaty debate had brought to the surface were soon to break out in a fratricidal civil war. On 26 March 1922, the IRA called a General Army Convention at the Mansion House in Dublin. Only anti-Treaty IRA Volunteers attended. A new IRA constitution was drawn up stating:

The Army shall be known as the Irish Republican Army. It shall be on a purely volunteer basis. Its objects shall be:

1. To safeguard the honour and maintain the independence of the Irish Republic.
2. To protect the rights and liberties common to the people of Ireland.
3. To place its services at the disposal of an established Republican Government which faithfully upholds the above objects.

The IRA Volunteers who were delegates to the Convention elected a sixteen-person Army Executive to whom they held themselves responsible. In turn, the Executive elected an Army Council with a Chief of Staff and his Deputy, an Adjutant General, a Director of Organization, a Director of Intelligence, a Quarter Master General and a Director of Engineering.[22]

They were to be assisted by a General Headquarters Staff (GHQ). The IRA was organized along British army lines into brigades, battalions and companies. With minor changes, this remains the structure of the IRA of today. Only the IRA's Army Convention, made up of representatives of all IRA Volunteers throughout Ireland, can decide on the issue of peace or war. Constitutionally, a campaign can only end when a General Army Convention decrees it. This still remains the case today.

Despite the fact that the Irish general election of 16 June 1922 returned an overwhelming pro-Treaty majority to the Dail, large sections of the IRA ignored the result, in particular those who had attended the Army Convention and pledged allegiance to the Republic they felt Collins had betrayed. The IRA split roughly fifty-fifty. Those who supported the Treaty were integrated into the new Free State army whilst those who resisted it remained in the IRA. They became known as the 'Republicans' and it is from them that the Republican Movement of today traces its descent. To the now legally constituted Free State Government, the IRA dissidents were known as the 'Irregulars'. Their leaders, the newly elected Executive of the anti-Treaty IRA, seized the Four Courts in Dublin and set up their headquarters, throwing down the gauntlet to Collins. He tried to persuade them to surrender but they refused. The British made it clear to the fledgling Free State Government that the challenge had to be met and defeated. In London, two IRA men had just assassinated Field Marshal Sir Henry Wilson, Chief of the Imperial General Staff and military adviser to the new Northern Ireland Government. The British Government was in no mood to tolerate a further outbreak of extremism in Ireland and 'the ambiguous position of the IRA.'[23] The British even loaned Collins two field guns to dislodge the IRA leaders from the Four Courts. On 30 June 1922, after two days of bombardment, the IRA surrendered, and its leaders were subsequently executed on the orders of the Free State Cabinet, one of whose members had been best man at the wedding of one of the condemned men. Such was the intensity of feeling.[24] The fall of the Four Courts marked the beginning of the bitter civil war. The ensuing week of fierce fighting in Dublin ended up with 300 wounded and sixty dead.[25] For ten months, comrade fought comrade and families were split down the middle. In the following two months, around 500 men were killed on both sides with the British providing the new Free State army with 10,000 rifles to make sure the anti-Treaty IRA was defeated.[26] Michael Collins was one of the victims, shot dead on 22 August 1922 in an ambush in the valley of Bealnablath ('The Mouth of Flowers') in his home county of Cork. It was thought he was in the area to talk with the anti-Treaty forces with a view to reaching an accommodation that would bring an end to the war which had brought him such pain. Collins' death as well as pressure from the British drove the Free State Government to introduce draconian measures to stamp out the 'Irregulars'. In just over six months, seventy-seven members of the anti-Treaty forces faced the firing squad, more than three times the number the British had executed during the Anglo-Irish war. The executions ended when de Valera recognized the hopelessness of his position and ordered the IRA to dump its arms.[27] By May 1923 the Irish civil war was over, but at tremendous cost. The IRA had been decimated but the ideal for which its leaders had fought was not buried with the many dead.

One of the unrecorded casualties was the hope, however slight, that the Treaty would eventually lead to Irish unity. If ever there had been any prospect of Stormont joining Dail Eireann as anticipated in an all-Ireland parliament, the blood-letting of the civil war put an end to it. Even before the civil war broke out, there had been severe disturbances in Northern Ireland. The Treaty had divided the two communities even more and inflamed sectarian tensions. Nationalists resented being cut off from their Irish brethren by partition and boycotted the institutions of the new state of Northern Ireland. Unionists feared the Treaty as the thin end of the wedge of Irish unity, not least because of the establishment of the Boundary Commission to re-examine the borders of 'their' state. Loyalist mobs attacked nationalist areas in scenes that were to be replayed half a century later. During this turbulent period between the Anglo-Irish war and the end of the civil war, 453 people were killed in Belfast alone – 257 Catholics and 157 Protestants – with rioting often along the same sectarian interfaces where it erupted in August 1969.[28] Overall, around 10,000 Catholics were expelled from their jobs and over 500 Catholic businesses were wrecked. Thousands of refugees streamed south, again as they would in 1969.[29] Although Collins, having signed the Treaty, was obliged to avoid any involvement in the North, he still sent weapons across the border to the Northern units of the IRA which came to the defence of the vulnerable nationalist population. By contrast, when history repeated itself in 1969, the IRA was not in a position to defend nationalists from what was seen, once again, as a loyalist pogrom.

Despite Collins' high hopes of the Treaty and Lloyd George's encouragement of those aspirations, Northern Ireland became a permanent fixture on the political map of Ireland, with a Protestant majority as determined to maintain its status as part of the United Kingdom as republicans were to change it. The Boundary Commission sat in 1925 with two of its three Commissioners hopelessly divided on what its true purpose was. The unionist representative argued that it was to consolidate the entity of Northern Ireland. The Free State representative insisted its purpose was just the opposite. The third member representing Britain not surprisingly came down on the side of the unionists. Had Collins known that this was to be the outcome, he would probably never have signed the Treaty. In the end the only recommended adjustment to the border was the transfer of part of East Donegal from the Free State to Northern Ireland.[30] Partition and the new state of Northern Ireland became permanent.

Majority rule meant Protestant rule until the day when Catholics outnumbered Protestants and in 1921 that day was too far distant to cause Protestants any concern. Northern Ireland's parliament at Stormont became known as a Protestant parliament for a Protestant people. The state had its own own police force, the Royal Ulster Constabulary (RUC), that was almost entirely Protestant. It in turn was supported by an armed paramilitary wing that was exclusively Protestant, the Ulster Special Constabulary, or 'B' Specials as they became notoriously known to nationalists. The prime function of the 'B' Specials was to make sure the IRA never got a foothold or raised its head again. Security of the new state was underpinned by a draconian Special Powers Act, that gave the Stormont Government power to intern people without trial and take whatever steps it deemed necessary to combat actual or suspected subversion. This legislation, which applied nowhere else in the United Kingdom, was targeted at the IRA in particular and the nationalist community in general. Most of the leaders of that community gave no allegiance to the state and chose to play little part in it.

But what of the IRA after de Valera had ordered it to dump its weapons in 1923 with the exhortation that 'other means must be sought to safeguard the nation's right'?[31] Sinn Fein candidates loyal to de Valera had contested the Irish general election of June 1922 and had won nearly a third of seats (forty-four out of 153) but refused to take them up as they did not recognize the legitimacy of Dail Eireann which they regarded as an illegal and usurpatory government.[32] This policy of 'abstentionism' remained at the heart of Sinn Fein's ideology for over sixty years, until its removal was successfully engineered by Gerry Adams in 1986 on the grounds that the principle was no longer relevant in the latter part of the twentieth century. De Valera finally withdrew from the political wilderness to which he had relegated himself and entered the Dail in 1927 as the leader of the new party he had formed – Fianna Fail, 'Soldiers of Destiny'. He pushed the Bible aside when required to take the oath of allegiance and simply signed his name in the book.[33] Six years later, the first Fianna Fail government came to power and in 1937 it introduced a new Constitution that abolished the oath of allegiance and, controversially, laid claim to the six counties that, since 1920, had constituted Northern Ireland. This territorial claim was always deeply offensive to unionists and was finally modified in the referendum in the Irish Republic that followed the Good Friday Agreement.

But de Valera's decision to enter the Dail and embrace constitutional politics caused a further split amongst those in the IRA who regarded his action as a further betrayal of the ideal of 1916. The IRA split again, with the militants staying together under the banner of the increasingly depleted Irish Republican Army. As the Northern state became ever more entrenched and the Government of the South paid only lip service to its constitutional claim, what was left of the IRA fought on with notable lack of success through the next four decades until it split once again. That was in 1969 when the 'Provos' were born.

Chapter Two

Commemoration

1966 was a memorable year. England beat Germany to win the football World Cup. North Sea oil gushed in. Freddie Laker's 'Skytrain' flew passengers across the Atlantic for next to nothing. Sir Francis Chichester sailed round the world, single-handed. The Beatles topped the charts. Skirts got shorter. London started to 'swing' and the 'feelgood factor' powered the pipe-smoking Harold Wilson to a Labour landslide in the British general election. But that was in England. In Ireland, things were different. The year dawned with apprehension on both sides of the border. 1966 was the fiftieth anniversary of the Easter Rising and the authorities, north and south, expected the worst. In reality, however, the IRA as a military force was virtually non-existent. A decade earlier, it had opened its border campaign, 'Operation Harvest', with the bold declaration that their generation would be the one to free Ireland from the British. But, yet again, it was not to be. The campaign never really got off the ground or much beyond the border: the nationalist people of the North had little interest; the IRA had no popular base and no issue on which to arouse support; even partition had long ceased to be a rallying call to arms. Furthermore, Sinn Fein had no deep-rooted political organization on which to build. As if these endemic problems were not enough, the Stormont and Dublin governments interned IRA men on both sides of the border so most Volunteers spent most of the time during this particular phase of 'the age old struggle' behind bars in Dublin's Mountjoy gaol or Belfast's Crumlin Road prison. Eamon de Valera, whose Fianna Fail party had been returned to power in 1957, gave the IRA no quarter. Historically, republicans have tended to deal more harshly with their own than the British ever did. Compared with the current IRA campaign, casualties were remarkably light. Eight IRA Volunteers were killed as were six officers of the RUC. The IRA knew it was going nowhere and finally on 5 February 1962 issued a Special Army Order, instructing all units to dump arms. Three weeks later, the campaign was formally ended with an IRA statement to the Irish people.

The guns were buried away in roofs, cellars and holes in the ground. No arms were handed over and there was no decommissioning. The IRA had to wait almost another ten years before the next phase began. One of the IRA men released from the Crumlin Road prison at the end of the border campaign was John Kelly, who subsequently went on to become a member of the Provisional IRA's GHQ staff. He relates that:

The IRA was in a state of disarray after the campaign had been defeated. The only thing that had been achieved was that the Republican Movement had struck a blow as they had done in every generation. That was the only achievement.

Was it thought at the time that the 'armed struggle' was dead?

There was a process of rethinking within the Movement. Perhaps the armed struggle was not the way forward on its own and that, quite rightly, there had to be politics. An armed struggle on its own was getting nowhere unless you had the political support of the population. That is why, basically, the 1956 campaign failed, because there was no political foundation for sustaining an armed revolution, an armed struggle.

But was the military campaign dead and buried for ever?

No, it wasn't dead and buried for ever. That was never part of republican philosophy. It was still there, on the back burner, to be used when necessary.

Although it never completely abandoned the tradition of physical force, the IRA's new leadership embarked upon a different strategy, recognizing that 'armed struggle' had serious limits. The lessons of the border campaign were staring republicans in the face. The Dubliner, Cathal Goulding, became the IRA's new Chief of Staff. He had spent most of the fifties in Pentonville prison with another young republican, Séan MacStiofáin, who was to become the Provisional IRA's first Chief of Staff. Goulding was blunt about the IRA's prospects.

The notion that the IRA was going to rise up some day and free Ireland and get rid of the British was a ridiculous pipe-dream, for the simple reason that we never had the support of the people north and south to do it ... We couldn't match the Free State army and we certainly couldn't match the British army. We could carry out a campaign possibly in the Six Counties for a while but not in the Twenty-Six Counties because people didn't like to see Irish policemen or Irish soldiers being shot.[1]

Goulding was nothing if not a realist. The lessons were plain – the IRA was declining, and to combat this Goulding wanted to become involved in politics and adopt a socialist agenda which would enable the movement to reach out to ordinary people. He was also scathing about the IRA's traditional policy of 'abstentionism'. Although it was an article of faith, he believed it was completely out of touch with reality, as IRA Volunteers 'still paid their income tax, still held driving licences and conformed in every way except they refused to enter into politics'.[2] The IRA's new Chief of Staff was anxious to take the Republican Movement back to its late-eighteenth-century roots when the father of Irish republicanism, Wolfe Tone, a Dublin Protestant, had endeavoured to forge an alliance between 'Protestant, Catholic and dissenter' to rid Ireland of the English Crown. Like Tone, Goulding was wedded to the principle of non-sectarianism: British Imperialism was the enemy, not the Protestant working class. However starry-eyed Goulding may have been about the prospect of Catholic and Protestant unity, he got his way on the Army Council. Politics not the gun became IRA policy. It was a far cry from the heroics of 1916 or the bloody deeds of Michael Collins, as Sinn Fein organized 'Fish-Ins' on private rivers to assert the right of the people of Ireland to fish. Power now flowed from the end of a rod not the barrel of a gun. IRA veterans like Billy McKee were appalled.

> I was utterly disgusted. Like many others who had come through the campaigns in the forties and fifties, we were still hoping against hope that a strong Republican Movement would come to the fore. We realized that if Goulding and this new leadership were allowed to carry on, republicanism would die a natural death.
> **Why?**
> Well because they had control. They had the reins. Anybody who wanted to join the IRA went to them. They took them in and schooled them for a while and then the next thing was they joined Sinn Fein and went fishing. They didn't know one end of a rod from another. They cast them into the river and the Guards (the Irish police) came along and took a few names. They thought that was a great protest.

But violence was never totally absent. Foreign companies and investors were targeted as the architects of 'economic imperialism': buses ferrying strike breakers were destroyed; farms owned by foreigners were attacked; and a foreign-owned oyster boat was blown out of the water.[3]

Veterans like Billy McKee and Joe Cahill, who had also spent most of the border campaign behind bars, did not follow the Goulding line.

To them, this change of direction was a betrayal. They were also bitterly opposed to the number of communists and Marxists who now swelled the IRA's ranks. The IRA remained at heart a conservative, Catholic organization, many of whose Volunteers attended mass, and Billy McKee still rises every day well before breakfast to do so. So does Gerry Adams, although perhaps not every day and not necessarily at that hour of the morning. To IRA men like Cahill and McKee, Marxism was the ideology of the ungodly. In 1964, Joe Cahill resigned from the IRA in disgust.

> I had a feeling that ultra-left politics were taking over. As far as I was concerned, the main purpose of the IRA and Sinn Fein was to break the connection with England and get rid of the 'Brits' from Ireland. They'd gone completely political and the military side of things was being run down. The Republican Movement was being led off the true path of republicanism. Sooner or later there'd have to be a showdown. A split was inevitable.

But to Goulding, Cahill and McKee were simply right-wingers living in a fantasy world and clinging to a romantic past.

As the fiftieth anniversary of the Easter Rising approached, the Dublin Government was taking no chances. Its worst fears seemed to be confirmed on 8 March 1966 when an anonymous republican group blew up Nelson's pillar in Dublin city centre. Although the IRA denied responsibility, it was an indicator of the general mood as Easter loomed. The toppling of Lord Nelson was regarded by many as a patriotic gesture and suggestions flowed in from all over Ireland and abroad as to whose statue would be an appropriate replacement. Patrick Pearse and Michael Collins headed the list.[4] In an atmosphere of growing tension, the Irish Cabinet was briefed on the state of the 'so-called IRA'. It was told that the number who would obey military orders was around one thousand, a number which had 'increased progressively' from an estimated 650 in 1962 when the IRA had ordered its cessation. There had been reports of 'a certain amount of drilling with firearms' although 'there was no more reason now than in the past four years to conclude that a campaign of violence is imminent or will commence within, say, the next twelve months'. Nevertheless, the Cabinet was warned that the IRA might use the Easter Commemoration to restart its campaign.[5]

Anxiety was already growing in Northern Ireland. The previous year the province's Prime Minister, Captain Terence O'Neill (ex-Eton and the Guards), had invited the Irish Prime Minister, Sean Lemass, to Belfast in a new spirit of co-operation between North and South. To the British Government, O'Neill was seen as a progressive unionist who would begin to heal the wounds of the partitioned island. But to extreme loyalists he was seen as a traitor prepared to sell Ulster's birthright and ultimately give 'Ulster' to the IRA. The composition of Dublin's official Easter Commemoration Committee confirmed unionists' worst fears. One of its members was Vinny Byrne, one of Michael Collins' gunmen who had wiped out the cream of British intelligence in Dublin in November 1920. Sinn Fein saw the 1966 Easter Commemoration as a perfect opportunity to remind the nation's youth of its heritage and duty. Taking its cue from the civil-rights campaign that was sweeping America, it planned to run a 'freedom train' from Dublin to Belfast to swell the crowds that would be marching to Milltown cemetery where the Republican Movement's dead lie buried. But the Dublin Government would have none of it. A 'strictly confidential' letter expressed the view of the Irish police. 'There will be trouble in Belfast if the train runs; opposition is mounting; even if the travellers do not provoke trouble, the opposition [the loyalists] will; the train should not be provided if at all possible.' The advice was taken and the 'freedom train' stayed in the station because of the belief that it was being used 'for IRA organizational purposes'.[6]

Britain also feared serious disturbance. The newly elected Labour Government under Harold Wilson was advised that both the Stormont Government and Scotland Yard were 'particularly concerned' about the threat of IRA violence. Secret British Cabinet papers reveal there were an estimated '3,000 trained members or supporters' who could be 'called out in an emergency'. These 'supporters' were engaged in military training in 'various places' in Ireland and were 'adequately supplied' with arms and ammunition. There were intelligence reports of thirty-four IRA training camps in Ireland, seventeen of which had been established since the summer of 1965. Some of these camps 'have been conducted fairly openly and the sound of firing has been heard over a wide area. Instruction at these sessions has included live firing practice, lectures on the use of explosives and the making of booby traps and advice on the mounting of attacks on government buildings.'[7] Wilson's Cabinet authorized plans for the army to assist the RUC 'if needed' and an additional infantry battalion was sent to Northern Ireland, 'ostensibly for training'. Harold Wilson, who emotionally favoured a united Ireland at this time, was anxious to keep any intervention as low key as possible to avoid giving the IRA the opportunity to depict any clashes as 'a people's uprising against the excesses of the Crown forces'.[8]

The Dublin Government, now led by the new Taoiseach, Jack Lynch, had good reason to fear that 'Paisley sectarian riots' might be used as a pretext by the IRA to restart its campaign. Eighteen months earlier, during the British general-election campaign of 1964 which had brought

Harold Wilson to power, Sinn Fein had set up its West Belfast election headquarters in an abandoned shop in Divis Street. One of Sinn Fein's election workers at the time was a young man called Gerry Adams. An Irish Tricolour was displayed in the office window. Technically such a display could be banned under Northern Ireland's Flags and Emblems Act, but the RUC, not wishing to provoke a confrontation, let well alone. But a young cleric, Ian Paisley, was not prepared to let it pass. A fundamentalist presbyterian preacher, Paisley's anti-Catholic and anti-republican rhetoric increasingly inflamed his growing band of supporters. He threatened to lead a march to remove the offending flag in person if the authorities did not remove it first. 'I don't accept that any area of Ulster is republican and I don't want to see the Tricolour flying here,' he declared. 'I intend to see that the Union Jack flies everywhere and that it keeps flying.' His supporters rallied to the emotional call, 'SOS To All Ulster Protestants'.[9] The threat had the desired effect. The following day fifty police moved in, broke down the door and seized the offending flag. Paisley called off the march and contented himself with a rally. The flag was defiantly reinstated and the police moved in again, smashing down the door with pick axe handles. Fierce rioting broke out, the like of which had not been seen in Belfast since 1935 when some twenty people died.[10] Three hundred and fifty RUC officers moved in with armoured cars and water cannon to quell the riot. The violence had a profound effect on the young Gerry Adams, as it led him to believe that 'the north of Ireland was a state based upon the violent suppression of political opposition'.[11] The incident and the rioting made Adams 'politically curious'. It had the same effect on many of the young men and women who subsequently travelled the same road. Marie Moore was coming home from work when she ran into the riot. It was her first experience of street violence.

Of course, I got involved in the riot and did some pushing and shoving and got some pushing and shoving back from the RUC and others that were there at that time. That was my very first memory of riots in the Falls Road, in my area.

Why did you get involved in that particular riot?

Well the RUC seemed to be going so vicious at some young men and young girls that were there. It seemed so hard. I was actually trying to separate them. That's how I felt. I was angry at the way that they were handling it, and the way that they were beating and pushing the young ones. Then they started to break up stones and stone the RUC.

All over a Tricolour?

All over a Tricolour which wasn't actually in the town or in an area that would cause friction. It was right in the heart of the Falls Road. Nobody had noticed it prior to that.

It was an early illustration of the way in which Paisley used a threat to force the authorities to act against those he saw as the enemy bent on destroying Ulster. It was a tactic he was to employ many times in the years to come. Two months before the planned Easter Commemoration, Paisley had made it clear he was not going to tolerate a republican incursion from the South, by train or anything else. 'Thirty thousand of them are going to invade this city,' he told a packed audience in Belfast's Ulster Hall. 'I want to say as hard as I can, we mean business. We are not going to be hammered into the ground.'[12] On the Sunday of the Commemorative parade, 17 April 1966, Paisley held a counter-rally in the Ulster Hall where he loudly attacked the Stormont Government for its weakness in allowing a Commemoration to go ahead that honoured those guilty of 'murder, treason and sedition'. To Protestants, 1916 meant something different but equally emotional. It was the fiftieth anniversary of the Battle of the Somme in which 20,000 British soldiers died, over 5,000 of them from the 36th (Ulster) Division, largely made up of the Ulster Volunteer Force recruited by Sir Edward Carson and reluctantly handed over to Lord Kitchener's army. Some marched to their death wearing orange ribbons and shouting 'No Surrender'.[13] The Somme was to loyalists what Easter was to republicans. Paisley declared to roof-raising cheers, 'Our forefathers suffered from bullets and bombs and won. We will do the same.'[14] Although there was violence in Dublin, the Commemoration march in Belfast passed off without incident, despite newspaper hoardings for the *Belfast Telegraph* announcing 'Full Scale Alert' and 'IRA Threat'.[15] For republicans young and old, the Easter Commemoration of 1966 was a watershed. Marie Moore's grandmother told her that such parades were normally banned by the Stormont authorities as they were deemed to be seditious.

We watched the parade coming up the road. Everyone seemed to be so proud and walking so straight. There were people cheering on each side. We joined at the back. My granny said, 'we've never got walking up this road before and now we're walking. This is great! We're starting to be part of something and all these people are here to celebrate. And what they're celebrating is us trying to be free, trying to be able to walk our streets. To be able to do what we we would like to do.' She told me that people had died previously for this and now we were being allowed to do it.

What did the IRA mean at that time?

Absolutely nothing. I hadn't heard of the IRA. There was no IRA activity on the streets. Absolutely nothing. It was just part of history.

For Billy McKee, the march meant that, despite all the setbacks, republicanism was still alive.

To me it meant that fifty years after the 1916 Rising those men were still being remembered and commemorated. It also brought back to the fold many men who had either retired or been semi-retired. It was a reminder that they still felt the same and hadn't changed their opinions or ideal. They were were still republicans.

Did you think that the IRA as you had known it was finished?

I believed that it was dead, completely dead. And it was except in the minds of myself and other old republicans. We lived in hope.

But the IRA was still there, although the secret intelligence reports of its military size and strength were almost certainly grossly exaggerated. It was still an organization that young men could join. The Easter Commemoration had a profound effect on the young Martin Meehan from Belfast's Ardoyne area. His father had been active in the IRA in the forties, but had seldom spoken of it to his family. The subject was taboo. In the early seventies Meehan became one of the IRA's most wanted men. I asked him whether 1966 made him aware of the IRA:

Very much so. It made me question what the IRA was about. It was something to look up to. It was something to be proud of and my objective after 1966 was to join the Irish Republican Army. It was something to be involved in that could be honoured and I wanted to participate in it to achieve the object of what the men and women in 1916 had died for and carry on that struggle.

How did you go about joining?

In those days you had a sort of auxiliary section of the IRA, you weren't actually a fully-fledged IRA member. You had to join the auxiliaries and then if you showed the qualities and the commitment and the resolve, then you were put up for membership by an older republican who was a kind of overseer of the auxiliaries. He told me and another comrade that we were two potential recruits for the IRA. Then we went to recruiting lectures that lasted for about ten weeks. There were twenty-seven of us at the beginning. The recruiting officer was very resolute and he put the fear of God into you. He told you that if you're joining the IRA, it was a total and absolute commitment. It required sacrifice and it required dedication and it required honour above all. He told us everything that was bad about joining: imprisonment, death, very little money in your pocket, very few friends; it was going to be a hard slog, and a long hard road ahead of us. So gradually people starting dropping off each week and at the end of the ten weeks, when we took the Declaration [to the Irish Republic of 1916] in front of the flag, only three of us turned up. And we had to come down in our best suits, in our ties and our shoes spit-polished. It was a big occasion, like joining the priesthood.

In the lectures, were you also told that you would have to be prepared to kill people?

No, not in so many words. Not everything you do in the IRA involves the ultimate of killing people. There's all sorts of other things you do. But that was one of the consequences of joining. You may have to face that reality.

The 1966 Easter Commemoration was a Rubicon for some loyalists too. The lines of battle were already being drawn. The previous year, in the wake of Prime Minister O'Neill's growing *rapprochement* with the South, around ten Protestants, mainly ex-servicemen, began meeting in the Standard Bar on Belfast's Shankill Road. They decided to form a loyalist 'army' to counter the IRA and defend Ulster and named it the 'Ulster Volunteer Force' (UVF), after the Brigade that had been wiped out at the Somme. All were violently anti-Catholic and had no problems in equating Catholics with the IRA. Their commander was a man who was to become a loyalist legend, Gusty Spence. It was Spence who announced the historic ceasefire by the loyalist paramilitaries twenty-eight years later on 13 October 1994. Today he has genuine regrets about what happened nearly three decades ago. Spence, as he himself admits, has seen the light. He recalls joining the loyalist equivalent of the IRA in 1965.

When I joined the UVF, I didn't have the maturity or knowledge that was needed [to know what was going on]. But there were 'clever' people who could see on the horizon the fiftieth anniversary of the Rising. And a lot of our fears were confirmed: all Catholic streets were decorated and had barricades erected. The IRA issued a few bellicose statements ... The whole of the UVF was stood to and they were armed and on duty at interface areas. There was a fair bit of tension.[16]

A month after the Commemoration, the UVF issued an ominous statement: 'From this day we declare war against the IRA ... Known IRA men will be executed mercilessly and without hesitation.'[17] Six days later, on 27 May 1966, the UVF picked their first target, Leo Martin, a well-known republican associated with the Belfast Brigade staff of the IRA. A four-man hit-team scoured the Clonard area of Belfast looking for Martin but could not find him. Frustrated, they came across a man who was obviously well oiled and wandering the streets singing republican songs. His name was John Scullion. They told themselves he must be an IRA man, shot him and left him for dead. John Scullion, an innocent Catholic, died a fortnight later.[18] It was the first sectarian killing of the current conflict. A month later, the UVF again tried to kill Leo Martin. Again, they failed to find their elusive target and ended up drinking in a pub, the Malvern Arms, off the Protestant Shankill Road. Whilst they were at the bar, four men came in, all of them with southern accents. They were working as barmen in a Belfast hotel. Gusty Spence identified them, erroneously, as IRA men. According to a statement later made to the police by one of Spence's co-accused, Spence said, 'these are IRA men, they will have to go'.[19] As the four men left the pub by the side door at 1.45am, they ran into a UVF ambush. One of the four, Peter Ward, was shot dead and the others were seriously wounded. Gusty Spence received a life sentence for the murder, although, to this day he denies that he killed Ward. The police allege that on his arrest Spence declared, 'so this is what you get for being a Protestant!'[20] The memory of the killing still causes Spence pain. It is an event he prefers not to remember. Ironically, the weekend of the murder, the Prime Minister, Captain O'Neill, was in France commemorating the fiftieth anniversary of the Somme and the sacrifice made by the original UVF. On his return to Belfast, O'Neill informed the Stormont parliament that the UVF would be banned. The IRA and the UVF were now on a par. Both threatened the stability of an already unstable state.

The year 1966 saw the ingredients being assembled for an explosion that was waiting to happen. Although the mixture was fuelled by memories of the past, fears of a resurgent IRA and the emergence of the UVF, the basic ingredient had been there since partition: discrimination. It stemmed from the political, economic and social conditions in which the Catholic minority in Northern Ireland lived. They were, in every sense of the word, second-class citizens. History had compelled them to inhabit a state which was not designed for them. Many Catholics did not have the vote since the franchise for local government elections in Northern Ireland only extended to ratepayers and to pay rates you had to be an owner or tenant of a house or flat. This discriminated against Catholics who were not only the minority population but also the poorest section of it. It was to be expected, as it would be anywhere else in the United Kingdom, that local councils reflected the political composition of the areas that elected them. Where there was a Protestant majority, there was a Protestant council. But what was *not* to be expected was that in an area where there was a Catholic majority, there was still a Protestant council. This happened in Northern Ireland because the electoral wards were gerrymandered into providing an artificial majority on the council. Perhaps this was not surprising given that the state itself had been gerrymandered to guarantee an inbuilt Protestant majority. Londonderry City Council was the most glaring example. In an astonishing electoral contradiction, 14,000 Catholic voters ended up with eight councillors whilst 9,000 Protestant voters ended up with twelve, thus giving a politically nationalist city a unionist council. The pattern in Dungannon, County Tyrone, the area that was to produce some of the Provisionals' most determined Volunteers, was much the same. Although Catholics had a narrow voting majority (53%), there were fourteen Protestants to seven Catholics on the Council.[21] Local authorities also discriminated in their allocation of public housing. The area that elected Fermanagh County Council was roughly divided equally between Catholics and Protestants, yet, as with Londonderry and Dungannon, unionists still controlled the council and saw to it that their own came first in housing allocation. In the twenty-five years after the end of the Second World War, the local authority built over 1,500 houses. Two thirds of them went to Protestants. But nationalist councils were not entirely blameless. Some played the same game. In the early sixties, 765 council houses were built in the predominantly nationalist border town of Newry. Only twenty-two were inhabited by Protestants.[22] There was widespread discrimination in jobs, too. Most of the province's employers were Protestants who tended to look after their own. Catholics often only had to mention their name or address to guarantee rejection. The most notorious example of job discrimination lay with the Belfast shipbuilders, Harland and Wolff. In a workforce of 10,000, only 400 were Catholics. When Catholics spoke about being 'an oppressed minority', they were right. There was plenty to be angry about.

But if blame is to be apportioned for the outbreak of violence, Wilson's Labour Government that was in power from 1964 to 1970 must accept a considerable part of it. The Labour Cabinet knew the condition of Northern Ireland, read the warning signs but did precious little about it, rashly pinning its hopes on the 'enlightened' Stormont Prime Minister, Captain O'Neill. But, to be fair, the Labour Government's attitude towards Northern Ireland was no different from that taken by all its predecessors since partition. British Ministers felt that since the province was self-governing, with its own parliament, its own Prime Minister and its own police force, it should be left to get on with the job without interference from the mainland.[23] It was a fatal mistake. The reason behind this hands-off approach was that history had taught British politicians that Northern Ireland meant trouble. The motto of a previous Prime Minister, William Pitt, who was responsible for the 1801 Act of Union, still held good. '*Quieta non movere*' – 'Let sleeping dogs lie.' The problem was the dogs were not sleeping any more.

In 1967, three Labour MPs who were leading members of the party's Campaign for Democracy went on a fact-finding trip to Northern Ireland to investigate discrimination, electoral practice and unemployment. Unionists described their visit as 'hostile and provocative', 'anti-Ulster', 'interfering and unwelcome'. The Labour politicians were appalled at what they found. One of its leaders, Paul Rose, was parliamentary private secretary to Cabinet Minister, Barbara Castle.

> I remember her patting me on the head and saying, 'Why is a young man like you concerned about Northern Ireland? What about Vietnam? What about Rhodesia?' I just looked at her with incomprehension and said, 'You'll see when they start shooting one another.' She was totally oblivious to this. I think their priorities were focused on other things to the extent that they were totally blinded as to what was going on in their own backyard.

The fact-finders submitted their report to the Home Secretary, Roy Jenkins, with its recommendation that a Royal Commission be set up to examine the situation in the province. Roy Jenkins who, having written a famous biography of Asquith, probably knew more about Northern Ireland than anyone else in the Cabinet, was less than enthusiastic. There was to be no Royal Commission. Jenkins left the House of Commons in no doubt as to why Northern Ireland should be left undisturbed, on the grounds that, historically, English attempts to resolve the situation in Ireland had always failed.

Few things indicated Westminster's desire to keep Northern Ireland at arms' length more pointedly than a parliamentary convention, in force since partition, that questions relating to the province could not be raised in the House of Commons. Stormont was considered the proper place, not Westminster. The time spent discussing Northern Ireland therefore averaged less than two hours a year. Technically, Northern Ireland did figure in the Home Secretary's dispatch box, alongside London taxis and wild birds. Its relegation summed up its importance in the British political mind.[24] Murderous civil conflict would change all that.

Chapter Three

Escalation

Growing up in Northern Ireland in the sixties was an entirely different experience from growing up anywhere else in the United Kingdom. By and large, the British public were as ignorant and apparently uncaring about the state of things in the province as were their political representatives at Westminster. Many of those who fought the IRA's 'war' and who came to make up the leadership of the Republican Movement grew up in that turbulent period and were conditioned by what they saw, heard and felt. Discrimination was part of their lives. Most of their parents accepted it with resignation and took it as part of their lot, the legacy of partition. Parents got on with their lives and made the best of it. Children knew little else. Although republicanism ran in many families, most were apolitical and had no reason to be otherwise when their nationalist political leaders had effectively opted out of the system. Parents were aware of sectarianism because so many had felt its discriminatory effect but children often only became conscious of it once battle lines were drawn. Whilst Catholics and Protestants tended to live in separate areas, there were not the bitter demarcation lines that exist today after nearly thirty years of conflict. Many estates were mixed and Catholic and Protestant children played and lived together, although attending separate schools. Nevertheless, experiences differed. The following are recollections of some of the men and women who went on to play prominent parts in the IRA and Sinn Fein and on whose lives this book is based. They come from Belfast, Derry and Tyrone.

Jim Gibney is from Belfast. He was interned in the seventies as an IRA suspect, gaoled in the eighties on the word of a 'supergrass' (see chapter seventeen) and is now part of the Sinn Fein leadership. There was no republican or nationalist tradition in his family, who were simply 'orthodox Catholics' doing what Catholics were expected to do: attend church regularly and fulfil their religious obligations. Politics were never discussed at home. The Gibneys lived on the predominantly Protestant Rathcoole housing estate in North Belfast which, over the years, became one of the most militant loyalist areas in the city. Today Rathcoole, with its towering blocks of flats, is entirely Protestant. Catholics who once lived there have long gone, either through choice or intimidation. But growing up in the sixties in Rathcoole, Jim Gibney remembers very little sectarian tension between Catholic and Protestant children and even helped Protestant friends collect wood for the 12 July bonfire. The 12 July is the most important anniversary in the Protestant calendar and the climax of their marching season. It marks the anniversary of the Battle of the Boyne in 1690 when the Protestant King William of Orange, 'King Billy', defeated the Catholic King James II. Traditionally, huge bonfires are lit in loyalist areas throughout Northern Ireland on the eve of the twelfth. The 'Orangemen' and the 'Orange Order' take their name from King William.

It was great fun and good crack, not knowing the significance of the bonfire. But I always have these memories at night-time on the eve of the 12th night, looking out my bedroom window at the bonfires burning in the middle of the grass square, with the effigy of the Pope on top. That was the only time in the house that you got any feeling that something may not be quite right. I remember, too, that Protestant neighbours of ours tended to be less friendly towards us as Catholic kids around the Twelfth. So at that stage I did have a sense of difference. I occasionally heard the word 'Fenian' addressed to me, not knowing what it meant.

'Fenian' is a historical term of abuse based on the Fenian agrarian rebels of nineteenth-century Ireland. The word 'bastard' is invariably added to it.

Gerard Hodgkins joined the Provisional IRA when he was sixteen, lying about his age to qualify as Volunteers had to be seventeen. He was subsequently gaoled and was one of the last IRA prisoners to join the 1981 hunger strike. After his release he was rearrested and sentenced for his involvement in the detention of a suspected IRA informer. As with many IRA men and women, his early childhood gives no hint of the path he would follow.

His early years were spent in Belfast in a two-up and two-down terrace house in the nationalist area of Beechmount off Belfast's Falls Road. Again, politics were never part of family life. His father was one of the few Catholics who worked in the shipyard but his employment was cut short when he fell sick through asbestosis. He received £5,000 compensation, a small fortune in those days and which he used to buy a house in a mixed area off the Springfield Road. It meant that most of Gerard's friends were now Protestants. It did not make any difference at first. They were all eight, nine and ten years old, playing together and 'doing the normal things that kids of that age do'. But when violence erupted, all that changed.

> Everybody suddenly woke up one morning, it's almost as if you realized you had a new identity. You were no longer just a kid growing up on the street. You were actually labelled. You were a Catholic or you were a Protestant. It was a shock because at that stage I knew nothing about politics. I'd been hanging about with fellas who were Protestants and when I went to school, fellas who were the same age would look at you differently because you knocked about with Protestants. I'd get into a conflict. They'd say, 'you're an Orange lover. You knock about with prods.' I hadn't a clue what a Protestant or a Catholic was until then.

> **And were you aware of the IRA at that time?**

> No, not really. The IRA would be a sort of folk memory. You would see on some walls graffiti, 'Join Your Local Unit', or 'IRA' or a Tricolour painted on the wall. It was just something you'd seen and you knew they were rebels. But really I hadn't a clue what they were.

Tommy Gorman had an even less likely family history for an IRA Volunteer. One brother was a member of the RUC and another was a British soldier, a combination probably unique for a family raised on the Falls Road. 'It gave me a broader perspective on things,' he recalls. His grandfather had been a Protestant who married a Catholic. It was only when he left school that Tommy became aware of sectarianism.

> I remember when I applied for a job, my father, who wasn't political in anyway, told us not to put 'Falls Road' as our address. We would put 'Broadway' which is a pretty neutral area close by. Our name, Gorman, was near enough neutral as well. We weren't O'Shaughnessy or Murphy.

Marie Moore, another native of West Belfast, put it bluntly:

> When I went for jobs, I found out that I was asked if I was a Catholic, not whether I had the qualifications. If I said I was a Catholic, I was told the job was not available.

Richard McAuley joined the IRA in the early seventies and was subsequently sentenced to ten years for possession of weapons. He later rose to prominence in Sinn Fein and became Gerry Adams' Press Secretary. His family was more nationalist than republican.

> My granny talked at times about the twenties and thirties and what was happening in West Belfast at that time. Right up to his death, my father always described himself as a labour man, a trade unionist. He would never have seen himself as a republican. I think, like most families, we used to have long arguments into the early hours of the morning, talking to each other about what was going on.

In Derry, discrimination was more keenly felt since nationalists were a majority in the city which historically Protestants had regarded as theirs. Derry became the symbol of Protestant resistance to the Catholic threat after the Apprentice Boys closed the gates of the walled city in 1689 to shut out the invading forces of the Catholic King James. The Apprentice Boys march through the city every year to commemorate the event. Derry became known as 'The Maiden City' because it remained inviolate. Gary Fleming spent four years in gaol in the eighties on the word of two Derry 'supergrasses' who alleged he was the Explosives Officer on the Derry Brigade Staff. He is now a senior republican in the city. The Fleming family has suffered heavy losses during the current campaign; four of his brothers joined the Provisional IRA. Paul served a life sentence for murder, Archie was charged with possession of firearms and served ten years, William was shot dead by undercover Special Forces and Kieran escaped from the Maze prison and subsequently died following an SAS ambush. Gary Fleming remembers his father telling him about discrimination.

> He talked often about particular housing problems. When he and my mother were first married and had their first couple of children, they lived in a one-bedroom flat. Houses were being allocated in a different area to single Protestants or newly married couples without children over the heads of people like my parents who had two children and who lived in the conditions that they lived in.
>
> He also talked often of his attempts to seek employment in the power station. I actually witnessed quite a few of the application forms when he filled them in. While he knew, and probably a lot of our people knew, that he was by far better qualified than many who were getting jobs, he was always denied employment in the power station for no other reason than his religion. It was hard for someone my age to understand, that an employer would employ someone just because of their religion as opposed to their ability to do a particular job of work.

You had to understand the whole nature of the Six County state, which I didn't at that early stage because I was so young. When you learn that it was basically designed to treat my parents, me, the rest of my family and our families to come, as second-class citizens, then you begin to see the nature of the beast. You decide that this can't be. It has to stop. We can't allow that to happen.

In County Tyrone, feelings were even stronger. The county runs along the border with the Irish Republic, touching Monaghan to the south and Donegal to the west. That is why, over the years, Monaghan has provided such a convenient operational base for the IRA. Tyrone has provided the Provisionals with many of its leaders and most determined Volunteers. Gerry McGeough joined the IRA in the mid-seventies, tried to buy surface-to-air missiles in America in the eighties, and stood trial in Germany in the nineties for involvement in the IRA's European campaign. Republicanism coursed through Gerry McGeough's blood. His maternal grandfather had fought for the IRA during the Anglo-Irish war and was taken out to be summarily executed by the 'Black and Tans' but was reprieved at the last minute. 'Other ancestors of mine would have been rebels or involved in anti-British activity over the centuries,' he says with pride. Tyrone is the seat of the O'Neills, the ancient kings of Ulster who resisted the forces of Queen Elizabeth I at the end of the sixteenth century. McGeough saw himself carrying on the fight against the soldiers of Queen Elizabeth II at the end of the twentieth. He lives and breathes history.

The centre of Celtic resistance in Ireland was in Ulster and the bastion of that resistance was in Tyrone. The policy was to break Ulster by first of all breaking Tyrone. It was something which I certainly was very conscious of from a very early age and something which instilled considerable pride in me. The fact was that I was of this Gaelic Irish stock which had for generation after generation resisted foreign rule in our country. I was conscious of Scottish planters, Protestant and presbyterian, being brought over and being given the land of the dispossessed or displaced native Irish Catholics. So this was something that, even though it had happened many, many generations before my birth, we were still very, very deeply aware of.

When did you first become aware of the IRA?

Very early on, when I was three or four years of age. The 1950s campaign was drawing to a close and I remember the RUC barracks had sand bags around the door so I was conscious of something amiss at that point. But actual awareness of the IRA really stemmed from 1966 and the fiftieth anniversary celebrations.

Tommy McKearney is a Tyrone contemporary of Gerry McGeough. Like Gary Fleming, he has lost three brothers. In the seventies, Sean McKearney was blown up with his own bomb. In the eighties, Padraig escaped from the Maze prison to meet his death in an SAS ambush at Loughgall and in the nineties Kevin who, unlike his brothers, had never been involved in the IRA, was shot dead by loyalists. The family name, McKearney, was enough to mark him out.[1] Tommy himself joined the IRA in the seventies and was given a life sentence for murder. He went on hunger strike for fifty-three days (see chapter sixteen). The IRA ran in the McKearney family with both his grandfathers having fought in the Anglo-Irish war.

> I come from a part of the world in County Tyrone where we have always been very conscious of the fact that Ireland was partitioned against our express wishes. It's a situation somewhat analogous to Israel's West Bank. We're part of a state which we never wanted to be part of.
>
> I was very aware of discrimination, in common with most of my contemporaries . . . We used to always say that even a Catholic graduate had two options – either to go and teach in a Catholic school or emigrate. It was as simple as that.

It was no coincidence that the civil-rights movement was born in Tyrone in 1968. The setting was an unlikely one, a terrace of pebble-dash council houses called Kinnard Park in the predominantly Protestant village of Caledon, a couple of miles from the border with the Irish Republic. The houses lie off the main street, out of sight, by the ruins of an old woollen mill which once made tweeds for the Royal Family. At the turn of the century, Caledon was a thriving village with the mill at its heart, until partition cut it off from its natural hinterland. By June 1968, Caledon had been catapulted from obscurity to fame due to an incident in Kinnard Park that re-ignited the ancient conflict. For several weeks, Catholic squatters had occupied two new houses, numbers nine and eleven. The squatters had moved in from outside the district because the unionist councillor in the area they came from had refused to build houses for Catholic tenants. In those days, it was customary for the local unionist councillor to allocate housing. When the squatting family in number nine eventually moved out, the house was allocated to a nineteen-year-old, single, young Protestant woman, Emily Beattie. She happened to be secretary to the local councillor's solicitor. The Cameron Commission, which the Government appointed to investigate why the 'Troubles' broke out, concluded that 'by no stretch of the imagination could Miss Beattie be regarded as a priority tenant'.[2] A few days before Emily Beattie was due to move in, the remaining squatters in number eleven, Mrs Annie Mary Gildernew and her daughter and baby, were evicted in full view of television cameras. Austin Currie, the nationalist MP at Stormont, raised the matter in the Stormont parliament but received no satisfaction. In a heated exchange, John Taylor (now a Westminster MP and Deputy Leader of the Ulster Unionist Party) staunchly defended the unionist councillor's decision. Currie protested and was ordered to leave the House, which he did, throwing his notes across the floor at John Taylor.[3] The following day, along with two others, Austin Currie occupied the house that had been allocated to Emily Beattie. On 20 June 1968, the three were evicted by a policeman who happened to be Emily Beattie's brother and was due to move into the house with her.

Caledon became a *cause célèbre* and a focus for the discontent felt by Catholics all over Northern Ireland. The civil-rights campaign began. A month later, on 24 August 1968, the first civil-rights march was held from Coalisland to Dungannon as a protest about Caledon and housing policy in general over the whole area. For the first time, the Northern Ireland Civil Rights Association (NICRA) became involved in a large demonstration. It had been formed eighteen months earlier as a pressure group similar to the National Council for Civil Liberties in Britain, taking up individual cases of discrimination.[4] To date, its profile had been low and its publicity scant, but that was to change. In line with its policy and tactics, Cathal Goulding's IRA had already been at work infiltrating the civil-rights movement. According to a confidential RUC intelligence report, thirty of the seventy people present at the first Annual General Meeting of Civil Rights in Belfast in February 1968 were 'known republicans or IRA'.[5] With some reluctance, NICRA agreed to become involved in the Coalisland to Dungannon march. The police were notified and raised no objection, but it was the last thing that unionists in Dungannon wanted. The propaganda reverses of Caledon were bad enough without drawing even more attention to Catholic grievances and unionist sectarianism by allowing a mass march to go ahead. The unionist Chairman of the Council told the police that there would be trouble if the march was allowed to proceed into Dungannon Market Square as the organizers proposed. The Square was unionist territory and no nationalist parade had ever entered it. John Taylor, Stormont MP, gave the same advice.

A confrontation became inevitable when a Paisleyite group known as the Ulster Protestant Volunteers announced they planned to hold a meeting in the Market Square the same night. They calculated that the Stormont Government would therefore ban the civil-rights march to avoid a violent confrontation. The Government did not but, under unionist and loyalist pressure, the police re-routed the parade. Around 2,500 people marched the five miles from Coalisland to Dungannon and were halted at a police barrier in the town centre. The RUC calculated that around seventy of the stewards were republicans and ten were members of the IRA.[6] Behind the police lines was a crowd of around 1,500, no doubt many of them potential counter-demonstrators. But the rally passed off peacefully with the marchers singing 'We shall overcome' for the first time, the song that was to become the anthem of the civil-rights campaign. In that summer of 1968, there was genuine hope that peaceful protest would highlight Catholic grievances and the Prime Minister, Captain Terence O'Neill, encouraged by the Labour Government at Westminster, would address them. It was not to be. The grievances were not addressed, not least because O'Neill, already under pressure from Paisley, feared the political consequences of appearing to weaken in the face of nationalist demands.

The first real confrontation between the civil-rights movement and the state came in Derry on 5 October 1968. The city had become the symbol of unionist discrimination. Various bodies, including the Derry Republican Club (Sinn Fein under another name) came together with NICRA to plan a march in the city. The umbrella body was known as the 'October 5 Ad Hoc Committee'. Its composition was largely republican and left wing. From the beginning, the route was contentious and an affront to unionists. The 'Ad Hoc Committee' declared its intention to assemble in Duke Street on the east bank of the River Foyle, which divides the city, and march across the Craigavon bridge to the west bank and the war memorial in the Diamond which Protestants regard as their inner sanctum within the ancient city walls. Four days before the march, the loyalist Apprentice Boys of Derry announced their intention to march on the same day over much the same route, also starting in Duke Street and ending up in the Diamond. In fact, the Apprentice Boys march never took place. It was, as before, simply a tactic to get the civil-rights march banned or re-routed. It half succeeded. The hard-line Stormont Minister for Home Affairs, William Craig, did not ban the march but ruled that no parade should be allowed on the east bank of the river or within the city walls. In effect this meant that the marchers' intentions were thwarted. They could not assemble in Duke Street or march to the Diamond to assert their right to equal treatment, or 'parity of esteem' as republicans of today would call it. Craig's restriction only publicized the march and created an issue attracting not only more demonstrators but, critically, television cameras and the media. That day, over 2,000 marchers assembled in Duke Street. They represented not only Sinn Feiners and left wingers but also moderate nationalists like John Hume who had been active in organizing a Credit Union and a Housing Association in the city and whose star was rising as the civil-rights campaign gained momentum. Also present were three Westminster MPs anxious to draw parliament's attention to the problem of Northern Ireland. The marchers insisted they had a democratic right to protest peacefully and moved off to be confronted by a cordon of police. Television cameras recorded the scene as police officers drew batons and charged the crowd, laying into them without provocation. The Cameron Commission laid the blame squarely at the feet of the police. Suddenly, Northern Ireland was front-page news. The genie was out of the bottle and there was no putting it back. The events of 5 October 1968 made Catholics more determined than ever to force the issue, and Protestants equally determined to resist. The violent attack by baton-wielding policemen on peaceful demonstrators was a propaganda coup for the civil-rights movement. It showed the state to be the repressive instrument republicans had always maintained that it was.

The shock wave from Derry reverberated around the province and the world. Armagh, the historic seat of the Catholic and Protestant churches in Ireland, was the scene of the next confrontation. Plans were announced for a civil-rights march into the centre of Armagh on 30 November 1968. Paisley and his supporters would have none of it and told the police as much, warning that plans had been made for 'appropriate' action. O'Neill, they said, had lost control of the situation and capitulated in Derry. They had no intention of allowing the same thing to happen in Armagh. The police were in no doubt that if they did not stop the march, Paisley and his men would. Paisley's attitude towards the RUC was described as 'aggressive and threatening'. Armagh was, after all, his birthplace and he was not going to countenance what he saw as a republican invasion of it. The police and citizens of Armagh were left in no doubt that there was going to be trouble. Two days before the march, twenty posters appeared with the headline, *'For God and Ulster'. SOS.* It warned:

> To all Protestant religions.
> Don't let the Republicans, IRA and CRA [Civil Rights Association] make **Armagh** another **Londonderry.** Assemble in Armagh on Saturday, 30th November.
> Issued by UCDC [Ulster Constitution Defence Committee].[7]

In the early morning of the day of the march, Paisley told the police that he planned to hold a religious meeting and had no intention of interfering with anyone. The police were not taken in and far from banning the march as Paisley wanted, took steps to protect it from his followers. At eight o'clock the RUC set up roadblocks to intercept the hundreds of Paisleyites who poured into Armagh. They uncovered two revolvers and 220 other weapons including bill-hooks, pipes hammered into small points and scythes.[8.] To avoid the inevitable confrontation, the police put up barriers between the 5,000 oncoming civil-rights marchers and the 2,000 counter-demonstrators with a seventy-five yard 'no man's land' in between. The route through the city had already been blocked by a lorry which the counter-demonstrators had placed across the road. The situation was ugly but contained. Whereas many of the Paisleyites were armed with cudgels, some of them studded with nails, there was no evidence that any of the civil-rights demonstrators carried weapons of any kind.[9] Francie Molloy was a steward on the march.

Men with cudgels and masks were actually blocking a peaceful demonstration. Paisley would have been in the very front row. It was a scene that I had never seen before.

City centres were seen as the bastions of unionist power and they were trying to hold on to that power. I think they were trying to show us that they had the power to stop us and the power to dictate to the RUC to stop us. They also had this idea that if you held on to the centre of a town then you dominated the politics and the control of that town.

After speeches, the crowd dispersed. There had been no violence but the stand-off raised the political temperature even more. Loyalists were determined not to give in and the civil-rights supporters were determined to keep on marching. Captain O'Neill knew how serious the situation was and how precarious his own position was becoming as opposition from loyalist extremists increased. He had already been summoned to London to talk with Harold Wilson who, in the wake of the growing violence, could no longer ignore the problems of the province. O'Neill agreed to a package of reforms which still omitted the civil-rights movement's main demand of 'one man one vote' in local government elections. O'Neill lost out on both counts. To nationalists, he did not give enough. To loyalists, he gave too much. For a brief moment, it appeared that the forces of moderation might be winning, as O'Neill sacked his hardline Minister for Home Affairs, William Craig, who had been urging not reform but a far tougher line with the civil-rights demonstrators. Another opponent was removed when Paisley was subsequently gaoled for three months for 'unlawful assembly' in Armagh. But such events only fuelled loyalist anger.

As 1969 dawned, a newly formed group of largely left-wing students from Queens University called People's Democracy, organized a civil-rights 'long march' from Belfast to Derry. They were dismissive of the dire warnings of violence, saying that loyalists would simply say 'Boo!' and 'Go Home!'[10]. On 1 January 1969, eighty marchers set out from Belfast City Hall. By the time they reached the outskirts of Derry four days later, the crowd had grown to several hundred. The atmosphere in Derry was already tense after serious rioting had followed a Paisley religious meeting outside the city's Guildhall. The Cameron Commission entirely blames Paisley's followers for the riot and not any elements connected with civil rights. In fact John Hume and others tried to calm the situation. The disturbances ended with Major Ronald Bunting, one of Paisley's more emotional lieutenants, calling on people to join the Ulster Protestant Volunteers and assemble the following morning at a church near Burntollet Bridge to 'see the marchers on their way'.[11] He urged loyalists who 'wish to play a manly role' to 'arm themselves with whatever protective measures they feel to be suitable'.[12] The scene was set for violence, and on the morning of 4 January the marchers, who had spent the night in the village of Claudy a few miles out of Derry, deliberated whether to proceed or call the march off, having heard of the trouble in Derry the night before. They were also warned by the RUC that there was a hostile loyalist crowd at Burntollet bridge. Nevertheless, the marchers decided to proceed. At Burntollet, the march walked into a carefully prepared loyalist ambush involving around two hundred counter-demonstrators waiting in the fields above the bridge. The loyalists, wearing white armbands for identification, attacked the marchers with cudgels and clubs. A number of the attackers were believed to have been off-duty 'B' Specials. Thirteen people were officially listed as injured although, given the ferocity of the loyalist attack, the actual total was probably far higher. Francie Molloy saw what happened and believed that the IRA should have acted.

> Marchers were being batoned. They were being stoned. They were being attacked by Orange marchers and demonstrators. The traditional role of republicans [ie the IRA] at that time would have been defensive and I believe they should have carried it out. I would have disgreed with our organization's point of view.

That night in Derry, reportedly fuelled by alcohol, policemen invaded the Bogside area of Derry and laid into the residents and their property. The Bogsiders erected barricades for their future protection and 'Free Derry' was born. The reports of police misconduct were not an exaggeration. The Cameron Commission concluded:

> . . . a number of policemen were guilty of misconduct which
> involved assault and battery, malicious damage to property . . .
> and the use of provocative sectarian and political slogans . . . not
> only do we find these allegations of misconduct are substantiated
> but that for such conduct among members of a disciplined and
> well-led force there can be no acceptable justification or excuse.[13]

As 1969 unfolded nationalists became even more alienated from the RUC
and the institutions they were there to uphold. More Bogside incursions by
the police followed. On 19 April a forty-two-year-old taxi driver, Samuel
Devenney, was savagely beaten by the police and subsequently died from
his injuries. Thirty thousand people came to his funeral in silent protest
against what they saw as 'police brutality'. A week later, Captain O'Neill
resigned. It made no difference. An enquiry into Samuel Devenney's death
was conducted by an English Chief Constable, Sir Arthur Young, who
regretted that he could not identify those responsible because of what
he famously described as 'a conspiracy of silence' among the police.
For many Catholics, any lingering faith in 'British justice' died with
Samuel Devenney. However much these actions were highlighted and
condemned by the Cameron Commission, it was too late. So, too, was
the final introduction of 'one man, one vote' a month after O'Neill's
resignation. The damage had been done. The RUC was seen as a loyalist,
sectarian force and no official enquiry could change it. Nationalists, in
particular in Derry and Belfast, increasingly felt themselves under siege
and defenceless in the face of further attack by loyalists and the RUC. No
distinction was made between the two. The violent forces that had given
birth to the state were now tearing it apart. The IRA was to become the
beneficiary.

Chapter Four

Explosion

On a summer's day in July 1969, as sectarian conflict intensified in the North, 5,000 republicans gathered in a cemetery in Mullingar in County Westmeath. They came from all over Ireland to pay their respects to two IRA men, Peter Barnes and James McCormick, the last IRA men to be executed in England. They had gone to the scaffold many years before, on 7 February 1940, having been found guilty of a bomb attack in Coventry the previous summer which killed five civilians, barely a week before the outbreak of war. Once Barnes and McCormick had gone to their deaths, their names lived on only in the memories of veteran republicans and the republican Roll of Honour. Until 6 July 1969, that is, when the Wilson Government, as a gesture of goodwill to Dublin, allowed their remains to be returned to Ireland and reinterred at Mullingar. The day is significant not just because it revived memories of the IRA as it once was but because IRA veterans who were deeply unhappy with current IRA policy, saw their hopes rekindled. To the consternation of the existing IRA leadership, Jimmy Steele, the veteran IRA leader from Belfast who had spent over twenty years in gaol for the cause, put thoughts into words in a speech that was to herald the coming split and the birth of the Provisional IRA. Steele's association with the IRA went back a long way. He had first been arrested in 1923.[1] Billy McKee, a close friend and staunch supporter, was at Mullingar and had kept a recording of Steele's oration. Within six months, McKee was to become leader of the Belfast Provisionals. He let me listen to the tape. The quality was remarkable and its content even more so given the momentous events that were about to unfold. The speech gives a real flavour of the time and an insight into the growing fracture within the IRA between Belfast and Dublin.

> Our two martyred comrades who we honour today . . . went forth to carry the fight to the enemy, into enemy territory, using the only methods that will ever succeed, not the method of the politicians, nor the constitutionalists, but the method of soldiers, the method

of armed force. The ultimate aim of the Irish nation will never emerge from the political or constitutional platform. Indeed one is now expected to be more conversant with the teaching of Chairman Mao than those of our dead patriots. [At this point there is applause and shouts of 'hear, hear' on the tape.]

From the graves of patriot men and women spring living nations, said Pearse. May we hope that from these graves of Barnes and McCormick will emanate a combination of the old and new spirit . . . a spirit that will ensure the final completion of the task that our martyrs were compelled to leave unfinished.

Surprisingly, there was no reference to the growing crisis in the North and the increasing threat to the nationalist communities in Belfast and Derry. Nor was there mention of the IRA's traditional duty to protect those areas from loyalist attack. The very idea was heresy to the Goulding IRA leadership to whom defending Catholic areas from Protestant attack was a sectarian act and sectarianism of any kind was anathema. It was not surprising, therefore, that when Belfast exploded the following month, the IRA was totally unprepared for what happened. Defending Catholic enclaves was no longer part of its remit. Jimmy Steele was not talking about the crisis in the North but the need to renew 'armed struggle' as the only way of finally driving the British out of the North. Billy McKee was delighted to hear his old comrade's call to arms.

The people that I was with in Mullingar were mostly the old people from all round the country. We all clapped and shook hands with each other. I was elated. We might have thought this was a a bolt from the blue, but I knew Jimmy had been working on that statement for a good while and I knew there was something good going to come out of it. But a few days after we came back from Mullingar, two men came to Jimmy's house. One was Jimmy Sullivan from Belfast. [Sullivan was Adjutant in the IRA's Belfast Brigade.] The other was from Lurgan. I was in Jimmy's house at the time. They said they wanted to speak to him, so I left thinking it was a private talk. When I met Jimmy a few days afterwards he told me they had come up to tell him he had been dismissed by GHQ in Dublin because his speech was against army policy. We all knew that and were glad.

Joe Cahill was another IRA veteran from the forties and fifties who listened to Jimmy Steele at Mullingar. Cahill had already resigned from the IRA because of policies with which he did not agree. He went on to become OC of the Provisional IRA's Belfast Brigade in the early seventies and is now the father figure of the Republican Movement. At Mullingar, Steele said what Cahill and many Northerners in the crowd wanted to hear.

Jimmy Steele ruffled feathers a week before the Protestant marching season in the North approached its climax. Midsummer 1969 was always bound to be a flashpoint, given the violence and tensions of the previous six months. Confrontations tended to occur whenever a loyalist parade passed a particularly sensitive nationalist area. Marchers would hurl sectarian abuse and onlookers would often hurl stones. In Belfast, the nationalist Unity Flats, sitting at the bottom of the loyalist Shankill Road, was inevitably one such flashpoint as the Shankill Orangemen marched by on their way to the city centre. On 12 July 1969, a number of Scottish bands stopped in front of the Flats and provocatively marked time, shouting abuse at the residents to wind them up. The taunting had the desired effect and bottles and stones were hurled from the forecourt and verandas of the Flats. Loyalists tried to invade the Flats to retaliate but were stopped by police. That evening, the police had to move in again to stop a full-scale confrontation between the two sides.[2] There were similar incidents elsewhere in Belfast, with families living on the wrong side of the sectarian divide leaving their homes to retreat behind their own lines.

As August 1969 approached this sectarian violence and intimidation heightened the tension, with police warnings that if the situation got out of hand, they did not have the resources to cope. The next flashpoint was the annual march of the Apprentice Boys of Derry, due to take place on Tuesday, 12 August, when fifteen thousand Orangemen were expected to parade through the city. Feelings were already running high in Derry after fierce sectarian rioting had erupted after the Orange parades on the Twelfth (of July). Ominously, the police had not been able to contain the riot and had resorted to throwing stones themselves.

Given the climate in Derry at the beginning of August as the Apprentice Boys' march approached, it is astonishing that the march was not banned. It was clear to any politician with even the most rudimentary knowledge of recent events that serious trouble was inevitable. Both sides were spoiling for a fight and the Apprentice Boys' parade was the last opportunity of the summer for a final showdown. Belfast looked on with foreboding. The Stormont Government did not ban the march because it feared being accused by its more extreme supporters of capitulating to nationalist violence. But the Labour Government at Westminster had no such excuse. It could have taken the decision out of Stormont's hands and saved its face. Harold Wilson was minded to heed the warnings but subsequently admitted that 'unwiser counsels prevailed', thought to have been expressed by the Home Secretary, James Callaghan.

Meanwhile, at least some elements of the IRA were prepared to go against the party line from Dublin and move to defend their beleaguered community in the Bogside. Sean Keenan, an IRA veteran of the same generation and persuasion as Joe Cahill and Billy McKee, became Chairman of the Derry Citizens Defence Association. Keenan's men knew what needed to be done. Street committees were formed with the defence of the Bogside in mind. Seven of Keenan's co-founders were members of the James Connolly Republican Club – Sinn Fein by another name.[3] Plans were laid to erect barricades at strategic points and Keenan announced that people were to defend themselves with 'sticks, stones and the good old petrol bomb'. Firearms were ruled out, at least at this stage. It was no surprise that the local dairy found that only a few 'empties' were returned on 10 August, even fewer on the eleventh and none at all on the twelfth. In the days leading up to the twelfth the local police were anxious to talk to Sean Keenan about his plans to keep the peace on the day of the Apprentice Boys' parade but, not surprisingly, Keenan was not anxious to talk to the police. The lines were drawn for what was to become famously known as 'The Battle of the Bogside'.

On Tuesday, 12 August, the Orangemen assembled for their annual parade. Before they set off, a few Apprentice Boys contemptuously tossed coins from the city walls into groups of Catholics in the Bogside below. The contempt was mutual and anger grew. At 2.30pm, a handful of nails was thrown at the police on the other side of one of the barriers they had erected. Those nails triggered two days and two nights of ferocious rioting which the best efforts of John Hume and his moderate colleagues proved unable to stop. By four o'clock, the Apprentice Boys themselves had become the target and fought back. Half an hour later, the Bogsiders had stormed the police barricades and were attacking the RUC with bottles and stones. The stewards, such as they were, had lost control. A baton charge was ordered and the police pursued the fleeing rioters into the Bogside, not knowing they were charging into a trap. It was not their first incursion into the area and this time the residents were ready. As the RUC advanced, they ran into a hail of petrol bombs hurled from the top of the Rossville Flats which towered over the approach to the Bogside. A water cannon was brought in to soak the rioters but it ended up trying to douse the flames of burning houses and shops. By the early evening of the twelfth, the police were taking heavy casualties. Two thirds of one unit, forty-three out of fifty-nine officers, brought in from County Down to reinforce the local police, were injured. As the police advanced into the Bogside, they were followed by a stone-throwing crowd of young Protestant hooligans. Both police and Protestants met with fierce resistance. The use of CS gas was authorized. It was the first time it had been used as a riot control agent in the United Kingdom.

The Battle of the Bogside was a dramatic initiation for many of the young people who later became prominent in the IRA and Sinn Fein in Derry. Tony Miller was fifteen at the time. He later became a very active IRA Volunteer.

> I was throwing stones, petrol bombs, bottles, everything. You name it. I remember having a serious hatred for the RUC at the time and just wanting to sort of take revenge because you saw people getting battered and choked with CS gas. I was on top of Rossville Flats with a full view of everything that was going on. There were hundreds of people below and you had a perfect view. On top of the flats was a thing constructed by the Bogside people at the time. It was like a huge catapult. We could put the petrol bombs on it and shoot the petrol right onto the spot where the RUC were actually congregating. It was made out of scaffolding and a tyre inner tube that people put the petrol bombs on. We'd pull the tube right back and launch the petrol bombs. It was a powerful feeling, like you were fighting an armed force. That was my first conflict with the RUC.

One of those also throwing stones was the young Martin McGuinness – it was the beginning of his 'political' education. Mitchel McLaughlin was already a member of Sinn Fein at the time of the Battle of the Bogside. He had joined after the fiftieth anniversary of the Easter Rising, encouraged by his mother's cousin who was 'a very active republican'. This meant that he was a rioter with some political understanding. Today McLaughlin is National President of Sinn Fein. In August 1969, he was in the thick of it, 'one of the hardy souls on the ground face to face with the RUC'.

> There was this sense of impending invasion. Barricades being thrown up. People were learning new techniques of resistance and coming up with new ideas. The battle line was drawn across the front of the Rossville Flats. Those on top dominated the situation so the RUC were forced to retreat even when they made successful forays. I discovered subsequently that my wife was one of the few on top of the flats. It was a bit like 1916. Everybody claimed to have been there.

At 7am on the morning of Wednesday, 13 August a senior police officer who visited the scene informed his superiors that army intervention would be required within twenty-four hours. The necessary steps were put in motion so the troops were ready to go if needed. The rioting continued throughout the day with the newly elected Westminster MP, Bernadette Devlin, urging the Bogsiders on and helping to break up paving stones to supply them with ammunition.[4] At nine o'clock that evening the temperature was raised even more when the Irish Prime Minister, Jack Lynch, made a famous television broadcast. In loyalist minds, already convinced that the insurrection was an IRA plot orchestrated from Dublin, the Taoiseach's words created the impression that an invasion was about to begin.

> The Stormont Government is evidently no longer in control of the situation. Indeed the present situation is the inevitable outcome of the policies pursued for decades by successive Stormont Governments. It is clear that the Irish Government can no longer stand by and see innocent people injured and perhaps worse.
>
> Very many people have been injured and some of them seriously. We know that many of them do not wish to be treated in Six County hospitals. We have, therefore, directed Irish Army authorities to have field hospitals established in County Donegal adjacent to Derry and at other points along the border where they may be necessary.
>
> Recognizing, however, that the reunification of the national territory can provide the only permanent solution for the problem, it is our intention to request the British Government to enter into early negotiations with the Irish Government to review the present constitutional position of the Six Counties of Northern Ireland.[5]

Under the circumstances, few words could have inflamed loyalists more with demands for 'the restoration of the historic unity of our country'. Fifty years of Irish history flashed before their eyes. Far from calming the situation, Lynch's speech poured petrol on the flames. To loyalists, the proposed 'field hospitals' were nothing more than a jumping-off point for an Irish army invasion.[6]

On the afternoon of Thursday, 14 August, with the rioting in Derry now into its third day, Stormont finally authorized the mobilization of the 'B' Specials. A party of around sixty was dispatched, armed with batons and pick-axe handles.[7] Predictably, on their arrival, the rioting intensified. By five o'clock the police were utterly exhausted and the hastily drawn-up plans for military intervention were put into action. A company of the First Battalion of the Prince of Wales Own Regiment, stationed in the province, had already moved from Belfast to the outskirts of Derry as a precautionary measure, and now arrived to separate the rioters. Mitchel McLaughlin was in the thick of the confrontation when news came that the army was on its way.

I had very mixed emotions. We were involved in a confrontation at that stage with a group of 'B' Specials on the city walls. A man came running up from the Bogside to say that it was over, that the British army was in. 'It's over' was wrong. It might have been the end of the Battle of the Bogside but I had the strongest sense at that moment that it was the start of something else.

Within two hours, some semblance of order had been restored as the army took over the police lines. Scarman notes that the arrival of the troops was welcomed. 'The city was tired and the army presence afforded a sound reason for going home.'[8] But not all the rioters wanted to call it off. Bernadette Devlin, according to one account, urged the Bogsiders to fight on as Stormont had not been suspended and the army had intervened on Stormont's side.[9]

For many young men who were later to become involved in the IRA, the three-day riot was a first taste of battle. For others, too young to get involved, it was a piece of theatre in which they were not yet allowed to take part. Fourteen-year-old Raymond McCartney watched from his grandmother's house which was close to what became known as 'Free Derry' corner. McCartney subsequently joined the IRA and served life for murder. He, too, went fifty-three days on hunger strike.

From my granny's you could have watched what was happening without actually being out on the street or in danger. My father would have allowed me to watch but he would have said, 'look, I don't want you throwing stones, I don't want you getting hurt, I don't want you getting injured'. You witnessed over that period a community rising up and saying, 'we're going to change this state by hook or by crook'. They just stood up and said, 'no more'. And not only did they say, 'no more', they pushed the RUC out of the area and changed the nature of the Northern state forever.

But the young Hugh McMonagle had other ambitions as he watched the soldiers arrive.

I remember running down and seeing the soldiers had sealed off William Street. I remember being fascinated by all these soldiers with their helmets and rifles and backpacks. I was totally amazed at them and excited by them. I said, 'I'm going to be a soldier someday.'
Did you join the army?
I didn't join that particular army, no. I ended up joining the opposition.

By the end of Thursday, 14 August, when the rioting in Derry died down, nationalist areas in many parts of the province were ablaze, with rioting in Strabane, Lurgan, Dungannon, Coalisland, Newry and, most seriously, Belfast. Most of the rioting in Belfast had broken out the previous day, encouraged by requests for demonstrations in other areas to divert police resources from Derry and Jack Lynch's provocative words. In the hours after Lynch's broadcast, Hastings Street and Springfield Road police stations were attacked by crowds protesting against 'police brutality' in Derry. Stones and petrol bombs were thrown and some shooting broke out on both sides. The RUC also came under fire, possibly from the IRA, in the Leeson Street area of the Lower Falls. The disturbances quickly spread and a car showroom was looted and burned, its cars dragged out onto the Falls Road and set alight. A Catholic witness described the scene as 'a mob out of control'.[10]

But these disturbances were minor compared to what happened the following night, Thursday, 14 August, along what was known as the 'Orange-Green' line that separated the two communities. The situation was extremely confused. It is too simplistic to say that Protestants attacked Catholics without provocation. There was indeed some provocation by nationalists since the strategy was to foment disturbances to draw police resources from Derry. But once unleashed, the Protestant backlash was ferocious. Protestants attacked Catholics partly because they saw them attacking the police, partly because they hated them and partly because they wanted to teach them a lesson for daring to challenge the state.

The IRA was in no position to come to the rescue. Despite all the warning signs, no preparations had been made for defence. Defence was not IRA policy. Nevertheless, veterans like Billy McKee and John Kelly responded as best they could with what few old weapons they could get their hands on. The police responded by opening fire with .30 Browning machine guns mounted on armoured cars and capable of firing 500–600 rounds a minute. One of these rounds killed a nine-year-old Catholic boy, Patrick Rooney, in his home in Divis Flats. He was shot through the head whilst asleep in bed. The bullet had come through two walls.

To Catholics, the death of young Patrick Rooney was confirmation that the police were on the Protestants' side. The feeling was further confirmed when they saw their homes being torched by loyalist mobs and the police doing nothing about it. From that day forth, the Protestant onslaught entered nationalist folk history as the 'pogrom'. In Conway Street, forty-eight Catholic houses were burned to the ground. Half a mile up the road, the Catholic Clonard area also came under heavy attack. Bombay Street was devastated by loyalist mobs with sixty per cent of its houses destroyed by fire. Catholic houses in Cupar Street,

Kashmir Road and Clonard Gardens were also set alight. Close by, a Protestant mob of around 200 poured down Percy Street, crossed Divis Street and petrol-bombed the Roman Catholic school and some of the neighbouring houses. There were fears that if the school was destroyed, the next target would be St. Peter's church which stood just behind it. Shortly afterwards 'three or four' IRA men entered the school and opened fire at the Protestant mob in Divis Street with a Thompson submachine-gun and a couple of revolvers. It is the only recorded incident of IRA involvement in the rioting although there were others. Hospital records suggested that around eight Protestants received bullet wounds as a result. The young Brendan Hughes watched IRA veterans defend his school. He later became Commander of the Provisionals' Belfast Brigade, leader of the first prison hunger strike and a folk hero of the Republican Movement.

My old school was being attacked by loyalist crowds with petrol bombs. One of the IRA men who were there at the time had a Thompson submachine-gun and asked if anybody knew the layout of the school. I did and I went with this fella. Petrol bombs were coming in all over. There was a man on the roof of the school and people were shouting at him to fire into the crowd and he was shouting back that he was under orders to fire over the heads. That's exactly what he did. He fired a Thompson submachine-gun over the heads of the crowd and it stopped the school from being burnt down. That was my first contact with the IRA.

What impression did that IRA man with a Thompson submachine-gun have on you?

It gave me a sense of pride and a feeling that we had something to protect ourselves with. I wanted to be involved in that too because our whole community felt that we were under attack. I wanted to be part of that defence. From then on in, I got involved with the Movement.

At the end of two nights of ferocious rioting and gunfire, Catholic streets had been burned to the ground and five Catholics and two Protestants had been shot dead. Hundreds had been injured and thousands made refugees. The situation was out of control. Stormont and Westminster took the decision they had long been trying to avoid. Troops would have to be sent over from England to reinforce the battalions already stationed in the North. Above all, Stormont wished to avoid this commitment because it feared the constitutional repercussions: that the British Government, having committed troops, might abolish Stormont since it would not wish the army to be under its control. To unionists, abolishing Stormont would mean giving nationalists what they most wanted. The Wilson Government had already communicated this view to James Chichester-Clark, the Stormont Prime Minister who succeeded Captain O'Neill, when he visited London on 8 August 1969, a week before the Apprentice Boys' parade. Chichester-Clark had been left in no doubt that 'the extended use of troops would involve a consideration of Northern Ireland's constitutional position by the United Kingdom Government in Westminster'.[11] It was the last thing any Stormont Prime Minister wanted to hear.

But there was even less enthusiasm to commit troops on the part of the Wilson Government. Such a decision would risk Westminster becoming directly involved in the affairs of Northern Ireland, something it had spent many years trying to avoid. It was a phone call made from a bookie's shop on the Falls Road in the middle of the rioting that made Jim Callaghan, the Home Secretary, realize he had no choice. The call was made by the local nationalist Stormont MP, Gerry Fitt.

> There was a crowd of three or four hundred people, pulling my coat, screaming and shouting that they were going to be murdered in their beds and begging, begging me to get the army in. I quietened them all down and said, 'Look, before I lift the telephone and ring Jim Callaghan, what do you want me to say? You're all asking me to get the army in?' And they all said yes. So I picked up the phone and rang him. I said, 'I'm pleading with you, Jim. Send in the army.' And I'll never forget his reply. 'Gerry,' he says, 'I can get the army in but it's going to be a devil of a job to get it out.'[12]

But the momentous decision to call in the army was not made as a result of a phone call from a bookie's office on the Falls Road. It was made by senior police officers in Belfast when they realized that the situation was beyond their control. They made their recommendation to the Stormont Cabinet which, in turn, transmitted the request to London. That was at 12.25pm on Friday, 15 August. The British Government complied. It was a fateful decision. But despite all the warnings that had previously been given about the 'constitutional implications' of deploying troops, Stormont was left untouched. It was, perhaps, the greatest political mistake of the time. Although we now have the benefit of hindsight, had Stormont been abolished in August 1969 and Westminster taken over the running of the province, the brakes would probably have been applied to the deteriorating situation. Root and branch reform would have been introduced, the army would have remained under Westminster's control, and the IRA would not have been presented with opportunities that were the result of security decisions made to a unionist agenda.

Today Lord Callaghan is sanguine about the historic decision his Government took and defends its decision not to abolish Stormont.

> I never do believe frankly that anybody from this side of the water understands Ireland and I've never flattered myself that I understand the situation fully. I think very few people do. Certainly we didn't have enough understanding of it at that time.

It was a sad admission.

Those violent days in August 1969 were a turning point for the IRA. Despite the efforts of Billy McKee, John Steele, Martin Meehan and a handful of veterans to defend their areas, the IRA's reputation was severely damaged. Slogans appeared on the walls in Belfast, 'IRA – I Ran Away.' Martin Meehan remembers the slogan being chanted at a meeting when 'the IRA came in for a lot of stick'. Joe Cahill remembers the taunts hurled at him and Jimmy Steele. Seán MacStiofáin had a similar experience. Unlike Cahill, he had remained loyal to the IRA's then Chief of Staff, Cathal Goulding.

> I went up to Belfast shortly after the pogroms in August and I was told that I was the only one from 'down there' who was acceptable 'up here'. I tried to reason with them and I suppose I tried to make excuses for Goulding and the Dublin leadership. I was hoping against hope that the events of 1969 would restore some sanity in the Republican Movement and perhaps persuade Goulding and others that their policies were wrong and that we could remain united and face the future together. But things didn't work out that way.

They did not. The events of August 1969 forced the growing divisions within the IRA out into the open. The 'Provos' were about to be born.

Chapter Five

Provos

In the hot summer of 1969, the order to return to barracks in Ireland came out of the blue for British soldiers, as they lay on beaches listening to pirate radio stations or relaxed with their families and girlfriends during their summer leave. The 'Troubles', as they had become euphemistically known, figured nightly on the news and from time to time captured the newspaper headlines, but for most soldiers, as for most of the rest of the population, they could have been happening on the dark side of the moon, not on Britain's doorstep. The military mind was focused on the threat from beyond the Iron Curtain not beyond the Irish Sea.

The decade was coming to an end and with it the deployment of British troops to deal with insurgencies in the last outposts of Empire. Less than two years earlier, the army had left Aden as the Union Jack was finally lowered after flying over the colony for 128 years. One era was ending and another beginning, although few that summer could have guessed that it was one which would herald almost thirty years of bloodshed and near civil war in part of the United Kingdom. The IRA was something from history books or black and white newsreels of the fifties. Despite the violent clashes between loyalists and civil-rights demonstrators now so vividly captured by the television cameras, Ireland was still a place you went for your holidays. I remember talking to the army's General Officer Commanding (GOC) at the time, General Sir Ian Freeland, who commented how he was really looking forward to his new posting because of the shooting and fishing.

But, in the climate of August 1969, soldiers knew what they were going into Belfast to do. It seemed simple. Catholics had demanded civil rights, a concept made universal by Martin Luther King. Protestants resisted and attacked Catholics. The police could not cope. The army had to go in to separate the two sides and restore order. But troops basically felt they were going in to rescue the Catholics, which is certainly how the Catholics saw it as smoke was still rising from their burned-out houses. Soldiers, many of whom were to lose close friends in the following twenty-five years, or

suffer dreadful injuries themselves, remember their early days in Belfast
with nostalgic affection. The cups of tea were endless and film of soldiers
being fêted and fed by a grateful Catholic population captures a warm
and distant moment in history. I refer to most of the soldiers by their first
names to protect their identities, not because of what they felt when they
were first deployed but because of what some of them subsequently said
and did as the situation deteriorated after a few short, sad months. 'Dave'
summed up the reception the troops received when they marched into
a still-burning Belfast in August 1969.

> I felt like a knight in shining armour. It was marvellous. 'Cheers!',
> 'Nice to see you!', 'Hello soldier!' Kids were following you every-
> where. Tea? There was too much tea – and buns and sandwiches.
> Six o'clock in the morning and you'd have full breakfast. They'd
> be out there with trays. I must have put on about a stone. The
> reception was fantastic.[1]

But it wasn't all tea and buns. Confusions arose because, whilst most soldiers
knew who the victims were, few had any idea of the sectarian geography
of West Belfast, where one end of a street may be Catholic and the other
Protestant. The army's orders were to stand in the middle and assert Her
Majesty's authority. But the kit and the training with which they had to
do it had been designed with rather different conflicts in mind. 'Bruce'
remembers unpacking the boxes when his company arrived in Belfast and
taking out a huge, internal security pack called 'Keeping the Peace'.

> It was all about 'box' formations. All lovely stuff. You unfurled this
> banner and walked down the Falls Road in box formation. But when
> we unfurled the banner we found it was in Arabic. It had last been
> used in Aden.[2]

Many of those who subsequently joined the IRA and spent much of their
young lives in gaol were still in short trousers. The sudden appearance of
soldiers on their streets in Belfast and Derry was a cause of great excitement.
Their childhood heroes had come to town. Gerard Hodgkins had always
wanted to join the army.

> You grow up reading the *Victor* and the *Hotspur* and comics like that
> and watching John Wayne and Battle of Britain movies. You had a
> romantic notion about them and then, suddenly, 'bang!', they're on
> your street. It was great. I remember one Saturday afternoon, there
> were a couple of Saracens sitting at each end of the street and we

were actually sitting in the back of one with these soldiers and just
chatting away to them, drinking tea and having a bit of a banter. I
actually think that they were paratroopers because I remember one
of them getting me a wee set of wings, the cloth ones, you know.
I suppose you were mesmerized in a way. You weren't looking at
them and saying, 'well, you're British and I'm Irish and you're the
enemy', or anything like that. I think I was about ten or eleven then.
I had the mind of a child, and politics just wasn't part of my life.

But Gerard was to join another army. So, too, was Hugh McMonagle
from Derry who in those far-off days idolized the soldiers. In 1969, the
army had no difficulty in winning young hearts and minds.

I remember being fascinated – totally amazed and excited. They all
had helmets and rifles and had their backpacks on. I said, 'I'm going
to be soldier some day'. They set up an army camp beside me where I
lived in Bligh's Lane and they formed what they called the 'Red Cap
Club'. Me and a whole load of other people in my area all joined. It
was run like a sort of youth club. We got on great with them.
I used to go down to the fish shop and fetch five fish suppers and
four pies and chips. The fish shop used to be able to see us coming
down. We were all for the army like, doing their errands. I used to
say at that time, 'I wish I could join the army when I get older'. It
was my boyhood wish.

Neither Hugh nor Gerard came from republican families so there were
no warning voices from within. But even in families where there was a
republican tradition, people found it difficult not to be grateful for the
army's intervention. Richard McAuley saw his first soldiers on the Glen
Road in West Belfast.

I remember thinking, 'thank God'. I think like most people, I was
very glad to see them because houses and streets were being destroyed
and people were being killed. There was no way of defending the
areas against that. It just seemed as the days and nights would go
on, more and more people would die, and more houses would be
destroyed. Seeing British soldiers on the street, I got this sense that
there's someone there now to protect us, to defend us against these
incursions into our area.

Brendan Hughes too, was excited by the troops' arrival although his
republican father felt differently.

A lot of the troops that had actually come in were very young. Some of them were sixteen, seventeen, eighteen years of age and they set up sandbags in the corner of the streets. I remember people bringing tea to them at the corner of our street and my father objecting. I also remember talking to the British soldiers and actually feeling for them because they were so young and caught up in this situation. Most of them were frightened and they were sitting in the corner of these streets behind sandbags and you could have walked up behind them and said, 'Boo!' – which I did. I remember sitting at the corner talking to the British troops – sometimes at one, two, three o'clock in the morning.

Even IRA veterans like John Kelly who had helped in the defence of the Lower Falls, grudgingly welcomed military intervention. 'I would have to say that we were relieved to see them arrive, yes,' he said. 'But we did not anticipate that they would stay on as an occupying force to maintain the established position of Unionism within the Six Counties.' How did Billy McKee feel when he saw nationalists welcoming the army and giving them cups of tea?

Well, I didn't like it but I couldn't blame them. They were only ordinary folk and they were going through a state of shock. There were some elderly people who'd lived through the 1920 trouble when people were burned out of their houses. They'd thought that was the last they'd see of it. But they were wrong. There was one woman who said that this was the third time she'd been burned out of Cupar Street – 1920, 1935 and 1969. You couldn't blame those people if they took anybody in and gave them a cup of tea.

The IRA, or what there was of it, was also in a state of shock. Belfast veterans of the forties and fifties campaign like Billy McKee, Jimmy Steele, Joe Cahill and Jimmy Drumm felt the IRA had let the people down and people were not slow in telling them so. The growing split which first became publicly apparent in Steele's speech at Mullingar the previous month, now became inevitable. Seán MacStiofáin, the IRA's Dublin-based Chief of Intelligence, came up to Belfast to try to heal the wounds. Although he had remained loyal to Cathal Goulding's leadership and been rewarded by his election to the Army Council, he had never fully embraced Goulding's policy of taking the IRA 'into the never-never land of theoretical Marxism and parliamentary politics'.[3] MacStiofáin had been at Mullingar, heard Jimmy Steele's speech and agreed with the sentiments but felt that he should have kept them to himself and not made them public.

It was not long before the dissidents took matters into their own hands. Less than a fortnight after the army came in, they held a secret meeting on 24 August 1969 at the social club in Andersonstown's Casement Park Gaelic football club. Although they would not have been aware of it at the time, those present were to become the nucleus of the Provisional leadership that was to dominate the events of the next twenty-five years. Besides the veterans Billy McKee, John Kelly, Joe Cahill and Leo Martin were Seamus Twomey, who was to become the Provisional IRA's Chief of Staff through the most violent period of the seventies, and the young Gerry Adams, a rising republican star in the Ballymurphy estate in West Belfast, his home territory. Also present was David O'Connell from Dublin, another veteran of the IRA's fifties border campaign, who was to become the Provisionals' leading political strategist through the seventies until he was eclipsed by Gerry Adams and the new Belfast leadership. The group decided that they were going to issue an ultimatum to the existing pro-Goulding IRA leadership in Belfast, the OC, Billy McMillen, and his Adjutant, Jim Sullivan: unless Cathal Goulding and three of his key supporters on the IRA's General Headquarters' Staff in Dublin resigned, they would break away and go it alone. After the meeting, the IRA's fragmented structure in Belfast was consulted to ensure support for such a move. The dissidents did not want blood on the streets. Fourteen of the IRA's seventeen areas in the city agreed. As Joe Cahill reflected, McMillen and Sullivan 'didn't have a lot of choice because the vast majority of IRA Volunteers in Belfast were prepared to break with Dublin'.[4] As John Kelly admitted, they were planning a coup.

A month later, on 22 September 1969, the dissidents confronted the IRA leadership by bursting in on a meeting of the Belfast Brigade Staff being held in Cyprus Street. The surprise visitors were armed as it was thought unlikely that McMillen and Sullivan would simply stand down without a fight. The dissidents marched in and announced to the startled meeting that they were taking over as the existing IRA leadership had betrayed the nationalist people. Given the subsequent internecine history of IRA feuds, it was a miracle that there was no bloodshed. I asked Billy McKee what he had said to McMillen and Sullivan.

I said everything I could – and I wasn't the only one. I told them that they had failed the people, the nationalist people of the North. I told them that they used the money that they got from subscriptions for their own political ends, not for weapons to defend the people. And I also told them that over the three years previous, the writing was on the wall. The dogs were barking in the street that there was going to be sectarian trouble in Belfast. Paisley was stirring it up. But it was like hitting your head against a stone wall. They tried to make some of the flimsiest excuses but then eventually most of them admitted they had been at fault.

We weren't so much wanting to take over the IRA as determined to break from Dublin. We realized that the Dublin crowd and the Dublin leadership were nothing other than con-men. They were only using the North as a base, a springboard to help them in their left-wing political field. That was their intention – to use the IRA up here for that purpose. And they used it. So the Northern lads got together and we told them that we wouldn't have any more truck with the South and with the Dublin leadership.

A compromise was reached. There was to be a notional separation from Dublin, six of the dissidents were drafted onto the Belfast Brigade Staff and Billy McMillen was to remain Brigade OC in a move which kept the institutional link. The Dublin leadership had little option other than to agree, however reluctantly, 'for the sake of unity'. It offered to keep open the Belfast Brigade's seats on the Army Council should there later be a change of heart but McKee would not hear of it. 'The offer was refused,' he affirmed. 'There would be no truck with Dublin.'

With differences buried, if only temporarily, the new 'combined' IRA in Belfast continued its search for arms as there was no guarantee that the peace that, with the arrival of the army, had descended on the city, would last and an IRA without arms was, as recent history had all too painfully shown, an IRA unprepared. 'What did we do for weapons?' said McKee. 'We went out and looked for them. We stole them, begged them and bought them. Anywhere. From England, Scotland, Ireland, the continent and America. From anybody. Whoever had them for sale.' There were literally hundreds of old weapons all over the country that had been stashed away after previous IRA campaigns. Some were carefully oiled and wrapped in sheets. Others were just dumped and left to rust. After the trauma of August 1969 many now found their way to the North. But there was also hope that modern weapons would soon be on their way, purchased with funds covertly supplied by members of the Fianna Fail Dublin Government to be prepared for a 'Doomsday' situation that might arise in the North. John Kelly and the Derry IRA veteran, Sean Keenan, set off for America in December 1969 to meet supporters living in the Bronx. For a century, Irish America had given the IRA and its predecessor, the Irish Republican Brotherhood (IRB), material and financial support in their fight against the British. America's

later role in the current conflict was to be no different. John Kelly was
surprised at the reaction he encountered.

> We had been told by the Irish Government that money was available
> for the procurement of arms and we had told our Irish American
> supporters at that meeting that that was where the money was
> coming from. Surprise wasn't in it. Some of them, the more
> traditional republicans in New York, were aghast at the notion
> of taking money from the Free State Government to procure arms.
> We had a problem convincing them. We said that if they couldn't
> provide the money, we weren't going to argue or quibble about
> where the money was coming from.

The mission did not succeed as history prevented die-hard Irish Americans
from using 'tainted' Free State money to buy guns. Nevertheless, channels
of communication and lines of procurement were established, which the
Provisionals were later to use to devastating effect. Kelly and company then
moved on to Europe, acting on the advice of Neil Blaney, the Minister
for Agriculture in the Dublin Government. According to Kelly, Blaney
told them of 'a quicker route'. But their arms-buying adventures on the
continent ended in farce. They did procure weapons but the consignment
was seized on arrival at Dublin airport. As the dissidents were not having
much success as gun runners, in the months after August 1969 the IRA had
to rely on the ancient weapons that emerged from the dumps. According
to Martin Meehan, they came in in 'bucket loads'.

> They were coming from everywhere, mostly from old republicans
> who had buried gear in the twenties, thirties and forties. They
> were in perfect working order. We couldn't cope sometimes with
> the amount of gear coming in. It was unbelievable. There were
> submachine-guns, old .303 rifles and 'Peter the Painters' – a pistol
> on a sort of a handle to give you a better grip than an ordinary
> pistol would.

But not all republicans in Belfast flocked to the standard of the new
'combined' IRA with its growing arsenal of antiques. Some were
suspicious of McKee's intentions. Martin Meehan was originally one
such sceptic. Having resigned from the IRA in disgust after what he
saw as the fiasco of August 1969, he was wary about joining up again
until he was certain where the Movement was going. He had plenty of
time to think about it, as he was arrested on 22 August 1969 for riotous
behaviour and spent two months in gaol. Meehan initially suspected that

the 'joint command' was a purely cosmetic exercise designed by McKee and the 'old Brigade' to find out where the arms dumps were prior to making a complete break and setting up on their own. 'They had their own agenda,' Meehan remembers. 'They were simply playing for time. When they found out all they wanted to know, then they would make a move.' By now, most of the weapons had been brought in across the border. Billy McKee spoke to Meehan, explained his thinking and invited him to rejoin.

> He outlined what his plans were. He guaranteed first and foremost that the nationalist areas would be defended at all costs and that what had happened in 1969 would never happen again.
>
> **What did he tell you about the policy towards British soldiers?**
>
> He didn't indicate that there was going to be an immediate offensive against the British army. He said, 'these things take time. People have to be trained. People have to be motivated. People have to be equipped. All this won't just happen overnight.' But the intention was there and it sounded good to me.

Martin Meehan rejoined the IRA.

Little, if any, of this was known to the Labour Government, still heaving sighs of relief that they appeared to have contained the situation and had not been forced to take the drastic step of introducing direct rule. But they did not sit back and do nothing. They knew that the explosion had not happened without cause and that there were serious Catholic grievances needing to be redressed. For the first time, a UK Representative's Office was set up at Stormont, along the corridor from the office of the Prime Minister, Major James Chichester-Clark. Its first occupant was an urbane, former Foreign Office diplomat, Oliver Wright. He was known as 'The Big Fella along the Corridor'. Wright's job was to see that Stormont addressed the grievances and to tick them off one by one. By Christmas 1969, he thought they were making 'good progress'. The hated 'B' Specials had been abolished and an inquiry under Lord Hunt had been set up to examine policing and the composition of the RUC. The Hunt Report recommended the disarming of the police and the establishment of the Ulster Defence Regiment (UDR) which, as the years went by, became just as hated by Catholics as the 'B' Specials had been. The UDR was almost entirely Protestant in its composition because Catholics refused to join. Local government was to be reformed and fair employment practices introduced. Oliver Wright thought 'we were doing all right'.

I used to say, 'you've done that, so tick it off'. I'm an Englishman –
damn it! – and how can an Englishman be expected to understand
Ireland! We were making progress and I'm quite sure that at that time
the Catholic community saw the British Government as their friend,
trying to do their best to ensure that Stormont introduced the reforms
that they, the Catholic community, wanted. And we did it.

But the reforms were too late. The damage had already been done.
Furthermore, to loyalists, they smacked of capitulation to the enemy
and only served to fuel the growing sectarian tensions which were on
the point of further explosion.

As Christmas 1969 approached, the date when many soldiers had expected
to return home, their job well done, there was an earthquake in the
republican camp, although it hardly seemed like it at the time. The split
in the IRA which had become more and more inevitable as the months
rolled by, finally happened. Ironically it came about not over the failure
of the IRA to defend nationalists in August 1969 but over the principle
that had sustained the IRA for the previous fifty years: 'abstentionism',
the Republican Movement's cardinal article of faith. Although republicans
could stand in elections to the parliaments at Westminster, Stormont and
Dublin, no successful candidate ever took his or her seat since to do so
would be to recognize the legitimacy of these institutions. The IRA's
whole existence and self-styled legitimacy rested on its refusal to recognize
these parliaments which, to republicans, had no moral or legal authority. It
claimed that, as the Army of the Irish Republic, it owed its allegiance to the
all-Ireland parliament, Dail Eireann, established after Sinn Fein's sweeping
victories in the general election of 1919. Abstentionism was the moral
certainty on which the IRA had drawn for over a half a century. But to
the Goulding wing of the IRA, abstentionism was part of the baggage
of history which had become an impediment to the socialist revolution
the IRA was now committed to undertake through the political process.
This, of necessity, entailed taking seats in Leinster House, the seat of the
Dublin parliament. Ironically, it was this issue that was to split the IRA
again seventeen years later in 1986 when Gerry Adams persuaded the
Republican Movement to abandon the principle of abstentionism that
had originally caused the split and brought the Provisionals into being.
There were to be further defections, although not as serious, in 1997, after
Sinn Fein entered all-party talks. On a wet night in mid-December 1969,
the issue came to a head at an Extraordinary IRA Army Convention held
in an isolated country village in the heart of the Irish Republic. MacStiofáin,
as Director of Intelligence, knew what was coming and had a car and driver

standing by to take him to Belfast once the result was known, not that there was any doubt what that result would be. There were two main items on the Convention's agenda. First, a motion that the IRA should enter a 'National Liberation Front' in alliance with 'the radical left'. Second, that the policy of parliamentary abstentionism should be ended. Technically, the latter was a matter for Sinn Fein, but Sinn Fein could not have acted without the IRA first giving its agreement. The same principle applied to the second split in 1986. The meeting was packed with Goulding's supporters. There was no representation from Belfast as by then Belfast had broken with Dublin and other delegations who might have been expected to support MacStiofáin had not, for whatever reason, arrived. There were allegations that dissident delegates had been prevented from getting to the Convention – some were reported to have been left at a pick-up point – and that delegations known to be favourable to the leadership line were given extra representation. MacStiofáin tried, unsuccessfully, to get the second motion debated first before delegates' heads started to spin. The National Liberation Front motion was passed. On the second motion, MacStiofáin spoke last, urging the delegates to vote against it. But they did not. The outcome was a foregone conclusion. MacStiofáin recalls the historic decision.

> The Convention was packed. The atmosphere was very tense, unlike any Convention I can remember. The motion was steam-rollered through. I remember saying that this was the end of the IRA as we knew it.

MacStiofáin insists that reports that he broke down and cried are false. Nor, contrary to belief, did he walk out of the Convention. The atmosphere, he recalls, was unhysterical, given the dramatic decisions just made. He left at the end of the proceedings and gathered his supporters around him. Before he did so, Cathal Goulding approached without hostility and asked MacStiofáin to have a talk before he decided to do anything. The conversation was academic as the split was irrevocable. The decision was made to contact those IRA units who had not been represented at the Convention and to canvass support throughout all thirty-two counties of Ireland. MacStiofáin's priority was to go to Belfast as soon as possible and break the news to the dissidents who had not attended the Convention, having already broken with Dublin following their 'coup'. On a grey December morning, he walked out to his car and told his driver to head north. MacStiofáin was starving and tucked into cold chicken.[5]

Veterans like Billy McKee were appalled at the Convention's rejection of abstentionism. In his eyes, it removed the IRA's moral basis for killing and was a betrayal of all the IRA stood for.

Let's put it this way. If you start to recognize the Twenty-six County Government, you've no right to have an IRA there. You've no right to go out and rob banks or rob anybody. You've no right to take a life because they're your people and they're your government. If you recognize them as a government, you must fall in line with them. You've no authority to take a life. Then it would be murder. I wouldn't ask anybody to take a life in the Twenty-six Counties because he's guilty of murder if he recognizes the government.

So the real reason for the split was ideological. It wasn't anything to do with the failure of the IRA to defend nationalists?

No, no, it was nothing to do with that. It would have happened even if the IRA had been strong in 1969 and then decided for to break that rule. It was a very strong rule all through the whole history of the IRA.

But as far as MacStiofáin was concerned, those who had split from Goulding had no standing in the IRA's constitution without ratification by an Army Convention. In Belfast, he addressed a meeting of twenty IRA men and a special Convention was called. He could count on the support of nine of the thirteen IRA units in the city. Billy McMillen and Jim Sullivan were not amongst his supporters. The Convention elected a new provisional Army Executive which in turn elected a new provisional IRA leadership with Seán MacStiofáin as the new provisional Chief of Staff. They became known as the 'Provisionals' because that is precisely what they were. Those who had stayed with Cathal Goulding became known as the 'Officials' – or the National Liberation Front (NLF) – to those who had walked out of the meeting or already split with Goulding. The new 'Provisional' leadership agreed to hold another Army Convention within the next six to twelve months to place the organization on a proper constitutional footing. In fact, the Convention met nine months later, in September 1970, and ratified the change so that technically the 'Provisionals' ceased to exist. Nevertheless, the name stuck.

On 28 December 1969, the Provisional Army Council issued its first public statement in which it said that the split was:

> . . . the logical outcome of an obsession in recent years with parliamentary politics, with the consequent undermining of the basic military role of the Irish Republican Army. The failure to provide the maximum defence possible of our people in Belfast and other parts of the Six Counties against the forces of British Imperialism last August is ample evidence of this neglect.[6]

The statement said it all. But the parting of the ways was not complete until Sinn Fein had been through the same process, which happened a fortnight later. There was even less doubt as to the outcome this time. The difference was that now the divisions were out in the open as Sinn Fein, unlike the IRA, held its meeting in public, or at least in a public place. On 11 January 1970, Sinn Fein delegates met for their Ard Fheis (annual conference) at the Intercontinental hotel in Dublin. Delegates knew that the decision had already been made but MacStiofáin and Ruairí Ó'Brádaigh, the President of Sinn Fein, still tried to swing the argument against the rejection of abstentionism. Not surprisingly, they failed, as Ó'Brádaigh recalls.

> The atmosphere was highly charged. The press were excluded and the television cameras were mounted outside the doors. It was a very difficult time. According to the Sinn Fein constitution, a two-thirds majority was necessary. The 'Officials' did not secure that majority but pressed their luck and put forward a resolution giving recognition to the 'Official' Army Council. Whereupon Seán MacStiofáin countered by going to another microphone and announcing that he was giving his allegiance to the 'Provisional' Army Council. So there we had the crux.
>
> It was obvious that with their simple but not two-thirds majority, they would push this through and this would compromise those of us who disagreed. So I jumped up and said it was time to leave and we had to force our way out. In fact, we had to fight our way out. An attempt was made by the 'Officials' to overturn the cameras outside. It was all very, very tense and very highly charged. So we made our way to another venue and elected a caretaker Sinn Fein Executive [Ard Chomhairle] to carry on and reorganize the country.

The historic split was complete. The 'Provos' were born.

As 1970 dawned, few soldiers in Belfast had any idea of the changes within the Republican Movement. Cups of tea and 'hearts and minds' were still the order of the day. The troops who had arrived to a hero's welcome a few months earlier, left at the end of their tour with that welcome still ringing in their ears. 'Dave' who felt like 'a knight in shining armour' when he arrived, left Belfast with a heavy heart.

> It was a day of great sadness. I was leaving friends, people we knew. Leaving the girls behind was probably the saddest thing of all. The girls lined up to wave goodbye. It was like the Wailing Wall of

Jerusalem. I remember a hit at the time – 'Leaving on a Jet Plane'. You know, the lines about 'packing my bags and hating to go and don't know when I'll be back again'. We were all singing our head off and the girls were waving and throwing their knickers at us. God, bless 'em! And they were all shouting 'we'll wait for you!'

And when you did come back again?

Everything had changed. Attitudes had changed. It was sad. People were frightened. Didn't want to know us. No tea. No scones. No breakfasts. People shunned us.

By the summer of 1970, the soldiers who had come in to protect the Catholics were no longer seen by them as 'knights in shining armour' but instruments of the hated Stormont regime. Why did the honeymoon end?

Chapter Six

Defence

By February 1970, three of the eight extra army units deployed in Northern Ireland to deal with the emergency were withdrawn to Britain. The British Government clearly thought the situation had been brought under control. With luck, the dramatic events of the previous year would be seen as a brief nightmare and the province could now settle down to some kind of stability with the introduction of the long-overdue reforms. The likelihood of sectarian confrontation would, it was hoped, be minimized by the erection of a Berlin-type wall along the interface between the Protestant Shankill Road and the Catholic Falls Road to keep the two communities apart. It was euphemistically known as the 'peace line'. Journalists were withdrawn too, as their editors decided the story was over, at least for the time being, and back home a general election was on the cards that might spell the end of the Wilson era.

But in reality the violence was only just beginning. Its escalation was not due to manipulation by any particular force but because circumstances combined to trigger the explosion which no amount of belated good intentions by the British Government could, at this stage, defuse. History had developed its own momentum, accelerated by recent events. The situation was complicated by the fact that there were no longer just two parties to the conflict, Catholics and Protestants, but four. The other two were now the British army and the IRA, both Official and Provisional. In the atmosphere of 1970, action by any one of the parties was bound to provoke a response by one of the others, in turn provoking a further reaction. The question then was where the killing would stop. There were thirteen deaths in 1969, twenty-five in 1970, 174 in 1971 and 467 in 1972.[1] Whilst it would be wrong to think that the whole situation was manipulated by the IRA to further its own ends, there is no doubt the Provisionals took advantage of the opportunities presenting themselves, not least by the actions of the British army, which were at times driven by a mixture of ignorance, lack of discipline and imprudent political and military direction. These combined to end the honeymoon between the nationalist population and the army.

At the beginning of 1970, the Provisional IRA had three aims, agreed at the first meeting of the new Provisional Army Council. First, to make ready for the defence of the nationalist areas in preparation for the loyalists' summer marching season, in order to avoid a repetition of 1969. Second, to retaliate against the army should British troops harass the nationalist population. Third, to make ready for a final offensive against 'the British occupation system'. Getting the British out was the most important of the three aims and no one should have been surprised at it given the history of the IRA. But the offensive was only to be taken when the IRA was ready, which meant when the Provisionals had sufficient, properly trained and armed Volunteers. This would not happen overnight. Modern weapons had to be acquired and Volunteers had to learn how to use them. The 'Provos' were prepared to bide their time. Getting the British out was not a pressing priority in early 1970, although circumstances were to accelerate the process. In the meantime, because newly recruited Volunteers had to do something to maintain their motivation, selective sabotage operations were sanctioned 'at the discretion of the national and local leadership in the Northern areas concerned'.[2] Such operations against security and economic targets would keep up morale as well as hurting the British and unionist establishments controlling the commercial life of Northern Ireland. It was better than sitting around doing nothing. In those early, cowboy days, the IRA's operations were not known for their sophistication. Brendan Hughes recalls:

> When the campaign started in 1970, it was largely concerned with explosives. There wasn't a great deal of shooting going on. The basic idea was to blow police stations away. What the IRA literally did was to walk up to an RUC station, hang a five-pound bomb on the door, light the fuse and run away.

The IRA was an irregular army and operated as such with a constitution, a code of conduct and strict disciplinary procedures whose extreme penalty was death. It was above all a volunteer army, hence the name of its rank and file members, IRA Volunteers. There was never any compunction to join and Volunteers were always free to leave. When, for example, IRA prisoners came out of gaol, there was no pressure on them to return to the 'war'. If they chose to do so, it was their own decision. Many did, but many preferred to call it a day and spend time with their families. Whether they returned to the ranks was entirely a personal decision. To force young men and women into the IRA or to compel them to stay against their will was not only inimical to the intense comradeship that bound the Republican Movement together but was considered counterproductive and dangerous. An unwilling Volunteer was a dangerous Volunteer, vulnerable to recruitment as an informer.

Joining the IRA was not a straightforward process. There were no advertisements in newspapers or recruiting posters along the Falls Road. The IRA was a secret army and admission to it was tightly controlled. Any potential Volunteer was carefully screened to make sure he or she was 'sound' and not an agent working for army intelligence or the RUC's Special Branch. In the closely-knit nationalist community, potential Volunteers had no problem in finding out how to go about joining. They would approach a senior republican in the area and drop a word in his ear. Sometimes it would be weeks or even months before they received a reply. Then a meeting would be arranged at which they would be actively discouraged from joining with warnings of the fate that would probably await them, prison or death. Few were deterred. Once accepted, they were sworn in by declaring allegiance to the Irish Republic, proclaimed in 1916. Then they were trained. Brendan Hughes remembers the early lectures.

Everybody wanted to be involved with guns and there were gun lectures going on almost every night. People were being trained on whatever weapons were there and being trained at particular houses. It was done largely in the kitchen or bedroom or whatever room was available and with whatever weapon was available at that particular time.

A group of people would assemble and the Training Officer would come in and strip the weapon down and put it back together again. He'd explain what type of ammunition it took and so forth. All the basic training on the weapon itself would be done in that sort of way. The weapons would be transported about in prams or a woman would carry it in some way. British soldiers were very reluctant to stop and search a woman.

The houses were pretty well known to the British army. I remember one particular night sitting in a house in the Lower Falls with six or seven others and a well-known British army officer opened the door and just walked in and said, 'what weapons are you training on tonight lads?' That sort of thing happened during the honeymoon period. The army was basically gathering intelligence and we weren't as yet on a war footing. I think the army looked upon it as a sort of a joke – as if we were only a

bunch of wee lads and weren't any danger to the British army at
that time.

Even at the beginning of 1970, the atmosphere between the IRA and
the British army was remarkably relaxed. Neither saw the other as a
threat. Army officers would engage the IRA and the Citizens Defence
Committees – who were often one and the same – in dialogue behind
the barricades, not just to pass the time of day but to find out what was
going on. So tension-free was the mood that soldiers would go into pubs
and leave their weapons around, as Brendan Hughes recalls.

There's a wee pub just down Leeson Street and the troops used to
walk in and sit down and we used to sit down beside them. We used
to ask them about their weapons and how they worked and very
often they would give you a whole run-down on the weapon.
   **That was your basic training was it, with the British
army?**
   Yes, a lot of my training came from pubs, you know, from the
British army, British troops, young lads of eighteen and nineteen.
We weren't much older than that ourselves though. They were
quite happy to give you a run-down on the workings of the SLR
[Self-Loading Rifle]. We used to steal the ammunition all the time.
We used to sit in the pubs and lift a magazine or something like that.
A few rifles were stolen as well. They used to leave them sitting at the
corner of the street. That used to happen because they were so naive
at that period and they weren't in a hostile environment either.

A few months earlier John Kelly had been given a gun lecture from a
British army officer in Belfast.

He stripped down a machine gun and demonstrated how we should
put it together again. He probably did it because he was an intelligence
officer and wanted to find out how much we knew about weaponry.
I was a little surprised but in those days it was a sort of one-to-one
relationship and we took it as a matter of course.

But those days were numbered. Easter Week 1970 was the beginning
of the end of the honeymoon. Sectarian violence returned to haunt
the province and now sucked in the army. Following a republican
Easter Rising Commemoration in Derry on Sunday, 29 March, a crowd
attacked the RUC headquarters in the city centre and tried to storm its
gates. Twelve soldiers were injured in the clashes and seventeen arrests

were made. Rioting broke out and the army sealed off the Bogside.[3] The same day, at the Easter Commemoration in Belfast, an appeal was made for money to buy guns for the IRA. On Easter Monday loyalists attacked a republican parade in Armagh. Easter Tuesday was the point of no return. This is the day when, traditionally, the sons of Orangemen have their day out in Bangor, Belfast's Southend-on-Sea, playing the pipes and drums of their fathers and affecting their swagger. The Junior Orangemen's day out was 'a kindergarten Twelfth of July'.[4] Early that Tuesday morning, Junior Orange bands from the Protestant New Barnsley estate in Belfast decided to tune up and fire up along the top end of the Springfield Road which divides Protestant New Barnsley from the Catholic Ballymurphy estate. Ballymurphy's residents did not take kindly to being awakened at such an early hour to the sound of 'The Sash My Father Wore', the most provocative of Orange tunes, and having to listen to Orange bands for the following two hours. Anticipating trouble that evening when the Junior Orangemen returned from their outing to Bangor, the army deployed seventy men from the Scots Guards to the Ballymurphy estate. It appears they were not sure what to do should rioting break out, other than keep the two sides apart. Sure enough, the Junior Orangemen returned to New Barnsley to be greeted by a hail of bricks and bottles hurled by Catholics from Ballymurphy from behind the lines the Scots Guards had established. For two hours there was a full-scale riot with the soldiers not knowing quite what to do. The following evening, Easter Wednesday, the army was more prepared, and there was to be no repetition of its ineffective performance of the previous evening. No doubt there had been protests from Stormont. A full battalion was deployed to Ballymurphy, escorted by a squadron of one-ton Humber armoured cars with barbed-wire coils mounted on their bumpers. This time, each soldier was armed with a CS gun and gas grenades to quell any possible riot. Clearly the army was set on a display of firmness and, if necessary, force. The residents of Ballymurphy did not take kindly to what they saw as a display of military aggression and attacked the troops with whatever they could lay their hands on. There was a dreadful inevitability to it all. The Ballymurphy riots continued for three days, during which time thirty-eight soldiers were injured. Petrol bombs were thrown at the army and the troops responded with twenty-one canisters and four grenades of CS gas.

On the third night of rioting, as Catholics were driven back into the Ballymurphy estate, Protestants followed in the soldiers' wake and defiantly tore down a Tricolour. Significantly, the Provisionals did not come out to take on the army for the simple reason that they were not yet ready to do so. The local Citizens' Defence Committee, encouraged by Jim Sullivan who had sided with the Official IRA at the time of the split, tried to calm things down and even confiscated empty milk bottles which were being used for petrol bombs. Nevertheless, the damage was already done which was, of course, to the Provisionals' advantage. The rioting finally ended on Thursday night. On Friday the GOC, Sir Ian Freeland, warned that in future petrol bombers could be shot. To many of the residents of Ballymurphy, who had seen loyalists invade their estate behind British troops, the army was no longer neutral but clearly on the Protestants' side. This may have been purely a localized perception at the time, but it soon became widespread.

If the Provisionals were not ready to come out in Ballymurphy that Easter, as they had not expected Junior Orangemen to trigger so much trouble, they were ready to do so by the time the Orange marching season got properly under way in the summer of 1970. By now many loyalists thought that things were going their way. The army had got tough with rioters, and Ian Paisley had won a spectacular victory over his Unionist opponent on 16 April 1970 in a Stormont by-election at Bannside. It was a slap in the face for the Prime Minister, Major James Chichester-Clark, and the policy of reform forced upon him by the British Government. Paisley celebrated his victory by telling Harold Wilson 'to keep his nose out of Northern Ireland'.[5] By the time the marching season had begun, Protestants were even happier, having waved goodbye and good riddance to Harold Wilson's Labour Government. In the British general election of 18 June 1970, the Conservatives came to power and Edward Heath became Prime Minister. Protestants were elated. The Conservatives were, after all, the Conservative and *Unionist* Party. But the new Home Secretary, Reginald Maudling, and the Defence Secretary, Lord Carrington, were to have a baptism by fire. The Provisionals emerged centre-stage.

Again, the event was triggered by an Orange march. It was almost a replay of New Barnsley and Ballymurphy. Every year, the Protestant marching season begins with endless parades in which flags are raised and banners blessed, each ceremony accompanied by the obligatory band, tunes and march. On Friday, 26 June 1970, Belfast's Orange Lodge No. Nine raised its flag and marched down the Crumlin Road which runs between the Catholic Ardoyne and the Protestant Shankill, the interface which had been the scene of violent sectarian clashes during the rioting of August 1969. Predictably, rioting erupted as the Orangemen paraded down the Crumlin Road, passing the narrow side streets of Ardoyne. Sectarian abuse was hurled at the Catholics and they responded with bottles and stones. But that was just a warm-up for Saturday's big parade when the Orange Lodges of the Shankill, the Bone, Cliftonville and the Oldpark districts all joined forces for a huge and noisy display of Protestant solidarity. The route they were to follow passed some of the most sensitive Catholic areas in West Belfast, the Clonard and Springfield Road, the scenes of some of the fiercest rioting and burning in August 1969. Again, it seemed an astonishing error of judgement that Chichester-Clark did not ban or re-route the parade or that the new Conservative Government did not force him to do so. But, as Lord Carrington subsequently told me, the Tories were new in office and knew little about Northern Ireland. And they did not want to see their Northern Ireland Prime Minister toppled. Once again rioting erupted that Saturday afternoon and, as evening approached, spread to other parts of the city. Soon, most of Belfast seemed to be ablaze. Suddenly, for the first time, shooting started. Shots rang out around the Ardoyne.[6] Martin Meehan, a senior Provisional IRA leader in the area at the time, claimed that loyalists fired first. He believes that the shooting was the first practical illustration of the Provisionals' defensive strategy.

There was an Orange march coming down onto the Crumlin Road. It took people unawares and a serious riot followed. There was shots fired. I know for a fact that four shots were fired from the loyalist side of the Crumlin Road and the shots were returned.

By the IRA?

By the IRA. Three loyalists were shot dead and fifteen wounded. There were three or four nationalists wounded. No one was killed. [After the shooting] every door in Ardoyne was opened. The IRA had proved beyond a shadow of a doubt what they said they were going to do, they had done. The date – 27th of June 1970 – is more significant for that than anything else. As a result, the whole broad spectrum of the nationalist people actually supported what the IRA was doing. Everybody, man, woman and child came out and supported us in any way possible. I never saw support like it in my life. It was unbelievable.

By Saturday evening, as rioting spread throughout the city, the army was stretched to breaking point. Across the river where 60,000 loyalists lived in their stronghold of East Belfast, dominated by the giant cranes of Harland and Wolff, there were fears that a loyalist mob was preparing to attack the 6,000 Catholics in their enclave of Short Strand with its famous landmark, St Matthew's church. Around ten o'clock, petrol bombs were thrown at St Matthews, setting alight an outbuilding. A deputation went to the local RUC station to ask for help. An army company was called in to give added protection but with most of Belfast apparently ablaze, the army could offer little more than a presence. As the night drew on the attacks intensified but the soldiers still declined to intervene and separate the two sides, either because they felt they were not numerically strong enough or did not wish to get caught in the middle of a sectarian fight, in the darkness, with shots being fired by both sides. The Catholics of Short Strand, believing the situation desperate with their church under attack, sent out an SOS to Billy McKee, then commander of the Provisionals' Belfast Brigade. McKee made for the beleaguered enclave to assess the situation for himself.

> We went over to see what could be done and we realized that it was getting more serious as time went on. So we sent up to [IRA] Headquarters and asked them to send what weapons they could. It was a duty to stand by our people and defend them. I took it as a duty and the men who were with me took it as a duty. I would do the same again if I was in a position to do it. So we went in and helped our people.

If ever there was a situation for which the Provisional IRA was created, this seemed to be it. Potentially, it looked like August 1969 all over again. One of the young residents of the area who watched open-mouthed was Jim Gibney, who is now one of the Sinn Fein leadership.

> I saw neighbours, people I knew, coming down the street carrying rifles. I was just dumbstruck by this experience. I'd never seen such a thing before. They were much older than me, of course. I watched them take up position on the corner and fire up the street that I lived in. I was fifteen going on sixteen and it was incredible to witness this at first hand. On one level it was exciting of course, because of what you were witnessing. It was something that you only see on the television or in films. The gun battle lasted right through into the early hours of the following morning.
>
> I think the defence of the district was a mixture of IRA activists and the local Citizen's Defence Committee. I think they occupied all the key places including the church that night to defend it against the loyalist gunmen.

McKee and the Provisionals took up position in the churchyard of St Matthews and blasted away at the loyalist attackers. The gun battle lasted five hours and, according to McKee, the Provisionals expended 800 rounds. He knew the figure because the IRA Quartermaster subsequently told him. During the battle, a couple of loyalist gunmen managed to fight their way into the church grounds to take out McKee and the Provisionals. One of McKee's co-defenders, Henry McIlhone, who was standing next to him, was fatally wounded.

I told Henry to get behind a tree as a couple of men came forward. I told him fire and he did but I don't think he hit anybody. All I heard was a clomp like a wet log hitting the ground. It was like a big tree falling. I knew he was hit when he went down. He never said a word. He was hit in the throat. He was taken to hospital but died that night.

McKee himself was lucky to survive.

As I turned round to give Henry another order, I was shot in the back and the bullet came up through my neck. There was a lot of blood. So I spun round and got the wall. As I held it, two men came up to me. They thought I was gone but they fired a shot and hit me in the arm. I just clomped down and there was all blood everywhere. I think they thought I was shot in the chest and dead. I survived. Henry didn't.

Two Protestants were killed in the gun battle that raged around St Matthew's church. The death toll for that weekend was six dead, five Protestants and one Catholic, and 200 injured. Fifty-four had gunshot wounds. Ten soldiers ended up in hospital. Half a million pounds worth of damage was done. The following day, 500 Catholic workers were expelled from the shipyard by Protestants. Surveying the devastation in the wake of the fateful decision to let the parades go ahead, the UK Representative said wistfully that it was 'the greatest single miscalculation I have ever seen made in the course of my whole life'.[7] Tragically, there would be many more. The weekend was critical for the Provisional IRA. Jim Gibney witnessed history in the making.

I think that it added to the rebirth of the IRA and fitted in with the emergence of the IRA as a defensive force in nationalist Belfast. That's its significance. Had the IRA and the Citizens' Defence Committees not been on the streets, then I believe Short Strand would have been razed that night. I'm firmly convinced of that, such was the intensity of gunfire and petrol bombing taking place around the fringes of the district. But the people who defended the street stood their ground. The following morning there was just sheer elation and relief that the IRA were there to deal with that situation.

The defence of St Matthew's became legend and Billy McKee a folk hero. The Provisionals, through their actions in Ardoyne and Short Strand, now had a credibility and standing within the nationalist community that the IRA had not enjoyed for decades. And they now had five 'defensive' notches on their guns – three from Ardoyne and two from Short Strand. The following Tuesday, the new Conservative Home Secretary, Reginald Maudling, paid his first visit to the province. Those who met him were not impressed. 'Is he really as innocent as he seems?', asked one.[8] On the flight back home, the relieved Home Secretary famously remarked, 'For God's sake, bring me a large Scotch. What a bloody awful country!'

The Stormont Government was furious and embarrassed by the weekend's violence and the inability of the police and army to contain it. Five Protestants had been shot dead. It was probably most fearful of the prospect of a resurgent IRA. With right-wingers breathing down his neck, Chichester-Clark was determined to get tough and show the IRA who was in charge of the province. Again, fatefully, he used the British army to do so. At that week's meeting of the province's Joint Security Committee, attended by Stormont ministers, the Chief Constable and GOC, the message was clear: the reason for the chaos the previous weekend was that the army had not been tough enough; when the next opportunity arose, a show of force was in order. The opportunity came sooner than anticipated.

The authorities assumed, with good reason, that some of the weapons used by the Provisionals in Short Strand and elsewhere that weekend probably came from the Lower Falls. The fact that the area was Official IRA territory and not a Provisional stronghold was probably lost on the army. As far as soldiers were concerned, the IRA was the IRA whether Provisional or Official. The following weekend the whole of the Lower Falls was placed under military curfew to facilitate the search for the IRA's weapons. If St Matthew's was a disaster, the Falls curfew was catastrophic. The two events were separated by barely five days but they set the scene for the next twenty-five years. Like so many landmarks in Northern Ireland's history, what happened was not premeditated or planned but the result of a sequence of events, generated by the general atmosphere and attitudes at the time.

The second disastrous weekend began at tea-time on Friday, 3 July 1970 when, following a tip-off, soldiers of the Royal Scots sealed off Balkan Street in the Lower Falls to search No. Twenty-four for arms. The Official IRA had left them there some time before. The haul was small – fifteen pistols, a rifle, a Schmeisser submachine-gun and some ammunition.[9] As the troops were leaving with the weapons, they were jostled by the crowd gathered at the junction of Balkan Street and the Grosvenor Road, the main arterial route from the city centre into West Belfast. It was 5.30pm and in the confusion and rush-hour traffic, an army Humber one-tonner (known as a 'pig') reversed and crushed a man on some railing spikes. He died in hospital later that night.[10]

As ever, the rest was predictable. The crowd stoned the soldiers, who suddenly found themselves trapped. They radioed for reinforcements and another company of Royal Scots went in and went in hard. A full-scale riot was now underway. As with the riots in Ballymurphy the previous Easter, cannisters of CS gas were fired with even more disastrous results. The clouds of choking and suffocating gas drifted up the narrow alleyways and back streets of the warren that is the Lower Falls. The gas got everywhere, in through windows, under doors and into the residents' eyes, noses, throats and lungs. An hour later, gelignite bombs were being hurled at the army. The area exploded. Brigadier Hudson, commander of the army's 39 Brigade which covered Belfast, surveyed the chaos from a helicopter and decided he had no choice other than to order his troops to withdraw and re-group around the perimeter of the area. By this time, the residents had built make-shift barricades to seal off their area. The army sent in reinforcements and soon there were 3,000 soldiers swarming all over the Falls, two-thirds of all the troops in Belfast. As the sappers moved in to dismantle the barricades, the Official IRA, whose stronghold it was, opened fire. Billy McKee had previously telephoned the Official IRA commander in the Lower Falls and offered comradely assistance but the offer had been declined. 'We're going to take on the British army,' McKee had been told.[11] A fierce gun battle ensued in which the army alone fired almost 1,500 rounds. Suddenly, above the din, an upper-class English voice boomed down from a helicopter in the sky, informing the residents that the area was being placed under curfew and everyone was to get off the streets. But there were some Provisionals on the Falls who ignored the Officials' refusal of help and decided to break the cordon and engage the army. The initiative came from Brendan Hughes' cousin, Charlie Hughes, who was then commander of the Provisionals' unit in the Lower Falls, D Company, and Brendan Hughes' hero. Charlie Hughes was later shot dead in the bloody feud that broke out between the Provisionals and the Officials in March 1971. The Provisionals claimed that most of the fifteen British soldiers wounded in the subsequent engagement were shot by the Volunteers of D Company.[12] Brendan Hughes was with Charlie Hughes on the night of the Falls curfew.

Word went round that the British army were coming in to take the IRA's weapons and they were going to leave the Catholic people, the nationalist people, undefended.

Charlie said the curfew was going to be broken and that he was going to do it. That night a group of people left his house and there was a major gun battle in Cyprus Street. It didn't last very long because the people [the Provisionals] had only a couple of rifles, one Thompson submachine-gun, and a couple of short arms. I think the ammunition ran out and there wasn't any more. So people had to get away but there wasn't anywhere to go. They ran over yard walls and into houses to take cover. I ended up in someone's house and that's where I was over the period of the curfew, sitting there and not knowing when we're going to get out or what was going to happen.

I watched the British army kicking in doors and pulling people out and trailing them up the street. I watched a couple of my friends getting trailed out and I was just waiting for my turn over the few days that we were there and it didn't come.

We had no food in the house. We just sat there drinking tea and smoking cigarettes. We just sat and talked and waited for the door to come in but it never did. We didn't sleep. It was frightening because here you were in the middle of a major gun battle. You heard people squealing and you heard the shooting and there were dead bodies.

The curfew lasted from ten o'clock on Friday night until mid-morning on Sunday, with a two-hour gap on Saturday afternoon to let people out to do their shopping. Richard McAuley's wife, Christine, was living in the Lower Falls at the time.

We were all very forcibly ushered into our homes and told that you would be shot, man, woman or child, if you opened your door and put your foot out onto the footpath. I remember my mother sitting on the stairs and we were all huddled around her because she didn't want us out of her sight. She was frightened of one of us opening the door and going out. She knew the army meant business from the aggression of the soldiers, their concentration on the streets and the way they were ordering people about and shoving them around. So we sat for a long time on the stairs with mother.

We only had a certain amount of milk and bread in the house and that quickly ran out after a day, so you weren't eating. It was very, very hard and very frightening. The soldiers were right outside the door and at the windows. You knew that if you went outside you would be shot.

Five years later, Christine McAuley was arrested at a house in Cork by the Irish Special Branch and charged with possession of explosive components. She was sentenced to four years imprisonment.

Street by street and house by house, the army combed the area for guns, in some cases literally taking houses apart. No doubt for many soldiers, it was their first real opportunity to go in and sort out the IRA, who they knew were in there because the troops had just been engaged in a major gun battle. There was little respect for people's sensitivities or property. Some were disgusted by what they saw being done, not by the residents of the Lower Falls, but by their own colleagues. The disgust was expressed by both officers and men. 'John', a soldier from the north of England, was appalled by the conduct of some soldiers.

The company commander ordered me to position myself on a roof top in order to give cover to the troops that were down on Albert Street. I shinned up the drain pipe, onto the outhouse and then got onto the roof. But I found I couldn't get into a good position so I had to remove a few tiles. And in doing so, the thought occurred to me that this could be my mother's home. What right have I to destroy this property? And as the slates were rattling down the side of the roof into the garden below, a man came out and looked up at me and said, 'excuse me, do you mind, this is my home!' I felt so bad and I still do to this day. Here was I, literally invading the man's home. I felt guilty and ashamed.

And the place was still saturated with CS Gas. Children were coughing, I remember. I'm talking now about the toddlers, kids of three, four, five. It affected everyone but children especially. And you have to remember too that this was 1970, the children in 1970 are the adults today. There's no doubt in my mind that what happened in the Falls then had a lasting effect on them.

I think the major effect was that it gave the community in the Lower Falls the opportunity to see the IRA, who were, I think, just about beginning to flex their muscles, as their saviours and they saw the British Army as the enemy, a foreign occupying force. I didn't consider myself at any time as a foreign soldier in a foreign country. These people were watching all the TV programmes that I would see. They read all the newspapers that I would read and supported the same football teams. No, I didn't see myself as a foreign invader and I don't think they did either up until the curfew.[13]

The lesson was not lost on one young officer, 'Jonathan', who, only the previous Sunday, had marched his troops down the Falls Road, unarmed, to attend a service in a Catholic church.

It was absolutely clear that this was a turning point. It was felt at the time, militarily, that the best way to prevent any further bloodshed was to seal the place off, search the place thoroughly, remove all the weapons and ammunition and then get back to normal living. And that was the view taken at the time.

You found the weapons and lost the people?

We certainly found the weapons, a lot of them, but as you say, our relationships after that were very much more difficult. It was the last time the army would have marched down the Falls Road, unarmed, to church.[14]

On Sunday morning, the last day of the curfew, a group of women, led by Maire Drumm of Provisional Sinn Fein, marched from Andersonstown to the Lower Falls as a relief column. They carried bread, milk, tea and sugar. When they got there, they were confronted by a line of soldiers who did not quite know what to do, faced with a crowd of singing, cheering women carrying groceries. They let them through. The curfew was nearly over. Marie Moore was part of what became known in republican folklore as the 'Bread March'. The reception they received was ecstatic. 'People started to come out of their doors and they started to cheer,' she remembers. 'And I think most of us were crying.' Many of the women were carrying the emergency supplies into the Lower Falls in prams. They pushed them out full of the Official IRA's weapons the army had failed to uncover. Thus, according to Gerry Adams, many of the Officials' weapons ended up in the hands of the Provisionals.[15] When they entered the besieged area, Marie Moore and the other marchers were horrified at what they found. Judging from photographs of the time and accounts of house searches soldiers subsequently gave me, her description probably suffers little from exaggeration.

> Some of the houses I had seen were totally wrecked. Holy statues were smashed on the floor. Family portraits and pictures were smashed. Furniture was ripped and overturned. Windows were broken and doors off the hinges. Some of the people who'd been beaten were still lying there, bloody and bruised.

One civilian, as mentioned, had died just before the curfew had been imposed, knocked down by the army 'pig'. Two more civilians were killed during the curfew, one shot at his front door and another, an English visitor, shot at the back of a house. A fourth civilian, shot near his home, died from his injuries seven days later. All were shot by the army.[16] The troops did recover a sizeable quantity of weapons, many of which had been used against them. The haul amounted to 100 firearms, 100 home-made bombs, 250 lb of explosives and 21,000 rounds of ammunition.

The seizures were used to justify the success of the operation. The final insult to the residents was the sight of two Unionist politicians from Stormont being given a tour of the area by the army in the back of an open Landrover to survey the subjugated population. It reminded 'John' of 'the British Raj on a tiger hunt'. The army had done exactly as the Unionists' Security Committee had demanded four days earlier – it had got tough. The result was summed up by Gerry Adams. 'Thousands of people who had never been republicans now gave their active support to the IRA; others, who had never had any time for physical force now accepted it as a practical necessity.'[17] Unwittingly, the army had driven the community into the arms of the Provisional IRA.

Chapter Seven

Attack

After the Ballymurphy riots, St Matthew's church and the Lower Falls curfew, nationalists now felt they had two enemies, the loyalists and the British army. Events seemed to fit in perfectly with the Provisionals' strategy, mapped out by the Army Council at the beginning of 1970. They had proved their capacity to defend the nationalist community but were still not ready to take the offensive against the British army and begin the 'war of liberation', always their long-term intention. They had the recruits but, as yet, not the weapons. After the gun-running fiascos of the previous autumn, serious efforts were now made to procure weapons and ammunition.

In the spring of 1970, a member of the Army Council, David O'Connell, went to New York to put an arms network in place. In a coffee shop on Fifth Avenue he met George Harrison, the veteran IRA supporter who had supplied weapons to the IRA during the fifties campaign, and still had some left. Harrison told me they talked for two hours. O'Connell said that although the Provisionals wanted modern weapons, they would happily take 'anything that could shoot straight'. Harrison replied that he would do what he could. The contribution he was to make over the next ten years was crucial to the IRA's 'war' effort. Getting weapons in America in those days was easy, as all you needed was a driving licence as proof of identity, and gun shops were everywhere. Serious fundraising in America also got under way around this time. Irish Northern Aid (Noraid) was established in April 1970 at the instigation of Martin Flannery, an IRA veteran who had fought the Black and Tans in 1920 and emigrated to America after the civil war. Over the years, Noraid raised millions of dollars for the Provisionals. The funds were earmarked for supporting the families of IRA prisoners but there were enduring suspicions that some of the money was used to buy guns. Harrison denies this and the case has never been proved. He told me that there was a separate fund for guns, made up of donations given directly or obliquely to him and Martin Flannery for that specific purpose. Those funds, he insisted, were kept separately. Money, he said, was never a problem. In those days, the FBI had better things to do than pursue IRA gunrunners and fund raisers. In time, that was to change.

By the summer and autumn of 1970, weapons were beginning to come in. Tommy Gorman, who had become involved after August 1969, remembers a windfall of weaponry.

> In August 1969, the IRA had virtually no guns at all. A year later, there was any amount and they were very freely available. There were Belgian FN semi-automatic rifles, assault rifles, self-loading rifles, and M1 carbines. People didn't question where they came from. Just the fact that the weaponry was there made people feel a lot more at ease.

Nor, according to Gorman, was there any shortage of bomb-making material.

> A lot of explosives were home-made. At that time, the IRA in its ingenuity was manufacturing its own 'Co-op Mix', as it was called. It was a combination of fertilizer and benzenes and sugars and stuff.
>
> **Were people aware of the risks that they were running doing this sort of thing?**
>
> I think they were aware but the risks became secondary because of what they had witnessed of what had gone on. We felt it would have been wrong to sit back and do nothing.
>
> **And did people think about the morality of killing people, shooting people, blowing people up?**
>
> I don't think at that point in time we were talking about attacking people. Our motivation was more defensive than anything else. If it meant attacking someone who was attacking the IRA, then so be it. But it wasn't actually going out and attacking targets as such.

But although the explosive mixture was in plentiful supply, inexperience on the part of the bomb makers led to the Provisionals' earliest casualties or 'own goals' as the army and loyalists referred to them, with black humour. In Derry during the weekend of the defence of St Matthews church, three Volunteers of the IRA's Derry Brigade died when incendiary devices they were making on the city's Creggan estate exploded. Two children of one of the IRA men, Thomas McCool, aged nine and four, also died in the blast. Initially the blaze was thought to be a house fire and it was only three days later when McCool was given an IRA military funeral, that people realized what had happened. Just over two months later, on 4 September 1970, a Provisional IRA Volunteer, Michael Kane, was killed when the bomb he was planting at an electricity transformer in Belfast exploded prematurely. MacStiofáin, who gave the oration at his funeral, referred to him as 'the first IRA casualty of the campaign' although statistically he was not.[1] The operation in which Kane had been involved was part of the Provisionals' growing sabotage campaign which had begun in August 1970 when nationalist anger was running high after the army had shot dead nineteen-year-old Daniel O'Hagan on 30 July, during a riot in Belfast's New Lodge area. The army said he was a petrol bomber, although local residents denied this. On 2 August 1970 there were three simultaneous attacks on 'strategic' targets: a customs post near the border in County Armagh, a telephone exchange in Newcastle, County Down, and an electricity board office in Lurgan. A week later, there were bomb attacks on an electricity sub-station in Belfast, an explosion at another customs post, and two more attacks on electricity sub-stations in Belfast and Magherafelt. Hard-line unionists now began to call for internment as Chichester-Clark's position became increasingly shaky. But, despite the excesses of the Falls Road curfew and the shooting of Daniel O'Hagan, the Provisionals had still refrained from making soldiers their targets. The recently disarmed RUC was a much easier proposition. On 11 August 1970, two policemen were killed by a booby-trap bomb as they examined an abandoned car near Crossmaglen. It was seen as the Provisionals' retaliation for the army's killing of O'Hagan and marked the beginning of the border village's notoriety. The same day, in Belfast's Milltown cemetery, the Provisionals buried the IRA veteran, Jimmy Steele. He had died of natural causes, having lived just long enough to see the birth of the Provisionals. Ten thousand turned out for his funeral, among them Gerry Adams. It marked the end of one era and the beginning of the next.

Amidst the growing violence of the summer of 1970, the Social and Democratic Labour Party (SDLP) was born, which for the following twenty-seven years would remain steadfastly opposed to the IRA's campaign of violence. Sinn Fein immediately called upon nationalists to boycott the new party. Its founder members, Gerry Fitt, John Hume and Austin Currie and those like Seamus Mallon who subsequently rose to prominence within it, were to became familiar voices and faces on radio and television as the conflict intensified and false dawns came and went. The SDLP, as the roll-call of its leaders suggests, was born out of the civil-rights movement. For years it attracted the cliché, the 'mainly Catholic SDLP' because one of its founder members and leaders, Ivan Cooper, was a Protestant. But the founding notion of a non-sectarian socialist party committed to the reunification of Ireland by peaceful means proved, in reality, to be a non-starter. In time it became the 'nationalist SDLP'. The Alliance Party, essentially a moderate unionist party committed to encouraging both communities to work together, was also formed in the spring of 1970, perhaps reflecting the mood of optimism generated by the Derry songstress, Dana, when she won the Eurovision Song Contest that Easter with 'All Kinds of Everything'. Alliance seemed to reflect the song.

In September 1970, the Provisional IRA held the General Army Convention it had bound itself to hold after its split. As ever, the location was secret. Its purpose was, according to MacStiofáin, 'to regularize the framework, representation and leadership of the reorganized movement'.[2] This it did with the Belfast delegates to the fore, and MacStiofáin was re-elected Chief of Staff. The following month, as became custom, Sinn Fein held its annual conference, the Ard Fheis. Again, it took place openly, this time in Dublin's Liberty Hall, where Ruairí O'Brádaigh was re-elected President of Sinn Fein.

> The delegates were told that this ended the 'provisional' period and that everything had now been regularized. From then on they would be in business simply as the Irish Republican Army.

From that moment on, the 'Provisionals' technically ceased to exist but the name and the nickname the 'Provos' lived on, although Gerry Adams, with strict regard for republican history, has always disliked the name.[3]

Both wings of the Republican Movement, the Provisional IRA and Sinn Fein, now claimed the republican mantle. They saw themselves as the only true heirs of the men of 1916. A dramatic moment came at the Ard Fheis when General Tom Maguire, one of the few survivors of the period from the Easter Rising to the Anglo-Irish war, was introduced to the delegates. Maguire was a County Mayo man who said that 1916 had been 'the turning point in my life. I will never forget my exhilaration. I thanked God for seeing such a day.'[4] Maguire was the last surviving member of the all-Ireland parliament that had been established by Sinn Fein after the 1918 general election. To tumultuous applause, Maguire gave the Provisionals his blessing.

For the remainder of 1970, the Provisionals carried on with their campaign of sabotage whilst increasingly tightening their grip on those elements within their community who were 'anti-social' or who might think that the honeymoon with the army was still on. 'Criminal elements' or young women who 'fraternized' with the 'Brits', either on the streets or at the army's discotheques, were disciplined in a barbaric and humiliating way, with a punishment known as 'tarring and feathering'. It was done publicly and served as a dreadful warning to others. One soldier, 'Chris', I spoke to witnessed the result. He was horrified.

> As part of the 'Hearts and Minds' campaign, we used to allow some of the local ladies to come into the discos. When one unfortunate young lady left the disco she was captured by a load of yobbos belonging to the Fianna Eireann which is the 'Boy Scout' movement of the IRA. She was tied to a lamppost and tarred and feathered. Can you imagine somebody putting hot tar over a lady's head having shaven the hair off and then putting all the feathers on her? To get that poor young lady clean again is probably a medical job. It's horrendous.
>
> We were called within twenty minutes of it happening. The first thing I saw was the body of a limp person tied to the lamppost. When we arrived, she was on her knees in a very bad state of shock. I always remember that she had a very light, summery dress on and her hair, or most of her hair, had been cut away. The tar actually ran down her neck and the front of her breast and her hands were badly affected where she'd clawed at her face to get it off. And the feathers were just stuck to the tar.
>
> We had to cut her away from the lamppost and take her to the hospital. She was very badly burned. As you can imagine, pitch not only sticks to the skin but causes horrendous burns. I felt utter revulsion for the type of person that had the mentality to do it — just because a human being decided to go and dance for a couple of hours at an army barracks. It's just unbelievable.

This reaction, which most people would share, not only illustrates the incomprehension and horror that most young soldiers felt at the barbarity of some republicans but helps explain why 'Chris' and others subsequently behaved in the way they did towards the residents of what they regarded as 'hard' IRA areas. The deaths of their comrades, often in horrendous circumstances, further increased the hatred many soldiers felt towards the community which they believed harboured the gunmen and bombers.

The fact that the first British soldier was not killed until February 1971 was more accident than design, although Seán MacStiofáin insists that the IRA did not actively take the offensive until after internment on 9 August 1971. As far as he is concerned, the deaths of a dozen British soldiers before then were 'retaliation' for army actions. Soldiers would have laughed at the semantic distinction. Martin Meehan, whose area was covered by the IRA's Third Battalion, perhaps gives the most realistic account of IRA thinking at the beginning of 1971.

If I can recall, the situation was spontaneous. As far as I am aware, nobody actually said, 'do that' or 'don't do that'. It was a spontaneous sort of situation that arose. People on the ground were to take action as they saw fit. I don't believe there was any orders sent or word from anybody in high rank. I think they were spontaneous gestures.

How independent were military operations at that time?

I would say that the Volunteers on the ground would have been taking actions that were not authorized. I think the leadership then would have been of the opinion that there were a couple of years before there could be a full-blown military campaign. But after the events of 1970 and with the aggression the British soldiers were showing in early 1971, it was like holding back a pack of wild horses. It was like the tide coming in. You couldn't stop it. It was inevitable at that stage.

And the leadership had to go with the tide?

I would say so.

The first British soldier to be killed in the current conflict was the victim of an IRA retaliatory attack. He was Gunner Robert Curtis, who was shot dead in the early hours of Saturday, 6 February 1971. He was the first British soldier to die on duty in Ireland since 1921. There had been no plan or pre-meditated decision to kill him or any other soldier. The shooting happened during the course of a riot that had begun that Friday afternoon with stone-throwing on the Crumlin Road between Catholic and Protestant schoolchildren. Tension had been building all week following arms searches by the army in the Clonard area of West Belfast. Rioting erupted on the Falls and there were gun battles in the Crumlin Road and Ardoyne. The violence continued for the rest of the week with John Taylor, then Stormont Minister for Home Affairs, supporting the army's tough line and declaring, 'we are going to shoot it out with them. It is as simple as that.'[5]

By Friday evening, 5 February 1971, the disturbance that had begun with schoolboys throwing stones escalated into a full-blown adult riot. Martin Meehan remembers what happened.

There was a serious riot in Ardoyne that night. Nail bombs were actually thrown at the British Army Saracens, one of which was engulfed in flames. Soldiers jumped out and fired shots into the rioters at the bottom end of the street and a civilian called Bernard Watt was shot dead. I think he was loosely connected with the auxiliaries [IRA 'helpers'] at that time. He was wearing a white shirt. Two or three of our people were wounded.

'Barney' Watt was twenty-six years old. The press reported that 'an army marksman shot and killed one rioter who had thrown two petrol bombs at an armoured car'. There was never any evidence that Watt was responsible. Not surprisingly, a gun battle did break out following the death of 'Barney' Watt and a known Provisional, James Saunders, was shot dead. He was admitted to be a 'staff officer' in 'F' Company of the Provisionals' Third Battalion. He was nineteen years old. Outnumbered, the army looked on as his coffin was brought out of the terraced house in Ardilea Street and shots were fired over it by masked and uniformed IRA men. Later, as the funeral cortège wound its way into Milltown cemetery, a soldier on top of an army Ferret car gave a salute in respect.[6] The rioting continued into the early hours of Saturday morning, by which time it had spread to the adjacent nationalist New Lodge area. Help was summoned from the Provisionals and Billy Reid, a Volunteer from the Third Battalion's 'C' Company, is said to have arrived on the scene with a submachine-gun. The crowd of rioters stepped aside and Reid opened up at the soldiers. A ricochet hit twenty-year-old Gunner Robert Curtis from Newcastle – and known as 'Geordie' – and killed him almost instantly. His unit had just completed a six-week tour along the border and had returned to Belfast for a break. The troops were taking their kit off the troop ship where they were billeted in Belfast harbour when they were suddenly rushed to the riot. They had been trained to cope with rioting whilst stationed in Germany but were totally unprepared for what ensued. 'Norman' was standing beside Gunner Curtis when he was hit.

> The crowd was in front of us, throwing bricks, bottles, petrol bombs, everything that was going. Then all of a sudden the crowd parted and this chap just popped out with a machine gun and just opened up. There were sparks everywhere. Bullets were just ricocheting all over the place and that's when 'Geordie' Curtis got hit. He was standing right next door to me. He just gave a slight scream and then he was on the floor. The bullet must have come up the street, hit the wall, bounced off it and hit him. It was deflected into his chest and killed him instantly.
>
> We got six soldiers shot that night. One dead. Our first night in Belfast. We was told they would give us a welcome party, or a going away party. So we sort of expected it. But we didn't expect to be shot at. Nobody told us they were using weapons. Nobody trained us for that.

The following day Major James Chichester-Clark, Prime Minister of Northern Ireland, went on television to declare that 'Northern Ireland is at war with the Irish Republican Army Provisionals'. Billy Reid, the IRA Volunteer who is said to have killed Gunner Curtis, was himself shot dead three months later on 15 May 1971 in a gun battle with the army. Ironically, he died within a stone's throw of Curtis Street. To the Provisionals, the killing of Gunner Curtis was direct retaliation for the army's killing of 'Barney' Watt.

The next killings which were believed to have been carried out by the Provisional IRA were so shocking to its own community that they were disowned by the Belfast Brigade. On 10 March, three young Highland Fusiliers, two of them brothers, aged seventeen, eighteen and twenty-three, were picked up whilst drinking off duty in Mooney's, a Belfast city pub, presumably on the pretext that they were being taken to a party for a good time. Off-duty soldiers were as yet not officially IRA targets. They were driven to a country lane above Ligoniel just outside the city and got out of the car to relieve themselves by the roadside. They were then shot in the back of the head. One of them was said to have been found grotesquely propped up with his half-empty beer glass still in his hand.[7] No one was ever convicted for the killings but there were suspicions that Provisionals from Ardoyne were responsible and had taken it upon themselves to carry out the operation in retaliation for British army 'repression' in their area. The public was horrified. There had been violence and death in Northern Ireland before but nothing as savage as this. The pressure on Chichester-Clark was now irresistible. There were demands for more troops, tougher security, the re-arming of the RUC and the immediate introduction of internment without trial. The Stormont Prime Minister could deliver none of these and the Heath Government declined to throw him a lifeline, fearful of alienating nationalists still further. On 20 March 1971, Chichester-Clark resigned to be succeeded by the unionist hard-liner, Brian Faulkner. Westminster was still playing for time as the situation deteriorated day by day.

By the spring of 1971, the Provisionals' bombing campaign in Belfast city centre had got fully under way although not yet with the savagery later associated with the IRA's murderous car bombs. Billy McKee, the Provisionals' Belfast Brigade commander until his arrest on 15 April 1971, insisted that civilian casualties should be avoided at all costs. To McKee, it was also a moral question: civilians were non-combatants. He also knew he could risk nothing that would alienate the community on whose support the Provisionals depended. Many operations were conducted at night when civilians were not around.

> We realized when the honeymoon period was over, when our people had been harassed and raided and everything else, we would have

to make our presence felt. Every time the British army attacked our people, we got Volunteers into the centre of the town and set bombs off there. Actually most were during the night. There was hardly a civilian casualty during that period, although I think someone lost a leg somewhere down the centre of the town, but I think that was the only civilian casualty there was. We took action against property over the abuse of the military. And it was done in places where there was practically no civilians about, you know. And we always gave notification.

Studying the statistics of the relevant period, it appears that McKee is right. There were no civilian deaths and many bombs did explode at night.

The new Prime Minister, Brian Faulkner, knew he had to act as the situation careered out of control, but he was also aware that he had to take the British Government with him to avoid being left out on a limb. In addition, he had to maintain credibility with the Unionist Party. He was Stormont's third Prime Minister in just over a year and he had no intention of stepping aside for a fourth. By the beginning of August 1971, five more soldiers had been killed, four of them by snipers and one by a time bomb left inside a police and army base. But the deaths of these soldiers do not give a true picture of the general mayhem that unionists saw engulfing their province. Since the beginning of the year, there had been over 300 explosions and 320 shooting incidents. Over 600 people had received hospital treatment for injuries. To Brian Faulkner, there was only one option: internment – locking people up without trial.

Faulkner finally persuaded a reluctant British Government and less-than-enthusiastic British army commanders that there was no alternative. The military deemed it a finely balanced equation. On 9 August 1971, internment was finally introduced under Section 12 of the Northern Ireland Special Powers Act, the draconian legislation that successive unionist governments at Stormont had had at their disposal since partition. The formal ground for arrest and detention was suspicion that the individual was acting, had acted or was about to act, 'in a manner prejudicial to the preservation of the peace or maintenance of order.'[8] However, internment took nobody by surprise, least of all the Provisionals, many of whose leaders had got 'offside' (gone on the run) after what they regarded, with some accuracy, as a series of dummy runs. Joe Cahill, who had taken over as Belfast commander following Billy McKee's arrest, told me that the Provisionals had a 'mole' in high places who tipped them off forty-eight hours beforehand that internment was coming. Brian

Faulkner had pushed hard for the controversial panacea and finally got it, but internment proved to be a disaster. In a simultaneous move across the province, 3,000 troops swooped at 4.15am on Monday and arrested over 300 republican suspects who were taken in for questioning. The problem was that very few of them were the men they were looking for. The key 'players' were anywhere but at home in their beds and many of those who were arrested were simply names on out-of-date RUC Special Branch files. 'Jonathan', the young officer who had marched his men to church down the Falls Road just before the Falls curfew was back in Belfast on internment morning.

> We were briefed to go to a whole series of houses and arrest known IRA men. And I have to say that many of the people we arrested were known but had not been active since about 1922. I remember arresting one elderly gentleman who was well into his eighties who was rather proud to be arrested. He said 'I'm delighted to think that I'm still a trouble to the British Government but I have to tell you I've not been active since the Easter Rising.' He had to be taken in but no doubt he was released shortly afterwards. I think that a lot of these names had remained on files for decades and had never been removed. Once a republican always a republican. The intelligence was very, very poor because the army hadn't built up its own store of intelligence by then and we acted on information we were given.

Internment was entirely one-sided. No Protestants were lifted. It was also carried out on only one side of the border. Dublin was appalled. Jack Lynch, the Irish Prime Minister, was given no prior warning. Internment had been devastatingly effective during the IRA's 1956–62 campaign because it had been introduced North *and* South. Now it was one-sided in more ways than one. Nationalist areas throughout the province erupted in an explosion of anger as fathers and sons were dragged from their beds.

The only members of the community who were both co-operative and understanding were the Protestants, delighted that at last Stormont and the British government had taken firm and decisive action. In the two days following internment, seventeen people died. Only one of them was a member of the Provisional IRA. The rest, except one UDR man, were civilians, most of them shot by the army in gun battles that echoed across the province. A week later, in a propaganda coup, the new commander of the Provisionals' Belfast Brigade, Joe Cahill, gave a press conference to show that the 'Provos' were alive and very much at large. John Kelly was on the platform with Joe Cahill.

It was MacStiofáin's idea. It was really a propaganda exercise to demonstrate to the British that they hadn't succeeded in breaking the Republican Movement or capturing those they believed were its leadership. It was very tense because there were a lot of soldiers on the ground, but it was very business-like. The logistics of getting all those cameramen and journalists there was another coup in itself.

The event over, Gerry Adams spirited Joe Cahill away.[9]

But the propaganda coup was nothing compared to the propaganda avalanche that followed the allegations of what was happening to some of those detained. A dozen IRA suspects were singled out for special 'in-depth' interrogation at secret centres within British army bases. Shortly after the internment operation had begun, a senior policeman and a British army officer came to see Brian Faulkner. The RUC and the army had already had discussions on the best way of getting intelligence from the detainees and were now seeking formal approval from the Stormont Prime Minister. They told him that the 'in-depth' techniques they planned to use were those the army had used before in colonial internal security situations. These, they said, were the methods most likely to yield the best results. They explained that the information that would flow from their application was absolutely vital to the success of the internment operation and most likely to deal a crushing blow to the IRA. They claimed that the plans had already been cleared with 'appropriate authorities' in London. The actual interrogations were to be conducted by army intelligence officers with RUC Special Branch officers standing by because of their specialized local knowledge. Faulkner agreed. He was hardly likely to object although he subsequently made it clear that the ultimate responsibility for the methods used rested with the army and the 'authorities' in London. Who the 'authorities' were was never specified. Faulkner never thought that 'Her Majesty's Government would ever authorize anything of dubious propriety'.[10] But Her Majesty's Government did. The interrogation techniques used were those which had operated many times before when Britain was faced with insurgencies in her colonies, including Palestine, Malaya, Kenya, Cyprus, the British Cameroons, Brunei, British Guyana, Aden, Borneo, Malaysia and the Persian Gulf.[11] There were 'rules' although they clearly had a degree of flexibility.

The following are prohibited:

1. Violence to life and person, in particular, mutilation, cruel treatment and torture.

   2. Outrages upon personal dignity, in particular humiliating and
       degrading treatment.

But these prohibitions are then effectively negated by the following
astonishing paragraph.

   The precise application of these general rules in particular circumstances is inevitably to some extent a matter of judgement on the part
   of those immediately responsible for the operations in question.

This caveat seemed to give the interrogators *carte blanche*. With good
reason it was seen by the community against which it was to be used
as 'A Torturer's Charter'. It was justified by the authorities because of
the need to obtain good, fresh intelligence to combat the terrorists.[12]

In-depth interrogation consisted of what were known as the 'Five
Techniques'. Suspects were made to stand spread-eagled against a wall
for long periods of time; hoods were placed over their heads to produce
sensory deprivation; there was a continuous high-pitched noise to 'enhance
the detainee's sense of isolation'; deprivation of sleep; and a bread and water
diet. Although only a handful of specially selected IRA suspects were picked
out for the full treatment, the techniques continued in one way or another
for the next two months until the Government's Committee of Enquiry
under the British Ombudsman, Sir Edmund Compton, produced its report
in November 1971 in response to the domestic and international outcry
which the allegations of torture and brutality had provoked.

   Liam Shannon was arrested on 9 October 1971, and interrogated at
Palace Barracks, Holywood, just outside Belfast. He says he endured all
of the 'Five Techniques', the only difference being that he said his
interrogators were police and not army. I met Liam Shannon twenty-five
years later and he relived the experience.

   The hood was tied tightly, securely around my neck. It was like a
   canvas bag and the strings of the bag were tied through the epaulettes.
   I could only breathe with difficulty. I continually tried to pull the bag
   off but it was tied too tightly around my throat and onto the epaulettes.
   It was impossible to get off. The sensory deprivation, or 'white noise'
   as they called it, was like compressed air or steam hissing from a
   pipe. The degree varied from time to time. Sometimes it was soft.
   Sometimes it got very loud. Almost ear piercing. It was terrible.
   I had the hood on for seven days. The whole week. It was only
   removed during interrogations. And the way they were done was

like something you see in KGB films. This massive bright light shone in your face and there was this figure behind a desk. The hood was pulled off and there was this person. You were sitting on a chair. You couldn't move. This bright light was cutting the eyes out of you. And the questions and the allegations were fired at you.

What sort of questions were you being asked?

Was I in the IRA? Who did I know in the IRA? What did I do? Did I know where guns or bombs were? They just spat out the questions at you.

Five years later, Liam Shannon received £25,000 compensation for his ordeal. 'It wasn't nearly as much as it should have been for what they put us through,' he said ruefully.

The Government appointed a Commission to investigate the allegations and the legality of the Five Techniques. The methods were stopped. The Irish Government subsequently took the British Government to the European Commission of Human Rights, and in 1976, the Commission found Britain guilty of torture but, when the case went to the higher authority of the European Court two years later, the finding of torture was dropped although Britain was still found guilty of inhuman and degrading treatment. To those on the receiving end, the difference was purely semantic.

The British army continued to hand the IRA more propaganda gifts by the unauthorized actions that some of its soldiers took. As they saw more and more of their comrades shot dead or blown apart, they took out their frustration and anger on the nationalist community. At the time such excesses were officially denied but with the passing of time, soldiers felt more free to speak out. Those I met were remarkably frank and most had no regrets about what they had done. The battle for hearts and minds had long been lost. 'Jim' lost five of his mates in Northern Ireland.

You see grown, hard men with tears in their eyes. You drink together, you know, and you get very, very close. Like brothers and probably even closer. And when you see these blokes being stretchered out of flats, or dying in gutters in a war which is not classed as a war, it makes you bloody bitter. It makes you angry, you know, and it fills you with hate.

I hated the people in those flats and the people in those areas with an intensity that used to make me feel almost physically sick when I heard them speak. You took all the bitterness that they flung at you and then all you wanted to do was fling it back at 'em. And I'm talking about women and children, no matter what.

What did you do?

We didn't kill any of 'em or anything like that, I mean we didn't stab 'em to death or anything silly. We took it out on them like by getting into their houses and breaking their telly sets and breaking their windows. If they were signalling on the ground with dustbin lids to let people know where we were, then we would break their windows, kick their doors in, and say, 'you cut that out and we'll cut it out'.

They used to throw milk bottles at us off the balconies of the flats as we were patrolling on different levels. They might be full of urine, or petrol, or whatever. We followed the milkman once and as soon as he put the milk down, we'd throw the bottles off the flats. And we'd say, 'when you stop your kids doing that, then we'll stop doing this.' It might sound pretty petty but when you get a bottle being thrown from three storeys onto your head, it's not funny. So we had to put a stop to it. It wasn't a case of winning hearts and minds with us. It was a case of staying alive.

Many soldiers would have been in their late teens and early twenties, the same age and generation as their Provisional IRA enemies. Soldiers' backgrounds, too, would have been similar, with many having been brought up in Britain's cities on council estates that were every bit as drab and depressing as Belfast's. Some respected the Provisionals' growing professionalism but most held them in utter contempt. Every action by one side intensified the hatred felt by the other. House to house searches continued to be one way in which troops got their own back. I remember one soldier telling me about searching a house in Ballymurphy. It should be borne in mind that he did many tours in Northern Ireland and was subsequently scarred for life in an IRA bomb attack in which he saw many of his mates die. His hatred for the Provisionals and the community that supported them was visceral.

We were going to search the house of a family that we believed was deeply involved. It was well known from the unit before us and the unit before them, too, that the woman in this house, who was probably in her fifties, was known to do this very, very good fit. Whenever you searched the house, she would throw a fit, complete with shrieking and howling, rolling eyeballs, vomit, foaming at the mouth, twitching and scratching – the whole business.

Now you cannot imagine the way some of these houses smell. They are absolutely disgusting. I just don't think I could really describe it. Awfully smelly houses, big, equally smelly people, to be honest. So you've got this old woman sitting there, shrieking and howling, foaming at the mouth, hurling abuse at all and sundry, rolling around the floor twitching her head off. Eventually when the search is done, the dog handler comes in to do his bit. And in the middle of the room was this sofa. I think it was green. It was a wreck, a horrible-looking thing. You wouldn't really want to sit on it but it was there. The dog walked once round the room, climbed on the sofa, lifted his back leg and just pissed all over it. At which point, this lady leaped up and started screaming about how this dog had ruined her sofa. Well, all the dog had done was to actually improve the sofa 'cos it smelled a hundred per cent better after the dog had pissed all over it than it did before.

Then, of course, you had to go through all the procedure. Search damage claim forms. She was gonna claim against the government for her sofa and we had to fill out all the paperwork. It was just one of these things that lightens up what was gonna be a dull four or five hours searching a house. And the way they described their furniture! This ceased to be a flea-ridden reject. It had suddenly become the only piece of Chippendale furniture in Ballymurphy. In actual fact, the urine had probably killed all the fleas.

'Chris', who had seen the results of tarring and feathering, had his own ways of getting his revenge. In the early days he'd arrested a young rioter with two nail bombs in his pocket and taken him home to his mother to face a torrent of abuse. On a subsequent tour, the teenager, now older, had opened fire on Chris when he was out on patrol. The gunman was pursued and caught.

I thought about him sitting in that doorway ready to extinguish my life. I did lose my temper to a certain degree. I did give him a good thumping. His genitals were black and blue for a while and I think I may have cracked a couple of his ribs.
But that's illegal. That's uncivilized.
I did get him medical attention afterwards. And a cup of tea with some sugar in for the shock. But that was the way you treat terrorists.

They are terrorists and that's the end of the story. No rank, no glamour. They are terrorists. What did we do in Kenya? We didn't call them Colonels or Majors or Brigadiers. We called them terrorists and they were hung. Same thing in Palestine. Terrorists there were caught and they were executed. No glory. Nobody cries over a dead body too long. A couple of days and they forget all about it.

However extreme this sounds, it is a reflection of the way that a good many of the soldiers on the ground felt, although not all gave vent to their emotions so frankly or did what some soldiers did. But there is another side to the picture. There were many acts of bravery and occasions when soldiers actually saved Provisionals' lives. 'Gordon' gave first-aid to a relative of Gerry Adams after he'd been wounded by the army. There was a Thompson submachine-gun at the scene. 'He was a young man who was injured and who needed help and it just happened that I was there to give him that help,' he said. 'Hiram' did the same to a suspected IRA man whom he himself had shot and wounded. 'We're not there just to let people die by bleeding to death,' he said. 'We're still there to save people's lives.'

But compassion and chivalry did not fit in with the Provisionals' perception of the British army or with that of the community that increasingly gave the IRA its support. If the Provisionals had justified most of their previous operations as either defensive or retaliatory, internment and the events that followed were to remove any restraint. The British army and the RUC were now targets, not only because of what they had done, but also because of what they represented to the Provisionals, British rule in the North. By the end of 1971, MacStiofáin had declared all-out 'war' and the Provisionals' real offensive had begun. The issue now was partition.

Chapter Eight

Enemies

For many teenagers across Northern Ireland, Monday, 9 August 1971 was a special date which had nothing to do with internment. It was the day their A-level results were announced. That morning, two young men destined to join the IRA and rise to prominence in the Provisionals were waiting for the postman.

Eighteen-year-old Tommy McKearney was asleep in his bed in the village of Moy, County Tyrone, where his father ran the local butcher's shop. He had been out the night before and was sleeping in. His father came into his bedroom to awaken him with the letter containing his results. They meant a lot to Tommy as they would effectively decide his future. His goal was Queens University, Belfast. Mr. McKearney gave Tommy the letter and told him internment was in. 'It was the most amazing conjunction,' Tommy remembers. 'There I was in bed, reading my A-level results and trying to take in the fact that the British Government, through its puppet regime in Belfast, had introduced internment without trial in the North of Ireland.' Tommy was from a family with a long republican tradition. In the 1920s, his maternal grandfather, Tom Murray, had been Adjutant General of the IRA's North Roscommon Brigade and in 1969 had come North to live with the family in Moy, giving Tommy and his brothers and sisters his particular analysis of the events they saw unfolding before them. Words like 'puppet regime' would have been part of the language of the McKearney household since the unionist government at Stormont was simply seen as an adjunct of the British Crown. Tommy lay in bed thinking. He had passed three A-levels but the results were not good enough for Queens. His future stretched out before him with, as he saw it, few options for a young Catholic from County Tyrone. He could go to college and become a teacher as many of his contemporaries did, or emigrate to England or elsewhere, as did a good many others. In 1971, discrimination was still endemic and job prospects, even for bright young Catholics with degrees, were limited. Tommy was acutely aware of the explosion in the North and the circumstances that had triggered and now fuelled it. Lying there, he thought about his future.

> I remember thinking that Queens wasn't on and I'd have to look for a second choice. But at the same time I was saying to myself, 'Do I have another choice?' Not in the academic world, but in the real life of politics in Ireland. I realized that with internment in, we – that's myself and the republican community in Tyrone of which I was a part – were at a crossroads. But it wasn't just one issue – internment. It was everything that had gone before. In my view, internment was like a straw which broke the camel's back. Three to four hundred people lifted in a swoop on Monday morning and then brutalized, as it soon emerged. That moment was also decisive in my own evolution. I had reached an age where I was capable of taking an independent decision. I decided to join the Provisional IRA.

Tommy joined and was sworn in. Unlike most of the many IRA Volunteers I spoke to, Tommy told his mother, who still remembers the day.

> Tommy came and said he was anxious to join the Movement. He said if I was dead against it or it would upset me too much, he wouldn't. I said he was eighteen and old enough to make his own mind up. I warned him that it would be a very hard life. I'd seen what my father had been through. He would never have a day's comfort and face nothing but hardship. But if that was to be his decision, so be it.[1]

She was surprised but not shocked at what Tommy said. 'So many young men were joining, any son of mine could have joined because of the tradition in our family and what was going on all around them,' she added. Tommy also recalls the decisive moment.

> My mother wasn't greatly surprised. She was extremely apprehensive and she was worried. She never adopted the approach of the Spartan mother. She never said, 'Come home with your shield or on it'. She would have welcomed me home without my shield. There's no question about that. She has never withdrawn her support, throughout my life.
>
> **Did you seriously think about what joining meant?**
> I was quite aware of what was involved. But let me say this. Coming from the community I come from, and came from at that time, with the history we have, being in the IRA is not seen as a

criminal activity and I didn't see it as criminal. I didn't see it any different from any other man joining an army to take part in a defensive war would. Nor was I so naive not to realise that war involves destruction and death. That we did take on and made no apologies for it. We believed that war had been foisted on us and we were willing to take part in it.

Were you prepared to kill people?

I was prepared, yes. As part of an army and part of an armed Irish Republican Army, yes.

Tommy was subsequently given life for the murder of an off-duty UDR man.

Fifty miles away in Belfast, Richard McAuley was also eagerly awaiting the postman. But the postman never came.

Probably like most others, I was extremely nervous because your future hangs on your A-level results. I didn't get much sleep and probably didn't get to sleep until about three o'clock in the morning. Consequently I didn't hear the noise at four o'clock when the British came into the area. I was awakened about half seven, went downstairs, there was a barricade at the top of the street. It was incredible. In our street! Barricades! I didn't understand it. Stories were going around that people were being lifted out of their homes and the word was that internment was in. And there was I asking people, 'What's happened to the postman?' They were all saying, 'His van's probably at the top of the street'. And my A-level results were with him. Then I thought to myself, 'Internment? Obviously, people will react. It'll galvanize opinion. They can't do it. They wouldn't be so daft.' But they did and I couldn't believe it. I then clambered over the barricades with some friends and went up to school to get the results.

Richard's A-level results were good and he went to St Joseph's College in Belfast to study to be a teacher, his childhood ambition. But he also joined the Provisional IRA, initially combining his military activities with his studies. The studies came second and he never graduated. Like Tommy McKearney, he realized that he may have to kill and thought about it a great deal.

Ultimately at that time it was about war. And in a war one does things that under other circumstances one would never consider doing. People outside this situation will look at republicans and see people that they don't understand. But yet if they were in our situation, they would probably be doing exactly the same thing – or maybe not. But we all have to make those choices. For me it wasn't an easy one. It wasn't something that I did on the spur of the moment or very quickly. I was aware of both the risks and the consequences of that action. I was prepared to accept them.

I knew that becoming an active republican was going to put my teaching career at risk. But it was a risk that I was prepared to take. My own recollection of it now is that even if I hadn't been arrested when I was, I probably would have failed my exams subsequently because I wasn't doing the work at college that I should have been doing.

Richard McAuley was otherwise engaged. He was arrested in January 1974 whilst moving weapons within his area, Andersonstown. 'We unintentionally drove into a British army checkpoint and were stopped and searched. They found the weapons and were clearly delighted to take them.' At his trial he refused to recognize the court, like most republicans at the time, on the ideological grounds that the courts were the judicial arm of an illegal occupying power. He was sentenced to ten years.

McAuley and McKearney were both teenagers when they joined the Provisionals but in the watershed year of 1971, older men joined too. After internment, Terence 'Cleeky' Clarke returned from Coventry where he had been living, to help with the 'resistance' in Ardoyne where he had been brought up. Bernard 'Barney' Watt, who had been shot dead by the army the night Gunner Curtis was killed, had been one of his best friends. Internment was the last straw. Clarke felt he had to help his community and reported back to Martin Meehan. To his surprise, Meehan attacked him for his activities in Coventry where he had been selling *The United Irishman*, the newspaper that was the organ of the Official IRA with whom the Belfast Provisionals had had a bitter feud earlier that year. In England, Clarke had not been aware of the difference.

At that particular time you could have said maybe half of the young men of Ardoyne were in the IRA or were working with the IRA or for the IRA. Whenever I'd have been walking down the street, or somebody had been walking down the street, you'd have got a wee woman coming up with a message that the 'Brits' were coming round the corner. 'Watch yourself, son', she'd say whether she knew you or not. So you had wee women in the street involved in watching for the British or warning people. And before you left a house, they would throw holy water and say, 'watch yourself, son'. The whole of Ardoyne at that time was solely dependent on the IRA. They were the defenders. They were the people that they needed, so they were going to assist them in any way that they could.

Clarke's activities in Ardoyne were curtailed at the end of 1971 when he was arrested and charged with possession of a gun. On 16 November 1971, whilst in Crumlin Road gaol awaiting trial, 'Cleeky', along with eight others, escaped and went on the run. The escapees were known as the 'Crumlin Kangaroos' because they had jumped over the prison wall. Clarke did not figure in the original escape plan and was only asked to assist. But he saw his chance and went over the wall with the others. He spent the first five or six days in an attic of a safe house in a loyalist area of Belfast before going across the border to Dublin. But he was keen to get back to Ardoyne and the 'war'. Clarke, like many of his contemporaries, saw the 'struggle' in simplistic black and white terms. The priority was to get the 'Brits' out and the only way to do it was by sending their sons home in coffins. Sinn Fein existed in the shadow of the IRA and was of little interest to most IRA Volunteers. The fact that the party had a political platform and a policy for the governance of Ireland following a British withdrawal went completely over the top of most young heads that were full of other things. Over the weekend of 25 October 1971, the Sinn Fein Ard Fheis approved the party's recently announced plans for Eire Nua, a New Ireland, to be made up of the four ancient provinces of the country, each of which would have its own regional parliament. Eire Nua was the brainchild of Ruairí Ó'Brádaigh, Sinn Fein's President, and David O'Connell, the IRA's Director of Publicity. Ó'Brádaigh and O'Connell, comrades from the 1956 border campaign, were the Republican Movement's leading strategists and political thinkers. The Provisionals conceded that the Ulster parliament could have, if necessary, a Protestant majority. But to the 'Cleeky' Clarkes of the time, Eire Nua and politics were of little relevance.

I was politically naive. Barren of political thought. I thought I was doing the right thing because it was for my people. I'm not ashamed of what I was then, although I've had regrets about different things. I hadn't a political thought in my head other than that I knew what we were doing was right because it was to get the 'Brits' out of Ireland. The more you hurt them, I thought, the more fed up they'll get and want to get out. At that time there were British politicians saying, 'Why are we there? Why are our boys dying?'

I remember on one occasion a certain person telling Seán MacStiofáin that he was a gunman not a politician. MacStiofáin hit the roof. He was going to have his scalp. But that was indicative of how we all felt then. We were gunmen and he was saying, 'We

just want to shoot. We don't want to talk or find out.' It's a sad
reflection on us at the time.

Clarke was recaptured a year later in October 1972 and finally tried. He
refused to recognize the court and told the judge, Mr Justice McGonigal,
who was notoriously unsparing of IRA suspects, that he had no right to
try him for the 'crime' of defending his country. He was sentenced to ten
years. Clarke ended up spending more than twice as long inside, a total of
twenty-one years. His last sentence was linked to his involvement in the
events that led to the killing of the British army corporals, Derek Wood
and David Howes, on 16 March 1988, when their car ran into an IRA
funeral. 'Cleeky' Clarke is now Gerry Adams' chief of security.

On 19 September 1971, a disused RAF camp just outside Lisburn
opened its gates to receive its first inmates, a batch of the detainees
arrested in the internment swoop the previous month. Of the 300 men
who had been lifted, seventy were released. Initially, all of them were
Catholics although Protestants soon fell within the police and army net.
In the summer of 1971, the Ulster Defence Association (UDA) was in the
process of being formed whilst the UVF was becoming increasingly active
in response to the IRA's campaign. Both groups were soon to embark
upon their campaign of sectarian slaughter, sometimes using their own
names, sometimes operating under 'flags of convenience' to confuse the
security forces. Their rationale was to hit Catholics so Catholics would put
pressure on the IRA to stop. On 4 December 1971, a group calling itself
'The Empire Loyalists' bombed McGurk's bar in Belfast, killing fifteen
civilians, all of them Catholics. In fact the atrocity was the work of the
UVF. Gradually, the number of loyalist internees grew. They were, of
course, held in separate compounds. To have done otherwise would have
resulted in a bloodbath on Her Majesty's premises.

The internees were held either on board an old troop ship, the *Maidstone*,
moored in a corner of Belfast harbour, or in the Nissen huts of Magilligan
outside Derry or Long Kesh outside Belfast, named after the village close
by. The Second World War huts inside the compounds, or 'cages' as
they became known to republicans, with their watch towers and high
barbed-wire fences, were a propaganda godsend. The Provisionals claimed
they were prisoners of war and it seemed that the British had provided them
with an authentic POW camp to prove it. Most of the senior Provisionals
who came to lead the Republican Movement through the eighties and
nineties were graduates of 'Long Kesh'.

Paul Holmes was one of those sent to the *Maidstone* after his arrest in
December 1971. Like 'Cleeky' Clarke and Martin Meehan, he came from
Ardoyne. According to Holmes, the army raided his house, kicked in the

door – 'there wasn't much door left from the earlier times they'd booted it in' – and took his shirt off. They were looking for a bullet wound which confirmed that he was the man they were looking for. He was carted off to an army barracks where he alleges he was 'systematically tortured' for a period of three or four days.

> They beat the shit out of me. There's no two ways about it. They actually played 'boom de de boom boom' with my head on a wall and they played the response 'boom, boom' by banging the wall with the kid's head next door.

A man in a white coat, whom Holmes did not believe was a doctor, took a note of his injuries. 'I thought they were just taking the piss,' he said. Then he was dispatched to the *Maidstone*. To his astonishment, he was released a year later. To the British, internment was a regrettable but necessary measure to stem the tide of IRA violence but, stung by the international criticism it provoked, the Government moved to place it on some kind of quasi-judicial footing. It therefore set up what were known as 'Tribunals' under a Commissioner, which would decide whether there was good reason for an individual to be detained. The Tribunals also reviewed cases of men already held. Witnesses, invariably soldiers and policemen, gave evidence from behind a screen to protect their identity. To republicans, the Tribunals were a farce. Paul Holmes' case was one of those reviewed.

> You had this diplomat from God-knows-where sitting there and they had these screens with the Special Branch men who beat the shit out of you sitting behind them, saying all sorts of things. 'We suspect him of doing this and we suspect him of doing that.' All they were doing was justifying the fact that you're there. Then I said to this guy in charge of the Tribunal, 'to be honest with you, these guys sitting behind the screen should be sitting where I am and I should be away home. These people beat the shit out of me and these are people who are supposed to be upholding the law.'

The Commissioner asked if there were any medical reports and to Holmes' astonishment, they were produced.

> It transpired that the guy in the white coat actually *was* a doctor and he *did* take notes and they *did* show the extensive bruising to my spine, legs and upper arms. And there was a mark on my face where they'd been playing that rapping game on the wall with

me and the other guy next door. The Commissioner believed the doctor's report. The doctor was fair. The doctor was honest.

Perhaps British justice was not all that unfair, although it was an admission few Provisionals would be prepared to make. Paul Holmes was released at nine o'clock that night. A few weeks later, he was heading for London to plant the Provisionals' first bombs in England. He was arrested on 8 March 1973, the day the bombs were planted, and subsequently spent twenty-one years in English gaols.

Paul Holmes had been interned on board the *Maidstone* prison ship and on 17 January 1972 had watched the Provisionals' 'Magnificent Seven' crawl through a porthole, swim ashore and escape. Like the 'Crumlin Kangaroos', the 'Magnificent Seven' soon entered republican myth and song. On the propaganda level such escapes, and there were many more to come, gave a huge boost to morale and enshrined the notion that republicans were prisoners of war with a duty to escape like RAF POWs in the Second World War. On the practical level, they ensured that many of the Provisionals' most experienced gunmen, bombers and planners were returned to the front line of the 'war'. Tommy Gorman was one of the 'Magnificent Seven'.

We managed to get hacksaws on board and we sawed the bars on the porthole on the seaward side of the boat. I, for some reason, was picked to go out first. We blacked ourselves out with boot polish and butter to protect us from the cold and we put socks on our hands and our feet to protect us from the metal hawser we were going to slide down. I got out the porthole and slid down into the water, wearing nothing but my underpants. I swam as far as I could under water and then slowly came to the surface. At that moment, I thought I was just going to be shot dead because it seemed like daylight with the lights shining over the water. But there were no shots so I slowly swam for about twenty-five minutes to the shore. With all the excitement, I didn't feel the cold really at all.

Then I just squatted below a small jetty on the edge of the water waiting for my friends to come behind me. I must have sat there for half an hour and nobody came. You have to realise the whole thing about being on the ship was the never-ending jokes and pranks that were played. Then it suddenly dawned on me that the others were all probably back on ship roaring their heads off.

The other six eventually joined him. One of them had nearly drowned, not being the best of swimmers. They hijacked a bus, made for Belfast

and then Dublin where they gave a triumphant press conference. They
then returned to the 'war'.

By this time, the beginning of 1972, there were plenty of weapons to do
the fighting with. The network set up by George Harrison and others in
America had started to deliver the goods. They had originally been put
in place by the IRA's General Headquarters Staff (GHQ) in December
1969 and January 1970 at the time of the Provisionals' split from the old
IRA. Ancient hardware had now been replaced by sophisticated Armalite
rifles covertly shipped across the Atlantic on board the QE2, half a dozen
at a time. In the early days, in 1971, there was a regular run every two
weeks, the time it took to cross the Atlantic and back. The Provisionals'
supporters on board the QE2 stashed the Armalites away behind panels
in their crewmates' lockers so, if the weapons were detected, they were
in the clear. When the liner docked in Southampton, the gun-runners
would come ashore with the Armalites folded up and tucked down their
trousers. 'Over the time, there were quite a few crew members with
limps,' one of those involved told me. 'On occasions, you could even
see the barrel poking out of their trousers.' This QE2 run continued for
almost five years. I was told that ten IRA Volunteers were involved in
five cells: one in America to procure the Armalites; one in New York
to smuggle them on board; one on the liner itself to hide them; one in
Southampton docks to collect and arrange the transfer to Belfast; and one
in the Lower Falls to collect them. Neither cell knew the identities of the
others involved. The QE2 run ended around 1975, not through fear of
detection, but because the quantities of Armalites were getting too big for
seamens' lockers. The IRA then switched to containers. As the operation
became bigger, control moved up the IRA's hierarchy, first to Northern
Command and then to the Provisionals' GHQ in Dublin.

The operation was initially masterminded by the 'D' Company of the
IRA's Second Battalion based in the Lower Falls. Brendan Hughes, then
second in command, was a key figure. He knew from the start that the
Armalite was a weapon the IRA had to get hold of.

> I remember sitting in a house and this guy who was in the Merchant
> Navy came back from America with this booklet on the Armalite.
> It really praised this weapon. It could be folded up, dumped in
> rivers, buried, almost anything. Everyone was talking about it —
> this 'Super Weapon'. The brochure said if a person was shot in
> the arm, it would break every bone in his body. It was light and it
> was powerful. Everyone went wild about it because up until then
> there were only M1 carbines, .303's and old Second World War

weapons. Everyone was saying, 'this weapon is going to change the whole war'. The Armalites came in and that I think helped change the whole situation because then the IRA had a weapon that was effective, easily dumped, easy to handle and easy to train on. If it did half the things that it was supposed to have done, the war was going to be over in a couple of years. At that time most people didn't think long term. They thought of next year or next month or six months time. But that was it. No one was thinking of ten years, or five years or even three years.

How did the Armalites get to Belfast?

They were transferred from Southampton to Belfast in cars. People would hire a car in London, drive it to Southampton, take the panels out of the side, put the Armalites in and drive them back. I remember a car driving up. The boot was opened and there were ten to fifteen Armalites in it. The magic Armalites were there. Fifteen of them. I remember the people who were there being amazed at their fire power. It was a big jump from a couple of M1 carbines. I know people felt, 'This is it. We're really moving up a stage here with these things'.

In 1971, the Provisional IRA shot dead forty-two British soldiers. In 1972, this figure rose to sixty-four, most of them killed by snipers. In other words the Provisionals were shooting dead, on average, a British soldier a week. In the same period, soldiers shot dead twenty-six members of the Provisional IRA.[2] Sometimes the Provisionals' targets were carefully chosen. An army foot patrol's routine would be carefully monitored to see if it betrayed a pattern. Army vehicles would be watched to see how much they varied their routes. Hoax warnings would be given to lure soldiers into a trap. But in those wild days of the early seventies, Provisional IRA gunmen sometimes just went out on the off chance. Brendan Hughes referred to it as the 'float'.

There would probably have been a group of twelve to fourteen Volunteers in a particular area, plus back-up. Some would meet in a house that particular morning. There'd be an Operations Officer there whose job it was to pick particular operations for bombings or for shootings or for ambushes or for robbing a bank if money was needed at that time. It was called 'jumping the counter'. It would be normal enough for five or six operations to go ahead in one day. Plus, they would put a 'float' out. That's two men in a car with one man driving and one man in the back with a particular weapon. They'd be 'floating' around the area just waiting until targets came along. Men would be picked to do the particular operation. Someone would be sent to steal or hijack a car, someone else would hold the driver whilst someone else carried out the operation, whether it was a bombing in the town or a 'float'. The circumstances at the time would dictate what operations took place.

Were the operations carefully planned or were they carried out on an opportunistic basis?

Some would have been opportunistic. I remember one occasion when a jeep drove through the area. I could never understand why. I used to think that maybe it was done for a bet. There were four British soldiers in it and it was an open jeep. They drove through the area which was a suicidal thing to do because at that particular period, the area was heavily militarized by the IRA and the only time the British army came in was when they came in in convoy with Saracens and whatever. The 'float' happened to be out that day and there were a few people with weapons in it and they just shot the whole jeep up. That was an opportunistic operation.

Certain harrowing incidents are permanently etched in the memories of both soldiers and Provisionals. The horrific death of a young, nineteen-year-old soldier, Gary Barlow, is one. He was shot dead by a Provisional IRA gunman on Sunday, 4 March 1973 when his patrol was on duty in the Lower Falls.'[3] This is the account of 'Chris', one of the soldiers who remembered what happened.

It was the very last patrol of their tour and they were suddenly called to an incident. When this happens, the Commander usually yells, 'Follow me!' and they make off at a helluva rate of knots. Unfortunately this soldier was left behind. He didn't think nothing of it. It was getting dark and he thought, 'Well, it's best to stop here. They'll come back and fetch me on the way back.' Of course, they didn't. The women in the area very quickly realized the young lad was on his own. They surrounded him.

'Chris' was not a member of the patrol, but was in Royal Victoria Hospital at the time when Gary Barlow's body was brought in. That was when 'Chris' first saw him and registered a 'look of terror' on his face. He saw the body again in the mortuary. Gary Barlow's rifle and ammunition had been taken away by the IRA. He had apparently been shot three times and later died in hospital. Brendan Hughes, in whose area the incident took place also remembers it vividly.

There was a gun battle that took place that day and this young soldier was left behind. He was killed and I remember feeling very, very sorry for him and I don't think it should have happened. He was killed by local IRA people and I am told by people who were there at the time, that he was only a kid and the young fellow was crying for his mother. It certainly had an effect on me when it happened. I always felt sorry for him and I regret it very much. It bothers me when I think about that young soldier sometimes.

In fact, the evening before the programme in which the incident was featured went out, new evidence came to light that affected the picture of what had happened. A particular family and group of friends from the area tried to save the soldier, despite being called 'soldier-lovers' or worse by the crowd of women who had gathered nearby, but who had not actually 'surrounded' him, as 'Chris' believed. Some of the women who tried to protect Gary Barlow rang me and said that they had alerted the barracks, but that it was too late to save him. One woman stayed there throughout to comfort him and was at his side when a young gunman appeared and shot him through the head. She has lived with the horrific memory for almost twenty-five years. Death was to become a way of life in Northern Ireland, many of them as horrific as that of the young soldier, Gary Barlow. There were over three thousand more deaths to come.

Chapter Nine

Bloody Sunday

The 'resistance' in Derry mirrored that in Belfast although in a much more concentrated form and in a much smaller area. Two nationalist estates dominated the city, the Bogside which nestled beneath Derry's ancient walls and the Creggan which rose above it. The Bogside was a warren of Victorian terrace houses built to accommodate the Catholic workers and their families who arrived in Derry in the nineteenth century to work in the linen mills that were once the basis of the city's prosperity. Significantly, they were herded into an area outside the walled city which was the bastion of Protestant supremacy. It was called the Bogside because it was wet. The Creggan was a sprawling post-war housing estate whose spectacular views of the River Foyle and the hills of Donegal beyond helped compensate for its bleakness.

Despite the geographical differences, the IRA in Derry had established itself and grown in much the same circumstances as in Belfast, with one notable exception. The imperative to defend the nationalist areas from loyalist attack was never as strong because in Derry nationalists were in the majority and separated from the minority Protestant population by the River Foyle, which acted as a barrier between them. With the odd exception, Derry has never experienced the depth of sectarian hatred that has scarred Belfast. Nevertheless, the IRA in Derry still saw itself in a defensive role, defending the community not from loyalists but, as recent history had taught it, from the army and RUC. It was the RUC, after all, that had 'invaded' the Bogside in 1969. There were incidents, too, like the shooting of 'Barney' Watt in Belfast, that convinced nationalists that the army was no longer a peace-keeping force. The army's Red Cap Club faced falling rolls and the youths of the Bogside and Creggan no longer ran soldiers' errands to the fish shop. During a confrontation in the early hours of the morning on 8 July 1971, a soldier from the Royal Anglians shot dead twenty-eight-year-old Seamus Cusack, an unemployed welder from the Creggan. It was the fourth night of rioting in the city and the Anglians had already logged sixty shots that had been fired at them, whilst firing only three in return. The army said Cusack had been seen 'carrying a rifle'. He was hit in the femoral artery which caused massive bleeding. When troops arrived at the spot where he fell, there was a huge pool of blood but no sign of Cusack. He had been spirited across the border to a hospital in Letterkenny.[1] To the soldiers, this was evidence enough to prove that he must have been an IRA gunman. The reality, however, was that many of the Derry men and women who were injured in the endless rioting and shooting were treated across the border where their names would not be given to the security forces. Not all were members of the IRA. Local people insisted that Cusack was not armed and had never had anything to do with the IRA. In the rioting that followed that afternoon, another Anglian soldier fired a single shot at nineteen-year-old Desmond Beattie. According to the Anglian's log, the target 'fired at him'. Beattie died almost instantly. A priest who was standing next to him told the inquest, 'I saw the lad drop to his knees with blood pouring out of him. I could see the hole in his chest.' He said he could see no trace of a bomb or weapon. Nor was there any forensic evidence that Beattie had been handling firearms or explosives.[2] The city erupted in anger. At a rally in Derry the following Sunday, Sinn Fein's Maire Drumm told the crowd, 'It's a waste of time shouting "up the IRA", the important thing is to join.'[3]

John Hume, whose own power base was in Derry, urged the newly formed SDLP to withdraw from Stormont in protest. This it did. For the party not to have acted would have isolated John Hume and handed the initiative to Sinn Fein which, as the years unfolded, was to become the SDLP's rival for the nationalist vote. With the deaths of Cusack and Beattie, Derry had its first martyrs. A month later, the Provisionals shot dead their first British soldier in Derry, twenty-three-year-old Paul Challoner who was on foot patrol in Creggan. It was the day after internment began.

But the alienation of the nationalists of the city caused by the killing of Cusack and Beattie and internment within a month of each other was nothing compared to the impact of 'Bloody Sunday', the tragedy with which Derry is synonymous. Sunday, 30 January 1972 was the day on which soldiers of the First Battalion, the Parachute Regiment, under the command of Lieutenant-Colonel Derek Wilford, shot dead thirteen unarmed civilians. The shooting took barely thirty minutes but the impact was seismic. To this day, it is difficult to convince nationalists in the city that the killing of their fellow citizens was anything other than pre-meditated murder by the army, authorized by Stormont and the British Government. How else, they ask, would soldiers slaughter thirteen innocent people taking part in a peaceful anti-internment march? The only explanation that makes sense to them, and there remain few voices to the contrary, is that there were orders from on-high to teach the rebels of 'Free Derry' a lesson they would never forget. This lesson, as the evidence of their eyes told them, was to send a good number of the marchers back home in boxes. After much research, I do not believe this 'conspiracy' theory to be true. 'Bloody Sunday' was a dreadful mistake and should never have happened, but there were no orders or directives from on high instructing the paratroopers to do what they did.

But 'Bloody Sunday' cannot be seen in isolation. It was a tragedy waiting to happen. For many months, there had been endless rioting in the city. Every day at tea time, there would be a confrontation at the corner of William Street and Rossville Street between soldiers guarding the entrance to the city centre and the rioters operating out of 'Free Derry'. Day after day soldiers would stand there being pelted by rioters and the stone throwers would get in plenty of practice. For both sides it became a regular fixture and was played with a certain good humour. The junction was known, with good reason, as 'aggro corner'. But however relaxed the regular battalions were about the ritual, it was anathema to Colonel Wilford and his men. They were the army's resident Battalion in Belfast seventy miles away. The Paras were eighteen months into their two-year tour and took pride in the fear their presence instilled whenever they were dispatched to the trouble spots of Belfast. They had seen plenty of action. Whenever One Para arrived on the scene, the trouble soon stopped. Kid gloves were not their style. Colonel Wilford took command of the Battalion in June 1971 and had been involved in trying to contain the post-internment explosion. A cultivated man who, on the face of it, was a most unlikely commanding officer for one of the toughest Battalions in the British army, Wilford was an accomplished painter and a lover of the Classics who bemused his men by reading the Roman poet Virgil's epic war story, the *Aeneid*, in Latin. But Wilford was as tough as the men he led, and could not afford to be otherwise. He had no illusions about Northern Ireland. His priority was to see that his men stayed alive.

In my view, this was a war. If people are shooting at you, they're shooting not to wound you but to kill you. Therefore we had to behave accordingly. We blacked our faces, we took our berets off, or at least our badges from them, and put camouflage nets over our heads. We always wore our flak jackets and when we moved on the streets, we moved as if we were moving against a well-armed, well-trained army. Now that might have been a compliment to the IRA but it wasn't really. It was a compliment to my soldiers. I wanted my soldiers to stay alive and I actually said to them, 'you will not get killed'. That was really my coda throughout my period of command.[4]

The lessons were not lost on his men. One who disregarded his Commanding Officer's instructions was shot by a sniper in Ballymurphy whilst getting out of his armoured vehicle to light a cigarette. He was paralysed for life. But Derry was a world away. Wilford was appalled at the way the army handled the troublemakers at 'aggro corner'.

> I wasn't pleased at all that British soldiers could line up behind plastic shields and just stand there and let people throw rocks at them and do nothing whatsoever about it. We thought it was a peculiar way for soldiers to behave. They just stood there in the road like Aunt Sallies and never went forward. It was quite horrifying. I actually said publicly that my soldiers were not going to act as Aunt Sallies. Ever! We did not carry shields. We did not wear cricket pads. As far as I was concerned, it was not a game of cricket that we were indulging in.

Derry's Protestant business community shared Colonel Wilford's view. Its representatives had recently held a meeting with the army's Commander of Land Forces in the province, Major-General Robert Ford, and left him in no doubt as to their feelings. The rioting, they pointed out, had already done nearly four million pounds worth of damage and it was creeping ever nearer to the centre of town. Army commanders knew what the business community was talking about. There was a line drawn on their military maps known as the 'containment line' separating 'Free Derry' from the city centre. On one side of the line the Queen's writ ran. On the other side it did not. The line was, literally, a series of big, black dots on the map. It was a cartographical *cordon sanitaire*. When the Adjutant of One Para first set eyes on it, he was appalled. There were no such 'containment' lines in Belfast, either on maps or on the ground. He has a clear recollection of its significance.

> On one side of the line were the nationalist areas where people did what they wanted. The line said, 'we stop them here'. That map was a clear statement of the philosophy. It was clear to us, and I think, very clear to Colonel Wilford, that the formal, open crossing of this line was going to be a very significant action by the security forces. It is something that had not been done for quite a long time. One might assume that the IRA would see it as an invasion of what they had come to regard as their own territory. The inference to be

drawn from this was, of course, that the reaction could be violent and very dangerous.

Colonel Wilford's assessment was the same and he left his men in no doubt as to the risks they were likely to run if the line was crossed.

I pointed out they were going into a situation that was totally alien to them. The Bogside was a 'no-go' area dominated by the IRA and the army was peripheral. Soldiers never went in. In the arrest operation, we were likely to step over the 'containment line' which would then take us into territory which had previously been declared 'no-go'. That was potentially very, very dangerous because the IRA for the first time would be faced with something they had not come up against. This was bound to make them behave aggressively.

It was clear to everyone that trouble was expected. The previous weekend, a civil-rights march to Magilligan internment camp, situated on a headland twenty miles from Derry, had ended in violence and hand-to-hand fighting. Marchers trying to reach Magilligan clashed with soldiers on the beach despite the remonstrations of the Derry civil-rights leaders, John Hume and Ivan Cooper, who had been anxious to avoid a confrontation. The estimated 3,000 marchers found themselves facing not only locally based soldiers from the Second Battalion of the Royal Green Jackets but also the hard men of One Para brought in from Belfast to deal with any trouble that weekend. Some of the demonstrators unwisely tried to force the army's barbed-wire barrier and fierce fighting erupted. The army fired volley upon volley of rubber bullets into the crowd. These 'baton rounds', which enterprising youths would sell to visiting journalists, are solid, hard and potentially lethal if fired at close quarters. Many demonstrators were injured, with some being forced into the sea. Television cameras captured the scene and the images had a powerful effect on the nationalist population, not only of Derry, but of the entire province. They saw it as a peaceful demonstration being met with excessive and unwarranted army force. The images only strengthened the determination of NICRA not to be intimidated. The following Tuesday, 25 January 1971, the Derry branch of NICRA issued a statement calling on its supporters to gather for a huge anti-internment march the following Sunday. Despite the fact that after internment, Stormont had made *all* marches illegal, the intention was to parade from Creggan to the Guildhall Square at the heart of the city centre, within Derry's walls.

Tension and anger on both sides mounted in the week after Magilligan. Two policemen were shot dead in Derry, the first to be killed in the city since the outbreak of the 'Troubles', and two bombs exploded inside the perimeter fence of Holywood Barracks in Belfast where One Para was based. Given the build-up, it was inconceivable that Sunday's march was going to be without trouble. But influential figures in the community went to considerable pains to ensure that it would be. They met the Provisional and Official IRA leaders in the city and asked them to remain inactive that day. They agreed. Dr Raymond McClean, a Derry General Practitioner, was one of those who made the contacts.

> Prior to Magilligan, it was very difficult to take people onto the streets because at that stage the Provisionals had taken over a very prominent role. We were, quite frankly, afraid because we wouldn't be responsible for what would happen. On this occasion we explained our difficulty and said that we would like to have a massive demonstration against internment. The message came back that if we wanted the demonstration, the IRA would leave that day to us and leave us alone. They weren't using us. We believed what they said.

The army, for its part, was preparing to get tough but not to the extent that people with hindsight believed. Once again, One Para was to be brought in from Belfast. Not all army officers thought it a good idea given what had happened at Magilligan the weekend before. One of the Royal Green Jackets' senior officers had phoned the Brigade Commander, Brigadier Robert MacLellan, to say it was 'mad' to bring the Paras in, only to be told by the Brigadier that he had his orders and he was going to carry them out.

The secret Brigade Operational Order of the day directed that if rioting broke out during the march and the mob crossed the 'containment line', the Paras were to go into action as an arrest force 'to conduct a "scoop-up" operation of as many rioters as possible'. This operation was only to be launched, the Brigade Order stressed, 'either in whole or in part on the orders of the Brigade Commander'. The Order went on ominously to warn that there may well be 'IRA terrorist activity to take advantage of the event, to conduct shooting attacks against the security forces'. It warned that 'almost certainly snipers, petrol bombers and nail bombers will support the rioters.' Memories of how Gunner Curtis had met his death were probably still fresh in most soldiers' minds. The unit chosen to carry out the 'scoop-up' operation was One Para's Support Company. It consisted of three units – the Mortar, Anti-Tank and Machine-Gun Platoons. Collectively they comprised the cream of the Battalion's most experienced privates and NCOs, many of them veterans of Aden. The

Mortar Platoon's sergeant, who says he 'dropped' three gunmen on 'Bloody Sunday' was, and remains, defiantly proud of his Battalion.

> We were very experienced and very highly motivated. The whole training of the Parachute Regiment is built on aggression and speed of movement. You know you can't afford to hang around. This comes through to the blokes and they get very hard-minded about their work. Under Colonel Wilford, I don't think there was a better Battalion at that time in the world, never mind the British army, in terms of internal security. Derry was nothing out of the ordinary other than the actual amount of dead.

Support Company was ready and more than willing to do the job. Its Company Sergeant-Major (CSM) had been as appalled as Colonel Wilford at how the rioters of Derry had been allowed free rein.

> Our philosophy was that a guy can't throw a stone if he's running away from you and therefore [in Belfast] we used to get stuck into them. The rioting in Derry had got totally out of control. I thought it was about time somebody went across there and did something about it – somebody with a bit more 'go' about them than the resident Battalions in Londonderry. It was time it was stopped.

The Sergeant-Major has a vivid recollection of the briefing his men received before they were sent into the front line. It no doubt conditioned their minds as to what they were likely to encounter should they breach the 'containment line' and deploy into the heart of 'Free Derry'.

> The one thing that stuck in my mind was the fact that we were warned about sniper fire, possibly from the Rossville Flats. Sniper fire is very, very accurate, very pinpointed. It's feared by soldiers. A sniper can fire through a window from ten feet inside a bedroom and you can't see him at all. It's something to be very, very wary of. The majority of soldiers up to that period killed in Belfast and Derry had been killed by very, very accurate sniper fire and none of the people in my Company wanted to be killed by a sniper.

The statistics confirm that between the beginning of 1971 and 'Bloody Sunday', IRA snipers had killed twenty-four soldiers. Eighteen had been shot dead in Belfast and six in Derry. The twenty-fifth sniper victim was to die on the day of the 'Bloody Sunday' march from injuries he had received in Derry four months earlier. However, the soldiers were not told that, of the nearly 2,000 shots fired at the army in Derry over the preceding three months, only nine came from Rossville Flats. Colonel Wilford also has a vivid recollection of the briefing. He remembers asking Brigadier MacLellan what would happen if there was shooting.

> I got really what was a very sparse reply to the effect that, 'Oh well, we'll deal with when it comes.' It's my greatest regret that I didn't actually pursue that question and say, 'What do you want us to do if we're shot at?'

Why didn't you pursue the question, given its critical importance?

> We were the Belfast Battalion. There we behaved in a recognized way. It was never necessary to ask that question. I asked it there in Derry because we were on new ground. But when I got the reply that I did, I accepted that we'd deal with it when it comes, assuming that there'd be specific orders. But I regret now, of course, in retrospect that I didn't pursue it.

So, if shooting did break out, how were your men trained to react?

> If someone starts shooting at you, you can behave in a variety of ways. You can run away – which, of course, on the whole, soldiers don't. You could take cover behind your shields and just sit in an area until it all passed over. Or you could do what my Battalion was trained to do – move forward, seek out the enemy and engage them.

Thus the scene was set for the tragedy. What happened on 'Bloody Sunday' was not, as I have said, in my view a conspiracy but an operation that went terribly and fatally wrong. Basically, the officers, sergeants and corporals of One Para lost control of their men.

The march began in a carnival atmosphere as it gathered around the shopping centre in Creggan at around two o'clock that Sunday afternoon. The organizers estimated the number to be around 20,000. The authorities put the figure at a good deal less but there was no doubt it was a huge crowd. The mood was so relaxed that Dr McClean decided to leave his first-aid kit at home rather than lug it around the winding streets of the Bogside. Bishop Daly (then Father Daly) joined the march.

> People from all walks of life took part. Yes, the march was illegal but marches were at the time. People felt they must put down a marker and say, 'we do not accept internment'. The huge turn-out was an

indicator of the way people felt about the Stormont Government at that time.

There were IRA men around but this would not have surprised any of the marchers as the IRA was, after all, part of the community and some of its members would be acting as stewards. Tony Miller was a member of the Provisional IRA at the time and remembers the order his unit was under.

> There was no action to be taken whatsoever. The march was to go ahead and there was no IRA units out. That was an instruction from the IRA in the town. There was to be absolutely no activity by the IRA that particular day. And there was none. None whatsoever.
> **Where was the IRA that day?**
> I would say most of the IRA personnel would have been taking part in the march. Or maybe they would have been home with their wives and children.
> **Was the IRA on standby with its weapons just in case?**
> No. No, not that I'm aware of, anyway.

Just before four o'clock, as the procession wound its way down from the Creggan, an incident happened that was to have a profound effect on the course of events during the next forty minutes. A single high-velocity shot rang out from the Bogside and struck a drainpipe running down the side of a church where soldiers from One Para's Mortar Platoon were stationed on the roof. The shot did no damage, except to the drainpipe, but its significance was huge. It suggested to the Paras that what they had been warned about at their briefing was true. There were guns in the Bogside and the IRA was waiting. The Mortar Platoon's sergeant saw the shot strike the pipe and Colonel Wilford heard it in his temporary command post nearby.

> One of my senior officers who was standing with me at the time said, 'That shot was aimed at us, sir.' We thought it came from the Glenfada Park area because my men could see the windows being moved. Its significance was that there was at least one weapon on the other side. And if there was one, then there were probably others.

The shot came ten to fifteen minutes before the Paras actually went into action and crossed the 'containment line' into the Bogside. Denis Bradley, who was then a priest, was near the point from where the shot was fired.

I remember coming across a couple of people whom I knew were actually in the Provisional IRA. They told me a shot had been fired. I said, 'You're not that stupid, are you?' They said, 'It's not us, it's the "Stickies"[5] [the Official IRA]'. I think the gun was taken off him and he was told to get out of the area.

The march proceeded down William Street and, finding access to the city centre blocked by army barricades, turned right and entered the Bogside along Rossville Street and past Rossville Flats to where a rally was to be held at 'Free Derry' corner. However, some of the 'hooligan' element broke away from the main march and started stoning the troops behind one of the barricades, despite efforts of some of the marchers to restrain them. This was the action that triggered the Paras' invasion of the Bogside. The stoning ran true to form and it was the moment Support Company's 'snatch squad' had been waiting for. They were getting impatient, some of them had been waiting around since daybreak. Wilford's Company Commanders kept urging him, 'Now's the time. Let's go, sir.' But Brigade Headquarters, who alone could give the order, told them to hold back. According to Wilford, the scene at the barricades was 'a bloody shambles' with soldiers (who were not Paras) playing their usual role as 'Aunt Sallies'. The order finally came at 4.07pm. Wilford gave the command, 'Move! Move! Move!' Major General Robert Ford, only an observer at the scene as Brigadier MacLellan was in operational command, urged the men on with the words, 'Go on, One Para. Go and get them and good luck!' Support Company's CSM described the tension among his men.

I recall a soldier cocking his weapon as he leaped into the back of the armoured car in front of me. I earmarked him and thought, 'When I get back, I'll kick his arse, because cocking a weapon like that is contrary to orders.' But I could understand it. The guy was probably tensed up in view of the briefing we'd had.

The original intention of the operation had been simply to 'scoop-up' the rioters around 'aggro corner'. It was never intended that the operation should be extended into the heart of the Bogside, but that is precisely what happened. The Paras leaped into their armoured vehicles, roared down Rossville Street and dismounted in the open area by Rossville Flats. Raymond McCartney saw the dramatic scene unfold before him.

There was this almighty charge and this almighty sense that something was happening that had never happened before. The next thing

you knew, there were shots being fired and you knew from street
knowledge that there were live rounds. You just felt you had to get
yourself out of the way. I can actually remember running through
the car park and round the back of Rossville Flats and lying in an
alleyway with three or four friends.

What did you see?

I didn't see too much at that moment but I saw the aftermath.
There were people lying on the street whom you knew to be dead
but I didn't actually witness anybody being shot. I just remember
the panic of people running. You just heard the shooting and you
heard the screaming and you heard the shouts.

The 'containment line' had been not only crossed but smashed. The
scenario was dramatically changed. This was the point at which the
Paras maintain they came under fire. Colonel Wilford who went in
with his men says he never saw any gunmen but remembers 'a couple
of shots', although nothing like the 'fusillade' the army referred to in
its subsequent statement. The sergeant of Support Company's Mortar
Platoon tells a different story.

It suddenly changed from an arrest operation to 'Hey, someone's
trying to kill me! Let's find out who it is and do the job back.' We
identified targets and started 'dropping' them.

The sergeant claims to have identified three gunmen and fired at them,
one in the courtyard of Rossville Flats and two in the flats themselves.

I've seen weapons fired at me before, in Aden and places like that,
over the previous ten years. I know when a hand-gun's firing at
me. You can see the kick of it. You can see the flash. The man
[in the courtyard] was firing at me with a pistol, I have no doubt
about it – no doubt whatsoever. It was the highest concentration
of fire I'd personally heard in Northern Ireland.

Bishop Daly who was in the courtyard of Rossville Flats is equally certain
that the Paras did *not* come under fire.

I am satisfied in my own mind from the behaviour of the soldiers
themselves that they were not being fired at. I'm quite satisfied too
that each individual was picked and targeted. But even if there were
shots, I do not think that what the Paras did was justified. I believe
it was murder.

However, Bishop Daly, who was part of a group tending the dying seventeen-year-old 'Jackie' Duddy, does state that he saw a man with a pistol in the area, but only *after* the Paras had started firing.

> We screamed at him to clear off. We were frightened that the Paras might have thought that the gunfire was coming from the group of us in the middle of the courtyard.

The television pictures of a crouching Father Daly, waving a bloodstained white handkerchief in front of the men carrying 'Jackie' Duddy, is one of the most harrowing images of the 'Troubles'.

Even twenty-five years on, it is impossible to say with certainty whether there were any IRA gunmen who opened fire either before or after the Paras did. If shots were fired, the triggers were almost certainly pulled by members of the Official IRA and not the Provisionals. Both organizations had withdrawn their weapons to the Creggan, the Officials having loaded them into the boots of two cars. However, it seems that the Officials did leave some weapons behind in the Bogside whether by accident or design, either for 'defensive' purposes or 'unauthorized use'. The most that former Officials I spoke to would admit was that, 'there was always the possibility that somebody had a short arm and used it on their own initiative.' They told me, no doubt pointedly, that at that time, the Official IRA's Standing Orders had just been changed, permitting weapons to be fired only 'in defence and retaliation'. 'Offensive' operations were ruled out. The breaching of the 'containment line' and the invasion of the Bogside by an armoured column of Paras may well have been more than enough to justify 'defensive use'.

In the half hour following Colonel Wilford's command to 'Move! Move! Move!', the Paras fired 108 rounds and shot dead thirteen civilians. Fourteen others were wounded. They claimed that they were firing at gunmen and nail bombers. Eyewitnesses stated that none of those injured or killed were armed or carrying nail bombs or any other offensive weapon. In the wake of 'Bloody Sunday', the government set up a Tribunal of Inquiry under the Lord Chief Justice, Lord Widgery. To the astonishment and fury of the people of Derry, Lord Widgery exonerated the Paras.

> Civilian, as well as army, evidence made it clear that there was a substantial number of civilians in the area who were armed with firearms. I would not be surprised if in the relevant half hour as many

rounds were fired at the troops as were fired by them. The soldiers escaped injury by reason of their field-craft and training . . .

. . . in general the accounts given by the soldiers of the circumstances in which they fired and the reasons why they did so were, in my opinion, truthful.[6]

Derry was outraged and the Ministry of Defence's own internal assessment of Lord Widgery's findings only intensified the community's anger and resentment. The MOD concluded that five were killed when there was 'reasonable evidence that they were using or carrying a weapon'; two as a result of a 'genuine mistake'; two 'probably accidentally'; and four as a result of firing 'bordering on the reckless' (Lord Widgery's phrase).[7]

Nevertheless, however deep the regret, no soldier I spoke to could bring himself to apologize directly even to those families whose loved ones were adjudged in the words of the MOD to have been shot dead 'probably accidentally' or as the result of 'a genuine mistake'. To do so would be, in their eyes and the Ministry's, tantamount to an admission of murder. No soldier was ever prosecuted which is, above all, why Derry was outraged, and Widgery was dismissed as a whitewash. A quarter of a century later, the people of the Bogside and Creggan are more convinced than ever that all thirteen were innocent victims murdered in cold blood by the British army. They point out that the results of the forensic tests used at the time, whose limitations were acknowledged even then by Lord Widgery, would never be accepted in 1997.

To this day, 'Bloody Sunday' has haunted not just Derry but some of the Paras who took part in the operation. I interviewed the CSM of Support Company and asked him what really happened. Still serving in the Parachute Regiment when I met him, he was startlingly honest in his answers. When Support Company returned to barracks, each soldier had to account for every round he had fired. The CSM noticed that one of his men had actually fired two rounds more than had been issued to him.

I said, 'What the hell were you doing?' And he said, 'I was firing at the enemy. I was firing at gunmen.'

Did you believe him?

I didn't know what to think at the time.

Did you believe him?

No. Knowing the soldier as I do know him, I don't believe he was firing at gunmen.

Did you see any gunmen?

No.

Did you see any weapons?

No.

Did you see any nail bombers?

No.

Do you believe, all these years on, that all the dead were gunmen and bombers?

No, not at all. I feel in my own heart that a lot of these people were innocent. I feel very guilty about the subsequent effect of that day. I think it was badly handled. By everybody. By me, the Platoon sergeants, the individual soldiers and our superiors. There was control from above prior to the deployment. It was contained. But after the deployment, it became quite chaotic.[8]

After the interview was shown in the documentary, *Remember Bloody Sunday*, I received several letters from people in Derry saying how much they appreciated his honesty. At last, they said, someone had been prepared to tell the truth and come close to saying they were sorry. Although the CSM never uttered the word, his demeanour and tone of voice were enough. It was a remarkable and courageous interview that clearly had an effect on some Catholics of the Bogside and Creggan. No one from the Government or the Ministry of Defence had ever said as much. They asked me to pass their letters on to the CSM, which I did. I later spoke to him and asked how his interview had been received by the Parachute Regiment. I knew he had been concerned about how his colleagues might take his breaking ranks. To his surprise, he had been widely congratulated. It was if a great weight had been lifted from his and the Regiment's shoulders.

The events of 'Bloody Sunday' had a profound effect on Colonel Wilford. I met him again twenty years later. He had retired from the army in 1981, a disillusioned man, after a series of desk jobs which had taken him from Whitehall to Nigeria.

There has to be a scapegoat and I was the one. I'm not bitter about it. The only good thing about being a scapegoat is that you protect other people. I adored my soldiers and I protected them because I believed they were right.

Are you still protecting them twenty years later?

I suppose so.

You can see the pain as the memories flood back. I asked him what 'Bloody Sunday' had done to him. There was a long, deep sigh.

It's an event which is in my subconscious all the time and occasionally it comes to the surface. If anything, I suppose it's made me anti-war. I would like to think that out of that tragedy – which it was, however you look at it – something more positive could have happened. Instead it just became something that went into the history books.

I'm sure I'd be censored for saying so if it comes into the open, but I really believe that we should find a more positive solution than hyperbole to a situation which has gone on for twenty years and will go on for another thirty – because there is no desire by either side to end it. I hear people saying, 'Troops out of Ireland'. It's like 'Troops out of Aden'. There we did make a positive decision and I think we need to make a positive decision now about ending the war in Northern Ireland.

But wouldn't that be a victory for the IRA?

Yes, but only a partial victory. It would be a victory for common sense, wouldn't it? We could claim a victory as well. And we would.

The supreme irony of 'Bloody Sunday' is that the Commanding Officer of One Para who had believed he had joined battle with the IRA twenty years previously, ultimately came to share their view of troop withdrawal.

But historically the most lasting impact of 'Bloody Sunday' was the effect it had on that generation of young people in Derry, many of whom were on the march that day. As a result, hundreds joined the Provisional IRA, eager to seek revenge for the murders they believed the British army had committed and the cover-up they were convinced had been perpetrated by Lord Widgery. If any young men had previously held back because they felt morally uncomfortable about killing, 'Bloody Sunday' removed any lingering restraint. Raymond McCartney was one for whom that day finally tipped the balance. But it was still not a decision he was prepared to rush into. His cousin, Jim Wray, was one of the victims.

It was the first time that that sort of grief had visited our home. I actually remember the three days of the wake. Our family was very, very close and we were being fragmented. I think the older people in my family sensed how I was feeling and what was going through my mind. I remember my oldest brother saying that this wasn't time for emotion to cloud decisions. He said that whatever I was thinking about, I should take time to make up my mind so that no one could ever accuse me of letting emotions cloud my judgement, so no one could say, 'you're joining the IRA just because of "Bloody Sunday".'

About two or three months passed and by then I had made up my mind. I actually approached a a very senior republican in Derry whom I knew very well and confided in him what I was thinking. And I remember him actually giving me a couple of books and saying, 'I want you to go away and read them. I want you to go away and think about it so as when you come back you can honestly tell me that you know all that's involved; that it's not something you're doing because your friends are doing it or out of romanticism or whatever. You have to be doing it because you want to do it.' So again I went away, maybe took another two or three weeks and went back and said, 'Look, I feel that I have weighed up everything in my mind and I'm making this decision for the right reasons, namely that I want to be part of a movement that's going to create change in this country.'

'Bloody Sunday' had given the Provisional IRA the biggest boost in its history.

Chapter Ten

Ceasefire

Although Harold Wilson's Government had made the fatal mistake of not abolishing Stormont when British troops intervened in 1969, it did set up a 'UK Representative's Office', as we have seen, in the Stormont parliament buildings to maintain closer contact with the unionist government and shades of opinion in Northern Ireland. It was also HMG's eyes and ears on the ground. Remarkably, the UK Representative's Office became a sort of Embassy of the United Kingdom within the borders of the United Kingdom itself. The Office later moved to a house at Laneside – an attractive villa on the shores of Belfast Lough at the end of a quiet lane, where in later years Ministers and officials held discreet meetings with republicans, loyalists and others, away from the inquisitive eyes of the rest of the world. Laneside was perfect for quiet meetings. In 1971, the UK Representative was a Foreign Office diplomat, Howard Smith, subsequently Ambassador to Moscow and Director General of the Security Service, MI5. By the autumn of 1971, Smith had decided that in the wake of the upheavals of internment and the violence and controversy that followed, he needed a Deputy as his work load was too great and his staff too small. Smith heard that an official called Frank Steele, whom he knew, was on leave in London at the time and asked for him to be his Deputy. Steele was a member of Her Majesty's Secret Intelligence Service, also known as MI6. MI6 had come to Northern Ireland with Whitelaw. Although the service is concerned strictly with foreign intelligence operations the representatives of its domestic counterpart, the Security Service, MI5, were no more prepared for the emergency than were their colleagues in the Home Office's Northern Ireland Unit, and were equally overwhelmed. It was the legacy of years of neglect and non-interference on the the part of the successive British Governments in the affairs of the self-governing province. When serious violence erupted, the Government decided that the skills of its foreign intelligence agency, MI6, were the ones best suited to deal with the emergency once British troops were deployed to restore order.

Steele was destined to play an important role in the historic secret meeting between the leadership of the Provisional IRA and the British Government. Previously he has never spoken in any detail about his work in Northern Ireland and his contacts with the IRA. I remember meeting him in the summer of 1972 at Stormont Castle where I assumed he was a Northern Ireland Office (NIO) official. A quarter of a century later, I met Frank Steele again, now retired and willing for the first time to record for posterity his recollections of that critical period in Northern Ireland's history. He wanted to set the record straight. In discussion about his posting, Steele pointed out that having spent years abroad, in Libya, Iraq, Jordan, Lebanon and Kenya, he knew very little about Northern Ireland. He was asked what he knew about Faulkner. He had read that morning in *The Times* something about a politician called Faulkner who was Minister for Agriculture in the Dublin Government. He produced this nugget, only to be told that the Faulkner his interviewers had in mind was Brian Faulkner, the Prime Minister of Northern Ireland. 'That means you've got an untrammelled mind,' they told him. 'You'll be unbiased, so you're just the man for the job.'

Because Northern Ireland was part of the United Kingdom, and theoretically the responsibility of MI5, Steele was precluded from doing intelligence work such as running agents but was expected to use his experience of conflict situations in the Middle East and Africa where he had spent most of his career. He also took it upon himself to get to know grass roots and extremists in both communities, in particular republicans in Derry and loyalists in Belfast. There were – and still are – those who thought that the British Prime Minister, Ted Heath, had sent an MI6 officer to Northern Ireland to establish a secret line of communication with the IRA. Steele emphatically denies this on the grounds that 'HMG didn't want to communicate with the IRA. It wanted to beat the IRA.'

When he arrived in Northern Ireland in October 1971, Steele, in his ignorance, was astonished at the situation.

One forgets what it was like in those years. The place was a shambles. Areas like Belfast and Derry were almost in a state of anarchy and civil war. There were sometimes around a thousand security incidents of one sort or another each month. The army hadn't learned how to cope with civil unrest in the UK and how to use minimum and not maximum force. Many nationalists believed that HMG had lent the British army to the unionist government to keep them in power and keep the nationalists under control. There was very little co-ordination of whatever intelligence was being produced by the RUC, the army and MI5. Internment had been a disaster. It barely damaged the IRA's command structure and led to a flood of recruits, money and weapons. It was a farce. And as for the special interrogation techniques, they were damned stupid as well as morally wrong. Such methods are counter-productive and do you enormous damage when they get out, as they inevitably do. And in practical terms, the additional usable intelligence they produced was, I understand, minimal.

The unionist government seemed to be just soldiering on and incapable of solving the problems facing Northern Ireland. The obvious answer was the introduction of Direct Rule from Westminster, which Harold Wilson's Labour Government had shunned when the troops were sent in in 1969. However, this presented considerable difficulties for HMG. The Unionist Party was linked to the Conservative Party and Direct Rule would cause uproar amongst unionists and Tory backbenchers. Furthermore, there was a belief, assiduously spread by the opponents of Direct Rule, that the problems were so complex that they could not be understood by mere mainlanders and were best left to the inhabitants of Northern Ireland to solve.

By the beginning of 1972, the powerful base established by the IRA in the nationalist community was the result not of intimidation but of a series of mistakes and miscalculations made by the unionist government and the British over the previous two years, of which 'Bloody Sunday' was the latest and most catastrophic. On the afternoon of the banned civil-rights march in Derry, Steele was at Laneside with Howard Smith listening to the reports coming in about the march.

When we heard the mounting number of deaths, we couldn't believe it. It was typical of the use of maximum instead of minimum force. I think it was when we got to seven dead that Howard and I looked at each other and said, 'Right, that means Stormont has to go.' Of course, when it got to thirteen deaths, Direct Rule was inevitable.

What effect did 'Bloody Sunday' have on the IRA?

It built them up even more. Nationalists – even those who disapproved of the IRA – said yet again, 'we need the IRA to defend us against the British army.' Once more, as with internment, it led to a flood of Volunteers, money and weapons going to the IRA. It was a humanitarian, political and military disaster. The only good thing about it was that it enabled us to bring in Direct Rule.

Within two months, the Heath Government was able to introduce Direct Rule. It was an increasingly bloody period in which much was to happen, all of which made the end of Stormont more and more inevitable. There was little else the British Government could do to try to stabilize the situation and make a fresh start. Both the Official and Provisional IRA intensified their campaigns in response to 'Bloody Sunday'. Both wings, in particular the Provisionals, had more than enough Volunteers and resources to do so. The avalanche of recruits was so great the organization could barely cope. On 22 February 1972, the Official IRA planted a bomb at Aldershot, the home of the Parachute Regiment, in revenge for 'Bloody Sunday'. The bomb was placed near the Officer's Mess but it did not kill a single soldier. Its victims were five women working in the kitchen, a gardener and a Catholic army padre. Three days later, the Officials struck again, trying to assassinate John Taylor, Stormont Minister for Home Affairs. He was hit with six bullets from a submachine-gun as he got into his car in Armagh. Miraculously he survived but his face still carries the scars. The Provisionals too, intensified their operations. One bomb was to have a particularly disastrous result. On Saturday 4 March 1972 there was an explosion at the Abercorn restaurant in the centre of Belfast. It was tea time and the place was packed with women and children having a break during the afternoon's shopping. No warning was given. Two women were killed and over a hundred customers were injured, many seriously. Two of them were sisters out shopping for a wedding dress. Both lost both of their legs. The Provisionals were blamed for the carnage but denied responsibility. Séan MacStiofáin suggested that the attack was the work of loyalists and stated, 'the restaurant itself had no value as a sabotage target. It was a direct attack on civilians . . . The IRA had nothing to do with it and said so in very clear terms.'[1] However strong the denials, in the eyes of the security forces and most people, the blame rested squarely on the Provisionals. The incident at the Abercorn had an indirect political effect, triggering the first contact between senior British politicians and the IRA since the beginning of the campaign. The initial approach was made by an unlikely intermediary, a former British army officer from Northern Ireland, Tom Caldwell, who had become a Unionist MP at Stormont. Caldwell had bumped into a senior Provisional at the Dublin Horse Show the previous year and exchanged pleasantries but nothing more.[2] He had subsequently talked to the Official IRA only to be told by Harold Wilson, now leader of the Opposition, and whom he met at Westminster in January 1972, that he was 'talking to the wrong guys'.[3] When the Abercorn bomb went off, Caldwell was determined to talk to the 'right guys', the Provisionals. On Sunday, the day after the bomb, he went to Dublin to meet Ruairí Ó'Brádaigh and Seán MacStiofáin.

The Provisionals expressed interest and Caldwell passed the message to London. Four days later, the IRA announced a three-day ceasefire to begin at midnight on Friday, 10 March 1972. Clearly, this was to give the British a violence-free window in which direct contact could be made. It happened the following Monday and, surprisingly, was made not by the British Government but by Harold Wilson and Merlyn Rees, the Labour Party's Shadow Northern Ireland spokesman. By this time, another intermediary was also involved, Dr John O'Connell, who was a Labour MP in the Dublin parliament. Dr O'Connell, through his Labour Party connections, knew officials in Harold Wilson's office whom he used as a message board. In March 1972, the message had come that 'friends of the IRA' were interested in talking.

On 13 March 1972 Harold Wilson, his Press Secretary Joe Haines and Labour's Shadow Northern Ireland Secretary, Merlyn Rees, flew to Dublin. It was the last day of the IRA's three-day ceasefire. The political formalities over, which provided the cover for Wilson's trip, the party was secretly driven to Dr O'Connell's house in Phoenix Park, Dublin, where ninety years earlier, previous Irish rebels had stabbed to death Lord Frederick Cavendish, the newly appointed Chief Secretary for Ireland. Rees says they approached the meeting with some trepidation, having Cavendish's fate in mind.

> I must say, at dusk, driving in a car to Phoenix Park and going up the steps of a big house, brought back memories of Phoenix Park and out of the corner of my eye I saw a car parked. I fervently hoped it belonged to the Irish Special Branch. We went up the steps and one of Harold's staff said to me, 'Harold would like you to go in first.' And I thought, 'I bet he does!' They said, 'He doesn't want to shake hands with them.' So I swiftly went up and went into the room.

Rees immediately recognized the men waiting in the room. The 'friends' of the IRA were the IRA. The delegation consisted of David O'Connell, a member of the IRA's Army Council, Joe Cahill, the IRA's Belfast Brigade Commander, and John Kelly of the IRA's GHQ staff. 'I knew they were members of the IRA,' Rees told me. 'There wouldn't have been much point in talking with them otherwise. It's the IRA who are causing the violence.' A table was set with sandwiches and soft drinks. Rees did as he was told to save Wilson's embarrassment and, to the 'amazement' of the three IRA leaders, 'twirled around the table' saying 'hello'. The encounter began at dusk and ended at midnight. Joe Haines recalls that 'a meeting of minds was clearly impossible. We were planets apart.'[4] John Kelly remembers Wilson asking one particularly pointed question.

> He puffed on his pipe in the way that he did and asked what the Republican Movement's intention would be towards a bombing campaign on the British mainland, in the event of there being no resolution to the conflict. We gave him a non-committal answer and said we didn't know and that it was not for us to answer that question.

Wilson tried to push for an extension of the IRA ceasefire to provide further room for manoeuvre but without success. At midnight, Kelly looked at his watch and said, 'It's too late. The ceasefire's over. It's started again.' With Kelly's words, the meeting came to an abrupt end. Wilson replied, 'Well, that's it then. Off we go.' A few hours later, the Provisionals in Derry returned to the offensive and started shooting at the army in the Bogside. The Provisionals were now ready to use one of their most devastating and indiscriminate weapons. The army had already come across what may well have been its prototype three weeks before the Dublin meeting with Wilson, but had not yet witnessed its horrendous results. On 20 February 1972 soldiers were carrying out an arms search in the Lower Falls when they discovered a vehicle packed with explosives. It was a car bomb.

Brendan Hughes claims the Provisionals discovered the device by accident following the death of Jack McCabe, an IRA veteran from County Cavan. McCabe had joined the IRA in the thirties and been active in the bombing campaign in England in the forties when he was the IRA's OC in Manchester.[5] He had been active in the fifties border campaign and had played his part in the current campaign from late 1969 when he had collected ancient guns from fellow veterans in the South and brought them North across the border. McCabe subsequently became the IRA's Quartermaster General, responsible for all weaponry and explosives. Just before Christmas 1971, whilst he was mixing explosives on the floor of his garage in Dublin, the spade he was using to shovel the mixture struck the garage floor and caused a spark that ignited the explosives. McCabe died on 30 December 1971. Brendan Hughes explained the consequences.

> Explosives were very, very hard to get, so people were experimenting, putting stuff together. There was a young Volunteer who was an explosives expert and an old IRA man, Jack McCabe, who went back years, who was involved in making the stuff. And to my

knowledge he made what was called the 'Black Stuff'. In the process of making that, he killed himself. The thing blew up on him. But he had already made a batch and it was sent to Belfast. The stuff was unstable so when it got to Belfast, it needed to be got rid of. It had to be destroyed. Someone took a decision to put it in their car and drive it into the town. He gave a warning and blew the stuff away that way. And that's how the first car bomb came about.

Seán MacStiofáin immediately saw the tactical and strategic advantages of the IRA's new weapon in that it 'provided an efficient container and an efficient delivery system. It yielded far greater administrative, industrial and economic damage for a given operation. And it required fewer Volunteers to place it on target'.[6]

On 20 March 1972, three months after Jack McCabe's death and a week after the ending of the IRA's three-day ceasefire, Belfast saw the devastating effect of the car bomb for the first time. A hundred pounds of explosives packed within a vehicle exploded, killing six people and injuring more than one hundred. It is not clear what the intended target was but the warning, if any, was imprecise. As people were being cleared from the street where there was believed to be a suspected device, the car bomb detonated in Donegal Street, to where they were being shepherded to safety. Two of the dead were policemen who had been escorting the crowd, the other four were civilians. Nineteen people were seriously injured. The Provisional IRA admitted responsibility but claimed they had given adequate warnings. The same defence would be given for the seemingly endless tragedies that were to scar the next twenty-five years.

Four days later, on 24 March 1972, the British Government announced that Stormont was being suspended and all law and order powers were being transferred to Westminster. In effect, Northern Ireland was to be administered by the British Government. Stormont, the 'Protestant parliament for the Protestant people' that had governed the province since partition in 1920, was finished. Direct Rule was introduced and William Whitelaw became the first Secretary of State for Northern Ireland. The Prime Minister, Edward Heath, announced that it marked the opportunity for 'a fresh start'. Loyalists did not see it that way. To them, it marked a victory for IRA violence and the beginning of the end of the Union. On the first count, they were probably right. There were huge loyalist protests and demonstrations but the Rubicon had been crossed and there was no turning back. I remember standing in the grounds of Stormont surrounded by a vast crowd of defiant, flag-waving loyalists, estimated to be 100,000 strong, as they cheered their former Prime Minister, Brian

Faulkner, who stood on the balcony with his Cabinet like the Queen and Royal Family at Buckingham Palace. I remember his words echoing out of the loudspeakers over the sea of faces and Union Jacks that stretched into the distance down the mile-long drive to the gates of Stormont.

> Our power is the power of our numbers. Our power is the justice of our cause. Our power is the responsibility of our conduct . . . Let us never play the game of the murderers of the IRA. Let us show the world that, so far as we are concerned, violence and intimidation are out . . . British we are and British we remain.[7]

It was a remarkable sight. We all knew that a chapter had ended.

The Provisionals were cock-a-hoop. They believed, with some justification, that it was their campaign which had brought Stormont down and that they now stood on the brink of victory. Their slogan, 'Victory '72', was more than just a morale booster. Martin Meehan, the Provisionals' commander in Belfast's Ardoyne, believed the slogan was true.

> Politics was a dirty word in those days. We actually believed we could drive the British army into the sea. It was raw determination, a gut feeling that if we kept up the pressure, we could do it. As young men, that was the thing that motivated us. We really thought that victory was just around the corner and that with one more push we could do it. All the signs were there that we were on the road and we had moved mountains.

To the Provisionals, Stormont was the first mountain moved. Tommy Gorman, on the run after his dramatic swim to freedom from the *Maidstone*, shared this view.

> Everyone felt we were very close to victory. The IRA at this period were actually going out chasing the British army instead of the British army chasing the IRA. Most people on the ground felt that it was only a matter of time before the British were going to finally admit defeat.

Seán MacStiofáin believed the IRA had never been as confident as it was in the spring of 1972.

> I think the IRA was in the best state it had been for fifty years in terms of men, ammunition, equipment and morale. We'd reorganized everything and thought we were winning. There was a report that

the British army said, 'give us a month in Belfast, a month in Derry, and then two months along the border, and it's over.' Well, they were wrong.

By the summer of 1972, there was just one IRA waging a campaign of violence – the Provisionals. The Official IRA had declared an indefinite ceasefire on 29 May 1972 following their killing of a British soldier, Ranger William Best, who was home on leave in Derry. Ranger Best was a Catholic from Creggan and his death outraged the community – thousands demonstrated in protest. This compounded the outrage already felt when the Officials bombed Aldershot in revenge for 'Bloody Sunday', killing kitchen workers not soldiers. The Goulding leadership of the Official IRA felt they were not only losing support but were being dragged into a 'war', increasingly sectarian and ideologically unsound. Whilst still reserving the right to defend nationalist areas from British army or loyalist attacks, the Officials explained that they had begun 'a new phase of civil struggle' in an attempt to divert a sectarian war and create political debate.[8]

Surprisingly, HMG was under widespread pressure in Northern Ireland to talk to the IRA. The Provos, too, were not unaffected by the mood for peace in Derry and elsewhere. The young Martin McGuinness and the veteran Sean Keenan, two of the IRA's most respected and influential leaders in Derry, went to Dublin and suggested to MacStiofáin that, given the Provisionals' position of strength and the prevalent mood of the nationalist community, it was time to test the water and see if the British were prepared to negotiate. MacStiofáin agreed and, disguised by a wig and moustache, crossed the border into Derry where, on 13 June 1972, he gave an audacious press conference with Martin McGuinness, the IRA's young Derry commander, Seamus Twomey, the IRA's Belfast commander and David O'Connell, who was the IRA's chief political strategist and acting Adjutant General at the time. It was a fortnight after the Official IRA ceasefire. MacStiofáin announced that the IRA was prepared to declare a truce and invited the new Secretary of State, William Whitelaw, to come to 'Free Derry' to meet the Provisional leadership and talk peace. Not surprisingly, Whitelaw declined. However, the SDLP leaders, John Hume and Paddy Devlin, went to the Provisionals to ask if their offer of a truce was genuine or merely propaganda. The Provisionals said it was genuine if the British would reciprocate.

This reply confronted William Whitelaw and his Ministers with considerable problems. They were well aware that there would be uproar both amongst the unionist community in Northern Ireland and in many quarters in Britain if it became known that HMG was talking to the IRA. There would be widespread criticism that HMG was talking

Tony Miller (blond, far left) and others reacting to a live round, Battle of the Bogside.

Gerry
Adams,
late 1960s.

Provisionals' press conference held in Belfast, after internment, by John Kelly (second right) and Joe Cahill, Commander Belfast Brigade (with cap), August 1971.

Gerard Hodgkins, early 1970s.

Gerard Hodgkins, 1997.

Frank Steele (right) in Derry, early 1970s.

Provisional IRA leaders (left to right) Martin McGuinness, David O'Connell, Seán MacStiofáin and Seamus Twomey, 1972.

Billy McKee and leading Provisional Proinsias MacAirt in Crumlin Road prison, 1972.

Billy McKee, 1997.

Peter Taylor (far left) and ITV *This Week* camera crew attacked by a loyalist mob at Lenadoon Avenue, 1972.

Reverend Ian Paisley remonstrating with Peter Taylor at Stormont, 1974.

Cathal Crumley (centre) on release from Long Kesh, 1980.

Cathal Crumley, 1997.

Hunger striker Raymond McCartney, 1980.

Bobby Sands' funeral, 1981.

to the terrorists instead of defeating them. Officials such as Frank Steele thought that, since it was not proving possible to defeat the Provisional IRA militarily, they would at some point have to be talked to. His foreign experience underlined his belief.

> My previous posting had been Kenya and the President of Kenya was the great Jomo Kenyatta who was one of our staunchest friends in the world. But it was not so long ago, when Kenya was a colony, that we'd interned Kenyatta because of his links with the Mau Mau. The Mau Mau's operational techniques and their obscene rituals made the IRA look like a Sunday-school choir. Not only had we interned Kenyatta, now our great friend, but a British governor at the time of the terrorist insurgency described him as 'a leader unto darkness and death'. Well, if you're prepared to talk to someone like that in Kenya, and leading members of the Royal Family willingly shake his hand, to people like me it seemed just pragmatic to talk to the IRA.

The subsequent exchanges were now conducted in the utmost secrecy. Press conferences were out. The IRA said they were prepared to meet the British to discuss a truce but only on two conditions: that 'political status' should be granted to their prisoners on whose behalf Billy McKee was on hunger strike in Belfast prison; and that the Provisionals should choose their own delegation, one of whom, they stipulated, must be Gerry Adams who had to be released from 'Long Kesh' where he was interned. To the Provisionals' astonishment, Whitelaw agreed. 'Political status' was granted, although the British called it 'Special Category'. This decision was to have momentous consequences (see chapters fifteen and sixteen). Adams was released from 'Long Kesh' and was as surprised as anyone at the news of his release. He was collected at the prison gates by Dolours and Marion Price, who were to be convicted a year later of the London Old Bailey bombings, and driven to meet his comrades in Belfast to discuss strategy. Brendan Hughes remembers being amused by the posture struck during the discussion by one of the most militant leaders of the IRA's Belfast Brigade, Ivor Bell.

> I remember a discussion taking place about what to wear for the meeting and I remember Ivor Bell saying that he wasn't going to wear a suit or a tie. He was going to dress as a combatant, as he always dressed. He said history had taught him that British politicians would try to make the Irish feel ill at ease. He was going to wear this gear to put *them* ill at ease.

In the end, Ivor Bell left his combat fatigues at home.

On 20 June 1972, the day William Whitelaw granted republican (and loyalist) prisoners 'special category status', Frank Steele and a senior NIO official, Philip Woodfield, made their way to a secret rendezvous just outside Derry to meet the Provisionals and discuss the mechanisms of a ceasefire and the logistics of a proposed meeting with William Whitelaw. After a few map-reading errors, they finally found the house, where they waited for Gerry Adams and David O'Connell. As Steele understood it, Adams was representing the IRA in the North and O'Connell the IRA in the South.

> They wanted to depict themselves as representing an army and not a bunch of terrorists. So we all had to have letters of authority. They had them and and we had them signed by a Minister or by Willie. I thought at the time it was simply ridiculous. I mean what on earth else were the four of us doing there? We hadn't just wandered in off the street to chat. We're obviously representing HMG and the IRA.
> **When you meet do you shake hands?**
> I can't remember now but I wouldn't have minded shaking hands. I mean because of my experience, one's shaken hands with with some fairly unpleasant characters over the years.

The meeting was businesslike without polemics or animosity. The details of a ceasefire were agreed. IRA operations were to cease and booby traps were to be 'de-boobed'. The army was to leave IRA suspects alone and cease its activities in nationalist areas. A telephone 'hot-line' was to be established between O'Connell in the South and Steele at Laneside to defuse tension and sort out misunderstandings where necessary. Steele remembers with a degree of affection the relationship he established with O'Connell over the 'hot-line'.

> Dave O'Connell had the endearing habit of ending all his conversations with 'good luck, good luck'. Everything was 'good luck'. He was a very quiet, self-contained and self-disciplined man. I know it's an unfashionable thing to say but I liked him. I could do business with him.

Before the meeting, Steele had been briefed that the young Gerry Adams had been an effective Commander of the Provisionals' Ballymurphy Battalion and was a senior officer of the Belfast Brigade. He was therefore expecting to meet 'an arrogant, streetwise young thug' and was surprised when Adams turned out to be 'a very personable, intelligent, articulate and self-disciplined man'. Steele believed that these were the qualities that made him 'so dangerously effective'.

> Gerry Adams obviously had a terrific future ahead of him whatever he did because of his qualities. As we were about to leave, I said, 'You don't want to spend the rest of your life on the run from us British. What do you want to do?' He said, 'I want to go to university and get a degree.' I said, 'Well we're not stopping you. All you've got to do is to renounce violence and you can go to university and get a degree.' He grinned and said, 'No, I've got to help to get rid of you British first.'

On 22 June 1972, two days after Steele and Woodfield's preliminary meeting in Derry, the IRA declared its suspension of offensive operations from midnight on 26 June. There was relief throughout Northern Ireland and, no doubt, the Northern Ireland Office. IRA Volunteers were relieved too. At last, after nearly two years of 'war', there seemed to be a real prospect of peace. Brendan Hughes summed up how many Volunteers felt.

> Most people never lived beyond the next month, never mind the next year. There was no strategy, no long-term strategy to fight the war. And when the British troops were taken off the streets in 1972 because of the IRA ceasefire, obviously people thought, 'this is it'. No one before had fought the British Government to a position where they were negotiating with IRA people. So there were expectations that the war was over. I think there was a need to believe it, a wish to believe it and a desire for it to happen.
>
> Most people involved had been on the run and being on the run means living from hand to mouth and depending on people to feed you. It means not seeing your kids, it means not seeing your wife, and it can be a very, very difficult situation to be in. People wanted it to end then. They wanted back to their wives and they wanted back to their kids.

At midnight on Monday, 26 June 1972, the IRA ceasefire came into operation. A few minutes before midnight, IRA gunmen shot dead a policeman in Newry as he tried to prevent them planting a bomb. Nevertheless, the plans for the historic meeting between the Provisionals and the British Government went ahead. It was to be top secret and held at the London house of Whitelaw's Junior Minister, Paul Channon, in Cheyne Walk, Chelsea. The only members of the Cabinet to know of the encounter were the handful of Ministers who sat on its Northern Ireland sub-committee. Whitelaw and Heath finally agreed to this high-risk strategy, persuaded by the argument that it would illustrate the lengths to which the Government was prepared to go to bring about peace. The same political rationale was applied to the secret dialogue held between John Major's Government and the Provisionals over twenty years later.

Frank Steele had the task of collecting the IRA delegation and escorting them to London. According to MacStiofáin, who as Chief of Staff was in a unique position to know, all six of the Provisionals who were to fly to London were members of the IRA – including Gerry Adams, despite his oft-repeated denial of IRA membership. There would be no Sinn Fein representation on the team. The IRA delegation consisted of Seán MacStiofáin, David O'Connell, Seamus Twomey, Ivor Bell, Gerry Adams and Martin McGuinness. Frank Steele was to be their 'minder'. At eight o'clock on the morning of Friday 7 July, Steele made his way to the agreed rendezvous in open country to the north-west of Derry near the border with Donegal. He was in a minibus with brown paper taped over its windows, driven by an army captain in civilian clothes. By now, Steele had something else on his mind, having heard that the previous night, two off-duty British officers had wandered into the Bogside and been 'arrested' by the IRA. He was obviously concerned for their safety and determined to extract a promise from MacStiofáin that they would not be harmed. But there was no sign of MacStiofáin or any other members of the IRA delegation. They waited. And waited. Steele began to think that all the effort that Ministers had made in bringing themselves to talk to the IRA and the effort that had gone into putting the operation in place, had been wasted. 'My God,' he thought, 'the IRA have changed their minds and they're not going to come.' But Steele was not to be disappointed.

Then suddenly up drove a car at a rate of knots, absolutely bulging with IRA. They explained that they'd set off in two cars but had had trouble with the second car and they hadn't been able to repair the thing. It was a puncture or something. So after trying for a bit, they all bundled into this one car. They then got into the minivan and we drove off to the field where the helicopter was going to come down and pick us up and take us to RAF Aldergrove airport outside Belfast.

Steele raised the matter of the 'missing' British soldiers to seek an assurance that they would be safe. 'Great,' said MacStiofáin who had no idea what had happened, 'they'll be our hostages in case anything happens to us.' It was en route for the airport that, as Steele remembers, they encountered the first obstacle.

> And as we drove along this narrow country lane, what should happen but a herd of cows floods out from a field on the right. Some of them take up station ahead of the minibus and some of them take up station behind the minibus. They were escorted by a stolid, Northern Irish farmer who wasn't going to get a move on for anyone. And MacStiofáin, whom I never think of as being a funny man, must have made one of the few funny remarks of his life when he said, 'I do think the British army could have given us a better escort.'

At Aldergrove airport just outside Belfast, the delegation was transferred to an RAF Andover for the flight to England. At Aldergrove, the RAF had laid on a 'meeter and greeter' whom Steele remembers 'standing to attention and doing the courtesies with his jaw hanging open at the sight of those he was shepherding.' The delegation boarded the aircraft and were flown to RAF Benson about fifty miles to the west of London, where they piled into two Special Branch cars and began the drive to Chelsea. It was a stunning July morning, and as they drove through Henley-on-Thames, it occured to Steele that his charges might be hungry so he stopped and bought a bag of apples.

> I got back into the car and handed the apples to the three IRA men who were sitting in the back seat. They all looked at each other. 'My God,' I thought, 'perhaps they think they're drugged!' So I took one at random and took a great bite out of it. Then I handed the bag to the Special Branch driver and he did the same. I then passed it again to the back. I think they were satisfied.

The British team at Cheyne Walk consisted of Whitelaw, Channon, Woodfield and Steele. The meeting was not a success, despite Whitelaw's attention to personal detail. The Secretary of State pronounced Séan MacStiofáin's name correctly in Irish as he shook hands. Adams noted that Whitelaw's hand was 'quite sweaty'. MacStiofáin was impressed and noted that 'he had done his homework'. In fact MacStiofáin had been born in Leytonstone of an English father and Irish mother. His real name was John Stevenson. MacStiofáin thought Whitelaw looked 'just like he did on television – smooth, well fed and fleshy'. The IRA delegation was asked if they wanted a drink. Thinking Whitelaw meant alcohol, they declined, perhaps suspecting, as with the apples, a British plot to dull their senses. In fact, it could have been water on a hot July afternoon. Whitelaw must have swallowed hard as he said a few words of welcome. He knew he was sitting down with men whose organization had been responsible for the deaths of many British soldiers but he was resigned to the fact that British governments had talked to 'terrorists' before and no doubt would do so again. He then asked MacStiofáin if he would like to open the meeting. The Chief of Staff produced a paper from which he read out a list of demands. They were:

1. The British Government should recognize publicly that it is the people of Ireland acting as a unit that should decide the future of Ireland as a unit.
2. The British Government should declare its intention to withdraw all British forces from Irish soil, such withdrawal to be completed on or before 1 January 1975. Pending such withdrawal, British forces must be withdrawn immediately from sensitive areas.
3. Internment must be ended and there should be a general amnesty for all political prisoners, internees, detainees and wanted persons.

Steele was surprised at what he heard. Unlike the reasonable attitude of O'Connell and Adams at the preliminary meeting, MacStiofáin behaved differently.

He was like the representative of an army which had fought the British to a standstill and as if we British wanted out. He behaved like Montgomery at Luneberg Heath telling the German Generals what they should and shouldn't do if they wanted peace. By demanding that the future of Northern Ireland should not be treated separately but as part of the future of Ireland as a whole, he was asking HMG to withdraw the guarantee it had given to the people of Northern Ireland – that their status within the UK would not be changed except with the consent of the majority. When Whitelaw pointed out that what was being demanded went against this guarantee, MacStiofáin, who had obviously done his homework, said, 'Well, this guarantee is enshrined in the 1949 Government of Ireland Act and all you've got to do is to change it.' He talked as if he thought all Willie Whitelaw had to do was to wander down to the House of Commons one day and say, 'My dear fellows, you remember in 1949 we gave this guarantee to the people of Northern Ireland. Now we want to withdraw it and do so in a hurry.' None of the IRA delegation seemed to have any concept of the consequences of this and the uproar it would cause not only amongst the unionists but in the House of Commons and the mainland in general.

Although relations were formal and businesslike, one of the IRA delegation, a Dublin solicitor called Miles Shevlin who was the Provisionals' legal adviser noting the meeting, deeply irritated the British side. Steele dismisses him as 'a creep'.

> He seemed more intent on demonstrating his worth to the IRA delegation by trying to score debating points rather than addressing himself to what we saw as the main object of the meeting: how to take Northern Ireland and all its peoples forwards rather than backwards.

The meeting was inconclusive. Whitelaw said he would bear in mind what had been said but was depressed at how intransigent the IRA delegation was. I suggested to MacStiofáin that the IRA's demands were totally unrealistic. He smiled. 'Maybe', he replied.

On the flight in the RAF Andover back to Belfast, Steele was so 'appalled at their naivety and lack of understanding of political realities' that he deliberately joined the delegation for a meal to try to point out how wrongheaded they were. He said he hoped they were not going to start their 'bloody stupid campaign of violence again'.

> I said if they really wanted a united Ireland, they were wasting their time shooting at British soldiers and bombing Northern Ireland into an industrial and social slum. They should be trying to persuade the Protestants and the unionists that they would have some sort of satisfactory life – jobs, housing and so on – in some sort of linkage with the South. But their basic line was, 'so long as you're there, we'll never come to a sensible agreement with the unionists. They'll always shelter behind HMG and, in particular, behind the British army. Therefore in order to come to a sensible agreement with the unionists, we've got to get rid of you British first. And the way to get rid of you British, as has been proved all over your Empire, is violence. You will get fed-up and go away.'

Steele said that Northern Ireland was not a colonial situation, that violence would not drive the British out and that the government would leave only if and when a majority of the people of Northern Ireland wished it to do so. Steele knew he was wasting his time and felt that all that Seamus Twomey and Ivor Bell in particular wanted to do was to get back to the IRA's simplistic doctrine of physical force in the belief that 'one more heave and the Brits would be out'. However, he sensed that Adams, who had said little either at the meeting or during the journey (although he was taking everything in) felt that this was not enough. Steele believes that the experiences and discussions of that day and the meeting at Cheyne Walk increased Adams' recognition of the limitations of 'armed struggle' and the need for the IRA to have a parallel political policy if it was ever to get anywhere. The Sinn Fein of today, with Adams as President, is the result.

The IRA delegation arrived back in Derry on Friday evening, 7 July. The two British soldiers who had wandered into the Bogside were released unharmed and subsequently disciplined by the army. Twomey went back to Belfast and held a meeting of the Brigade Staff. Martin Meehan was one of those present.

> Twomey outlined what was on offer from Whitelaw and the Republican Movement's interpretation of it. He said, 'There's not going to be an old 1921 sell-out here. The men and women on the ground that are doing the fighting will be fully informed. There'll be no underhand deals. But above all, my gut feeling is that it's not going to last.' I remember him telling us to 'keep the guns well oiled'.

There was to be no time for the guns to get rusty. The Belfast members of the IRA delegation returned on Saturday to find a crisis about to explode in the Lenadoon area of West Belfast. The Twelfth of July Orange march was approaching and tensions were running even higher than usual. The annual flashpoint was even more explosive than usual this year, as loyalists felt they had lost their parliament and lost out to the IRA. In response the UDA, the loyalist paramilitary group that had been formed the previous summer, was recruiting thousands of members throughout the province. Intimidation of Catholics in Protestant areas was rampant. I was in Belfast at the time, trying to film one of the few Catholic families left in the Protestant Rathcoole estate being forced to leave their home. They had been petrol-bombed the night before and told to get out. We were told to get out too. We did not argue. There had been 300 Catholic families on the estate. There were now only a dozen left who had no intention of staying. The dislocated Catholic families congregated in West Belfast and prepared to move into empty houses at the bottom end of Lenadoon Avenue. The problem was that the houses were in loyalist 'territory' and loyalists were not prepared to allow Catholics to continue their onward march down Lenadoon Avenue. The UDA threatened mayhem if the families moved in, causing army intervention to prevent this. Steele believes that Seamus Twomey must have thought the crisis ready-made for what he wanted. Either the army backed off and allowed the Catholics to occupy the houses, causing a consequent boost to the IRA's reputation and damage to the army's credibility, or the army would not back off and the ceasefire would end in circumstances which made the IRA seem to be in the right. For Twomey, it was like a win-win situation.

On Sunday 9 July, the families, with the backing of the IRA, prepared to move in. O'Connell telephoned Steele on the hot-line to Laneside to announce the imminent breakdown of the ceasefire unless the army allowed the families to move in to the empty houses. Steele said the IRA could not be allowed to railroad Catholic families into these houses and that O'Connell should tell Twomey to back off. He reiterated his position in a later conversation, saying that the army would use any force necessary to prevent the IRA railroading Catholic families into the empty houses. At one point, Steele was telephoned by someone claiming to speak for the Belfast IRA and threatening the end of the ceasefire. Steele was not sure if this was Twomey. Because of the IRA's attitude at the London meeting, Steele was determined that the IRA should not think that HMG would do anything just to preserve the ceasefire, and was therefore deliberately laid-back about the escalating crisis in Lenadoon Avenue. When, in his final telephone conversation with O'Connell, O'Connell said the ceasefire was breaking down, Steele said it was a pity, but he hoped to see O'Connell again sometime.

By the time of this conversation, the large crowd that had assembled at the top of Lenadoon Avenue prepared to march down the hill. At the head of the procession was a lorry stacked with the possessions of one of the families. I stood at the bottom end of Lenadoon Avenue, behind the barbed-wire line drawn up by the army, fearing the worst. The moment I saw the crowd coming round the corner and marching down the hill with the lorry in front, I knew the ceasefire was finished. It was only a matter of time. It took about half an hour to be precise. The lorry halted at the army line and there was an altercation between Seamus Twomey, who was at the head of the procession, and the soldiers. An army Saracen rammed the lorry to prevent it going any further. The crowd attacked the soldiers who retaliated by firing rubber bullets at the crowd. I watched the Protestant crowd cheering the army on. We were trying to film the confrontation but when we turned our cameras on the triumphant loyalists, they turned on us (see plate section for photograph). Within minutes the shooting had started. The Provisionals were armed and ready at the top end of Lenadoon Avenue with guns, as instructed by Twomey, 'well oiled'. They fired over 300 rounds at the troops. The ceasefire was over. The IRA Army Council issued a formal statement to that effect that evening when they also disclosed some information about the talks with Whitelaw.

Remarkably, nine days after the end of the ceasefire, Harold Wilson tried to put it together again. In the intervening period, forty-two people had died. Ten of them were soldiers killed by the IRA and three were Catholics killed by loyalists. The UDA and the UVF had begun to intensify their campaign of sectarian killing. Merlyn Rees believes that Wilson cleared the meeting with Heath first, but was told that he (Wilson) would not be acting on the Government's behalf. On 18 July 1972, an IRA delegation led by Joe Cahill, this time without David O'Connell and John Kelly, was flown to England to meet Harold Wilson and Merlyn Rees at Wilson's cottage in Great Missenden. Rees referred to the delegation as 'the second eleven'. Like Frank Steele, he could not stand Miles Shevlin, the lawyer who was with them and who had previously accompanied the IRA delegation to Cheyne Walk. 'Whatever I said,' remembers Rees, 'he said, "you're worse than Mr Whitelaw". Instinctively I preferred soldiers to lawyers. We didn't get on very well.' The talks got nowhere. The IRA had let slip the dogs of war and saw no reason to call them off. The same day, Rees heard that the hundredth British soldier had been killed, shot dead by a sniper in Ballymurphy. His name was James Jones and he was eighteen years old.

Frank Steele believed there was never 'a cat in hell's chance' of the ceasefire surviving, let alone being reinstated so soon after it had broken down.

> Of course, I and the army were blamed by the IRA and other republicans for the breakdown of the ceasefire at Lenadoon. We were accused of being intransigent and of being dilatory in trying to contact Whitelaw to try and persuade him to allow the Catholic families to move into the empty houses. But if the ceasefire had not ended at Lenadoon, it would, I am sure, have broken down over some similar incident. The difference between what HMG wanted – peace – and the unrealistic demands of the IRA, were too great to be bridged.
>
> There were too many people who could influence the continuation of the ceasefire, who didn't want it. The unionists didn't want it as they wanted the British army to go on knocking hell out of the IRA. The RUC didn't want it as they wanted to be able to fight with the British army against the IRA and restore some of their credibility and morale which had taken such a knock over internment. The Protestant paramilitaries didn't want it as they saw

themselves fighting alongside the British army against the IRA. Part of the British army didn't want it as they reckoned the IRA could still be beaten militarily. The hard-line IRA didn't want it. I know this sounds a callous thing to say, but I don't think either community had suffered enough to want peace, to make peace an absolute imperative. And so we entered into something I don't think anyone expected: twenty-five wasted years of killing, maiming and destruction. We may have got fed-up but, contrary to IRA expectations, we have not gone away.

Before he left Northern Ireland in 1973, Frank Steele remembers that while he and some colleagues were having a drink at Laneside, they had a go at devising a suitable coat of arms for the Northern Ireland Office. This included a quartering of hooks to get caught on if you were not careful. They also decided it needed a motto. They came up with 'It seemed a good idea at the time'.

Frank Steele died in the autumn of 1997 after a long illness. Although bedridden and aware of only the short time he had left to live, he talked to me for hours, with great lucidity and wit, about his historic encounter with Ireland. Sadly he never lived to see the Good Friday Agreement, whose seeds he had sown more than a quarter of a century before.

Chapter Eleven

Setbacks

Mrs Jessie McDowell is a proud, neat Protestant woman. Her living room is adorned with pictures of her children and grandchildren, all of them as neat and clear-eyed as she. You can imagine Jessie going to church every Sunday morning, prayer book in hand, never a second late for the service.

At 2.15pm precisely, on Friday, 21 July 1972, she returned to her little shop in the middle of the parade on the Cavehill Road in North Belfast where she sold ladies' and children's clothes. It was the kind of place where people probably spent more time chatting than shopping. On her return from lunch, Jessie found a car parked on the pavement outside her shop window. She was not annoyed, but slightly surprised that cars were being parked closer and closer to the shops. However, the congestion was always worst on a busy Friday afternoon. She did, however, think it 'a bit cheeky' as the car was blocking her window, thereby allowing no shoppers to see in. Jessie had been inside for half an hour when the woman from the shop next door came to see if the driver was in Jessie's shop. He was not. A neighbour said the car had been there since one o'clock. Jessie thought she had better ring the police, who told her to look inside.

> I looked in and discovered the box sitting on the back seat with a tarpaulin over it and wires coming out of the side. I didn't know what to think. I had no idea what a bomb was like. So I went back in and explained to the police that it was a box of wires. They said, 'Get out immediately and lock your door in case anyone comes in. Warn as many people as possible to get out.'

There were two customers in the shop and Jessie told them to get out fast. She ran outside and shouted at the top of her voice, 'There's a bomb in that car in front of my shop!' She noticed a boy looking into the car and shouted to him to get away. He appeared to take no notice. She then ran down the parade from the hairdresser's at the top to the baby shop at the bottom, warning everyone to get out. Then the bomb went off.

I didn't feel anything. I just looked and the blood was running down my leg and my arm. I don't know what hit me. It could have been the ceiling or the fluorescent lighting. As I was being carried out, I looked up at my shop and foolishly handed the keys to someone. I didn't need keys. The shop was on fire and the car was on fire and that was the last I'd seen of that. We had no idea how devastating a bomb could be.

Three people were killed in the blast. Two were women and one was the young boy, Stephen Parker, whom Jessie had last seen looking into the car. He was blown against the wall and left in pieces. Stephen, who was just fourteen, was posthumously decorated with the Queen's Commendation for bravery. He had been warning people about the bomb when it exploded.

Jessie McDowell had no idea that there were bombs all over Belfast that afternoon. At three o'clock, a car bomb also tore through Oxford Street bus station, killing two soldiers, who had come to diffuse it, and four civilians, two of them teenagers aged fifteen and eighteen. The bomb injured over a hundred people. Television images of charred torsos and limbs being swept up like black jelly and dumped in bags brought home the horrific reality of the carnage caused by a bomb. A police officer near the bus station at the time of the explosion has never forgotten the scene.

At first there was almost like a silence. Then you could hear people screaming and crying and moaning almost as if they were winded. The first thing that caught my eye was a torso of a human being lying in the middle of the street. It was recognizable as a torso because the clothes had been blown off and you could actually see parts of the human anatomy. One of the victims was a soldier I knew personally. He'd had his arms and legs blown off and some of his body had been blown through the railings. One of the most horrendous memories for me was seeing a head stuck to a wall.

A couple of days later, we found vertebrae and a rib cage on the roof of a nearby building. The reason we found it was because the seagulls were diving onto it. I've tried to put it at the back of my mind for twenty-five years.

The Provisional IRA planted twenty-two bombs in Belfast city centre that day, which became known as 'Bloody Friday'. They insisted that ample warnings had been given and the intention had never been to kill civilians, but the excuse sounded hollow. There *were* warnings but they were hopelessly inadequate. The RUC's Belfast Regional Control received a warning at 2.42pm that there was a bomb at the bus station. There was no indication as to the precise location or description of the vehicle it was in. The bomb exploded twenty minutes later at 3.02pm. By then, there were bombs and warnings all over Belfast. The city centre was in chaos. The police and army had never had to deal with an onslaught on such a scale before and they could not cope. 'Bloody Friday' still remains a painful memory for Provisionals like Brendan Hughes.

> What happened on Bloody Friday was a disaster. It was largely the fault of the IRA. I think they overestimated the British army's capabilities of clearing that particular area that day and it resulted in that disaster. When the IRA put bombs into the town, they were giving warnings. To my knowledge there was never an attempt at any time to kill people with the car bomb because the people who were putting the car bombs there had their own families shopping there as well.
>
> **Did 'Bloody Friday' change IRA tactics?**
> I think it certainly made people much more careful about what they were doing, in particular with regard to car bombs in the town.

Remarkably, given the scale of an IRA operation that, according to the police, must have involved dozens of IRA Volunteers in Belfast, no one was ever gaoled. Five years later, however, one man was charged with conspiracy to cause an explosion in connection with the 'Bloody Friday' bombs. He was Daniel Jack and he was arrested at 6am on 20 June 1977. During his interrogation at the RUC's Castlereagh holding centre he admitted hijacking one of the cars. He had been seventeen at the time. He told the police that at a meeting following the explosions, someone had said the whole operation was 'a fuck-up' and should never have happened. Others, he said, laughed and said it would 'toughen the bastards up'. Jack said there was 'drink on the go' but he did not have any. In court, Jack's defence was that he had only signed the statement after being beaten up for two of his four days in police custody. There was medical evidence to support these allegations, provided by Dr Joe Hendron (later the SDLP MP for West Belfast), who had examined him after his interrogation. Hendron found three large bruises and was left in no doubt Jack had been ill-treated. Daniel Jack was given a suspended sentence and released.[1]

For years, 'Bloody Friday' remained in the subconscious of Belfast even though most of its citizens had either forgotten or been too young to remember it. On Remembrance Sunday, 5 November 1972, the Reverend Joseph Parker, father of Stephen Parker, the young boy killed by the bomb in the shopping parade, held a service outside Belfast City Hall in memory of all those who had died in the 'Troubles'. A miniature white cross was planted on the City Hall lawns in memory of each person killed. At that first service in 1972, 436 crosses were planted.[2] In 1974 the Reverend Parker announced he was emigrating to Canada, 'a sad, lonely and disillusioned man'.[3] The services continued until they were abandoned through lack of interest – had they continued, by Remembrance Day 1997 there would have been almost 3,250.

Ten days after 'Bloody Friday' British troops invaded the IRA 'no-go' areas in Belfast and Derry, in the biggest British military operation since Suez. It was code-named 'Operation Motorman'. The IRA did not stand and fight but – I understand by prior agreement with the British through intermediaries – evaporated over the border or went on the run. But there was no cessation to the violence. As long as they had sufficient support in the community, the Provisionals could operate without the notional security of the 'no-go' areas to protect them. With this permanent affront to unionists removed, William Whitelaw was able to proceed with the beginnings of his political initiative. On 30 October 1972, the Northern Ireland Office published a Green Paper for discussion, 'The Future of Northern Ireland'. Over the next two decades, many similar papers were to follow. Significantly, Whitelaw's Green Paper reassured unionists that the status of Northern Ireland would never be altered without their consent, but also recognized for the first time that there was an 'Irish Dimension' to the problem and that 'whatever arrangements are made for the future administration of the Province must take account of the Province's relationship with the Republic of Ireland'.[4] Whitelaw's document was to be the foundation of British policy for the next twenty-five years, culminating in the Good Friday Agreement of 1998.

The purpose was 'to provide a firm basis for concerted governmental and community action against those terrorist organizations which represent a threat to free democratic institutions in Ireland as whole'. The Government also announced that it planned to hold a plebiscite on the border. This was held throughout Northern Ireland on Thursday, 8 March 1973. The Provisionals shot dead a soldier guarding a polling station and exploded eleven bombs. They had also planned a spectacular incident to mark the day of the Border Poll and the escalation of their campaign. Shooting and bombing in Belfast were no longer national news. Bombs in London were.

The Army Council had long been considering extending its campaign to England as the IRA had last done in the forties. According to Billy McKee, it was not a question of if but when.

There had been a discussion early on about bombing England. I thought we should wait until there was a crisis before we should start. I agreed with the strategy but I didn't agree with bombing civilians, pubs that were full of people and so forth. I didn't condone that. Blowing up the Houses of Parliament wouldn't have made any difference to me but not ordinary civilian people.

Why bomb England?

Well, why bomb Belfast? Our people were suffering. The English people were telling us that they knew nothing about the situation. It's time they were made to find out what was going on here and not to brush it under the carpet.

At the beginning of 1973, the Provisionals were experiencing the crisis to which Billy McKee referred. Between November 1972 and January 1973, the Provisionals' senior leadership had been dealt a series of crippling blows, not just by the British security forces but also by their counterparts in the Irish Republic. In its 1972 Christmas message, the British army announced that it had arrested 200 Provisional IRA officers since 'Operation Motorman' the previous summer. They included the Derry IRA veteran Sean Keenan (3 November) and Belfast's Martin Meehan (27 November). Across the border, the Gárdái had been equally active, striking at the leadership of both wings of the Republican Movement. They arrested Maire Drumm, Vice-President of Sinn Fein (5 November), and, in their biggest coup, Séan MacStiofáin, the IRA's Chief of Staff (19 November). MacStiofáin was charged under Section 30 of the Offences Against the State Act and sentenced to six months' imprisonment for IRA membership. Under the Republic's special legislation, no evidence beyond the word of a Special Branch officer was required. MacStiofáin went on hunger strike for fifty-eight days before being ordered off by the Army Council. The Commander of the Belfast Brigade, Joe Cahill, briefly took MacStiofáin's place as Chief of Staff. On 30 December 1972, the Provisionals were dealt a double blow. Ruairí Ó'Brádaigh, President of Sinn Fein and former IRA Chief of Staff, was charged with IRA membership in Dublin and subsequently sentenced to six months in gaol. The same day, Martin McGuinness, then the twenty-two-year-old Commander of the IRA's Derry Brigade and his Deputy, Joe McCallion, were arrested in County Donegal. After 'Operation Motorman', McGuinness and other Derry IRA leaders had taken refuge across the border in Buncrana, County Donegal, an IRA haven a few miles from Derry. McGuinness and McCallion were charged with possessing 250 lb of gelignite and 4,757 rounds of .303 ammunition.[5] The weaponry was found in a Ford Cortina which had been abandoned as it approached a Gárdái checkpoint. Undeterred by the loss of three of its senior Commanders, in a defiant New Year message the Provisionals' Derry Brigade declared that they would fight on 'as long as the British maintain their control in Ireland'.[6] McGuinness and McCallion were both given six months for IRA membership. McGuinness told the Court:

> For over two years, I was an officer in the Derry Brigade of the IRA. We have fought against the killing of our people. Many of my comrades have been arrested and tortured and some were shot unarmed by British troops . . . I am a member of Oglaigh na Eireann (the IRA) and very, very proud of it . . . We firmly believed we were doing our duty as Irishmen.[7]

The erosion of the Provisionals' command structure continued into the New Year, with the arrest of Anthony 'Dutch' Doherty (8 January) in Dublin and the IRA veteran, Leo Martin (13 January), in Belfast. A month later, John Kelly, who had been a member of the IRA's GHQ Staff, was arrested in Dublin (5 February) and charged with IRA membership.

This decimation of the Provisional IRA's leadership was nothing if not a crisis. The Army Council finally took the decision to bomb London. The team selected for the mission was a mixture of mature and inexperienced Volunteers, none of whom had ever operated 'behind enemy lines' before. The eleven-person team included Gerry Kelly, now a senior member of the Provisional leadership; Dolours and Marion Price, daughters of the veteran Belfast republican, Albert Price; Martin Brady, who had worked in a restaurant in the West End and had an invaluable knowledge of London; Roy Walsh, who had joined the IRA in the wake of August 1969; and Paul Holmes who had joined at roughly the same time. Holmes had just been released from 'Long Kesh' but had no hesitation about joining the bombing team and running the risk of being sent to gaol for even longer.

> The fact that the bombs were going off in England was bringing home to the British people what was happening in the North. You could actually see the logic of what the Irish Republican Army was trying to do – basically bring home to the British people the fact that there is a war going on here and that there is more than one participant that's going to have to suffer.

The team was given strict instructions to avoid civilian casualties and to make sure that adequate warnings were given. The lesson of 'Bloody Friday' had not been lost. The month before the attack, two members of the team, Dolours Price and Martin Brady, travelled to London to reconnoitre targets, hotels and parking places for the cars that were to carry the bombs. Four cars were hijacked in Belfast in the middle of

February 1973 and resprayed in the city. They became a blue Vauxhall Viva, a bronze Hillman Hunter, a green Ford Cortina and a green Ford Corsair. The cars were then driven to Dublin to be fitted with false number plates and loaded with their bombs.[8] The team crossed on the ferry and drove to London where the cars were parked overnight in a garage in Dolphin Square. Four targets had been selected: the Cortina was to bomb the Old Bailey; the Viva, the British Forces Broadcasting offices in Westminster; the Hunter, the Army Central Recruiting Depot in Whitehall; and the Corsair, New Scotland Yard in Victoria. By 8.30am, the four cars were in place with the bombs timed to explode at three that afternoon. An hour's warning was to be given. But, unknown to the team, the Metropolitan Police had intelligence that an IRA operation might be afoot. At seven o'clock that morning, members of Scotland Yard's Special Patrol Group (SPG) were given a briefing at Cannon Row police station in the West End about the possibility of an IRA attack. They were told to keep their eyes peeled for any suspicious-looking vehicle. Constable Stanley Conley and an SPG colleague were patrolling the area around Scotland Yard when Conley spotted the green Ford Corsair. He had been on the SPG for six years and had a policeman's alert eyes and nose. He noticed the Corsair had no tax disc and was a 1968 model with 1971 number plates. On closer inspection, he discovered that there were four drill holes in the number plate instead of the usual two.

> We decided we'd have to have a closer look because of what we'd been told. We went over and had a look round it. Somebody had forced the key-lock and the paint had been scraped off. The inside of the boot was black when the colour of the car was green. I said to my mate, 'I don't like the look of this'. Then we saw a couple of wires going up towards the back seat. There were 175 pounds of explosives under it.
>
> **If this bomb had gone off, what would have happened?**
> There'd have been carnage. I was told by one of the explosive boys that it'd have blown in every window in Scotland Yard, right up to the thirteenth floor. And possibly drawn most of the people out through them because of the blast and the vacuum caused by the explosion.

The Corsair was the first car bomb to be discovered in England and the first to be defused. Scotland Yard immediately gave the order to 'Close England' to make sure the bombers did not escape. At 1.56pm, the IRA telephoned a warning to *The Times*. The police had an hour in which to act. The bomb at British Forces Broadcasting was identified and rendered safe but the two other bombs, at the Army Recruiting Centre in Whitehall and the Old Bailey, were not defused in time. Both exploded shortly before three o'clock The police had not been able to clear the area and 180 people were injured in the blast. One man subsequently died of a heart attack. By this time England had been closed and ten of the bombers had been arrested at Heathrow. Roy Walsh and his colleagues were obvious suspects.

We just turned this corner to board the plane and we saw this queue with several men questioning people. I thought, 'Well, it's too late to turn back' because I thought we were being observed in the Main Terminal. We were stopped getting onto the plane and asked for identification. I didn't have any identification at all nor did any of my friends. We said we were over in London for work. We were detained there and then.

What went through your mind when you were stopped?

Initially, that's the end of my involvement as an activist in the Republican Movement. I knew I was going to prison.

What was your reaction when you heard that nearly two hundred people had been injured by your bombs?

I was shocked that there were so many casualties because our intention was never, never to injure anyone.

But if you're going to plant bombs, you also risk injuring and killing people.

We believed our warnings were adequate. We thought an hour was plenty of time. We gave the description of the cars, their registration numbers and where they were parked. I think it was the slowness of the police reaction that caused the injuries.

One of the team got away. He or she has never been identified. The Border Poll went ahead, although the London bombs got bigger headlines. The result of the poll surprised no one. Nearly sixty per cent voted in favour of Northern Ireland remaining part of the United Kingdom. Most nationalists boycotted the plebiscite.

The London bombers were tried and sentenced on 14 November 1972. Eight of them got life, including Roy Walsh. He was released with two of his colleagues in 1993, having spent twenty years in English gaols. The three London bombers were the longest-serving prisoners of the 'Troubles'. Did Walsh have any regrets?

No. The only regret I've got is getting caught, and I would say that every republican prisoner regrets getting caught. For actually doing what I did, no, I've no regrets.

Throughout 1973, security forces on both sides of the border kept up their offensive against the IRA by land and sea. On 28 March the Irish Navy arrested Joe Cahill just off the coast of County Waterford on board a Cyprus-registered boat, the *Claudia*. In its hold were 250 rifles, 240 small arms and a quantity of anti-tank mines and explosives. They had come from Libya following trips to Colonel Khaddhafi's revolutionary regime by the IRA in the summer of 1972. MacStiofain, then Chief of Staff, had ordered the IRA's Director of Supplies to 'go to the Middle East and get new contacts for arms'. He warned the person concerned, 'don't come home until you succeed'. I understand the first consignment reached Ireland in early November 1972. They not only needed a back-up to their American arms supplies but also heavier weaponry which, unlike US gun shops, Colonel Khaddhafi would have. The consignment was believed to have been tracked by British intelligence until the point where the Irish authorities swooped. There were reports from the Provisionals on board the *Claudia* that there had been sightings of a submarine, presumed to be monitoring their progress. As the Irish Defence Minister, Patrick Donegan, colourfully put it, 'We gave her a good kick up the transom!'[9] On 21 May 1973, Cahill was convicted of IRA membership and illegal importation of arms and sentenced to three years 'penal servitude'. Four others were convicted with him. As Cahill later admitted, the interception of the *Claudia* was a disaster for the Provisionals, although it appears that Middle Eastern arms had already reached Irish shores.

The security forces kept up the pressure during the summer of 1973. On 25 June, they announced that in a period of five days they had arrested twenty-three known IRA Volunteers and thirteen known IRA officers.[10] The arrests continued. On 19 July, seventeen members of the IRA in Belfast were lifted, among them three of the most wanted men in the city. Their biggest catch was Gerry Adams who had been on the run since his visit to Cheyne Walk and the ending of the ceasefire at Lenadoon. With him were Joe Cahill's brother Tom and Brendan Hughes, who was believed to have been on the Belfast Brigade Staff. Hughes and Adams had been targeted for some time by the army's 14 Intelligence Company whose role is undercover surveillance. The unit had been watching a house on the Falls Road in which the Provisionals were gathered. But the Provisionals were watching too. Noticing a 'dodgy' car near the house, Hughes climbed over the back wall and asked a couple of local republicans from the Beechmount area to check it out. They came back over the wall to relate that they had seen two people get into the car and drive off. Hughes concluded that it was not 'dodgy' after all, but was wrong.

Within seconds the whole house was surrounded. The British army kicked the door in and arrested myself, Gerry and Tom. There was a lot of shouting and bawling as soldiers do in a situation like that. They didn't know what to expect. But they certainly knew that I was there and they knew who I was as soon as they came into the house. So it was a matter of putting your hands up and and surrendering. They were quite enthusiastic about the whole thing. They knew who they'd got.

The three were taken round the corner to Springfield Road RUC station for questioning. During their interrogation, both Hughes and Adams say they were badly beaten. It appears Tom Cahill was spared because of the gunshot wounds he had previously received in a feud with the Officials. Adams says the men who beat him were in plain clothes. Hughes – whom the security forces christened 'The Dark' because of his swarthy appearance – claims to have received extremely painful treatment.

I was taken to a small Portacabin where they tied my feet and arms to a chair. They then systematically started to beat me with their fists. They produced a weapon, a .45 automatic, cocked it and put it to my head. They told me I was getting killed. No one knew where we were. They were going to dump me in a loyalist area and put a statement out saying the UVF had done it.

They then untied me and put my hand on a table and held it. They then took a small metal toffee hammer and just constantly beat my fingers until they swelled up. Then they did it with my other hand as well. They were constantly asking me questions: about the safe houses, where the weapons were, and where I'd been for the past eighteen months or two years. They weren't wanting statements, just information. I was then untied from the chair and spread-eagled against the wall and constantly kicked and punched between the legs.

I found it difficult to believe that Hughes had really undergone the treatment he described and that soldiers would really behave like that. Hughes said I was naive.

I have no reason to tell lies. Possibly if I had been killed or shot by one of those soldiers, I would have no reason to complain. I'm not telling the story now to get sympathy from the British people. I'm not crying or complaining about it. I'm just telling what happened to me.

After their interrogation, Adams says the three were photographed by their captors who wanted souvenirs of their 'trophy'. I asked one of the 14 Intelligence Company officers involved in the surveillance operation if he had seen the photographs. He said he had and that Hughes and Adams seemed 'in a pretty bad way'.

Pressure on the IRA leadership was maintained in the Republic throughout the summer of 1973. Seamus Twomey had taken over as IRA Chief of Staff following Joe Cahill's arrest on the *Claudia*. But Twomey's reign was equally short-lived. He was arrested in County Monaghan on 1 September 1973 and sentenced to three years for IRA membership and possession of £1,500, the proceeds of an armed robbery in Kerry.[11] In court he shouted, 'Up Belfast! Up the Provos!' Just over a fortnight later, the Provisionals were dealt another blow when Kevin Mallon, the IRA leader from Tyrone who was believed to command the Provisionals' border units, was also arrested in Monaghan. Twomey and Mallon joined another senior Provisional and IRA veteran, Joe 'J B' O'Hagan, in Dublin's Mountjoy gaol. But the three did not stay behind bars for long. On 31 October 1973 they escaped in a cel-ebrated break-out. A helicopter landed in the prison yard and, to the aston-ishment of the guards, lifted the three 'Provos' to freedom. It seemed some compensation for all the setbacks. The following month, 'The Helicopter Song,' recorded by the Wolfe Tones, sold 12,000 copies in Ireland.[12]

By the summer of 1973, Martin McGuinness had been released from gaol and made a defiant address to 10,000 supporters at the annual commemoration at the grave of Wolfe Tone at Bodenstown. He proclaimed the Provisionals to be stronger than ever and that they would not end their 'just war' until British troops were withdrawn and their demands met. McGuinness was now free to return to the campaign and the prosecution of the 'war'.

What had marked Derry out from Belfast was the lack of civilian casualties caused by the IRA's bombs. On 'Bloody Friday' the IRA had also set off three large car bombs in Derry which had caused severe damage but not a single injury. The Derry Brigade was under the strictest orders to avoid civilian casualties. From 'Bloody Friday' until the summer of 1973, the centre of Derry was blitzed in a bombing campaign that did not cause a single civilian death, although there were injuries.[13] At one stage, only twenty of the city's 150 shops were left trading. McGuinness made no secret of the purpose of the campaign, which was to leave Derry with a crippled economy. Tony Miller was one of the IRA Volunteers involved in carrying out the policy and flattening the city centre.

> Targets were picked, you just went out and did your operation and reported back on the target that was hit. You didn't ask questions why you were bombing this or why you were doing that. You just went out and did your job and that was it.

But the commercial centre provides jobs for the people of your city, the commercial centre provides wealth for the people of your city, it generates the economy of your city, why bomb it?

Because the IRA instructed me to bomb it.

You didn't question the orders?

No.

Were you given orders on civilian casualties?

Bomb warnings were phoned in. The bombs had times set. You were attacking a building and not people. Volunteers let people know that they were leaving a bomb.

What sort of warnings did you give, how long?

Sometimes three-quarters of an hour. Sometimes half an hour. But it was normally sufficient for civilians to be cleared. I have to say that sometimes you had very narrow escapes. I don't think that in the commercial bombing campaign in Derry there were any civilians killed at that time. I'm thankful, like, but the IRA in Derry were very, very efficient at that time.

The centre of Derry was flattened.

Yeah, that's what I mean, very efficient.

Tony Miller's early career as a bomber came to an end on 29 November 1973 when he was arrested on a charge of causing explosions and sentenced to eight years. He says he was 'about eighteen' at the time. I said eight years did not seem long, given what he had done, to which he replied that it was a lifetime when you were eighteen.

By the the time of Miller's arrest, the Provisionals had a new target in their sights. William Whitelaw had worked hard in 1973 to persuade the Unionist Party, the SDLP, the Alliance Party and others, to share power in a new Executive that would govern Northern Ireland. On 21 November 1973, the parties finally agreed to go along with Whitelaw's initiative but the Unionist Party split. The former Prime Minister, Brian Faulkner, had decided to accept power sharing, seeing no other way of making political progress and ending the violence. In the process he left many of his fellow unionists behind him. The Provisionals were equally hostile to Whitelaw's initiative, accusing the SDLP of being 'arch collaborators' and warning that the 'armed struggle' to bring about a Thirty-Two County Irish Republic would be 'pursued and intensified'. It threatened that 'the IRA will destroy the new Northern Ireland Executive as it destroyed the old Stormont'.[14]

On Thursday, 6 December 1973, the British Prime Minister, Edward Heath, opened a four-day conference at the Civil Service Staff College at Sunningdale, Berkshire, attended by the British Government, the

Northern Ireland political parties and the Irish Government. It was a historic occasion, the first time such a meeting had taken place between the British and Irish governments to discuss the future of Northern Ireland since the Boundary Commission wrapped up its abortive business in 1925. The outcome, known as the Sunningdale Agreement, was effectively what the SDLP had demanded as a quid pro quo for its participation in Whitelaw's new power-sharing Executive. Sunningdale provided the Irish dimension required by the SDLP. A Council of Ireland was to be established consisting of a Council of Ministers and a consultative assembly made up of representatives from Dail Eireann in Dublin and the new Stormont parliament, recently elected on 28 June 1973. Prophetically it mirrored the Good Friday Agreement of 1998 which the SDLP's deputy leader, Seamus Mallon, referred to as 'Sunningdale for slow learners'. For unionists, it was a bridge much too far. Paisley described Sunningdale as 'a massive confidence trick, an experiment to bluff the people'. He said Faulkner and his 'Republican Unionists' had been 'out-flanked, out-manoeuvred and out-witted'.[15]

Whilst agreement was being hammered out at Sunningdale, Brendan Hughes escaped from 'Long Kesh'. Like prisoners of war during the Second World War, an IRA prisoner's first duty is to escape, not just to embarrass the authorities but to get back to the 'war'. Brendan Hughes could not wait.

> I thought I'd something more to offer on the outside and I didn't want to carry on living in gaol. I didn't know what was going to happen on the outside but I wanted to have some further input into that. So I began to train and get fit – fit to escape.

Over the years, 'Long Kesh' must have resembled a rabbit warren, there were so many tunnels beneath it. Hughes and his colleagues tried to add more but abandoned the digging in favour of another plan. An old mattress was rolled up and left outside the 'cage' for collection by the prison refuse collectors. It was thrown in the back of the dustcart along with the rest of the compound's garbage. The lorry then trundled around the prison picking up rubbish. What the rubbish collectors did not know was that Brendan Hughes was wrapped up inside the mattress like a sausage in a roll. Once outside the prison, he fought his way out of the mattress, jumped off the lorry and hitched a lift to Newry. He then took a taxi across the border to Dundalk from where he was driven to Dublin. There, Hughes 'The Dark' was given a new identity and began the next stage of his legendary career.

> I got my hair dyed and a new ID. I become a man called Arthur McAllister. The real Arthur McAllister died when he was a baby. Had he lived, he would have been about the same age as meself. So

we built an ID around him. I became Arthur McAllister, travelling salesman.

What were you selling?

Toys. I used to drive around Belfast and set up a whole new arrangement for myself. I moved into Myrtlefield Park off the Malone Road [in the city's stockbroker belt] and was stopped almost every other night by British troops. But I was able to get by with the ID that I had. Arthur McAllister always wore a suit and a tie. Every morning he would leave the house in Myrtlefield Park in the car, dressed in a grey-checked suit.

Arthur McAllister's career as a toy salesman lasted for five months. Hughes was high on the army's wanted list. Newspaper reports said he was believed to be the new leader of the Provisional IRA in Belfast and the man behind the wave of shootings and bombing.[16] The *Sun* headlined him as 'IRA Terror Boss. Power-crazy, ruthless rebel' and issued what amounted to its own wanted poster.

Wanted for questioning into murders, bombings and shootings. He holds little brief for politicians and is convinced the only way to a united Ireland is through the bomb and bullet. Now a massive hunt is on to catch him. His photograph has been circulated to all army units with the direct order: Find at all costs.[17]

The net was closing in once more, North and South. In the Republic, Martin McGuinness was arrested again in Buncrana on 11 February 1974 and sentenced a second time for IRA membership. He was released on 13 December 1974 having served nine months of his twelve-month sentence. In Belfast, informers were clearly earning their money. On 28 April 1974, Ivor Bell, who had been part of the IRA's delegation at Cheyne Walk and was now believed to have become the Commander of the Belfast Brigade, was arrested in a flat in Malone Avenue close to Hughes' residence in Myrtlefield Park. Bell had also escaped from 'Long Kesh' by changing places with a prisoner going out on parole to get married. When Bell was arrested, Hughes is thought to have taken over as Belfast Brigade Commander.

On 10 May 1974 the house in Myrtlefield Park was raided by police acting on a tip-off, possibly from the same 'source' who had provided the intelligence about Ivor Bell. Arthur McAllister came quietly.

That was the end of Arthur McAllister. They came to the door and they knew right away who I was. I was protesting about the fact that they were raiding this house when the Special Branch man turned round to me and says, 'Oh come on, Brendan, you've had a good enough run.' I knew that was it. They were quite friendly this time. I was put in the back of the jeep and taken to Castlereagh. I wasn't punched and I wasn't insulted.

How did the authorities know that you were there?

I don't know. At that period we had Lisburn Army Headquarters bugged. And every three days I would receive tapes of phone conversations that went in and out of there. We'd cut into the lines and were listening to the incoming phone calls. We knew there was an agent operating within the group of people that were around us. Someone wasn't right. We had a good idea who it was. And I think that person gave the information that I was there.

Was the agent or informer identified by the IRA subsequently?

I went to gaol after that and from what I am told he was, yes.

And what happened to him?

I don't know.

There is no record of any killing subsequent to Hughes' arrest that would indicate the 'execution' of an informer. Perhaps his police or army handlers had spirited him out of Northern Ireland before he could fall into the hands of the IRA's 'internal security' unit from which he would have been unlikely to escape. The 'agent' would have earned the break.

In Myrtlefield Avenue, the police hit the jackpot. They not only uncovered Arthur McAllister but four rifles, a submachine-gun, two pistols and more than 3,600 rounds of ammunition. Hughes was sentenced to fifteen years. Fleet Street had a field day. 'Pin-stripe Provo chief seized at £50,000 HQ', triumphed the *Daily Telegraph*.[18] And there was more. Documents were found in the house that the media proclaimed was the IRA's 'Doomsday Plan'. Hughes maintains that the plan was not as the media made out. Memories of August 1969 had not gone away.

It was actually a plan for the defence of nationalist areas at that time. In 1969 Catholics were left practically defenceless. In this situation, it was an attempt to make sure that that didn't happen again. It was *not* a plan to attack loyalist areas or whatever. At that time there was a great fear among Catholic and nationalist people that civil war would soon break out.

In the atmosphere of May 1974, the Provisionals' fears were not without foundation. A loyalist *coup d'état* was on the cards.

Chapter Twelve

Contact

At 5.30pm, at the height of the rush hour on 17 May 1974, a week after Brendan Hughes had been arrested in Myrtlefield Park, three car bombs ripped through the centre of Dublin killing twenty-two people and injuring over a hundred. Ninety minutes later, another car bomb exploded in Monaghan town, killing five and injuring twenty. There were no warnings. The death toll was the greatest of any single day during the 'Troubles'. But these were loyalist not IRA bombs. Two of the cars had been hijacked earlier that day in Protestant areas of Belfast. Although both the UDA and the UVF denied any involvement, the UDA's press officer announced, 'I am very happy about the bombings in Dublin. There is a war with the Free State and now we are laughing at them'.[1] No one was ever brought to justice for the slaughter. In fact, it was the UVF who were responsible. One of the wilder conspiracy theories was that the bombs were the work of British Intelligence to force the Dublin Government to be tougher on the IRA. Arrests made in the Republic during the previous eighteen months showed that the authorities were being anything but soft.

But no conspiracy theories are needed to explain the bombs. They were the response of the loyalist paramilitaries to Whitelaw's power-sharing Executive and the Sunningdale Council of Ireland. They believed that both were the fruits of IRA violence and the gateway to a United Ireland. The UVF was hitting back at Dublin, whom they refused to distinguish from the IRA. Given the amount of Catholic blood now on the loyalist paramilitaries' hands, no one should have been surprised that they were prepared to strike across the border. In 1972 alone loyalist paramilitaries had murdered eighty-one Catholics. The Dublin bombs served to increase tension in an already tense Belfast. The power-sharing Executive had taken office at the beginning of 1974 in the teeth of bitter opposition from the non-Faulkner unionists. The opposition gathered momentum when Edward Heath called the 'Who governs Britain?' election in February in a showdown with Britain's militant miners and Whitelaw was summoned back to London to help calm things on the home front. Not for the last time, British domestic considerations took priority over the future of Northern Ireland. The unionist alliance opposed to the Executive and the Sunningdale Agreement, the United Ulster Unionist Coalition (UUUC) made up of the non-Faulkner unionists, Paisley's Democratic Unionist Party (DUP) and William Craig's right-wing Vanguard Party, fought the 'Who governs Britain?' election on a single issue summed up in their manifesto: 'Who governs Ulster? The Irish Republic? The IRA? The SDLP? A Council of Ireland?' To loyalists, they were all the same. At the general election on 28 February 1974, UUUC candidates swept the board, winning eleven of the province's twelve Westminster seats. The days of Whitelaw's initiative were numbered in the face of such widespread opposition from the majority Protestant community. The election also swept away Heath and Whitelaw, bringing Harold Wilson's Labour Government to power once again and installing Merlyn Rees as the new Secretary of State for Northern Ireland.

Few Northern Ireland Secretaries can have entered office with a bigger potential crisis on their hands. Opposition to Sunningdale had now moved from the political arena onto the streets. All might have been different had the SDLP been prepared to hold back on the implementation of the Council of Ireland, but John Hume and his colleagues who were Ministers in the Executive were unwilling to do so. Merlyn Rees realized that Sunningdale was a political time-bomb and that Faulkner was a unionist leader without a unionist army. To his former supporters, Faulkner, the hard-liner who had introduced internment, had gone soft. Rees read the writing on the wall.

> When I first arrived in the province, within a day or two Brian Faulkner came down to see me and told me in so many words, 'I cannot carry the Unionist Party on Sunningdale whatever happens.' He says, 'I cannot carry it. I have lost my reason to be. I'm beaten, overwhelmed by the vote against my sort of unionism, or the unionism I'm trying to carry out.'

As opposition to Sunningdale mounted, resistance crystallized around the Ulster Workers' Council (UWC), a group of trade unionists controlling most of the key services in Northern Ireland, from power stations to sewerage. They were backed by the loyalist paramilitaries of the UDA and UVF. On 15 May 1974, the UWC called for a general work stoppage. Gradually, the strike gathered support, no doubt encouraged by widespread intimidation by the loyalist paramilitaries whose road blocks, manned by masked men with cudgels, dissuaded many from going to work. The fear that the province was on the brink of a *coup d'état*, the premise on which

Brendan Hughes' 'Doomsday' document was based, was heightened by the sight of the UWC's Co-ordinating Committee giving out passes to those required to carry out essential services, enabling them to bypass barricades, obtain petrol and continue with their work. The new Labour Government was furious at the challenge to Westminster's authority but took only limited action. The army, which could run some but not all of the essential services, advised Rees that it would be folly to intervene and try to smash the strike in the face of such widespread opposition from the majority community. Rees was realistic.

> It could not be done. We couldn't do a Prague.[2] You can't put down a popular rising by killing people. We're not Russia. The weakness of Sunningdale was that it was signed up over in stockbroker Sunningdale. They ought to have met in Belfast and learnt the realities of life. When people in the south said, 'put it down', they didn't know what they were talking about. Even the police were on the brink of not carrying out their duties as well. And the middle classes were on their side. This wasn't just an industrial dispute. This was the Protestant people of Northern Ireland rising up against Sunningdale. They could not be shot down.

Having decided not to tackle the strike head on, the Government's only weapon was words. Rees accused the eleven UUUC MPs of trying to set up 'a provisional Government in Northern Ireland' and on television, in the most scathing attack on the majority community ever made by a British Prime Minister, Harold Wilson accused the Protestants of being 'spongers'. The following day, loyalists stuck pieces of sponge in their lapels as a sign of their contempt and the insult only strengthened their determination to resist. Three days later, on 28 May 1974, Brian Faulkner, who had courageously tried to lead his party into a new era, resigned, his position being untenable. The Executive fell and Sunningdale with it. If the Provisionals brought down Stormont, the loyalists smashed Whitelaw's initiative and consigned it to history. In 1974, Protestants were not ready for power sharing and cross-border institutions. Merlyn Rees had to start all over again.

Two weeks prior to this collapse Rees had legalized Sinn Fein and the UVF (the UDA having never been proscribed). His long-term plan was to set up a constitutional Convention consisting of all the parties in Northern Ireland, including Sinn Fein and any party that might represent the loyalist paramilitaries, to work out the future for the province, free from British interference. For the Convention to work, Rees realized that the IRA would have to end its campaign of violence and Sinn Fein become part of the political process, and he believed that contacts would eventually have to be made with the IRA's Army Council to encourage this. As far as he knew no such approaches had been undertaken at Government level since the abortive Cheyne Walk meeting in 1972 – from which the political backlash had been so severe that Whitelaw had proscribed any further contact between officials and 'terrorists' while violence continued. Rees was obliged to continue this directive. Furthermore, for most of 1974 Wilson operated a minority Government so few risks could be taken,[3] although Wilson and Rees had met members of the Army Council, both in Dublin and at Wilson's home in Great Missenden, before and after the IRA ceasefire that led to the Cheyne Walk talks. But at that time Labour had been in opposition. Rees knew that no such dialogue could be risked by the new Government, given the political circumstances at home.

It may have been many months before his officials told him that the dialogue had been underway for some time – though it is a reasonable assumption that the Prime Minister, as Head of the Security and Intelligence Services, was informed and had allowed it to continue. The Secret Intelligence Service, MI6, had been carrying on the work that Frank Steele had started, establishing relations with a variety of community leaders. As we have seen, after Direct Rule was introduced in March 1972, Frank Steele became the MI6 officer attached to the Government's team at Laneside. Steele was briefed to look at all aspects of the political situation and was inserted as a nominal assistant to the UK Representative, Howard Smith, who had become Whitelaw's Political Adviser.

In the socially deprived nationalist enclaves Steele quickly became known to leaders as the accessible and responsive member of Whitelaw's new team. He could deal with local crises, minimize army excesses or misunderstandings and address community concerns. Steele used his skills in a largely overt role and had a profound – and unrecognized – effect in developing the Sunningdale initiative and bringing the nationalist politicians to the negotiating table. He also helped to save lives by ensuring that when the army invaded the IRA's 'no-go' areas on 31 July 1972, there was no confrontation with the IRA. When Frank Steele left Laneside in May 1973 his overt position was taken by a senior Foreign Office official, James Allan, whilst his MI6 responsibilities were inherited by a younger colleague, Michael Oatley, whose instincts, like Steele's, seem to have been to head for the troubled areas of the province and make as many contacts as he could. Community Relations officers working in both loyalist and republican areas still remember his requests to be shown around, his interest in gaining some first-hand understanding of local problems. MI6 agents do not wait for memoranda telling them what to do.

Steele and Oatley knew what their job was and how to do it within the broad lines of Government policy. Steele had played his part in the Cheyne Walk talks but was afterwards barred from making any approach to the IRA. After his departure, the political constraints imperceptibly loosened and, with or without authority, Oatley clearly responded. By the latter part of 1973 he was involved with a range of contacts on both sides of the sectarian divide. Over the next twenty years, Oatley was to play a vital role in the secret and often interrupted liaison between HMG and the Provisionals' Army Council (PAC), always operating in the shadows, as his profession demanded. In the many years when no dialogue was taking place, the PAC – or perhaps only one or two members – knew that wherever in the world Oatley happened to be serving, they had a point of contact who had not let them down, should the need arise to communicate. At critical points he reappeared, to present himself in the right place at the right time. For example, much later, in early 1991, Oatley went to Derry just before he retired and spent a long night talking with Martin McGuinness – a talk which, from the British side, can be seen as the catalyst to the peace process. As we will see, on the nationalist and republican side, the process had been long under way. Precisely how much of its hand MI6 disclosed either to NIO officials or to Ministers remains unresolved. Although MI6 operates under tight political control and in close liaison with interested Whitehall departments, neither Merlyn Rees nor later Sir Patrick Mayhew (Northern Ireland Secretary during the secret talks of 1993) seem to have had much idea of what was going on and what was being said in their name. Presumably others in Government, or at the very head of it, did.

People in the nationalist areas of West Belfast and Derry told me that from late 1973 onwards Oatley was looking for contacts in the republican community who could familiarize him with the IRA and its intentions, in the hope that a channel of communication could be opened to its leaders. Although he appears to have been assisted in these highly sensitive endeavours by people well respected in the community, he was running fearful risks. The odds against his survival seem, in retrospect, to have been high. As a result of his efforts, from November 1973 onwards members of the PAC became aware that British officials were willing to develop channels of communication to them, provided the utmost secrecy could be guaranteed. Three such channels were apparently in place around this time, all of them very tentative and eventually leading back to Laneside's leafy lane. One was through West Belfast, involving a senior IRA commander; one through Derry; and one, soon abandoned, through Dublin. In the end it was the Derry link that proved most productive in ultimately delivering a ceasefire in 1975, although the Belfast connection also played its part. Remarkably, this Derry link continued to function, to a greater or lesser extent, through the long and bloody years that followed until the peace process of the 1990s got off the ground nearly two decades later.

Who were the individuals who made these vital links with the PAC and how were they found? In a way, they emerged and evolved from the patient groundwork that Frank Steele had carried out as he negotiated with community leaders and sorted out endless problems in the most troubled areas. He is still remembered with respect and some affection. When I mentioned his name, people would smile and ask how he was. Steele himself once asked me to pass on congratulations to a certain individual for 'becoming a statesman'. The individual seemed quite touched. Nationalists had been accustomed to being treated as second-class citizens by the combined forces of unionism. They had seen civil-rights marchers attacked by loyalist mobs and the police and experienced, through intimidation and arson in whole areas of Belfast and Derry, treatment little short of ethnic cleansing, while an apparently acquiescent Westminster Government stood by. They were therefore greatly impressed – and no doubt surprised – when one of Whitelaw's senior lieutenants arrived in their midst apparently prepared to listen and take action on their behalf. Michael Oatley followed in Frank Steele's footsteps and gradually built up the trust that his predecessor had enjoyed. Community leaders were inclined to respond.

The pattern of what followed has never been revealed but it seems that just as Oatley was undertaking the delicate process of developing a channel of influence and communication to the IRA leadership, within his brief, individuals on the nationalist side were also keen to find a way of conveying to the UK Government the reality of the Provisional IRA. They were anxious to explain its origins and aims and the possibility of reaching an accommodation: they wished to impress on the British Government that slogans need not necessarily be taken at face value and that the men behind them were not the mindless psychopaths portrayed by British Army and tabloid propaganda. Of necessity, such intermediaries had to have impeccable republican credentials. Even so they took enormous risks, as communicating a British point of view or reply to a Provisional argument – however reasonable both might seem – could look dangerously like treachery when discussed in the back rooms of Derry or Dublin, risking the IRA's well-known response of a bullet through the head.

The fact that this secret dialogue developed most effectively and durably through Derry reflects the achievement of a unique individual whose identity remains a secret and whom I shall simply refer to as the Contact because of his pivotal role between the two sides. Although confidence in him was damaged from time to time, it was invariably restored and endured for over twenty years. PAC members who dealt with the Contact recognized that he was genuinely concerned to have their objectives and principles fully understood by the Government whilst, on the British side, he was evidently accepted as someone completely committed to trying to end violence. Both sides no doubt found him honest and reliable as a channel of communication.

Both in 1973–5 and again some twenty years later, it was the Contact who made the secret dialogue possible by acting as the conduit between the British Government – represented at first by MI6 and Foreign Office officials and later by MI5 – and the individuals representing the Provisional Army Council. He would not only convey messages between the two sides and interpret them where necessary but also facilitate the face-to-face meetings, at which he would invariably be present. Occasionally he stepped outside his remit and took on a more pro-active role to break deadlocks and push the process along. For many years, often putting his life at risk, he worked with great devotion and ingenuity, offering options to either side that might create circumstances through which peace might be found. For two decades this remarkable man was at the centre of an astonishing and untold story. Whilst John Hume worked tirelessly centre stage to bring about peace, the Contact worked clandestinely and occasionally to powerful effect in the wings. Like many of his contemporaries who had watched the Provisional IRA emerge from the loyalist violence provoked by the civil-rights campaign, the Contact had become increasingly depressed at the incessant spiral of killings on all sides. Internment, 'Bloody Sunday' and the loyalist sectarian killings all added to his conviction that something had to be done.

By late 1973 several of the Provisional leaders and most notably David O'Connell were looking for a way to end the campaign. They saw its limitations and felt growing pressure from the nationalist community in the North in response to the increasingly bloody loyalist assassination campaign. Around this time messages from Laneside, apparently originating from Oatley, started to arrive in Dublin where the Provisional leadership was based, via the three different channels. These messages recognized the Republican Movement's possible willingness to look for a new way forward, explained the obstacles to even secret negotiation, and offered a range of encouragements to a unilateral ceasefire. Through the Derry connection, however, things went a little further and Ruairí Ó'Brádaigh, President of Sinn Fein, was encouraged to believe that while no negotiation or dialogue could take place immediately, a reliable and acknowledged channel of communication might be established for future use.

By the time Merlyn Rees became Secretary of State in March 1974 the channel of communication had been active for some time. There had been discussions over Thomas Niedermeyer, the German industrialist and West German consul in Northern Ireland who had been kidnapped on 27 December 1973, although such discussions unfortunately were too late to save him; his remains were found on a rubbish tip in West Belfast more than six years later. There had also been a sustained exchange through the Contact with Ó'Brádaigh, and through him with O'Connell, about the possibility of legalizing Sinn Fein in time for candidates to be nominated for the general election on 28 February 1974. A message encouraging Sinn Fein to move into political activity had even been inserted, by agreement, in a speech by Whitelaw's successor Francis Pym. Nothing much came of all this but Ó'Brádaigh valued the fact of dialogue and its potential for further development as well as recognizing that it had strengthened his argument for the pursuit of a political rather than a purely military strategy by the Republican Movement. The Government, in its turn, was evidently impressed by the secrecy with which the IRA guarded the link and the discussions it brought about, and were later encouraged to make more vigorous use of the connection when it felt freer to do so.

By the end of May 1974, with the Sunningdale initiative over and the departure of Brian Faulkner, the province was back to square one. But the experienced and imaginative team of officials assembled in the NIO under Rees's energetic Permanent Secretary, the tough and pragmatic former fighter pilot Frank Cooper, had more ideas to offer. Under the circumstances of the time, launching Sunningdale had been an astonishing achievement which had proved that Northern Ireland was not locked irrevocably in the pattern of its history, and the power-sharing Executive had given a brief glimpse of what political life in the province could be like when the representatives of the two communities worked together. The Government's next move was to call an all-party Constitutional Convention to map out the province's future, whilst low-level dialogue with Ó'Brádaigh and his colleagues continued through the secret channels. By the summer of 1974, the Contact's credibility and recognition of his value to both sides had been greatly enhanced by his role as an intermediary on two critical occasions in June when his action may well have saved lives. He first intervened to prevent the Provisionals killing the elderly Earl and Countess of Donoughmore, who had been kidnapped from their home in County Tipperary by one of the IRA's units. As a result, they were set free, unharmed, four days later. The Contact did not wish them to suffer the same fate as Thomas Niedermeyer. Later the same month, his intercession helped free a British soldier taken by the IRA and held across the border in Donegal. There was much to talk about on the political level, too, from the aftermath of the UWC strike, to the White Paper Rees had published on 4 July, which outlined his plans for the Convention and the possibility of troop withdrawals in the event of a reduction or permanent cessation of violence.

In a further gesture of encouragement to the Provisionals, Rees announced his intention to end internment which had been one of the IRA's demands at Cheyne Walk. Rees hoped the IRA might be enticed into talks with the hint that given 'a genuine and sustained cessation of violence', anything might follow. These words were to become a mantra which, as Rees said, 'could have been emblazoned in neon lights over Stormont Castle'.[4] What that 'anything' might be was not specified and was perhaps deliberately left vague in the hope that the Provisionals would take it to mean talks about British political disengagement. Troop reductions, Rees implied, might begin with withdrawal to barracks in Northern Ireland and then, given the right circumstances, eventual withdrawal from the province. By June 1974 it seems that the PAC was ready to call off its campaign if given direct encouragement to do so – as later appears to have been the case during the secret discussions with the British in 1993. Dialogue between the two sides no doubt played a key role in this. Ruairí Ó'Brádaigh, released from gaol in the Republic the previous year after a conviction for IRA membership, was encouraged towards this view by the dramatic impact he believed the UWC strike had had on British Government thinking. He believed the strike marked a watershed.

> It threw British policy totally into the melting pot. It swept the decks clean. It was back to the drawing board. The word coming through was that every solution was up for consideration.

The word 'coming through' was transmitted by Oatley via the Contact. How sincere was it? What was said? What was transmitted? Oatley's business was clearly to keep the Provisional leadership in play. How much did Merlyn Rees know at the time about Michael Oatley's role?

> He was a member of the 'liaison' staff who moved around the province and talked to people, with no instructions from me, but certainly with no instructions to initiate policy. They are not speaking on behalf of 'the Government' in that sense of the term. They talk to people on both sides of the divide and keep contact.
> **Did you know he was MI6?**

Yes.

And what was his role as a member of MI6 in the province?

To talk. To talk with both sides of the divide and to explain. He was an intelligent man. He wouldn't have overstepped the mark.

Did you know that Michael Oatley initiated contact with the IRA?

Yes, though I wouldn't have had a bit of paper telling me. That's what they [MI6] were for.

Did you authorize that renewal of contact with the IRA?

Not formally, no. But there was no need. As I say, that's what they were for.

And how did that fit into Government policy?

Well, that section of the White Paper which talked about security policy was, you know, a bit of paper on which they could work.

To Ó'Brádaigh and the IRA leadership, Michael Oatley was the 'British Government Representative' but they made an 'educated guess' that the representatives they were dealing with had direct or indirect links to the British Intelligence services. They would not have expected anything else.

By the end of 1974 new pressures were being felt. On 10 October 1974, a general election returned Wilson to power with a narrow but workable majority which increased confidence to pursue his Irish policy. The prospect of the Convention election due to be held the following year also stimulated fresh debate among the IRA leaders as to whether or not there should be a fundamental shift to politics within the Republican Movement. Meanwhile, in Belfast in particular, IRA leaders and the nationalist community as a whole became increasingly conscious of the threat of further loyalist paramilitary killings. Once again, as in 1972, the IRA was at a crossroads.

In the streets and fields the Provisionals' military campaign continued. IRA Volunteers were not aware of the secret discussions between their leaders and the British and expected an intensification of their actions on the ground. The campaign had to be maintained if the Movement's military strength was to be preserved and the PAC, despite the political inclinations of some of its members, had no immediate intention of winding it down. If the Army Council was to negotiate, it intended to do so from a position of strength. Once again England was to be the target, to drive home the message in a way that could not be ignored.

Earlier in 1974, the IRA had launched its first attack on the mainland in which people had been killed. It was the first in a series of bombings that year that led to many deaths as well as a string of wrongful convictions which were overturned finally by the Court of Appeal some twenty years later. These miscarriages of justice were indicative of the mood at the time and no doubt due to the pressure on the police and forensic experts to secure convictions. The innocent suffered. The first bomb of 1974 was planted on 4 February in the boot of a coach carrying soldiers from Manchester to Catterick military camp in North Yorkshire. It weighed fifty pounds and exploded on the M62 near Bradford killing nine soldiers, one woman and two children.[5] Judith Ward was charged with the explosion and sentenced to thirty years in prison. Her conviction was finally quashed in June 1992 when the Court of Appeal accused the forensic scientists involved of having 'taken the law into their own hands'.[6]

On 5 October 1974, the IRA struck at what they claimed were 'military' targets, two pubs in Guildford that were frequented by off-duty soldiers. Four soldiers, two of them women, and a civilian were killed and fifty-four people were injured. The 'Guildford Four', who were sentenced for the murders in 1975, had their convictions finally overturned in October 1989, after spending fourteen years in gaol. The Court of Appeal decided that their confessions had been fabricated by the police. The 'Maguire Seven', convicted around the same time for their involvement in manufacturing the bomb, had their convictions overturned in June 1991 when the Court of Appeal ruled that the forensic evidence on which they had been convicted had been unsatisfactory. On 7 November 1974, the IRA bombed a pub in Woolwich used by off-duty soldiers from the Royal Artillery Training Centre. One soldier and one civilian were killed and twenty people were injured.

However, the most horrendous attack of all came two weeks later at 8.15pm on 21 November 1974, when two bombs exploded at pubs in Birmingham, the Mulberry Bush and the Tavern in the Town. A few minutes earlier a man with an Irish accent had phoned a warning to the local newspaper, the *Birmingham Post and Mail*, but it was far too late. Nineteen people were killed and 182 injured. The nation was shocked at the carnage and the way in which the 'war' in Northern Ireland was now being brought home so savagely. That was precisely what the IRA had intended although it almost certainly did not intend disasters like Birmingham. Birmingham, like 'Bloody Friday' was a horrendous mistake. The Provisionals denied responsibility, so embarrassed were they by the slaughter. I was told by someone who may have been in a position to know, that the bombs were planted on the orders of a local IRA man keen to seek revenge on Birmingham for the way he believed the city had gloated over the death of James McDade, an IRA Volunteer from the Birmingham area, who had been blown up by his own bomb exactly one week before. After the explosions, an Irishman was arrested in the city and five others were detained as they were about to board the Heysham–Belfast ferry.[7] They became known as the 'Birmingham Six' and were given twenty-one life sentences for murder.[8] Their convictions were finally overturned after the Director of Public Prosecutions announced in February 1991 that the forensic evidence on which the prosecution had been based had been dropped.[9]

Remarkably, the secret contacts continued despite Birmingham and the universal outrage that it and the other IRA bombs had caused. Bombs in England simply underlined the need for dialogue with the IRA. However, had it emerged, in the wake of Birmingham, that the Government was in contact with the IRA leadership – although no face-to-face meeting had yet taken place – there would have been a political storm that the Labour Government would have found difficult to ride out. It would have been charged with monumental hypocrisy, given that the Home Secretary, Roy Jenkins, had just introduced the Prevention of Terrorism Act, allowing terrorist suspects to be detained for questioning for up to seven days and, if deemed advisable, to be excluded from Great Britain.

In the wake of the Birmingham bombs another meeting took place that helped break the taboo of contacts with the IRA. It involved Protestant clergymen from the Irish Council of Churches and members of the Provisionals' Army Council. At the time the Government knew nothing about the secret meeting but it was eventually to provide a useful cover for the achievements of the covert dialogue, namely the ceasefire that was soon to be declared. The extraordinary encounter took place secretly on 10 December 1974, three weeks after the Birmingham bombs, at Smyth's hotel in the village of Feakle, County Clare. The meeting was held on the clergymen's initiative. The Provisionals introduced themselves as the political and military leadership of the Republican Movement. Their delegation included Ruairí Ó Brádaigh, David O'Connell, Billy McKee and the three helicopter escapees from Mountjoy gaol, Seamus Twomey, J B O'Hagan and Kevin Mallon, who were still on the run. One of the architects of the encounter, the Reverend William Arlow, claimed his purpose was to appeal to the IRA to call off its campaign on the grounds that every bomb made it less likely that Protestants would ever agree to a united Ireland and more difficult for the British Government ever to move in that direction. To their surprise the churchmen discovered that the IRA men were not the monsters their actions and the media would suggest. Billy McKee remembers the astonishment on the churchmen's faces.

I think they were expecting men coming in with trenchcoats and rifles over their shoulders and bayonets by their sides. But it wasn't like that. It was a very cordial meeting, and very, very good.

The feeling was reciprocated by Dr Arthur Butler, the Church of Ireland Bishop of Connor.

We were all most impressed by their attitude, with their fair-mindedness, and we were so pleased to find that they were talking seriously and deeply and with great conviction and had listened very carefully to what we had to say.[10]

The clergymen had drafted a document that they hoped, having cleared it with the Provisionals, to present to the British Government, which included the proposition that 'contingent upon the maintenance of a declared ceasefire and upon effective policing, HM Government will relieve the army as quickly as possible of its internal security duties'. The wording was not a million miles from Rees's White Paper.[11] The Provisionals made their by now familiar case although the clergymen did most of the talking. But discussions were abruptly interrupted when the Irish Special Branch raided the hotel, acting on a tip-off. However the IRA had been tipped off too and Twomey, O'Hagan and Mallon had already made a hasty departure, leaving Ó'Brádaigh, McKee and the others sitting downstairs by the fire comparing notes. The Branch men, armed with submachine-guns, rushed in and demanded to know where the 'others' were. McKee said they were 'upstairs'. The raiders dashed up the stairs and into the room where the clergymen were holding their own meeting. They lined them up against the wall, expecting to unmask Twomey, O'Hagan and Mallon and were embarrassed to discover that their suspects were Protestant clergymen. When they came downstairs, McKee remembers, 'their faces were dropped and they started whispering amongst each other'. The policemen hung around for half an hour and then left empty-handed. At least the clergymen had not been Catholic priests.

On 18 December 1974, a deputation from the clergymen met Merlyn Rees at the House of Commons and handed him the document which had been discussed with the Provisionals. They said these were points the Government would have to agree to if the IRA was to consider a permanent ceasefire. Besides the proposal about troop reductions, the document also contained the prophetic requirement that the Government should affirm that it had no 'political or territorial interests in Ireland beyond its obligations to the citizens of Northern Ireland'. Similar sentiments were to form the basis of the Downing Street Declaration nearly twenty years later.

Rees believed that the Provisionals were now prepared to move because of 'the ignominy of Birmingham' and because, as military intelligence suggested, 'they wanted time to re-group and re-equip'.[12]

The attitude of the Feakle clergymen towards the IRA leaders had a powerful effect on at least some of them, making them feel less isolated and more free to consider their options. They were conscious of the need to respond to mounting pressure from sections of their own people in the North, to end a campaign that was making life a nightmare as they were hemmed in by oppressive security measures of the British Army and exposed to the murderous sectarian campaign of the loyalist paramilitaries. On 20 December, ten days after the Feakle meeting, the Army Council announced an early start to its customary Christmas ceasefire and began looking for ways to bargain for its extension. The obvious channels for doing this were those established by Oatley, and a flurry of activity followed involving both the Contact in Derry and the other links in Belfast. After Feakle, the position of the moderates in the leadership was greatly strengthened but the PAC as a whole had no idea what prize for a cessation it might realistically be in a position to claim. This question was to be resolved over the next six weeks. Until the end of 1974 the British side, represented by Oatley, had not knowingly had any direct contact with PAC members – although one of the latter, who was not identified as such, had twice introduced himself at meetings in Belfast. As Christmas approached, communication with the leadership via the Contact had sharply intensified, strengthening confidence on both sides that real progress was being made. Face-to-face meetings and direct negotiations were now to begin in earnest. Eighteen months' work in the shadows would finally produce movement in the direction of peace.

The temporary ceasefire was partly a result of Feakle but mainly because of the secret dialogue with the Provisionals' Army Council which had been developing for well over a year. The ceasefire Oatley and his colleagues had been working towards finally came into being, although initially it was to last for only ten days over Christmas. The IRA issued a statement saying it was ordering 'a suspension of operations' from midnight on Sunday, 22 December 1974 until midnight on Thursday, 2 January 1975 in order to give the British Government an opportunity 'to consider the proposals for a permanent ceasefire'. The statement concluded by saying that if there was not 'a satisfactory reply' from the Government 'the Irish Republican Army will have no option but to resume hostilities'.

By Christmas 1974, it seemed as if there was a historic possibility of bringing a permanent end to violence. The 'Provos' held the ceasefire and the British held their breath.

Chapter Thirteen

Truce

On Christmas Day 1974, Ruairí Ó'Brádaigh was at home in Roscommon preparing for the domestic festivities when, looking out of a window, he was amazed to see the Contact getting out of a car. Friends might drop by but the last person he expected to see that day was the man from the North. He knew it must be important for the Contact to forgo his own Christmas Day celebrations and set out on the long and tedious drive south. He had brought a message in the form of a letter written in his own handwriting which he said had come from the British Government. The astonished Ó'Brádaigh read the letter which, he says, stated that the British wished to meet the Republican Movement to devise structures of British withdrawal from Ireland – or structures of disengagement from Ireland. He cannot remember the precise words. The message was the Government's response to the IRA's ten-day Christmas ceasefire which was now into its third day. Ó'Brádaigh immediately informed the Army Council as the deadline for the expiry of the ceasefire was only a week away. The IRA leadership decided that the Contact himself should come to an Army Council meeting to authenticate himself and the message. He had met individual members before but never the full PAC face-to-face. The Army Council met on 31 December 1974, three days before the ceasefire was due to end.

One of those present was Billy McKee, recently released from Crumlin Road prison on 4 September, after almost three and a half years in gaol. He had returned to command the Provisionals' Belfast Brigade and taken a seat on the Army Council. At that stage, British Intelligence was not aware that McKee, whose integrity they held in some regard, had risen to such heights. McKee had first heard that the British had been making approaches at an Army Council meeting in Dublin when someone mentioned that a 'James Allan from the Home Office' and a 'Michael Oatley' had been in touch with Sinn Fein in Belfast, wanting to 'get in touch with the leadership and talk about peace'. Seamus Twomey, now Chief of Staff after his escape from Mountjoy, also mentioned Oatley's name. McKee was taken aback and naturally suspicious as he had not known all that had gone on whilst he was in gaol. Nevertheless, he felt that the approach was worth following up – it was no use 'letting it lie' only to find out later that 'some good' might have come of it. Given the respect in which he was held by the military side of the Republican Movement, McKee had been a powerful voice in advocating the Christmas ceasefire.

At the Army Council meeting on 31 December at which the Contact was present, Ó'Brádaigh assured the members of the PAC that he had total confidence in him and believed that the message he brought was genuine. As far as Ó'Brádaigh was concerned, the secret dialogue that had been going on for over a year was not about playing games, having finally resulted in the brief, unilateral Christmas ceasefire and fuelled the leadership's deliberations about ending the military campaign and moving into the political arena. The Contact was closely questioned to make sure that his credentials and trustworthiness were as impeccable as Ó'Brádaigh had insisted. Billy McKee was still suspicious however, as to him the Contact was a complete stranger and he feared the IRA might be walking into an Intelligence trap. Other members of the PAC assured him that the Contact was trustworthy and in any case was only acting as 'a message boy'. The Contact said that British officials would like to talk with Billy McKee – without realizing that McKee was in the room. In those days, the OC of the Belfast Brigade may have been a household name but not a household face. McKee remembers the exchange.

> We asked him, 'Well, what's on the agenda?' He said, 'Withdrawal'. We said we were interested. He said this man [Michael Oatley] doesn't want to meet anybody except Billy McKee. Seamus Twomey said to me, 'Well, are you willing to go up?' I said, 'Not on my own. I'm not going to meet any British agent on my own'. I said I wanted a witness there to hear what's going on. Twomey agreed and another man was sent up with me.

The 'other man' was a senior IRA figure from Derry who was on the IRA's GHQ Staff. It was not Martin McGuinness.

Following its meeting with the Contact, the Army Council decided to extend the ceasefire deadline for another fourteen days until 16 January 1975. Ó'Brádaigh recalls that the purpose was 'to give the British Government an opportunity of developing the invitation and of being more specific'. In other words, to give the British more time. Again, the deadline was midnight. On 7 January 1975, a week after the Army Council meeting, Billy McKee and the GHQ IRA man travelled to Derry to meet Michael Oatley at a secret location. Derry was used for all meetings as it was on the border and easily accessible to members of the PAC coming from the Republic where most of them either lived or were on the run. On occasions they were picked up in Letterkenny by local people from Derry who were identified by the Contact as being willing to help. On other occasions, members of the PAC were dropped off near the border and made their way across on foot along familiar tracks. Often Seamus Twomey and David O'Connell would stay in Derry overnight or longer, whenever the talks reached a critical stage, so they could be on hand to be consulted and give advice. Billy McKee once spent nearly two weeks in the city, never leaving the house where he was staying except at night.

When Michael Oatley arrived at that first meeting with Ó'Brádaigh and McKee, he was apparently disconcerted to see another unknown face – that of the person from the IRA's GHQ. McKee told Oatley that he had refused to come alone and that the other person was his witness. 'I don't make any secret deals with you,' he warned. The Contact urged Oatley to stay because if the other man went, McKee would disappear too. With great difficulty he had brought them together and he did not wish to see his labours wasted. Billy McKee told me what Michael Oatley had said.

He said that the British Government wished to meet the leadership of the Provisional IRA. I asked him what was on the agenda and he said 'withdrawal' and he said that he needed our help.

Are you sure he said withdrawal?

Oh, he said 'withdrawal' all right. 'Withdrawal' was used during the whole negotiations by Michael Oatley and James Allan. They said that's what they wanted and they needed the IRA to help them so that there wouldn't be a bloodbath. They said they wanted us to meet the loyalists and we said that could be arranged all right.

But you're absolutely sure that Michael Oatley at that meeting discussed withdrawal with you?

Yes, if he had said anything else, we probably wouldn't have met. He certainly mentioned it. So did James Allan and the other men [who took over from Michael Oatley]. They spoke of withdrawal on different occasions, and I can tell you if they hadn't mentioned withdrawal, there'd have been no ceasefire, no truce at that time.

Seen in the present-day context, the suggestion that British officials, however deniably, were discussing a British withdrawal from Northern Ireland with representatives of the IRA is so extraordinary that I asked a senior former Government source with some knowledge of what happened to give his analysis of this encounter and the remarkable meetings that followed. He said they had to be seen in a particular historical context.

All sorts of things were said in those days to get the essential points across. You have to remember that the Provisionals' leadership of the time had very much less opportunity than their modern successors to be sensitive to the realities of the political situation. Oatley and Allan and the people who came after them were meticulously professional and I am sure that none of them ever discussed the possibility of a British political withdrawal from Northern Ireland in other than the most remotely hypothetical fashion. On the other hand, since it was a central preoccupation of their interlocutors (though recognizably, even to them, unattainable in the short or medium term) refusal to discuss it at all would have ended the conversation.

It would have been no good our people saying 'We cannot talk about that. It is impossible.' Instead they would say, 'Yes, we will talk about it. But if these are your aims you must recognize what has to be done to achieve them, and that is an accommodation with the majority population, which cannot be coerced.' The whole point of contacts of this kind in those days and subsequently has been to enlarge the political awareness of the IRA's leadership. Many people have contributed to this, not least the men themselves, and the effects have become obvious. I am perfectly certain that our officials in those days would never have suggested that HMG could abandon its responsibilities in Northern Ireland without majority consent. They may very well have discussed theoretical moves towards achieving that consent or other intermediate steps.

I am equally sure that the 1975 ceasefire took place without any belief on the IRA side that they had been offered any undertakings whatever about constitutional change. Indeed I doubt whether they asked for any. The fact is they were getting nowhere, wanted to stop and to become political, and needed help in doing so. The same was true in 1994. In the latter case, I much regret that the Government of the day reacted with suspicion rather than support. It was a total misreading of the situation. The achievement of the leadership in maintaining discipline during periods of ceasefire has been astonishing and we ought to support those who take a moderate stance, not ask them to disassociate themselves from the people they are seeking to bring with them.

I had previously heard about the Christmas Day letter and its alleged mention of 'structures of disengagement' without knowing the background to it and had always remained sceptical. Not only did I find it surprising that the letter no longer existed – strange for such a vital piece of evidence – but I found it extremely difficult to believe that the British Government would ever say such a thing, let alone that it would have been committed to paper, regardless of whose hand it was in. What made the story even more tantalizing was that I was inclined to believe Ó'Brádaigh, whom I had invariably found to be truthful. He tended to smile and offer no comment rather than tell a lie. Ruairí Ó'Brádaigh, as the British recognized, was a man of his word, whatever his IRA connections. Above all, I was puzzled by Ó'Brádaigh's insistence that the letter said that the British were prepared to discuss 'structures of disengagement' or words to that effect. If so, what did those words mean? Historically, it was vitally important to establish the truth, and to do so I had to find out precisely what had happened during the meetings that were to follow once the ceasefire was reinstated and whether the British had ever genuinely talked about 'withdrawal'.

The only way to find out what had been said was to gain access to the Republican Movement's minutes of those critical meetings, no easy task as no journalist had ever been given access to them before. Finally, someone, somewhere, agreed that I could see them and a complex logistical operation was put in place in which I had to travel to the minutes since they could not travel to me. I was not to know where I had been or where I had seen them and was instructed to go to a location far away in the Irish Republic where I was assured I would be met and taken care of. A car was waiting which drove me to a location by a circuitous route to avoid any possible Gárdái Special Branch surveillance and to make sure I could never find the place again. Down the years I had been on such ventures before – involving both republicans and loyalists – invariably at night, on one occasion lying in the back of a car in South Armagh covered by a blanket and on another being blindfolded and driven by loyalists through the darkness of East Belfast. This time it was daylight and there were no blindfolds. We finally arrived at a house in the country where I was ushered into a bedroom. The minutes were lying on a dressing table neatly arranged in a red file. I was brought tea and fruit cake and instructed that I could dictate sections into my tape recorder but on no account could I take the minutes away. I pulled up a chair and sat there for five hours, speaking into my recorder and at times scarcely believing what I was reading. I had to keep reminding myself that these were the Provisionals' minutes and their accuracy could only be authenticated by the equivalent minutes taken by HMG. Knowing that this was out of the question I had to read the Provisionals' version and make a judgement. Certain elements of the minutes tallied with what I already knew to be fact.

The minutes had been neatly typed on what appeared to be a fairly ancient typewriter. Word processors were a rarity in 1975. Someone was always in the room next door supplying refreshments and, more importantly, answering questions and providing guidance where necessary. I asked what records the typed minutes were based on and was shown some of the original, handwritten notes that had been taken at most of the meetings. The minutes seemed genuine. Some of the names were in code. I was told that 'Yellow Man' was Sir Frank Cooper – why, no one seemed to know. 'Michael' was Ruairí Ó'Brádaigh, 'S' was the Contact and 'Mr Kelly' was David O'Connell. More prosaically, 'A' was James Allan and 'O' was Michael Oatley. Oatley's MI6 successor was mysteriously code-named 'Hospital Man' ('HM'). The following account of the extraordinary things that the Provisionals maintained were said at some of these meetings throughout 1975 are based on my record of these minutes. They may be one-sided but there is no reason to believe they are fantasy.

Nothing of any real significance developed after the exploratory meeting with Billy McKee and Ruairí Ó'Brádaigh in early January 1975. Merlyn Rees did announce the release of twenty more republican detainees but that in itself was not enough to merit the continuation of the already extended ceasefire which had lasted for a record three weeks and two days. It came to an end at one minute past midnight on 16 January 1975. At two o'clock the following morning, Ruairí Ó'Brádaigh received a phone call from Belfast asking him to get in touch with the Contact urgently. Ó'Brádaigh left the house and, for security reasons, went to a telephone box in Roscommon to make the call. The Contact told him that, despite the ending of the ceasefire, the British still wanted to talk. Ó'Brádaigh never finished the conversation as the Gárdái arrived and arrested him in the telephone box. They might well have wondered what Roscommon's prime suspect was doing in a telephone box in the middle of the night. He was released shortly afterwards and immediately tried to pick up the threads. At seven o'clock that evening, he managed to reach the Contact again who told him that the British were keen to meet Ó'Brádaigh himself and had not done so to date because he was considered 'too prominent'. Perhaps it was a way of bringing the Provisionals back into play. A meeting was arranged.

The IRA leadership briefed Ó'Brádaigh to say that the Republican Movement was prepared to send two of its representatives to meet two representatives of the British Government to negotiate 'in specific terms' a bilateral truce – a ceasefire agreed by *both* sides – and to negotiate 'implementation of its three demands'. These were much the same as those made at Cheyne Walk: British forces should be withdrawn; the

Irish people should decide their future; there should be an amnesty for all 'political' prisoners and an end to detention without trial.

The meeting with Ó'Brádaigh was arranged with remarkable speed and took place two days later at midday on 18 January at a secret location in the North. It went on for two days. For the first time, Oatley was accompanied by his Laneside Foreign Office colleague, James Allan. Ruairí Ó'Brádaigh and Billy McKee represented the PAC. McKee had already met Oatley – a fact not recorded in the Republican Movement's minutes – and it is clear that the dialogue would not have continued without his approval. Although he was content to maintain a lower public profile than Ó'Brádaigh, he was very much more influential with the military wing of the Movement. He had been arrested on 15 April 1971 and, on his release from Crumlin Road gaol three and a half years later, he effectively held the balance in the leadership between O'Connell and Ó'Brádaigh on the one hand, and Twomey and the more hard-line Provisionals on the other. McKee could be as hard and ruthless as any but his instincts were moderate, as indicated by his remarks about not letting the opportunity of dialogue pass. He had been identified by the NIO, and through Oatley to the Contact, as a leader whom it would be appropriate to involve in discussions, both because of his personal prestige, and because it was thought that following his release from prison he had not returned to any official position within the Movement.

The meeting was largely taken up with 'a long general discussion' in which both sides put their case. It was Ruairí Ó'Brádaigh's first ever formal meeting with the British as he had not been a member of the IRA delegation during the Cheyne Walk talks with William Whitelaw in 1972. This is Ó'Brádaigh's recollection.

> In the beginning it was a 'getting to know you' meeting. We discussed generalities. Why the bilateral truce of 1972 went wrong and politically why it broke down. We discussed what we had to do if this situation were to be renewed and how a similar breakdown could best be avoided. We also discussed the terms of political discussions that would follow any mutual arrangements for a truce. The atmosphere was cordial. There was no hostility.

Oatley and Allan said they would convey what the Provisionals had said to their 'principals' and report back with an answer, 'possibly the next day'. They were as good as their word and at the meeting the following day, they gave a reply which they stated had been authorized by their

immediate superior 'Yellow Man', Frank Cooper, the Permanent Under
Secretary at the Northern Ireland Office. The minutes record the British
saying that there would be an 'open agenda' for talks and they would not
'exclude the raising of any relevant question' if a permanent cessation
of violence could be agreed. There would be 'two levels of business',
one conducted at Laneside with Sinn Fein and the other secretly with
Ó'Brádaigh and McKee. The 'real hard business' would be done at the
lower level. Oatley and Allan said they had 'Yellow Man's 'personal
assurance' that the Provisionals' position and the British response had
been considered 'right at the top'. But the priority at the moment,
they said, was to discuss 'tacking down' a truce. The minutes record
that the rest of the meeting was taken up with a general discussion on
'long-term British policy towards Ireland'. The Provisionals made their
position clear.

> . . . if the British Government wanted to disengage quietly from
> Ireland, the Republican Movement would help them. But if they
> wanted to restructure British rule in Ireland and make it more
> acceptable, then the Republican Movement would contest the
> ground with them.[1]

On 31 January 1975, Michael Oatley passed a message via the Contact
saying that he was concerned about the violence that had broken out
since the ending of the ceasefire a fortnight earlier, noting that there had
been 'three acts of violence' that day alone and warning 'how politically
difficult this makes our task'. There had been two bombs inside the
security cordon in the centre of Belfast and a policeman had been killed
in a machine-gun attack in County Tyrone.[2] The British subsequently
spelt out that a 'genuine and sustained cessation of violence' would have
to include an end to *all* violence, including kneecapping, armed robberies
and the procurement of weapons. If, on this basis, it was clear that violence
had come 'to a complete end', the Provisionals were assured that two things
would happen. The rate of release of prisoners would be 'speeded up with
a view to releasing all detainees' and 'the army would gradually be reduced
to peacetime levels and withdrawn to barracks'. It is important to note that
there was no mention on the British side of 'political' disengagement.

But a problem was arising which neither side had foreseen. On 30
January 1975, the Government had published a report by Lord Gardiner
who had been asked to review anti-terrorist measures in Northern Ireland.
He concluded that the special category status conceded by William
Whitelaw in 1972 following Billy McKee's hunger strike, was 'a serious
mistake' and recommended its abolition. He also said that an immediate

start should be made to the building of new 'cellular accomodation'.[3] Both recommendations were to have momentous repercussions in the years that followed. Merlyn Rees wasted no time and within a week he announced that work would begin immediately on the new 'cellular' accommodation for 200 prisoners, which would be ready by the autumn.[4] Interestingly, there is no mention in the minutes of this hugely important change in prison policy until six months later. Clearly, at the time, the new policy was not seen to be particularly significant. Its full implications had not yet sunk in.

On 7 February, the two sides got down to the business of 'tacking down' the truce. Whilst violence raged outside it was the truce, not penal policy, which was the most urgent priority. Oatley and Allan stressed that this time 'practical arrangements had to be made to ensure that any ceasefire did not break down' as it had done in 1972 and enumerated what would follow 'a genuine and sustained cessation of violence'. To the Provisionals, the most important points were:

1. No restriction on freedom of movement and no question of those wishing to return home to live in peace being harassed by the security forces.
2. Permits to be granted for people to carry arms for self-defence, taking account of the risk to individuals. The need to protect those who may be at risk of assassination is recognized.
3. There is no question of the security forces undertaking provocative displays of force.
4. Misunderstandings must be avoided between the security forces and others to ensure that a sustained ceasefire will not break down. This will require practical and effective arrangements.
5. If there is a genuine and sustained cessation of violence and hostilities, the army would gradually be reduced to peacetime levels and withdrawn to barracks.
6. Discussions will continue between officials and representatives of Provisional Sinn Fein and will include the aim of securing permanent peace.

Both sides broadly agreed on the above general terms for a truce. Remarkably, as I sat reading those six points, it seemed like two warring armies were making peace. So much for never 'talking to terrorists'. But to Ó'Brádaigh and McKee, the key lay in the last two paragraphs – troop withdrawal and continuing discussions to secure a 'permanent peace'. To the Provisionals, these were the overriding issues but it was a more pressing detail which almost held things up – two dozen arms permits for key IRA Volunteers. The vexed question was resolved when a message came from 'Yellow Man' declaring 'if all that stands between us and the successful conclusion of our present arrangements is twenty-four permits – we shall find a way round that difficulty.' The problem was resolved and the permits were issued, on condition that the IRA did not flaunt the remarkable concession by walking around openly displaying their weapons. Finally, with the truce 'tacked down', the IRA issued a statement on 8 February 1975 announcing a new ceasefire to begin at six o'clock the following evening.

> In the light of the discussions which have taken place between representatives of the Republican Movement and British officials on effective arrangements to ensure that there is no breakdown of a new truce, the Army Council of Oglaigh Na Eireann has renewed the order suspending offensive military action.

Ironically, the day of the announcement, a soldier, twenty-two-year-old William Robson, who had been shot two days earlier by an IRA sniper in Fermanagh, died in hospital.

One of the main features of the truce was that it was to be monitored through a series of 'incident centres' manned throughout the province, by Sinn Fein, to avoid the kind of confrontation that had brought the 1972 ceasefire to an end. The incident centres had a hot line to a desk first in Laneside and later to the Northern Ireland Office at Stormont, manned twenty-four hours a day by officials who had, if necessary, immediate access to the Secretary of State. In this way, it was hoped that any problems could be sorted out before they became serious. The centres were set up in Enniskillen, Armagh, Derry, Newry, Dungannon and Belfast. They were a watershed in the public perception of Sinn Fein, giving it a political standing in the nationalist community and, more importantly, a physical presence, as Tom Hartley, one of the Provisionals' leading political strategists, recognized.

> They began a trend of actually taking Sinn Fein out of the back rooms and putting it onto the main arterial routes. As long as we were in the back rooms, people wouldn't see us. We wouldn't be seen as a political force. As the old saying goes, out of sight out of mind. In 1975, the whole of West Belfast knew where the Sinn Fein rooms were. Every day they passed the office as they passed by in a black taxi [the 'People's Taxis' that provided cheap transport] up and down the Falls Road and people would say, 'there's the Sinn Fein office'. The incident centres gave the party a physical presence.

Marie Moore, one of Sinn Fein's original workers in the Falls Road incident centre, was acutely aware of Sinn Fein's inferior status as the IRA's political arm and was depressed by the fact that young people never gave it a thought.

> Sinn Fein was classed as a second-class citizen. It was the secondary thing you went to. My own view was that if you didn't have a political solution, then what solution was there? What did you do? If you fought the Brits until they got out, what did you put in its place? There had to be some sort of political initiative that, if necessary, had to go along with the armed struggle.

Loyalists, already deeply suspicious about the Government's intentions, were bitterly opposed to the incident centres, regarding them as capitulation to the IRA. The SDLP also had grave reservations, seeing them as providing a political boost to Sinn Fein at their expense. Whilst the SDLP only expressed their concern, the loyalist paramilitaries gave vent to their opposition by slaughtering Catholics. In the week after the IRA announced its ceasefire, loyalists murdered five Catholics in a series of gun and bomb attacks. The killings continued with growing intensity throughout the period of the ceasefire, making it increasingly difficult for the IRA not to respond. Getting the IRA to break the truce was one of the tactical purposes of the loyalist campaign. Among the most horrendous murders were those committed by a notorious gang known as the 'Shankill Butchers' who tortured their innocent Catholic victims and carved them up with butchers' knives. The gang had started killing Catholics in 1972 and in 1979, eleven members were finally brought to justice and sentenced to a total of two thousand years imprisonment for nineteen murders.[5]

A month into the truce, the Provisionals were unhappy and told the British so. At the formal meeting on 5 March, they complained that 'the undertaking given regarding the movement of troops out of Ireland has not been fulfilled'; that the release of prisoners to date has been 'derisory'; and that there has been no movement as had been hoped on the transfer of the 'Winchester prisoners' – the Price sisters, Gerry Kelly and others who were serving life for the 1973 London bombings – from English gaols to prisons in Northern Ireland. But Oatley and Allan were more interested in trying to persuade Sinn Fein to take part in the elections for Merlyn Rees's Constitutional Convention that were to be held on 1 May 1975. They said it was a sign that the Government, 'no longer wants to dictate events in Ireland and wants Irishmen themselves to "get on with it" '. Ó'Brádaigh and McKee were not interested, knowing that the chances of any agreement emerging from the Convention were zero. The situation was getting serious and the Army Council told their representatives to give the British the ominous warning that, 'we achieve more in wartime than in peacetime'. The IRA instructed ÓBrádaigh and McKee to speak from the following brief.

> The Army Council of Oglaigh Na Eireann has reviewed the truce situation. After four weeks of genuine and sustained suspension of hostilities, the response by the British Government is considered unsatisfactory.
>
> We formally informed HMG that the duration of the truce depended on the progress made towards securing a permanent peace. Negotiations on the three basic demands of the Republican Movement for a permanent peace have not made any worthwhile progress. We therefore demand the initiation of such talks on a realistic basis. Any matters of a truce supervisory nature must be handled by a separate team of negotiators.[6]

At the formal meeting on 16 March, Oatley and Allan got the message. They said that the IRA's concerns were 'carefully noted and taken very seriously', and insisted that, 'despite problems, progress had been achieved'. They then attempted to mollify the Provisionals by saying the Government acknowledged 'the patience in negotiation and the discipline of the Republican Movement' and insisted that they wished to continue with the meetings and 'build up trust'. 'We must get through our difficulties', they concluded. Two days later the Price sisters were transferred from Durham prison to Armagh gaol. It was one of the confidence-building gestures the IRA was looking for. In March 1975, Michael Oatley prepared to leave Northern Ireland and as he said goodbye to the Provisionals' delegation he gave them gold-plated Cross pens as momentos. McKee subsequently complained that the Government might have afforded the real thing. 'HM', Oatley's replacement, then took over.

The bloodshed continued. By the end of March, loyalist paramilitaries had murdered six more Catholics and, in the vacuum created by the IRA ceasefire, bloody internal feuds broke out amongst the republican and loyalist paramilitaries. British officials would doubtless have shed few tears at all the bloodletting, but by this time, the Contact was getting worried. He would have known how tenuous the ceasefire was becoming due to the lack of political progress as well as the increasing pressure on the IRA to retaliate in the face of the loyalists' campaign of sectarian murder. The Provisionals had come into being as the defenders of the nationalist community against loyalist attack and now they found themselves standing by whilst Catholics were being butchered. In desperation, the Contact took it upon himself to act and, on 29 March, he exceeded his brief and wrote a letter to the Prime Minister, in the form of an Easter message from the leadership of the Republican Movement. It was potentially a dangerous thing to do but the Contact covered himself by first showing it to 'Mr Kelly' (David O'Connell), whom he went to see at a meeting in County Tyrone. O'Connell said they were the sentiments he himself would have expressed. The surrogate letter began by reminding Wilson of how there had been 'one hundred days of effective peace on the part of our forces'.

> During this period, the representatives of the Republican Movement have earnestly tried with your representatives to pave the way towards a permanent and lasting peace in Ireland and a permanent end to this age-old conflict. We feel that Her Majesty's representatives on the ground are too close to the day-to-day problems of administering Northern Ireland to fully appreciate the historic importance of the past one hundred days . . .
>
> It is our compelling belief, that our Irish problem will be solved only by Irish men, free from British direction and political constraint. We have accepted that the Irish problem cannot be solved 'at a stroke' but the progress to date falls far short of what we consider the minimum necessary to satisfy our Movement and our people . . .
>
> In the face of the lack of real movement: the continuing arrest and imprisonment of our members both in Northern Ireland and England; the almost total lack of real response from Her Majesty's forces on the ground; the punitive 'dribble technique' of releasing political prisoners; and the discernible drift towards the restructuring of British rule in Northern Ireland [via the Convention]; can we honestly be expected to maintain our present position?
>
> We trust that you, Mr Prime Minister, will take the opportunity of this historic Easter time to make a truly positive initiative which will bring to an end the necessity of the continuing reoccurrence of hostilities between our peoples and secure an honourable and a permanent end to such hostilities.[7]

The following day, Easter Sunday, some 4,000 Provisional IRA supporters marched to Belfast's Milltown cemetery for the annual commemoration of the 1916 Rising. To the fury of loyalists, the crowd was addressed by the IRA's Chief of Staff, Seamus Twomey who, unlike his fellow escapees, J B O'Hagan and Kevin Mallon, was still at large. Twomey said there could be no permanent peace until the Provisionals' three main demands were met. In Carrickmore, County Tyrone, David O'Connell made a similar speech, saying English rule must be ended, even if it meant another five years of hard fighting. The army made no attempt to arrest either IRA leader. At least in this respect, the truce seemed to be working. In Dublin, the Army Council issued an Easter message stating that the IRA would settle for no permanent agreement unless it included a programme of planned and orderly withdrawal of the English establishment from Ireland, and that there was a limit to the patience of the Army Council in relation to the present ceasefire.[8]

Three days later, on Wednesday 2 April, the Provisionals showed they meant business by bombing a travel agents in the centre of Belfast. It was the first breach of the ceasefire and was claimed to be in retaliation for two recent breaches of the truce: British army house searches and the wounding of two Provisional Sinn Fein members on 13 March in the Lower Falls. The army had said they were firing into a crowd. Local residents said they were unarmed.[9] The day the Provisionals bombed the travel agents, a formal meeting was held between Ó'Brádaigh and McKee on one side and James Allan and 'HM' on the other. Whilst I studied the file on this meeting, I saw before me, for the first time, the words I had been looking for – 'structures of disengagement' – and crucially these were minutes of a formal meeting between the two sides, not a message passed through the Contact. As I read on, I could hardly believe what the British representatives were reported by the Republican Movement to have said. The minutes of that astonishing meeting – if accurate – record the following. The British first tried to soothe the Provisionals' injured feelings.

The acceptability of the Republican Movement as a respectable movement has greatly increased. It is now viewed as a serious political movement which should be listened to. This is an enormous gain. It would be lost if the Republican Movement goes back to war. There is no magic way forward. The only way is slow . . .

This is an extremely historic moment. It may not happen again for a long time. The responsibility on the Republican Movement is enormous. History and the future of the Republican ideal are at stake . . . [the] rate of progress . . . is slow but will increase as it goes along.

Finally, with reference to Seamus Twomey's speech in Belfast at Easter, a firm [public] undertaking is totally and absolutely out of the question. This would lead to a Congo-type situation which both Brits and the Republican Movement wish to avoid.[10] Grave statements lead to the opposite happening.

If on the other hand the Republican Movement helps the Government to create circumstances out of which the *structures of disengagement* [author's emphasis] can naturally grow, the pace quickens immensely once the groundwork is laid. The only way to develop is to get the groundwork right. HMG cannot say they are leaving Ireland because the reaction would prevent that happening. They cannot make a stark definitive statement.

If one looks at events: Harland & Wolff [which had been in serious financial trouble] have been nationalized but are retained separately from the other British nationalized industries. The tendency is towards eventual British disengagement. The hits [presumably on the Provisionals' agenda] are there but will stop if the Republican Movement goes back to war. The whole British army in Ireland is programmed for fighting the Republican Movement. The difficulty is to reprogramme it quickly. The important thing is to believe in each other's sincerity.[11]

However carefully phrased the words, did the British really say them? I still found it difficult to believe. Were the minutes a deliberate distortion by the Provisionals or a misinterpretation, given what they wanted to hear? I had no reason to believe that the earlier minutes were inaccurate so why should these be any different? The truth only lies locked away somewhere in MI6's files. I could not believe that Merlyn Rees, the Secretary of State, would ever have countenanced such things to be said. Did the British representatives really mean it? Or was it all part of a brilliant Intelligence operation to string the Provisionals along and leave them damaged and split when all came to naught? Since I had already interviewed Lord Rees by the time I gained access to the minutes, I rang him and put some of the above quotes to him. Did he know what had been said and if so, had it been said with his authority? He was astonished at what he heard and said that he did not know that such things had been said and they had certainly not had his authorization. The Secretary of State clearly did not know what was going on. Both of us were equally incredulous.

In April 1975, the sectarian killings reached a new intensity. On Saturday 5 April, loyalists threw a bomb into McLaughlin's bar in the nationalist New Lodge area as customers were settling down to watch the Grand National, and two Catholics were killed. By now the pressure on the Provisionals to retaliate was too great to resist and five hours later, in a tit-for-tat attack, the IRA threw a bomb into the crowded Mountainview Tavern on the Shankill Road, killing five Protestants. One of the dead, William Andrews, was a member of the UDA. That evening, loyalists struck back, killing a sixty-one-year-old Catholic, Thomas Robinson, on his way from a social club in Ardoyne.[12] By the end of the month, loyalist killers had murdered fourteen more Catholics. Nevertheless, despite having retaliated once, the Army Council was still intent on getting what it could from the truce, although it was becoming increasingly restless about the lack of any tangible political progress. It accepted the lull in the run-up to the Convention election but once this was over, it expected real progress. The election produced the predictable triumph for the loyalist coalition, the UUUC, which won forty-seven of the Convention's seventy-eight seats. The SDLP won seventeen. As the UUUC had stood on a platform opposed to power sharing and any Irish dimension, there was no chance of any accommodation. The IRA regarded the clear failure of the latest British political initiative as a bonus that played directly into their hands. Now they expected things to move. They decided to press the Government to make its declaration of intention to withdraw so the Convention could draft a constitution in this context. The Provisionals were nothing if not optimistic. They said this would 'give a purpose to the Convention and rescue something from the shambles', repeating that 'permanent peace is possible only in exchange for British disengagement. The delivery on the ground of the amnesty [the freedom of movement given to IRA Volunteers] is not enough'.

Volunteers clearly enjoyed the freedom. Many took the opportunity of the truce to return home, thinking the 'war' was over. On the ground, the IRA began to relax. Few of its members, including those inside the prisons, had any detailed knowledge of what was going on during the secret meetings between their representatives and the British. It was a lesson not lost on the leadership in the period leading up to the 1994 cessation. One of the Volunteers who returned to Derry was Shane Paul O'Doherty. He had been on the run in Donegal and returned to his home in the city on 8 May 1975. He was planting a cherry-blossom tree in his front garden when two plain-clothes policemen came to arrest him and pointed guns at his head.[13] O'Doherty was astonished, believing that the truce gave him freedom to return to Derry and freedom from arrest. To the IRA's Derry Brigade, it was a clear breach of the truce. Two days later, a sniper shot dead a twenty-year-old policeman, Constable Paul Gray, who had been on foot patrol in the city centre, in retaliation for the arrest of O'Doherty. The killing dominated the next formal meeting on 14 May, with the British representatives saying that the shooting was 'a totally disproportionate action to the arrest of Shane O'Doherty' and which they regarded as 'an act of political folly because no Government can accept that kind of incident if it hopes to survive'. What the Derry Brigade had done, the British said, was 'to put a stop to progress. Troop reductions cannot now be considered.' Frustration grew on both sides. To the British, IRA violence had not ended. To the Army Council, there was no sign of the political progress they had hoped for in the wake of the Convention result. Both sides withdrew to reconsider their positions.

Gradually, through the Contact's intervention and skilful encouragement, the process was put back on track. The minutes of the formal meeting of 22 June 1975 were again astonishing to read.

[The British representatives] restated very firmly that Brits were going and it would be a tragedy if anything happened. Two roads were leading in the same direction, only the Republican Movement was travelling faster on its road than the Brits were on theirs . . . There had been a lack of generosity by the Brits up to this time and British problems were always emphasized. There should be public recognition of the Republican position. Peace has been taken for granted and no credits were going to the Republican Movement. This must be altered.

Two days later 'HM' rang the Contact and 'sounded excited'. As a result of the phone call, the Contact said that 'progress had been made and there was a good breakthrough. The Brits now accepted that they had been ungenerous.' The Contact was asked to meet James Allan and 'HM' the following day but, as the Contact reported back to McKee and Ó'Brádaigh, it was not a happy encounter. Scant progress was being made. The British were offering the release of more prisoners but this did not 'begin to meet the minimum of requirements'. The Contact related that one of the British representatives sympathized with the Provisionals' position and had remarked, 'the whole bloody world knows that the British never move until it's too bloody late. It's not finished yet.' The Contact said he then left the room quietly, went outside and kicked his car to vent his anger and frustration. One of the British team apparently came out and apologized, saying 'I can see you are obviously upset. We must do our homework better.' The Contact believed that 'damaging his car had more effect than all the previous days of talking'.

By July the Army Council was still looking for tangible signs of progress and demanded 'visible' and 'meaningful' indications that the talks were getting somewhere. They wanted withdrawal of British troops from nationalist areas in Belfast and Derry; the dismantling of two army bases – 'Fort Monagh' and 'Silver City' – in the Provisionals' stronghold of West Belfast; and an end to screening and surveillance. The Army Council concluded:

The implementation of these reasonable demands during the next two to three weeks would be viewed by the Republican Movement as an expression of HMG's sincerity. It would also be progress towards a public declaration by the Government of withdrawal from Ireland. The leadership repeats once more that until that declaration is forthcoming, coupled with self-determination for the whole Irish people and a general amnesty for all political prisoners, there is no prospect of a lasting peace.

The leadership added that it was alarmed at the Government's silence on the growth of the loyalist assassination squads, or what it called 'sectarian forces'.

On 31 July 1975, there was a bloody illustration of what the IRA leadership meant. Members of the Miami Showband were returning to the Republic from an engagement in Banbridge, County Down, when they were stopped at what they thought was an army checkpoint. The men who waved them down were wearing UDR uniforms, but in fact they were members of the UVF, intent on killing Catholics. They gunned down three members of the band whilst two escaped. As the killers were planting a bomb in the Showband's van, it exploded prematurely, killing two of them. At least one of the UVF men *was* a member of the UDR. The same day, another formal meeting was held. Studying the files, I was surprised to read that the British were advising the Republican Movement on how to brush up its image. It should stress that *it* was non-violent and it was the loyalists who were doing all the killing. Remarkably, the British suggested that the Provisionals might talk to two of the most respected journalists who covered Northern Ireland – Derek Brown of the *Guardian* and Mary Holland of the *Observer* – with a view to getting their case across.

But the Provisionals were not interested in public relations. They wanted to talk about the declaration of intent which, to them, was the whole point of the truce. Allan and 'HM' said the Government could not now give this for three reasons: the Convention 'must be given a chance publicly'; the Government was waiting for 'a consensus of opinion to emerge in Britain'; and there was the danger of 'a Congo-type situation resulting'. The minutes then record the following exchange.

The Republican Movement asked, why continue to fight in Ireland when withdrawal is on? Is the loss of life justified? The Brits replied that there is no British de Gaulle on the horizon. Mr Rees says it would be unhelpful to make a private or public statement at this

time with the Convention in session. The trends are all in favour
of such a statement.

Then, for the first time, the Government's plans to abolish special category
status were raised. The British representatives said the Government had
'no intention of depriving those who have it at present' and added that 'no
date has been given for its termination on new convictions'. Ominously,
the Republican Movement gave a warning that 'any attempt to do away
with it would be resisted'. No one at that time could ever have imagined
how dramatic that 'resistance' was to be six years later with with ten
men dead on a hunger strike and its leader, Bobby Sands, being elected
to Westminster.

On 13 August 1975, the IRA retaliated for the Miami Showband
killings with a bomb and gun attack on the Bayardo Bar on the Shankill
Road, a place believed to be a haunt of the UVF. Six Protestants were
killed, one of them a member of the UVF.[14] One of the Provisionals
who was subsequently given a life sentence for the killings was Brendan
'Bik' McFarlane, who was to become a key figure in the 1981 hunger
strike before escaping from the Maze prison (the renamed 'Long Kesh')
in the mass IRA break-out of 1983.

The truce was now virtually over: sectarian killings spiralled, to which
the IRA retaliated, gradually returning to its campaign. On 1 September,
the South Armagh Republican Action Force, a flag of convenience for
elements of the Provisional IRA, shot dead six Protestants at the Tullyvallen
Orange Hall in Newtownhamilton, County Armagh. Two of them were
aged seventy and eighty. The gunmen claimed the attack was in retaliation
for the loyalists' assassination campaign against Catholics in Belfast where,
in August, they had shot dead ten. As the sectarian killings went on
endlessly, there were those in the IRA who felt distinctly unhappy at
the way in which the Provisionals were being dragged into a sectarian
campaign. That had never been part of the Republican ideal. Brendan
Hughes, now locked up in the compounds of 'Long Kesh' with Gerry
Adams and others, was one of those increasingly concerned.

In the 1975 period there was a great deal of disillusionment among
a lot of the people in the gaol, including myself and Gerry Adams.
When the ceasefire was on, the whole machine slipped into sectarianism and a lot of us were very, very unhappy with that situation.

I didn't believe that Tullyvallen and other attacks were going to
achieve anything. I believed they were counter-productive. Sectarian
bombings and sectarian killings were doing nothing except destroying
the whole struggle.

By the end of September the truce was effectively in ruins, destroyed by sectarianism, the resumption of the IRA's campaign and, above all, lack of political progress on the IRA's agenda. By this time, the Army Council had recognized that nothing of any substance would be forthcoming from the British, despite all the assurances they had received in the secret meetings. They decided there was little point in carrying on. They had been talking with the British for over a year and felt that nothing had been achieved beyond the release of a few prisoners. Their patience had run out. They told the Contact to tell the British, without giving any reason, that for the time being any more meetings were off. Merlyn Rees did little to give them encouragement, announcing on 4 November 1975 that special category status would be abolished and that all those convicted of terrorist crimes committed after 1 March 1976 would be treated as ordinary criminals. He also rejected any possibility of an amnesty. The Provisionals had had enough. On 10 November, the Derry Brigade gave its answer by blowing up the building in which their incident centre was based.[15] Two days later, Merlyn Rees announced that all the incident centres were to be closed down as they had ceased to serve any useful purpose. Although the final closure of the incident centres effectively marked the end of the truce, the secret dialogue did continue, despite the intensification of the IRA's campaign both in the North and in England. IRA operations on the mainland suffered a serious setback when its London unit was arrested on 12 December 1975 following a six-day siege at Balcombe Street in the West End. Its members subsequently claimed that *they* had been responsible for the Guildford bombing and that the men in gaol were innocent. In 1998, as part of the confidence building measures that accompanied the Good Friday Agreement, they were transferred to Portlaoise prison in Ireland. It was their appearance at the Sinn Fein Ard Feis that almost scuppered the Yes campaign (see chapter 26).

As 1976 began, the situation in the province seemed to be getting out of control as the cycle of sectarian killings accelerated and both sides indulged in an orgy of horrendous tit-for-tat killings. On 4 January loyalist gunmen shot dead five Catholics living in rural areas. The Provisionals retaliated the next day in horrific fashion at Kingsmills, South Armagh, by machine-gunning to death ten Protestant workers who were returning home in a minibus. The murders were claimed by the 'Republican Action Force' which was, like its predecessor the 'South Armagh Republican Action Force', a 'flag of convenience' for local Provisionals. Before opening fire, the gunmen asked if there were any Catholics on the bus. The driver stepped forward not knowing whether he was to be shot or spared. He was allowed to live and his passengers were mown down.[16] It is an episode and a period that most Provisionals prefer to forget as it disgraced every republican principle they claimed to stand for.

The truce and the dialogue with the British were over by the beginning of 1976, one having ended in bloodshed, the other in deadlock and frustration. The last formal meeting between the two sides was held on 10 February 1976. The Provisionals had not even begun to get what they wanted. It was not surprising that the younger members of the Republican Movement, many of whom were locked in the compounds of 'Long Kesh', saw the 1975 truce as the great betrayal, accusing the IRA leadership of naivety and inexperience in dealing with the 'Brits'. They believed that much had been given with little received in return. Gerry Adams and Martin McGuinness remained untainted by the truce as Adams was locked up in 'Long Kesh' for the entire period and McGuinness was in gaol in the Republic during its formative stages. Both observed from the sidelines and watched, in their eyes, the IRA being run down. Those who were to become the 'new' Provisional leadership, destined to lead the Republican Movement through the next two decades, regard the 1975 truce as the time when the IRA came closest to defeat and suffered irreparable damage. They vowed it would never happen again. The IRA declared that it would never order another ceasefire without the British Government first giving a declaration of intent to withdraw from Northern Ireland. It was to be almost twenty years before there was another sustained IRA cessation.

Chapter Fourteen

Counteroffensive

Remarkably, the compounds or 'cages' of 'Long Kesh' still stand today like a disused film set. Wandering amongst them is like walking back into history. The Nissen huts are bare but for the odd metal chair left abandoned in the middle and the empty tin of 'Smash' instant potato rattling around in the wind. On the wall of one hut is a fading list of prisoners: T W ['Cleeky'] Clarke – number 674. [Martin] Meehan – number 669. They are ghosts of the past. Perhaps some NIO official had ordered the compounds to be spared the bulldozer in case one day, when peace finally came, 'Long Kesh' might become a museum. A guide might point out where tunnels had been built and relate how Gerry Adams had 'streaked' around his compound naked except for his boots. The highlight of the tour could be the site of 'Cage 11' where Adams and his comrades devised the strategy that was to drive the IRA and Sinn Fein through the eighties and nineties. It was here, the guide might say, that the strategy was born of the 'Long War', which dramatically bore fruit more than twenty years later when Gerry Adams and Martin McGuinness were elected to Westminster. 'Cage 11' provided the nucleus of the Provisionals' Northern leadership that was to challenge and ultimately oust Ruairí Ó'Brádaigh and the Dublin leadership that had directed the Provisionals since the split in December 1969. Along with Gerry Adams, the strategists' names were to become part of future history: Gerry Kelly, Brendan Hughes, 'Bik' McFarlane, Jim Gibney, 'Cleeky' Clarke, Ivor Bell, Bobby Sands and many others.

Adams knew that a new strategy would have to be mapped out if the Republican Movement was to survive, let alone win. By the time internment ended, he knew the truce had been a disaster. The leadership, too, knew the damage that had been done. Billy McKee remembers talking to Seamus Twomey in early 1976 and discussing calling off the campaign.

> Things weren't going well. It was getting very rough. Different things happened during the campaign – it happened many a time

– we were short of money, short of arms and men were getting arrested. Things were getting a bit critical and we made plans about what way it would finish. I said to Seamus, 'If we do ever have to call it off, no matter what happens, one thing we can always say is that we got rid of Stormont.'

But you didn't call off the campaign?

No. We got another kiss of life.

The government's new penal policy was the life-saving kiss. Nevertheless, Adams did not criticize the leadership. To have done so would have been disloyal, sowed dissent and played into the hands of the enemy. The leadership made the decisions and stood or fell by them. Adams later wrote: 'For me it was becoming clearer that the main problem was that the struggle had been limited to armed struggle. Once this stopped, the struggle stopped.'[1] The current leadership of the Republican Movement learned the lessons. As a young Provisional in Derry, Mitchel McLaughlin saw first-hand the effect of the truce, although, like Adams, he refrained from direct criticism.

I think that there was a leadership there with the best intentions that was prepared to deliver on their end of the bargain. Their disastrous mistake was not to recognize soon enough that the British Government were not similarly engaged. They simply waited too long. It was the closest in my opinion that the IRA have come to being defeated.

The weakness was that the republican leadership was going into these negotiations – which were essentially negotiations on behalf of the people of Ireland – on their own. They were isolated from the rest of the body politic in Ireland. That was the crucial strategic position.

The only consolation for the Republican Movement during the truce was that internment had ended. On 5 December 1975, Merlyn Rees had announced the release of the last forty-six detainees.[2] He had finally achieved the ambitions he had harboured since his first visit to 'Long Kesh' with a parliamentary delegation in 1971. Rees had found the experience disturbing and the feeling had never gone away.

I found the idea of a concentration camp offensive. For me personally, ending internment was something positive that I had done and it was the right thing to do. If all I have is a footnote in history saying, 'Merlyn Rees ended internment', that will satisfy me. I doubt if anybody will give it any more praise than that but it deserves it.

But the compounds were not emptied. Prisoners who had been sentenced through the courts stayed on, still enjoying the special category status and POW lifestyle that was soon to come to an end. Life behind the wire continued just as it had before the last internees were released. By this time, Gerry Adams was a sentenced prisoner, having received eighteen months for trying to escape. Once internment was over, almost by accident, he began writing a weekly column for the Provisionals' newspaper, *Republican News*, under the pen name of 'Brownie'. As they evolved from late 1975 to early 1977, the 'Brownie' articles were to provide the ideological and strategic foundation for the Provisionals' direction over the next twenty years. Adams drew on the past to point the way forward. The Irish Republic which had been proclaimed in 1916 was still Adams' and the IRA's goal. Only the means of achieving it had changed.

Adams argued that the building of the 'Socialist Republic' that Patrick Pearse and his followers had fought and died for, now had to begin by establishing the political structures that would develop whilst the 'war' continued, until the British finally disengaged. In Adams' opinion, republicans had to build a broad political base within their own community that would both accompany the 'armed struggle' and continue once it was over. Those who supported the Provisionals' 'war machine' had to be politically organized around it. Such structures were to be created, Adams argued, by a process he called 'Active Abstentionism'. That meant that republicans were to reject all forms of British administration and set up their own. Adams recognized that the process was already well underway but needed to be taken even further. Its purpose was to solidify and extend support for the 'armed struggle', the Republican Movement and the future. But none of this was to be at the expense of the military campaign. On the contrary, the 'armed struggle' was to remain at its heart, the base around which everything else was to be built. Adams termed it 'Active Republicanism'. He defined it on the eve of the sixtieth anniversary of the Easter Rising in 1976 and addressed his words to the Volunteers about to attend the Commemoration.

> Active Republicanism means hard work, action, example . . . It means fighting. It's hard to write that down because, God knows, maybe I won't fight again and it will be cast up at me, but it still needs to be said even by a coward like myself, because at least I will move aside for the fighters.
>
> How they fight is a matter of tactics and conditions, but fight they must. There can be no question of that. The enemy allows us no choice. It is an armed struggle because the enemy is armed. Because

he establishes and protects his vested interests by force of arms. The cabinet ministers, the politicians, the warlords, the business interests, the profit makers – the Establishment – have all agreed on their objects and the course they will follow. They are armed mercenaries. We must be armed revolutionaries. We must be Active Republicans.[3]

In his column the following week Adams admitted IRA membership. It was the one and only time he has done so. He was recounting a conversation he had recently had with a visiting priest. Adams had defended the use of force saying it was not a role the IRA chose or welcomed but one that had been forced upon it. 'I tried to explain it all like this,' he wrote.

Rightly or wrongly, I am an IRA Volunteer and, rightly or wrongly, I take a course of action as a means to bringing about a situation in which I believe the people of my country will prosper . . . The course I take involves the use of physical force, but only if I achieve the situation where my people can genuinely prosper can my course of action be seen, by me, to have been justified . . . I cannot complain if I am hurt, if I am killed or if I am imprisoned. I must consider these things as possible and probable eventualities . . . I have no one to blame but myself.[4]

On 14 February 1977, Gerry Adams was released from the compounds of 'Long Kesh'. Exactly one year and one week later he was arrested in West Belfast along with a dozen others and charged with IRA membership. Adams was alleged to have become the IRA's Chief of Staff (he denies this, as he also denies he was ever a member of the IRA) following the arrest of Seamus Twomey on 3 December 1977. Adams' arrest came the morning after the Provisionals planted an incendiary bomb at the La Mon House Hotel outside Belfast on 17 February 1978. The bomb was attached to petrol drums which caused a fireball to sweep through the restaurant full of diners. Twelve people perished in the inferno, all Protestants. The warning came only nine minutes before the explosion – it appears that the bomb exploded prematurely. Two days later, the IRA admitted responsibility and regret. The warning, it said, 'proved totally inadequate given the disastrous consequences. We accept condemnation and criticism from only two sources: from the relatives and friends of those who were accidentally killed, and from our supporters who have rightly and severely criticized us.'[5]

Seven months later Adams was released. The prosecution had argued that his participation in a military-style parade in the compound was evidence of IRA membership, but this was dismissed by the Lord Chief Justice of Northern Ireland, Lord Lowry, as insufficient evidence on which to proceed. Adams, therefore, was never acquitted of membership because the case never came to full trial. Nor could his membership of the IRA delegation that met William Whitelaw in London in 1972 (see chapter 10) be used as evidence, since I understand that all were privately given an assurance by HMG that they would not be prosecuted for IRA membership on this particular occasion.

By the time of Adams' last 'Brownie' column in February 1977, the IRA was being hit hard. By then the Government had put in place a whole range of structures designed to demoralize and defeat the Provisionals. The abolition of special category status for crimes committed after 1 March 1976 had been a severe blow to morale and changes in the configuration and role of the security forces posed problems for the IRA. In the early summer of 1976, a government document, 'The Way Forward', had recommended that the RUC be given primacy in the war against 'terrorism'. The army, which for years had been the lead agency, did not like the new policy but had to swallow it. It was to be implemented by the new Chief Constable, Kenneth Newman, who had come from the Metropolitan Police on 1 May 1976 to take over the RUC. The ending of special category status and police primacy were designed to have a psychological as well as a practical impact on the conflict. The IRA were to be considered and treated as common criminals and, significantly, those who were to pursue them and bring them to justice were policemen not soldiers. The change of structures and names was also designed to counter IRA propaganda and alter public perception of the conflict. It was not to be seen as a 'war' between the IRA and the British army but a 'normal' problem of criminal gangsterism to be combated by the police. However, the police were to be aided in the front line by the locally recruited soldiers of the UDR and RUC Reserve. If troops were to be in the front line, they were to be Ulstermen. The vast majority of the RUC and UDR were Protestants. 'Ulster' was now seen to be fighting its own battle. The Provisionals referred to the Government's new policy as 'criminalization', 'Ulsterization' and 'normalization' and fought tooth and nail to oppose to it. Many suffered and died in the process since IRA Volunteers refused to be branded as criminals. Although it is tempting to accept the Provisionals' analysis of the change – that it was a carefully planned and skilfully co-ordinated counter-insurgency initiative – the reality was less conspiratorial. As Merlyn Rees admitted, 'there wasn't a master plan. I'm not a master-plan chap. I don't believe in that sort of thing.' But whatever its origins, the policy was, in the short term, effective. Merlyn Rees was its architect but it was his successor, Roy Mason, who put it into practice. Mason became Secretary of State on 10 September 1976 and accepted the challenge with obvious relish, at one stage declaring he was going to roll up the IRA like 'a tube of toothpaste'. Unionists could not believe that at long last the Government had sent over someone who knew what needed to be done and was prepared to roll up his sleeves and get tough. Political initiatives were out. So were any secret talks with the IRA. Mason's intent was to hit the IRA until it reeled. If the media raised questions about how this was being done, then the media was the enemy too. Roy Mason hardly got off to a good start with the media when, at a private dinner at the Culloden Hotel attended by army and BBC executives, he suggested that the reporting of Northern Ireland should be censored. The army were said to have been delighted. BBC representatives, on the other hand, were horrified. I remember that after making a series of programmes for ITV's *This Week* in 1977 which raised questions about Goverment security policy, the Northern Ireland Office suggested to Thames Television that it might be better if another reporter covered Northern Ireland. My reports, they said, had painted 'the blackest possible picture of events in Northern Ireland'.[6]

Roy Mason and Kenneth Newman were as one in implementing the new policy. Newman restructured the RUC as resources were poured in to enable the force to carry out the task it was now being required to do. He established four new Regional Crime Squads whose specific job was to target the IRA's Active Service Units (ASUs), acting on information provided by the RUC's Criminal Intelligence Unit. Each Regional Crime Squad was made up of around twenty detectives including three or four from Special Branch. Each Squad was then sub-divided into four units of five detectives, with one Special Branch officer to each unit. Ironically, the composition of the Regional Crime Squads came to resemble the Provisionals' ASUs which they were set up to smash.[7] But even as Mason and Newman set about their work, something happened that was to have profound repercussions for the future although it was little noticed or reported at the time.

By the autumn of 1976, prisoners charged with offences committed after 1 March that year, were now being convicted and sentenced. The new 'cellular' accommodation recommended in the Gardiner Report was ready to receive its first inmates. This accommodation was known as the 'H-Blocks' because they were built in the shape of a letter 'H'. Each H-block had four wings, one along each leg of the 'H'. On 15 September 1976, in the week Roy Mason took over from Merlyn Rees, Kieran Nugent, the first IRA prisoner to be sentenced under the new policy, entered the Maze Prison and was ordered to put on prison uniform. Nugent refused, saying he was not a common criminal. Criminals wore uniform. He was a political prisoner. Political prisoners wore their own clothes. He was taken to his cell where he put on the blanket that was on the bed rather than stand around naked. Thus was the 'blanket protest' born. Other prisoners followed suit, one of whom was Gerard Hodgkins. Hodgkins had been jailed for fourteen years in December 1976 for a firearm and bombing offence and IRA membership. When he arrived at the Maze Prison, he too had been ordered to put on a prison uniform.

> The prison officer was there saying, 'Right, you're here to do your time. You can do it the hard way or you can do it the easy way.' He says, 'If you take my advice you'd get them uniforms on you now. If not, strip.' So you stripped there and then whilst you were being ridiculed and jeered at by the 'screws' [prison officers]. Well, we wouldn't wear the uniform. There wasn't a physical beating or anything at this stage.

Hodgkins put on the blanket. At that time, November 1976, there were only a handful of 'blanket men' in the H-Blocks. They felt a profound sense of isolation, alone in their cells and often in separate blocks. What went through Hodgkins' head as he stood there alone, naked except for a blanket, in a cell empty except for a chamber pot and a Bible?

> Believe it or not you were sort of hoping against hope that within a few months we'd get political status. Being honest about it, within a few months we really believed we'd get it.

Over the next four years, hundreds more 'blanket men' were to join the protest.

The driving force behind the Labour Government's new policy was the RUC's holding centre at Castlereagh on the outskirts of Belfast. 'Holding centre' is a euphemism for interrogation centre. There was a second centre at Gough Barracks, Armagh, which covered the south of the province. Castlereagh, and to a lesser extent, Gough, became notorious because of the stream of allegations of ill-treatment that flowed from them. Most came from republicans but some also came from loyalists. I first encountered these allegations whilst working in Belfast in the early summer of 1977. I initially dismissed them as 'Provo propaganda', which is how they were discounted by the authorities. However, I began to take them seriously when I talked to some of those who had been interrogated and released as well as the doctors who had examined them. It soon became clear that these allegations were not mere propaganda and that many of them were true. Some of the injuries were self-inflicted, as the authorities insisted, but I suspected that the majority of them were not. The injuries revealed a pattern: wall standing, wrist bending and blows to parts of the body where they were least likely to leave marks. The medical evidence was broadly consistent with what the suspects alleged. At the time there was great pressure to achieve convictions through the courts. Because it was virtually impossible for the police to persuade witnesses to give evidence and because forensic evidence was not always available, confessions elicited during interrogation were the most common means of bringing cases to court, securing convictions and filling up the new H-Blocks. This was made possible as a result of Lord Diplock's report of December 1972 which considered 'legal procedures to deal with terrorist activities in Northern Ireland'. He recommended that, as members of a jury were open to intimidation, as were witnesses, courts should consist of a single High Court judge sitting without a jury. These special anti-terrorist courts became known as the 'Diplock Courts' and they are still in existence today. Lord Diplock also addressed the problem of the admissability of statements made in police custody. Hitherto, all confessions had to be 'voluntary' in the literal sense of the word, that is, made without any encouragement, inducement or pressure from the police. If a suspect wanted to confess, he did. If he did not, he said nothing. As a result, Lord Diplock believed that existing 'technical rules and practice' governing the admissability of statements were 'hampering the course of justice in the case of terrorist crimes'. He recommended therefore that, in future, any confession should be accepted by the court unless it was proved, 'on the balance of probabilities' to have been extracted as a result of 'torture' or 'inhuman or degrading treatment'.[8] Lord Diplock's recommendations were incorporated in the Government's Northern Ireland Emergency Provisions Act of 1973. The interpretation of what constituted 'torture' or 'inhuman or degrading treatment' was left to the Diplock judge. In a famous, or infamous, ruling, Lord Justice McGonigal said that a 'blow' did not necessarily render a statement inadmissible. His judgement in that particular case became known to republicans as the 'Torturers' Charter' since it appeared to sanction a degree of ill-treatment as long as it was not excessive. It was astonishing that such abuses recurred after the British Government had been condemned by the European Commission and Court of Human Rights – in 1976 and 1978 respectively – for its interrogation practices in the months following internment in 1971. When the political storm over the ill-treatment of suspects finally broke over the Labour Government's head, Mr Justice Bennett was appointed to investigate the allegations. He concluded that 'the uncertainty . . . about what is permissable and what is not, short of the use of physical violence or ill-treatment, may tempt police officers to see how far they can go and what they can get away with'.[9] Some police officers clearly had been tempted.

Tommy McKearney was one of the 1,308 terrorist suspects charged in 1977 alone.[10] Many were sentenced on statement evidence alone and charged with offences committed long before their arrest. McKearney was arrested on 19 October 1977 and charged with the murder of an off-duty, part-time UDR man called Stanley Adams. Adams was a postman who had been shot dead by the IRA on 28 October 1976 whilst delivering a letter to a remote farmhouse near Pomeroy in County Tyrone. The IRA had sent the letter to the address so they could lie in wait and kill Adams. To the IRA, Stanley Adams was a 'legitimate' target as he was a member of the security forces and never off duty, collecting intelligence on his rounds and feeding it back to the army. This was the IRA's justification for targeting all off-duty UDR men, whether postmen, milkmen or school-bus drivers. They were now all considered 'soft' targets in the front line as a result of the Government's change in security policy. Today, McKearney remains insistent that off-duty UDR men were indeed 'legitimate' targets. When I put it to him that Stanley Adams was a postman delivering a letter who was shot down in cold blood, he rejected the notion. McKearney was willing to address the question whilst never admitting the crime.

> An off-duty UDR man is a member of the British army. Now it is very naive and stretching credulity to breaking point to suggest that a man delivering the milk, delivering the mail, or driving a school bus sets aside his [military] role while delivering or driving: that he would ignore what he sees through the day, that he ceases to observe, that he ceases to record, that he ceases to report. Now, by anybody's standard, an intelligence officer for a regular army is carrying out a very necessary function without which the regular forces in uniform cannot and do not operate. It is a key pivotal point.

McKearney was taken to Castlereagh and interrogated for seven days under the Prevention of Terrorism Act (POTA) that permits a suspect to be detained for questioning for up to a week. The Emergency Provisions Act allows a suspect to be held for only three days. POTA was reserved for the hard men.

> For the best of seven days I was subjected to physical torture. For hours on end, I had several Special Branch officers holding and bending my wrists. One would hold the elbow, the other would bend the wrist – both wrists. It's a particularly painful experience. So painful that I recall very clearly that it was the first time I ever fainted. It might have been the third or the fourth day. What I do

remember clearly was that when I started to recover consciousness, I started to see polka dots. It was like reading comics or watching films when people 'see stars'.

But the most traumatic piece of torture came towards the end of the seven days. I think, looking back on it now, that the interrogators believed that they would make one last attempt to have me break. They brought in maybe four to six hefty policemen in civilian clothing. They pressed me to the floor and brought in a bin liner and put it over my head and started to tighten it around me so that I couldn't breathe. It was through that that I sustained several injuries, notably a black eye which was the most obvious sign.

Why should people believe you?

Well I don't make a great play of what happened to me. As a matter of fact when I was brought from the interrogation centre I was most reluctant even to talk about my torture with the doctor who examined me in the holding centre.

Whilst investigating the allegations and writing *Beating the Terrorists?*, I interviewed Dr Irwin, the police surgeon who, along with his colleague Dr Elliot at Gough, had courageously done a great deal to expose what was happening at Castlereagh and Gough Barracks. Dr Irwin went into his files and produced the medical examination he had carried out on Tommy McKearney. He noted that at the beginning of the examination, McKearney had been reluctant to complain or say anything about his interrogation.

He was pale, nervous and exhausted. He had a black eye that looked fairly recent and bruises whose colour suggested that they were five to six days old. His forehead was swollen and many of the muscles at the back of his neck, forearm and abdomen were swollen and tender. His fingers were trembling.[11]

Dr Irwin was in no doubt that McKearney had been ill-treated at Castlereagh. Nevertheless, his statement – which he never signed – was accepted by the court on the word of an RUC Inspector. McKearney was sentenced to twenty years for the murder of Stanley Adams.

At the height of the Castlereagh allegations, Sir John Hermon was the RUC Deputy Chief Constable in charge of Operations. Soon after he became Chief Constable, in 1980, he examined the record of complaints of Assaults During Interview (ADI) and collated them with the teams of interrogators. There were some signs of 'pattern' and, he says, adjustments were made accordingly. With rare exceptions, the allegations never surfaced again. By this time close-circuit television cameras had been installed in the interview rooms and the RUC had developed other ways of cracking the IRA's cells. Sir John Hermon has now retired. I asked him about what had happened at Castlereagh. Castlereagh was important, he said, not just because of the damage it did to the IRA but for other reasons too. In the seclusion of the interview rooms, away from the gaze of their comrades, suspects could be propositioned and recruited as informers by Special Branch.

Castlereagh caused a high degree of consternation within the IRA. They would have been concerned because people who were taken in for interviews could very well have been turned into a source – a 'converted terrorist' – and they [the IRA] wouldn't have known it. Indeed that did happen, and they would have been worried about it and certainly wanted to denigrate Castlereagh at every possible opportunity.

Why were some suspects ill-treated at Castlereagh?

Well, it was never intended that any suspects should be ill-treated.

But some were.

I couldn't deny that because I would say that they were. This was certainly not a policy, nor was it normal procedure. I am satisfied that there were some incidents that were done in a very clandestine way by some small number of officers.

Hermon was keen to point out the pressures the RUC had been under at this time, without offering it as justification for what happened.

In the 1970s and early 1980s, the police officers involved [in interrogation] were seeing mass murder on the streets. You can imagine the emotions, with police officers being murdered also. These people are human, and although that's no excuse, you can understand that if anyone did fall below the standards you set, you could see a reason why. Emotions were running very high. At that time, we had a detective probably investigating three or four murders on his own. That was the background to a lot of it.

How did Castlereagh damage the IRA?

It damaged them in many ways. It did result in very professional interrogations and made many suspects aware of what exactly they were doing which could have converted them into sources of information. It revealed a lot of intelligence. Even those not directly involved in incidents had some information and this allowed the

RUC to build up a very considerable information base which was available to the army and the secret service.

In the face of the Government's new security offensive, the IRA had to reorganize and regroup to avoid defeat. When Gerry Adams was released from 'Cage 11', he knew what had to be done.

Chapter Fifteen

Reassessment

In his New Year message for 1978, Roy Mason declared that 'the tide has turned against the terrorists and the message for 1978 is one of real hope'.[1] He had good reason for saying so. A record number of people had been charged with terrorist offences – 1,308 – and shootings and bombings were dramatically down. The tube of toothpaste was certainly being squeezed. Furthermore, Mason and Newman had stood up to a second loyalist strike in May 1977 and seen off its leader, Ian Paisley. The strike had been called to demand tougher security and a return to majority rule. Paisley had said he would resign if the strike failed.[2] He never did. The Queen too, had visited Northern Ireland in her Jubilee year and, by declaring the province safe for Her Majesty, Mason had called the Provisionals' bluff. Nor were the Government's successes all one-sided. The RUC's Regional Crime Squads had virtually smashed the UVF's structure and brought to justice Lenny Murphy, leader of the notorious loyalist murder gang, the 'Shankill Butchers', who had slaughtered Catholics with butchers' knives. The optimism generated was summed up by the award of the Nobel Peace Prize to Betty Williams and Mairead Corrigan, the leaders of the 'Peace People', a grass-roots, cross-community, apolitical movement that had taken to the streets to demand an end to IRA and loyalist violence. Against this background, the problem of Castlereagh and the human-rights issues it raised seemed of little importance.

One of the biggest coups of the year for the security forces North and South was the arrest of the Provisionals' Chief of Staff, Seamus Twomey, on the run for almost four years. Twomey was picked up in Dublin, having avoided arrest for so long in the North. His freedom of movement in Belfast during the truce, most notably during his appearance at the Easter Commemoration in 1975, had outraged loyalists. Twomey's run finally came to an end on 3 December 1977 when he was arrested by the Gárdái. On searching the flat where he had stayed in Dun Laoghaire, a few miles from Dublin, police found a document stuffed in a pencil case. Its contents were a dramatic insight into the Provisional IRA after the setback of the truce. The secret document was an IRA GHQ 'Staff Report', detailing how the IRA had reorganized to stave off potential defeat. It was almost certainly written much earlier in 1977. The Report was also seen as recognition of how successful British security policy had been.

> The three and seven day detention orders are breaking Volunteers, and it is the Republican Army's fault for not indoctrinating Volunteers with the psychological strength to resist interrogation.
>
> Coupled with this factor, which is contributing to our defeat, we are burdened with an inefficient infrastructure of commands, brigades, battalions and companies. This old system with which Brits and [Special] Branch are familiar has to be changed. We recommend reorganization and remotivation, the building of a new Irish Republican Army.
>
> We must emphasize a return to secrecy and strict discipline. *Army men must be in total control of all sections of the movement* [author's emphasis].
>
> We must gear ourselves towards long-term armed struggle based on putting unknown men and new recruits into a new structure. This new structure shall be a cell system.[3]

Each cell was to consist of four Volunteers. The theory was that members of one cell would not know who the members of the other cells were. This meant that the information available to any potential RUC interrogator would be severely circumscribed. Cells were also instructed to operate outside their own areas as often as possible, 'both to confuse Brit intelligence (which would thus increase our own security) and to expand our operational areas'. But the cell was not, and could not be, totally isolated from the main body of the local Brigade structure. Brigades and Battalions were kept for both practical and administrative purposes. Orders, intelligence, guns and bombs had to come from somewhere. Each cell would have a leader. This person would take his orders from the Brigade Operations Officer and would be guided by the Brigade's Intelligence Officer. The weapons and explosives would be provided by the Brigade's Quartermaster and direction would be given by the Brigade's Explosives' Officer. This meant that despite tight security, potentially one person from each cell would be in touch with at least two and possibly four senior members of the Brigade Staff. This new cellular structure was an improvement on the vulnerable and visible structure it had replaced but it did have its limitations. When, five years later, the 'supergrasses' began to give evidence against their former comrades, names of scores of IRA Volunteers came tumbling out. The cells were not watertight. Inside the compounds of the Maze prison, the prisoners were just as aware of the need for reorganization as was the IRA leadership outside. Many of them were in gaol because of the shortcomings of the existing structure. A manual known as the 'Green Book' was produced that became the IRA's handbook. In future all Volunteers had to read, absorb and be tested on it before being sworn in to the organization. Its first page is a copy of the Proclamation of 1916, to remind Volunteers what they are fighting for.

The 'Staff Report' found in Dun Laoghaire was as important for what it said about Sinn Fein as it was for what it said about the IRA. It concludes with a paragraph on the role of Sinn Fein which mirrors the notions of 'Active Abstentionism' and 'Active Republicanism' advocated by Gerry Adams' 'Brownie' columns.

> *Sinn Fein should come under Army organizers at all levels* [author's emphasis]. Sinn Fein should employ full-time organizers in big Republican areas.
>   Sinn Fein should be radicalized (under Army direction) and should agitate about social and economic issues which attack the welfare of the people. SF should be directed to infiltrate other organizations to win support for, and sympathy to, the Movement. SF should be re-educated and have a big role to play in publicity and propaganda dept., complaints and problems (making no room for RUC opportunism). It gains the respect of the people which in turn leads to increased support for the cell.

The document leaves no doubt which wing of the Republican Movement was to be in the driving seat. Although years later, for tactical, political and presentational reasons, the IRA and Sinn Fein were to pursue a policy of 'separate development', with each wing insisting on its separate identity, the relationship between the IRA and Sinn Fein always has been and remains umbilical. There is no reason to believe that the connection between the IRA and Sinn Fein outlined in the 1977 'Staff Report' has ever changed. The difference was that over the next twenty years as Sinn Fein met with increasing electoral success, a vindication of Adams' strategy, Sinn Fein's esteem and authority within the Republican Movement was greatly enhanced. Sinn Fein was no longer second class but an equal partner with the IRA. This did not necessarily mean that all members of Sinn Fein were members of the IRA. Far from it, although some did hold dual membership. A 'partnership' is how one senior Provisional described the relationship to me.

Volunteers did not need Twomey's document, however, to tell them that something had to be done. They knew it from what they saw happening all around them. Tommy McKearney who, prior to his arrest in 1977, was a senior figure in Tyrone, knew the IRA was in trouble.

> Time and attrition inflicted by the British sapped some of our morale and the ceasefire, of course, had had its effect too. That left us in a situation where we found that numbers were smaller, and a smaller number of men were carrying more and more responsibility on their shoulders. And this led of course directly to the reorganization and it also led to a great self-questioning and a great debate within not just the IRA but within the entire Republican Movement of 'how do we make progress from here?' That debate went on in parallel with the reorganization.
>
> It wasn't just a question of getting more recruits for the IRA. It was a much wider debate than that. It was how to bring the struggle forward in every sense. But more recruits for the Republican Army was part of the debate. One couldn't be separated from the other. It was a question of how to involve the population, the republican population, in the struggle.

In addition to changes at ground level, there was a major structural change at the top of the IRA. The Army Council still continued to direct the campaign and the GHQ staff in Dublin continued to provide the logistical and financial back-up but a new operational tier was placed between Dublin and the IRA's structure on the ground. It was called 'Northern Command' and was established around the end of 1976. Although it was thought to be operationally necessary, it also gave control over the prosecution of the 'war' to the Northerners who were fighting it. It was not a new idea. In the campaign in the forties, the IRA had operated with a Northern Command. But now the situation was completely different. Martin McGuinness is thought to have become its first Commander. (He is also alleged to have become Chief of Staff in 1978 after Gerry Adams' arrest, a position he is said to have held until 1982 – McGuinness denies this.) Northern Command was precisely what it said. It covered not just the Six Counties of Northern Ireland but the five border counties of the Republic: Donegal, Leitrim, Cavan, Monaghan and Louth. This extended area constituted what was known as the 'war zone'. The actual 'war' was fought in the Six Counties. The South was definitely off limits. Nevertheless, the five border counties provided IRA units with jumping-off points as well as a logistical base for supplies. They also provided rest and recuperation for Volunteers on the run.

The concept of the 'Long War' was born inside the Maze prison, although obviously with input from the IRA outside. It was the culmination of all that Adams and his colleagues had thought about and discussed, learning from their experience through the seventies. The notion held by the Volunteers in 1972, that the 'Brits' were going to be driven into the sea, had long been abandoned. The experience of the truce, if the prisoners did not know it already, meant that the British had no intention of going. If victory and the goal of 1916 was ever to be achieved, new strategies would have to be devised. Politics had to march hand in hand with 'armed struggle' and it was going to take a long time. The IRA's restructuring was part of that process. Brendan Hughes, one of Adams' closest colleagues, knew there was no other way.

> Change was necessary because of the damage that was done to the IRA and the damage that it had done to itself [during the truce]. By 1976 you had people who had been in gaol for five or six years and who'd studied the situation for that long. They had an idea and a plan to rebuild the whole Movement and they did so out of necessity. Also people were coming into the gaol with more ideas and a better outlook as to where the whole thing was going. That was the 'Long War' scenario. It wasn't going to end quickly. The IRA didn't have to go on bombing everywhere to get what we wanted. They could do it – and they would do it – for twenty years. But it wasn't going anywhere without the involvement in politics and without a mass movement.

Richard McAuley, who was also in gaol in the seventies, was equally aware of the pressing need for change.

> The British obviously were very consciously and deliberately at all times looking at their strategy, looking at their tactics and changing them to suit what they saw as the threat from republicans. And then, as republicans adapted to what the British were doing, the British then changed. There's this sort of constant 'to-ing and fro-ing' going on all the time. I'm sure right up until now.

McAuley was right. The British army commissioned its own intelligence assessment of the reorganized Provisional IRA. The review was intended to cover not just the IRA's new structures but its weaponry, technology and tactics. The analysis, carried out by Brigadier James Glover of the army's intelligence staff, was called 'Future Terrorist Trends'. The report was marked 'Secret' and given a restricted circulation within the Ministry of Defence in November 1978. Its purpose was to identify the direction in which the IRA might be going over the next five years so the army could develop its own counter measures. The aim was to stay ahead of the game. Remarkably, and it is still not known how, the report fell into the hands of the enemy and was published in *Republican News*. 'Brownie' could not have believed his luck. General Sir James Glover (as he now is) has no doubt that Adams was one of the prime architects of the 'Long War' strategy and the reorganization of the IRA.

> For some time we'd always thought that, sooner or later, a charismatic figure would emerge from within the ranks of the IRA who would succeed in transforming it from being the old-fashioned organization that it was into something very modern. It became evident that Adams was starting to fulfil this role, both when he was in the Maze and probably even more so when he was outside. One of the things I've never really quite been able to understand is how, whilst he was locked up in the Maze, his influence spread outside into the North and obviously trickled down to the South as well. His cohort was Martin McGuinness.
>
> What did we think of Adams at that stage? Well, first of all, he was a man who had respectable – that's a contradiction – terrorist credentials. He had, I think, run Ballymurphy – the Second Battalion – for a time. He had been interned, he had been released, and he'd been imprisoned again. So he was acceptable to the rank and file of the IRA because he'd been seen to have been drawn from their midst.

Brigadier Glover's report was a realistic and prophetic assessment of the nature, strength and motivation of the Provisional IRA in 1978. It was free from the general view that the Provisionals were mindless terrorists with very little support, surviving through mass intimidation of the population. Although Glover recognized that PIRA had been badly hit by security force action, he knew they were still a potentially powerful and dangerous adversary. There may have been some shortage of recruits but the reorganized IRA did not need the large number of members who had flocked to join in the early days. His report said:

> PIRA's organization is now such that a small number of activists can maintain a disproportionate level of violence. There is a substantial pool of young Fianna aspirants [the junior wing of the IRA], nurtured in a climate of violence, eagerly seeking promotion to full gun-carrying terrorist status and there is a steady release from the prisons of embittered and dedicated terrorists.

Brigadier Glover realised that the leadership had good material to lead.

Our evidence of the calibre of rank and file terrorists does not support the view that they are merely mindless hooligans drawn from the unemployed and unemployable. PIRA now trains and uses its members with some care. The active service units are for the most part manned by terrorists tempered by up to ten-years operational experience.

The mature terrorists, including, for instance, the leading bomb makers, are usually sufficiently cunning to avoid arrest. They are continually learning from their mistakes and developing their expertise. We can therefore expect to see increased professionalism and the greater exploitation of modern technology for terrorist purposes.[4]

Brigadier Glover's analysis was uncannily prophetic. He also calculated that the IRA was likely to extend its range of targets beyond members of the security forces, to 'top government officials, members of the judiciary, and senior members of the RUC and the Army'.

The report did not please all of Brigadier Glover's senior colleagues, however. It was not what they wanted to read but it was, as far as Glover was concerned, what they ought to know. That was its purpose.

It didn't find all that much favour and I always found it slightly ironic because I was accused of encouraging the enemy. I think it revealed for the first time the strength of the IRA's commitment to the 'Long War' and their own confidence in their ability to sustain it politically and their confidence that they had the wherewithal to sustain it with the people, the weapons and the public support.

It wasn't a message that British Governments really wanted to hear, was it? It wasn't a perception they held of the IRA.
No. Perhaps underneath it all, everyone realized that this was the likely way in which things were going to go. But, yes, at the time, it hadn't really been paraded in front of them in such an overt and, I hope, persuasive way.

Despite his predictions, General Glover never thought the 'Long War' would last so long. Few people did. But how were the IRA to be defeated?

One of the messages that was in that Report was that we believed they could not be defeated militarily. That again was a slightly unpopular message at the time because there was a school of thought that they could be brought to their knees by military means alone, which of course they can't. 'Defeated' is perhaps the wrong word. Peace will only reign when there is a political solution and the military situation has been contained. The IRA will never be totally defeated. The cause of republicanism will remain as long as the island of Ireland is divided.

Glover's report also left open the possibility of an unforeseen event, such as another 'Bloody Sunday', which could have incalculable repercussions on the situation. Such a situation was already developing in the Maze prison.

In the H-Blocks, the 'blanket men' were also reassessing their position. By 1978 there were nearly 300 'non-conforming' prisoners refusing to wear prison uniform. But the protest had failed to make any significant impact outside the prison walls beyond the blanket men's natural supporters. A 'Relatives' Action Committee' was formed and parades were held on the Falls Road and elsewhere, led by women wearing blankets surrounded by posters declaring, 'Free the Prisoners. Free the People.' But in the areas through which they marched, they were appealing to the converted. The Government, meanwhile, saw no reason to act as the prisoners and the protest were not a problem. Hell would freeze over before Roy Mason would ever contemplate the reintroduction of special category status. To him, 'people who may once have claimed an ideal are thugs and gangsters'.[5] The forces of law and order seemed to be winning and the blanket protest was seen by the Government as a last, desperate attempt by the IRA to salvage something from the wreckage. But that is not how it was seen inside the H-Blocks. Over the months and years the protest gathered a momentum of its own as the prisoners bonded ever closer, determined to maintain the principle that had led them to refuse to wear prison uniform. Outside, the IRA hit back on their behalf, targeting prison officers who were seen as the instruments of the Government's 'criminalization' policy. By the beginning of 1978, six prison officers had been killed since the abolition of special category status on 1 March 1976.

In the autumn of 1977, I made a programme called *Life Behind the Wire* that examined conditions inside the Maze prison. A feature of it was a remarkable interview with Desmond Irvine, Secretary of the Prison Officers' Association (POA) and who had worked at 'Long Kesh' since it opened in 1971. He had actively wanted to take part in the programme despite the Northern Ireland Office's wish that he did not. I remember saying goodnight to him at the end of a long talk about the prison and the proposed interview. He left saying he was looking forward to it. In the programme he talked about how the sentenced prisoners in the compounds saw themselves not as criminals but as men who had been fighting a war. He described their drills, military training and command structures. He said that prison officers were dealing with an army. Remarkably, for a loyalist prison officer, he said, without any sign of bitterness, that he understood why IRA prisoners felt the way they did.

> If one studies the history of republican prisoners, you will find that this was always a very strong point with them, that they would not wear prison clothes. So I don't think they do it mainly for publicity but they do it because it is their belief.

Do you respect them for doing it?

> I suppose one could say that a person who believes sincerely in what he is doing and is prepared to suffer for it, that there must be a measure of respect for him.

He then spoke movingly about the price paid by some prison officers. Six of them, he said, were now dead.

> One can think of wives who are now widows. Children who are now fatherless and parents who have lost sons. That's the cost to the members of the Prison Service. We have paid for devotion to duty by the life blood of some of our members.

A week after the programme, Desmond Irvine wrote to me, aware of the controversy his remarks had caused. What he had said in the interview was not Roy Mason's line. In his letter, dated 29 September 1977, he said that he had found the programme to be 'an accurate description of life at the Maze'.

> Regarding my own interview I have no complaints . . . you succeeded in giving an authentic representation of the views expressed by me. Congratulations have poured in from many sources including many messages from Great Britain.
>
> I was concerned about the reaction but there was praise from both staff and prisoners.
>
> I believe the programme will ease the burden borne by my members. *To be told by the spokesman of the Provos they respected my frank answers to your questions and they would act in a reciprocal manner, gives me grounds for believing we are entering a new phase when co-operation between staff and prisoners will improve* (author's emphasis).

A fortnight later the IRA shot Desmond Irvine dead. I felt sick. I received a phone call from a newspaper journalist in Belfast, asking how I felt about being responsible for his death. I went to his funeral and watched his coffin being lowered into the grave on a windy hillside on the outskirts of Belfast. I could not express my condolences to Irvine's widow as I was told she did not want to see me. I felt like stopping my reporting of Northern Ireland. I later received a verbal message from the IRA, saying they knew how I felt but Desmond Irvine had been killed because he was Secretary of the POA, not because he had appeared on television. In the chronology of deaths in the conflict, Desmond Irvine is yet another statistic: '7 October 1977. Off duty. (38). Shot shortly after leaving trade union office, Wellington Park, Malone, Belfast'.[6] Twelve more prison officers were to be killed. The most senior was Albert Miles, the Deputy Governor of the Maze, shot dead outside his home on 26 November 1978. To the prisoners, the IRA Volunteer who pulled the trigger was a hero. 'Bik' McFarlane later wrote that Miles' 'execution' gave him 'comfort' as he had been 'the chief perpetrator of the regime in the Blanket Blocks' and was killed in 'response to the barbarity of the screws by our comrades outside'.[7]

By the time Albert Miles had been shot dead, the protest had entered a new phase as blanket men were beginning to recognize that their protest was making little impact. This coincided with the arrival of Brendan Hughes in the H-Blocks. Hughes had been the IRA's OC in the compounds but had had to leave in 1977 when he was sentenced to five years for assault during a fracas with prison officers.[8] As the offence happened after 1 March 1976, Hughes lost his special category status and found himself shipped off to the H-Blocks and confronted with a prison uniform. It was a dramatic change from life in the 'cages'.

> Every morning I would go out from the cage and negotiate with the Governor. He would call me 'Brendan' or 'Mr Hughes'. It was a military situation where I was the representative of the prisoners and I got all the respect I was entitled to. One morning I was taken to court and sent back to the gaol, only this time I was put into the H-blocks. I was told to strip and given a prison uniform. I was called 'Hughes 704'. That morning I was called 'Mr Hughes'. And there I was that same afternoon being told that I was no longer a political prisoner and that I was 'Number 704. Hughes'. And obviously I refused to wear the prison uniform. It didn't matter whether it had arrows on it or Mickey Mouse, it was still the prison uniform.

Hughes was locked up in H5, the new block opened to accommodate the increasing number of non-conforming prisoners. His arrival was greeted enthusiastically by the blanket men. He was already a legendary figure and highly respected. He was bombarded with requests for news from outside, which the protesters were starved of. They had no radios, television or newspapers because they refused to conform to prison rules. Normally they would have got news from visits but because visits entailed putting on a prison uniform, they were out of the question. Some men had not seen their families for months. Soon afterwards, Hughes became OC of the 'Blocks'. He told his men what they knew already: that the blanket protest was going nowhere and changes had to be made. He suggested that they give it up, put on prison uniforms and make the prison system unworkable by sabotaging it from within. Bobby Sands, who had become the prisoners' Public Relations Officer (PRO), conveyed the suggestion to the prisoners and was met with a 'resounding and highly charged reaction'.[9] Hughes' proposal had no takers.

The protest had by now developed its own dynamic and it was this, perhaps more than anything else, that carried it forward. Allegations mounted of brutality by prison officers against the protestors. Many of them were probably true. The prison officers were loyalists and the prisoners were the enemy who had been slaughtering their fellow loyalists outside as well as their fellow prison officers. The blanket men did not enjoy a lot of sympathy. The Prison Service was twenty per cent understaffed and, as the number of prisoners increased as Castlereagh and the Diplock Courts – the 'conveyor belt system' as the Provisionals dubbed it – filled up the H-Blocks, there was an urgent need for new prison-officer recruits. I later asked one senior Prison Service official about the allegations of brutality, to be told that, given the manpower crisis, the screening of recruits was not as rigorous as it should have been. Historically, the UDR had the same problem.

Following the rejection of Hughes' suggestion of wearing prison uniform, the prisoners had to decide what to do. In March 1978, the 'no-wash' protest began which, to the world outside, became known as the 'dirty protest'. The prisoners felt 'no-wash' was more dignified. There are different accounts as to how it began but all prisoners are agreed that it was the result of prison officers' brutality. According to Hughes, men refused to leave their cells to wash and go to the toilet because every time they did they were 'harassed' by prison officers. Refusing to leave their cells was a protest in itself. The prisoners, therefore, urinated and defecated in the chamber pots with which they were provided. The prison officers would then come round with a 'big bin' which they would fill from the pots in the cells. The situation escalated when prisoners refused to empty their urine and excreta into the bin. Prison officers then, according to Hughes, started to kick the pots over, spilling their stinking contents all over the cell floor. Finally the prisoners poured their urine under the door and built bread dams to stop it running back in again. But that left the problem of what to do with the excreta. In the end, Hughes, as OC, ordered them to daub it on the walls.

> It was me that gave the order to do that. Anybody who felt they could not do it, was not ordered to do it.
> **Whose idea was it?**
> I don't know whose idea it was or where it came from. Other people were suggesting that we smear excreta on ourselves. If the first step hadn't come about, that was the alternative – to smear ourselves with excreta. It was a step that I wasn't prepared to take.

To outsiders, it may seem petty that the situation was allowed to escalate in this way. The problem was that neither side was prepared to give in. Each needed to show the other that it was the stronger. Prisoners felt they held the moral high ground. Prison officers considered them scum. The intensity of the situation, with men locked in their cells for twenty-four hours a day, being beaten, they claimed, by prison officers on a regular basis, was a recipe for further conflict not compromise.

The moment when prisoners first smeared their excreta on the walls remains a disturbing memory for many. Gerard Hodgkins, who had lied about his age to join the IRA during the truce, was only nineteen years old. He had no idea that joining would come to this.

> I just smeared it on the wall. I ripped off a lump of the mattress to do it with. You were going against your whole socialization of how you were brought up. You were going against everything you'd ever learned about basic hygiene and manners and stuff like that. I lived like this from 1978 to 1981 – for three years. After a time, you became accustomed to it.
> The maggots, for example. I mean, nobody likes maggots. You'd be repelled by them. I don't think I could touch a maggot now. If there was one sitting here, you know, I'd flick it away or get somebody else to do it. But you became so accustomed to them being in the cell, especially when winter was coming in and it was cold. They must sense where warmth is. You were literally waking up in the morning and there were maggots in the bed with you. It just gets to the stage where you just brush them off. I think the human spirit can become accustomed to any environment.

On 31 July 1978, four months into the 'no-wash' protest, Cardinal Tomas O'Fiaich, the Roman Catholic Primate of All Ireland, visited the H-Blocks. The Cardinal understood the IRA and, being himself a nationalist from

Crossmaglen, knew what motivated the prison protest. The church was becoming increasingly concerned about the lack of resolution to the protest and the continuing violence which it believed it fuelled. He was appalled at what he found and did not mince his words in the statement he made when he left.

> Having spent the whole of Sunday in the prison, I was shocked at the inhuman conditions prevailing in H-Blocks three, four and five, where over 300 prisoners were incarcerated. One would hardly allow an animal to remain in such conditions, let alone a human being. The nearest approach to it I have seen was the spectacle of hundreds of homeless people living in sewer pipes in the slums of Calcutta. The stench and filth in some cells, with the remains of rotten food and human excreta scattered around the walls, was absolutely unbelievable. I met two of them and I was unable to speak for fear of vomiting.

In the prison, morale soared. Here at last was someone prepared to tell the world what conditions were really like inside the H-Blocks. Cardinal O'Fiaich's standing within the community meant that people would listen. Irish America had a field day as money and support for the protest began to pour in from across the Atlantic, to the dismay of the British authorities.

Conditions inside the Blocks continued however, becoming so unbearable that in time some prisoners came off the protest, unable to stand it any longer. They became known as 'squeaky booters' because of the noise their new boots made as they walked off down the prison wing to a cleaner life and a prison uniform. The name was spat out with venom by those who stayed behind. Did Gerard Hodgkins ever consider becoming a 'squeaky booter'?

> No. I had my times when you'd be depressed. You'd be going into depressions and you'd wonder about it. Is this ever going to end? But I just couldn't bring myself to wear the uniform, you know. There's times where you get depressed and you question what you're doing and the thought crosses your mind. But I just couldn't do it. I don't think I could have lived with myself. It was a unique experience. That whole period of history within the prisons was something that nobody planned. It wasn't sort of, 'right, we'll do that and then we'll go to bed and then we'll go to sleep'. It all just happened and there was a camaraderie that came with it and I've never experienced a bond like it since then.

One of the first orders that Brendan Hughes gave on becoming the Block's OC was that visits should be taken once more, despite the fact that this meant putting on prison uniform. If prisoners were to beat the system they could not do so without communication and support from outside. The 'uniform' would be put on for the visit and taken off again immediately the visit was over. Mothers now saw their sons, in some cases for the first time in over two years. Phelim O'Hagan, son of the veteran Army Council member, Joe 'J B' O'Hagan, had been sentenced for the murder of a policeman in 1977. When his mother, Bernadette, received the permitted visit immediately after her son received his sentence, he told her he would not be putting on a uniform to come out on visits and therefore he may not see her again for a long time. Bernadette did not believe he was a criminal, and respected her son's decision. But she had no idea it would be two years and three months before she saw him next. What she eventually saw horrified her.

From what I could see of his face behind the beard, he was like marble. It's still very vivid in my mind what he looked like, with the long, straggly beard and the long, fine hair and the white face behind it. It was really shocking after him going in as a fresh-faced youth of twenty-two. I saw somebody that I couldn't put an age to. The most remarkable thing about him was his hands. They were really, really, cold – again just like cold, white marble.

You used to think, 'God, it must be terrible when they finally come out and when you come face to face with them on a visit. But at no time ever in all of my visits did I ever detect anything obnoxious. There was never any bad smell. Nothing. I don't know how they managed to keep themselves so clean and so presentable when they did come out on their visits. It was remarkable.

Thankfully I didn't cry. I have never, ever cried, in front of any of my children. Any tears I shed were at home.

But Brendan Hughes' call for visits was not out of any sense of philanthropy but so that messages could be passed secretly between the prisoners and the leadership outside. The messages were known as 'comms' (communications). They were written, both inside and outside the prison, in the tiniest writing on roll-your-own cigarette papers or toilet paper, wrapped in cling film and then transferred during visits, often during a kiss. If there was danger of detection, the 'comm' would be swallowed to be excreted later. In this way contact was once again established with the world outside. But it was not just 'comms' that were smuggled into the H-Blocks. Writing materials, tobacco, and even

tiny radios were all smuggled in, not orally but anally. Brendan Hughes
became an expert.

> If the packages were small enough, they could be swallowed or kept
> in the mouth under the tongue. The bigger parcels, like the pens
> and tobacco and other things, had to come in another way. If you
> could, you saved a bit of margarine or butter from your breakfast
> that morning and took it with you when you were brought out
> of the cell. They took you up to a small room at the top of the
> wing and all the uniforms were lined up there. As soon as you got
> the trousers on, you ripped the bottom off them to expose your
> back-end. Before you went out to the visit, you rubbed a bit of the
> margarine or butter on your rear-end. So when you got the parcel
> on the visit, you had to get your hand in between your legs and pass
> the thing up your rear-end. That's how most things came in. Radios
> came in that way. Everything came in that way. It took a wee bit
> of skill and sleight of hand to do it. And you had to be quick.

And weapons could come in that way?

> Weapons could have come in in that way. Small weapons. Yes.
> So that's how we started to organize.

Of course the prison authorities realized what was happening and knew
that there was a limit to what the human mouth could hide or the throat
swallow. If they found a radio in the H–Blocks, they knew there was only
one way in which it could have come in. Counter measures were put
in place known as the 'strip' or 'mirror' search. The description suggests
what happened. A prisoner had his anus searched for contraband goods.
The normal way was to make him stand over a mirror with his legs apart
whilst a torch was shone up his back passage. If anything was discovered,
it was pulled out with rubber gloves. Occasionally a trip to the prison
hospital was necessary, where forceps would be used. But, according to
some prisoners, there was an even more humiliating procedure where
a man was up-ended, his legs thrust apart and a gloved hand pushed
down his anus. These searches often resulted in violent confrontation
between prisoners and prison officers. Tommy Gorman recalls suffering
at the hands of one particular officer who was subsequently killed by
Gorman's 'comrades outside'.

> This man took great delight in torturing people throughout his time
> when he was in the prison. His particular forte was when he took
> part in the mirror searches. We were forced over a mirror and he
> would probe your anus with rubber gloves. He would then ask you

to open your mouth to check inside and when you opened your mouth he'd put his fingers in. He didn't let up. He rejoiced in people's suffering – until the IRA finally caught up with him.

But the reason those sort of searches were being done was because prisoners were smuggling materials in up their back passage. The searches had to happen to stop the prisoners getting what they were getting.

No. We seen the searches as part of the whole attempt to demoralize us and torture us.

Forced washing was another point of violent confrontation. The prison authorities feared that conditions inside the H–Blocks had become so insanitary that an epidemic might break out. Contractors were brought in to steam-clean the cells, only to find that when the prisoners returned they would cover them with excreta once again. Because the protestors refused to wash, they had to be forcefully scrubbed down. Leo Green, serving life for the murder of an RUC Inspector, was forcibly washed many times.

You were dragged to the top of the wing, where you were held in a chair and your head was shaved and your beard was shaved. Then you were dragged over to the bath and dropped into it and told to wash. Nobody washed. So then prison staff, the 'screws', would have soaped up and down your legs and used a wee, hard brush with a handle on it to wash your testicles. They held you standing up and ran this brush up and down your testicles. Then you were dragged out of the bath and painted head to foot with some sort of disinfectant. You were then dragged to an empty wing and put in a clean cell.

But if you conformed, if you had done as instructed, then you wouldn't have had to live in these conditions would you?

Well, if you had done what was instructed, you would have accepted that you were a criminal.

According to the prisoners, beatings by the prison officers became a way of life. They admit that not all of the officers were brutal but insist that many of them were. Laurence McKeown, serving life for murder, says that he was often a target.

It seemed to be turned on and off. Certain people seemed to get more beatings than others. It could happen any time a prison officer decided to do a cell search. Sometimes even getting a beating was a relief because you were sitting there expecting it to come. When it did come, it brought a sense of release and you thought, 'Well, at least that won't happen to me again for the rest of the day'. But sometimes it did.

But you were hardened IRA men.

Well, we were hardened IRA men but that word sounds like something out of a novel or something like that. But the average age of people there was about twenty years of age, which meant that there were people there who were seventeen or eighteen. Seeing them together as a collection in the canteen or for mass, they looked anything but like 'hardened IRA men'. They're naked for a start and they're ordinary, because these are the kind of people who are in the IRA, ordinary people. They're young and they're in a situation where their captors are all either ex-British army or they're from loyalist areas or loyalists themselves. So they're at the mercy of a group that doesn't wish to show any mercy and in fact is delighted to have an opportunity to have a go at these IRA men who are now unarmed and naked in their cells. How they behave towards them is totally at their whim.

The hatred prison officers and prisoners felt for each other was mutual and lasting. Nothing brought it home to me more forcefully than a production of Bobby Sands' epic 'The Crime of Castlereagh' which I watched in a parochial hall in West Belfast. It was staged by former prisoners and prisoners out on parole or home leave. One scene depicted a prisoner being turned upside down whilst a prison officer with rubber gloves gloatingly searched his anus. As the officer was walking off stage, a shot rang out and he fell down dead. It was a dramatic piece of theatre. The packed audience, among whom were many of the Republican Movement's most prominent figures, including members of the leadership, broke out in spontaneous applause and cheering. It was a chilling moment.

But the 'no-wash' protest failed to move the British Government, and had little effect on the British public. But if, after almost three years, the demand for 'political status' had made no impression on the Labour Government, it was even less likely to affect the Conservative Government that came to power on 3 May 1979, when Margaret Thatcher became Britain's first woman Prime Minister. The prisoners had only one option left. The Hunger Strike. Most of them had never heard of the 'Iron Lady'. They soon would.

Chapter Sixteen

Hunger Strike: Fighting

On Monday morning, 27 August 1979, General Glover was flying back from Derry to Army Headquarters at Lisburn. It was a very misty morning and the haze hung over the ridge of the Sperrin mountains that separate the east from the west of the province. Even in summer, hailstones sometimes lash their top. Sitting in the helicopter, a distorted message came over the headset. Something about a Lord somebody or other being murdered in the South. The name was indistinct over the crackling radio. Glover tried unsuccessfully to find out more. When he landed on the heli-pad at Army Headquarters, an officer rushed up and asked if he had heard that Lord Mountbatten had been murdered in an IRA attack in Mullaghmore, County Sligo. Sir James still remembers the shock. It was exactly the kind of attack he had predicted in his report only nine months earlier. The target was prestige and the remote-control bomb was technically sophisticated.

Lord Louis Mountbatten, the Supreme Allied Commander in South-East Asia during the Second World War and the last British Viceroy of India, had spent holidays in the coastal village of Mullaghmore every summer for the past thirty years. He had never had a bodyguard. He had clearly been watched by the IRA. That morning, as the seventy-nine-year-old Earl went out on his thirty-foot boat, *Shadow V*, with his fourteen-year-old grandson, the elderly dowager Lady Brabourne and a young boatman, a fifty-pound bomb exploded on board, triggered from the shore by a remote-control device. All four were killed in the blast.[1] The bomb had been placed under the floorboards of the boat.

Whilst the army was dealing with the aftermath of Mullaghmore, word came through of a second disaster. The carnage was even greater. That same afternoon, a convoy of soldiers from the Second Battalion, the Parachute Regiment, were driving from the army base at Ballykinler at the tip of County Down to Newry in County Armagh in order to relieve the Queen's Own Highlanders who, their tour of duty over, were eagerly awaiting their return to Britain. The dual carriageway ran along the side of Carlingford Lough, the stretch of water separating Northern Ireland from the Republic. As the convoy of two four-ton trucks and a landrover passed a hay lorry at the side of the road near Warrenpoint, the lorry exploded with devastating effect. The explosives, estimated to be half a ton, were packed in milk churns and triggered by remote control from the IRA's vantage point in the safety of the Republic across the water. The mechanism was simple: a radio transmitter. Six soldiers died in the blast. Many, like 'Jim', received horrendous injuries.

> I don't remember a sound as such. It's a sensation. It's as if you were stood next to Niagara Falls with your eyes shut and didn't know you were there, there's this sensation of millions of gallons of water falling. But it's not a noise. It's a sensation rather than a noise. I can remember my legs being moved and then 'bang'. For I think about seven days, I had no recollection of anything.
> **What were your injuries?**
> The left side of my skull is plastic. I lost my left eye. I've got the greater part of my left forearm missing and there's a steel nail through the bone in my forearm.

Those who could ran for cover as they came under sniper fire and took shelter by the Gate Lodge of Narrow Water Castle close by. The Paras opened fire against the snipers on the other side, accidentally killing a tourist. The survivors immediately radioed the Queen's Own Highlanders in Newry for help. A Wessex helicopter arrived with a 'quick reaction force' and hovered cautiously above the horrendous scene before landing in the safest spot in a field behind the Gate Lodge. It was barely twenty-five minutes after the hay lorry had exploded. A second explosion ripped through the Gate Lodge, killing twelve more soldiers, including the Commanding Officer of the Queen's Own Highlanders, Lieutenant Colonel David Blair. This second bomb, estimated to have contained a ton of explosives, was also detonated by remote control from across the border. Colonel Blair was so close to the explosion that his remains were never found.[2] It was the army's single biggest loss in the 'Troubles' and the Parachute Regiment's worst since Arnhem. Despite personal feelings, General Glover had to admire the sophistication of the IRA's attack, 'arguably the most successful and certainly one of the best planned IRA attacks of the whole campaign.' To the Provisionals it was revenge for what the Paras had done on 'Bloody Sunday'. A slogan soon appeared on the wall opposite Sinn Fein's headquarters on the Falls Road, 'Thirteen gone and not forgotten – we got eighteen and Mountbatten'.

*   *   *

In the stinking cells of the H-Blocks there was jubilation amongst the protesters. Their 'comrades on the outside' had, in the space of a few hours, struck a devastating double blow at the British establishment and British army. Their OC Brendan Hughes was matter of fact.

> We were locked in the cells. We were getting badly treated. We were getting beaten and abused. As far as most of the prisoners in the gaol were concerned at that time, that type of military operation taking place on the outside was us hitting back at what they were doing to us. Certainly there was nobody going to cry over Mountbatten or the soldiers getting killed.

In January 1980, the prisoners issued a statement defining exactly what they meant by 'political status'. They explained it in the form of 'Five Demands':

1. The right not to wear prison uniform.
2. The right not to do prison work.
3. The right to associate freely with other prisoners.
4. The right to a weekly visit, letter and parcel and the right to organize educational and recreational pursuits.
5. Full restoration of remission lost through the protest.

To anyone not familiar with the history of the protest, the 'Five Demands' seemed eminently reasonable. That is why they were issued. Furthermore, as 'Bik' McFarlane pointed out, they contained no 'emotive terminology' so they gave 'the Brits plenty of room to manoeuvre'.[3] With the 'Five Demands' at the forefront, a campaign was begun to enlist broad support for the prisoners. Supporting their 'just' demands did not necessarily mean supporting the IRA. Tactically and skilfully, the two issues were divorced. It became a matter of supporting civilized conditions for prisoners, not supporting the 'men of violence'. Throughout 1980, Cardinal O'Fiaich, Bishop Edward Daly of Derry and other church leaders negotiated with the new Northern Ireland Secretary, Humphrey Atkins, to try to reach a way out of the impasse and avoid the hunger strike that was looming. It was the prisoners' weapon of last resort. The discussions made little progress and in February, thirty IRA women prisoners in Armagh gaol joined the protest, smearing their cells as their male comrades had done. The impasse remained. In June 1980, the Government gained support for its stand when the European Commission of Human Rights rejected a case brought by Kieran Nugent, the first 'blanket man', and three other prisoners, that conditions inside the Maze were 'inhuman'. The

Commission ruled that the conditions were self-inflicted and 'designed to enlist sympathy for the [prisoners'] political aims'. The Commission did also claim, however, that the Government was being 'inflexible'.

By the autumn of 1980, Cardinal O'Fiaich and Bishop Daly felt they had reached the end of the road. O'Fiaich felt betrayed. On returning from Rome, he had met Bishop Daly in London and gone to the Northern Ireland Office to discuss the growing crisis with NIO officials. They came away thinking that the Government had conceded the prisoners' right to wear their own clothes. They had either misunderstood or the officials had been imprecise. In fact, what the NIO officials had been talking about was 'civilian-type clothing'. The Government had moved a little but not enough for the prisoners. Perhaps the NIO quite honestly thought that this would be an acceptable compromise but if they did, they completely miscalculated the mood of the prisoners after four years of protest. One official told me that civil servants had all been 'rushing around buying Marks and Spencer's clothes'. The problem was not, he said, due to 'perfidious Albion' but excessive expectations on the part of the prisoners. Around that time I also spoke to another NIO official in Belfast, who opened a desk drawer and produced a pile of 'civilian-type clothing'. It was an example of what the NIO meant. There was a nylon shirt, still wrapped in cellophane, trousers and pullover. They had obviously been bought in some chain store. They were not particularly elegant but they were, undoubtedly, 'civilian'. What did I think? I said the prisoners would never accept it. If the NIO was going to provide these 'civilian' clothes, why not let the prisoners wear their own clothes and save money? There was a principle involved, claimed the official. Indeed there was for both sides. That was the problem. Four years into the protest, neither side was prepared to give in. The stakes were too high.

In the H-Blocks, discussion of a hunger strike was not new. It had been considered the previous year, in the summer of 1979, when Pope John Paul visited Ireland, but it had been rejected at that time. The IRA leadership was against it and, according to the IRA's General Order Number Four, Volunteers are forbidden to undertake hunger strikes without the express sanction of GHQ. The penalty for breach of this Order was dismissal.

The IRA leadership was against a hunger strike for several reasons. They feared it might dissipate resources and energies from the 'war'; they did not believe there would be sufficient mass support to sustain a long and traumatic campaign; and they were not convinced it was a battle they could win. There was always the abiding fear that if the British broke the men within, they would break the men without. The prisoners could not afford to be beaten. The H-Blocks had become the second front in the 'war'. The Army Council faced a dilemma: although it did not want a hunger strike and knew it could order the prisoners not to go ahead, it feared that given the intensity of feeling inside the Blocks, the order might not be obeyed. If Brendan Hughes and his men decided to proceed as a result of the prisoners' collective decision, the Army Council faced the prospect of revolt against its authority. Laurence McKeown, who was to go seventy days on hunger strike, to the point of death, was aware of the Army Council's dilemma.

The IRA has a bigger agenda than what's happening in the prisons. It had come out of the 1975 ceasefire, had started to get reorganized and by 1978–79 was again becoming fairly effective. In the IRA's eyes at that time, the prisons were a bit of a side issue, although the prisons had greatly held the struggle together during a difficult period.

If the IRA had ordered you not to go on hunger strike, would that order have been disobeyed?

I think at that time it probably would. By that stage, what had happened in the gaol was that the comradeship had built up so much that this had become totally our world. If the IRA had said, 'no hunger strike', it would have been an absolute disaster because people would have gone on hunger strike anyway and it would have caused a major split within the IRA. So, the IRA had to go along with it.

The Army Council had to accept the inevitable. The notion that the IRA outside manipulated the hunger strike and encouraged the prisoners to put their lives on the line is simply not true.

As OC of the H–Blocks, Brendan Hughes asked the OCs of H3, H4 and H5 for volunteers. By now there were around 500 prisoners on the protest. Everyone who considered putting his name forward knew that, failing recognition of the Five Demands, it was to be a hunger strike to the death. Seán MacStiofáin had lost credibility within the Republican Movement because he had not seen to the end his fifty-seven day hunger strike in the Republic's Curragh prison.[4]

Hughes discussed strategy with Bobby Sands, the prisoners' PRO, in the cell next door. They communicated by talking via the heating pipe running along the back of all the cells. The rest of the Blocks were kept informed by messages passed to other prisoners during visits. Hughes and Sands discussed how many people should go on hunger strike and how it should be run. Hughes wished to end the 'no-wash' protest, 'one way or the other'. In the end, 170 prisoners volunteered to go on hunger strike. Seven prisoners were selected who, geographically, represented the whole of Northern Ireland. Brendan Hughes was to lead the strike as the IRA's representative from Belfast. Joining him were Tommy McKearney from

Tyrone, Raymond McCartney from Derry city, Leo Green from Lurgan, Thomas McFeeley from County Derry, and Sean McKenna from South Armagh. The Irish National Liberation Army (INLA) prisoners had also decided to join forces with the Provisionals and added a seventh person to the hunger strike, John Nixon from Armagh city. Tactically it had been decided that the seven men would all go on hunger strike together, meaning that the strike was only as strong as its weakest link. It turned out to be a mistake. The other miscalculation that Hughes admits was misreading the new Prime Minister, Margaret Thatcher. 'If we had known anything about Thatcher and her personality perhaps we mayn't have embarked on the hunger strike at that stage.' With Hughes on the hunger strike, the role of OC passed to Bobby Sands and 'Bik' McFarlane took over as PRO.

On 10 October 1980, Sinn Fein announced that a hunger strike would begin on 27 October. The Government responded with an official announcement that they were scrapping prison uniform in favour of civilian-type clothing for prisoners. But that was only half a demand met; there were still four and a half to go. The prisoners were not interested. It was their *own* clothes or nothing.

After twelve days on strike, the seven were moved to A wing in H-Block 3, which had been set aside as a hospital wing some time previously in case an epidemic broke out. Although the move brought the hunger strikers together, it made communication with the other prisoners and the outside leadership more difficult. Priests and lawyers became the intermediaries. In the other Blocks, the prisoners were kept informed of events outside through a crystal set smuggled in by Sands. During visits Sands had also established contact with Father Brendan Meagher, a priest from Dundalk who was to become the mediator between the prisoners and the British Government. The prisoners code-named him 'The Angel'.[5] Sands gradually got the message from Father Meagher that 'own clothes' would not necessarily present an obstacle to a settlement.[6] On 1 December the hunger strike was joined by three female IRA prisoners from Armagh gaol: Mary Doyle, Mairead Nugent and Mairead Farrell. Mairead Farrell was to be shot dead by the SAS in Gibraltar eight years later. The Armagh women prisoners already had the right to wear their own clothes and it was thought that this, plus possible improvements in their regime, might prove a basis for resolving the conflict. The British showed no sign of moving, however, despite repeated representations made by Cardinal O'Fiaich and the Catholic church. Compromise was not a word in Mrs Thatcher's vocabulary. She had just lost one of her closest political colleagues, Airey Neave, in an INLA car-bomb attack and seen Lord Mountbatten and eighteen of her soldiers blown up on the same day by the Provisionals. 'I want this to be utterly clear,' she announced. 'There can be no political justification for murder or any other crime. The Government will never concede political status to the hunger strikers or to any others convicted of criminal offences in the province.'[7] Her Secretary of State, Humphrey Atkins, restated the Government's position on 10 December 1980. The prisoners' response was to add twenty-three more volunteers to the hunger strike. By this time, all the strikers had been transferred from the emergency hospital wing in H3 to the Maze prison hospital. The situation was becoming critical. Tommy McKearney was drifting in and out of consciousness.

> I was in extreme pain. I'd been vomiting. I was running a temperature and I had a severe headache. I hoped that a solution would be arrived at which would not end in death, but in some ways there was a feeling going through me that if this pain were to continue, death would be a welcome arrival. If I could only remove the pain, I would die happy.
>
> **You would have gone through with it?**
> Yes, I was prepared to go through with it. It's always impossible to say at the last crucial moment but I was very close to it.

His mother visited him on 18 December in what she thought were his final hours. He had been on hunger strike for fifty-three days.

> He was lying in the hospital bed. He was very thin and very frail. He was blind at that stage. He could still talk and he could understand what were you talking about. The doctor said he had roughly about twelve hours left to live. It was an awful time having to walk out and thinking you had to come back and put him in a coffin.
>
> **Did you ask him to come off, to end his hunger strike?**
> No. I didn't feel I had the right to ask him that.
>
> **What did he say to you?**
> He just said, 'Goodbye, Mother'.

Tommy McKearney was fading fast but Sean McKenna was fading faster. Death seemed only a few hours away.

But behind the scenes, things had been moving. An NIO official had visited the hunger strikers in the prison hospital and given indications of the kind of changes that might occur in the prison regime if the hunger strike were called off. The indications were made in writing. Brendan Hughes appears not to have said a great deal. By now a more important initiative was in play. 'The Contact', the person from the North who had played such a critical role as intermediary in setting up the 1975 truce, emerged from the shadows once again to reactivate the channel that became code-named the 'Mountain Climber'. It seems that the Provisionals' leadership got in touch and told him they wanted a settlement. The Contact then passed this message on to Michael Oatley, the MI6 officer with whom he had dealt before and during the truce. Oatley, presumably having consulted the Northern Ireland Office, who, in turn, may have consulted higher authorities given the sensitive nature of the mission, personally took a document over to Belfast, probably on 18 December. Speed was of the essence as by now Sean McKenna was close to death. That morning, Father Meagher had visited Brendan Hughes in the prison hospital to tell him he believed an honourable settlement was in the offing and that a document was on its way from London. He had seen a précis, he claimed. Hughes told the priest to visit the other hunger strikers and explain the situation. Any decision to be taken, had to be taken collectively. Father Meagher went round the other hunger strikers and relayed the message. No one can remember the precise detail of what he said – they had, after all, been on hunger strike for fifty-three days – but none of them had any doubt that the substance of the Five Demands was potentially there. Leo Green reflected what all of them felt.

> As I remember, it was an explanation that what we had set out to achieve in terms of the Five Demands would become available. In terms of the actual wording, I don't remember, but I certainly believed that it meant that we would have been allowed to wear our own clothes and there would have been no more compulsion to do prison work.

All the prisoners agreed they should wait for the promised document to see the offer in writing. Father Meagher said it was on its way and should be with them that evening. After the midday meal, Sands walked across to the prison hospital, giving the 'thumbs up' sign on the way. Later that afternoon, however, there was a crisis. Sean McKenna, who was lapsing in and out of a coma, was suddenly transferred to the military hospital at Musgrave Park. Was it brinkmanship with the 'Brits' turning the screw? What were the hunger strikers to do? Wait for the document to arrive and risk letting their comrade die, or call off the hunger strike on the word of the priest and save Sean McKenna's life? At around six o'clock that evening, Hughes took the decision to call off the hunger strike. The others agreed. Hughes was not prepared to let Sean McKenna die, believing that if anyone was to die, it should be him.

Meanwhile the document had arrived in Northern Ireland that afternoon. The Contact drove to Aldergrove Airport to meet Michael Oatley and Father Meagher, who was acting as the direct link between the prisoners. Oatley handed over the document to the priest. It was then taken to a safe house on the Falls Road where the Provisionals' leadership was waiting. They were dismayed by what they read. The document was over thirty pages long and much of it was a restatement of the Government's position. It was considered much too vague. As they were pouring over the fine print, Tom Hartley rushed in to relate that the hunger strike was over. The news was 'a bolt from out of the blue' and it was thought that the prisoners had got their demands. Father Meagher took the document, or a copy of it, and returned to the prison with it around midnight. The hunger strike was by now over. When the strikers read the document, it seemed to be much as Father Meagher had outlined that morning. The document suggested that once the hunger strike was over, clothing would not necessarily be a problem and there could be movement on the other issues like prison work. Sands went round the prisoners, the thirty-page document in his hand, and relayed the news. It was not what Sands and the Provisionals outside wanted − it was far too imprecise − but it was enough for the hunger strikers, confronted with the imminent death of their comrade, Sean McKenna. One of the prisoners, Seanna Walsh, remembered hearing Bobby Sands.

> Bobby said there was absolutely nothing concrete in the document but it was so wide open, he could drive a bus through it . . . that if he had got the Brits around the table to negotiate on the basis of the document, he said he could have 'taken the trousers off them'. If he negotiated now that it was ended, he just didn't know how much leeway he would be able to claw back.[8]

Hughes, Sands and McFarlane could no longer negotiate from a position of strength, but were at the mercy of the 'Brits' goodwill. Had they been outmanoeuvred? Had Sean McKenna's transfer to Musgrave Park been a clever move to break their will? In spite of such misgivings in the Maze, there was euphoria that night. The prisoners thought they had won. The following morning Danny Morrison, one of the Provisionals' leadership, went into the Maze and talked to Bobby Sands. He said the leadership wanted the document to be worked on the basis of a 'principled settlement'. They wanted the situation to end. Sands said he would work it.

It is difficult to know precisely why the issue was not resolved, given the willingness of the prisoners to 'work it'. The Governor of the Maze at the time, Stanley Hilditch, has never given his side of the story and, although I contacted him, he still did not want to talk. Looking at what subsequently happened, it is hard to avoid the conclusion that it was a mixture of intransigence and inflexibility on the part of the prison authorities that was to blame. Had they been prepared to work the agreement, which does appear to have been suitably vague, and had the Government encouraged them to do so, the situation would probably have been resolved. The failure to reach a solution, when one appeared eminently possible, is one of the great 'if only's of history. If agreement had been reached there would have been no second hunger strike with ten men dead, and no fresh avalanche of support for the IRA and Sinn Fein.

Discussion followed between Sands and Governor Hilditch, with each side suggesting a way to move forward. The Government had made it clear that no changes could be made in the prison regime until the prisoners ended their 'no-wash' protest which had continued throughout and after the hunger strike. But prisoners were only prepared to do this when they had got what they wanted. As they saw it, the administration wanted them to conform for thirty days before allowing them to wear their own clothes, which appeared to be a device to 'make us eat dirt and allow them to claim outright victory'.[9] Sands and the prisoners worked out various compromises, one of which being that they should go 'on the sick' so they could wear pyjamas and dressing gowns whilst they were transferred to clean wings. Another was that they should be allowed to wear football kit whilst the transfer was made. Neither was acceptable. Christmas 1980 came and went without resolution. The prisoners were still not wearing their own clothes. However, by mid-January, with frustration growing by the day, Sands and Hilditch seemed to have come to a workable compromise which was also acceptable to the leadership outside. Hilditch had told Sands that the prison regime was 'not static and was indeed developing'. In return, Sands had agreed to give the authorities 'a week's grace'.[10] Two wings were selected, in H3 and H5, for removal to clean and furnished cells. Twenty men would be involved. They would end their protest, move to their new accommodation and prepare themselves for work of an educational or vocational nature. The families of these twenty 'conforming' prisoners would then be allowed to bring their clothes into the prison. The co-ordination and timing of the exercise were vital so that honour was seen to be satisfied on both sides. On the appointed day the operation swung into action. The chosen prisoners 'washed, shaved and prepared for work' and moved to the clean cells. Their families had brought in their clothes which the twenty prisoners expected to find after their transfer. But there were no clothes. They learned that the prison authorities expected full conformity. Only then would they get their own clothes. Prisoners thought that the administration had taken their readiness to compromise as a sign of weakness and had decided to 'put the boot in when we were down'.[11] When word got out what had happened, Sands gave the order to smash up the wing. 'We did so with a vengeance,' recalled one prisoner. 'It was war!'[12] It was back to square one.

There was a tragic inevitability to it all. Plans were laid for a second hunger strike. This time there was to be no compromise. Sands decided to lead it. If the Army Council had serious misgivings about the first hunger strike, it was even less enthusiastic about the second. The IRA's main concern was to prosecute the 'war' and a second hunger strike might prove an even more damaging diversion. But again, the Army Council could not go against its prisoners. The tail was wagging the dog. The Army Council sent in a 'comm' saying that if the second hunger strike went ahead, the IRA reserved the right to return to full-scale war. During the first hunger strike, it had carried out only limited operations. On 31 January 1981, Sands smuggled out a reply. In his 'comm' to the Army Council, Sands wrote:

> We fully accept . . . the right of the Army to carry on unlimited operations in pursuance of the liberation struggle and without handicap or hindrance. We accept the tragic consequences that most certainly await us and the overshadowing fact that death may not secure a principled settlement . . . We realize the struggle on the outside must also continue. We hope that you accept that the struggle in the H–Blocks, being part of the overall struggle, must also go on in unison.[13]

The Army Council was not bluffing. In the seven months of the 1981 hunger strike, the IRA killed thirteen policemen, eight soldiers, five members of the UDR and five civilians.[14] It was to be one of the bloodiest periods of the 'Troubles'. In total, sixty-one people died, thirty-four of whom were civilians.[15]

Sands was twenty-seven years old when he began his hunger strike. The IRA women prisoners in Armagh had requested permission to go on hunger strike too but this had been vetoed by the Army Council. This time, the pattern was to be different. As with the first hunger strike, there was no shortage of volunteers. Once again the INLA joined in. Prisoners were to embark on the strike one at a time and at staggered intervals. It was agreed that Sands would be followed by Francis Hughes from County Derry, Raymond McCreesh from South Armagh and Patsy O'Hara, the INLA OC from Derry city. In this way, the prisoners calculated they would arouse maximum support and put maximum pressure on the Prime Minister, Margaret Thatcher. As the hunger strike developed, it increasingly became a personal showdown between the 'Iron Lady' and the 'Iron Men'.

Chapter Seventeen

Hunger Strike: Dying

The fifth anniversary of the ending of special category status, on 1 March 1981, was to mark the beginning of the second hunger strike. Bobby Sands was to lead it – he stood down as OC of the H–Blocks and 'Bik' McFarlane took his place. McFarlane, who had once studied for the priesthood, had wanted to join the second hunger strike, as he had the first, but in both cases it had been ruled out. His conviction was for the murder of five Protestants drinking in a pub, the Bayardo Bar, in the Shankill Road during the truce on 13 August 1975. The attack was in retaliation for the UVF's massacre of members of the Miami Showband the previous month (see chapter 13). Although the pub had been targeted because it was thought to be a UVF haunt, the IRA leadership decided that the sectarian nature of McFarlane's conviction would be used against him by the British and thereby undermine the 'political' nature of the prisoners' demands. Their analysis would have been correct. The British lost no time in telling the world of Sands' 'criminal' record, as they did with the nine other prisoners who succeeded him. Sands, from the nationalist Twinbrook estate on the outskirts of West Belfast, had joined the IRA in 1972 at the age of eighteen. He had carried out a 'few petty robberies'[1], before being sentenced to five years for possession of four pistols. He was released from 'Long Kesh' in 1976, where he had been OC of one of the huts in Gerry Adams' 'Cage 11', but was arrested six months later with three others, after a gun battle following the bombing of a furniture showroom in Dunmurry. Sands was interrogated at Castlereagh where he had 'a very bad time' and was sentenced to fourteen years for possession with intent. 'We beat a stack of bomb charges,' he later said, 'because we'd kept quiet.'[2] A gun had been found in the car. Sands joined the blanket protest in September 1977 where he used his isolation and empty hours to begin writing, often in verse, about his IRA and prison experiences. As with Gerry Adams and 'Brownie', many of Sands' writings and poems were published in *Republican News*, under the pen name 'Marcella', a tribute to his sister of the same name.

A few days before Sands refused food for the first time, he was visited by

Father Denis Faul, one of the prison's visiting chaplains. He was known to the prisoners as 'Denis the Menace' as he had no time for the Provisionals' left-wing ideology. But he cared passionately about their welfare and prison conditions. As a priest, Faul had profound theological reservations about hunger striking and did his best to persuade Sands not to go ahead.

> I said first of all that he would cause great grief to his own relations and had to consider his own family. Secondly I said that it would cause convulsions in the community. And it did. There were sixty people killed outside during the hunger strikes and we had a duty to avoid that. But Bobby said to me, 'greater love than this no man has, than that he lay down his life for his friends'. And I had to say, 'I accept that Bobby and I won't argue with you any further.' I could have but he was in good conscience. He felt he was doing the right thing and for the right motives. I had to let him go ahead.

At first, it proved difficult to generate support on the streets outside. On the Sunday before Bobby Sands embarked on his hunger strike, 3,500 supporters marched through West Belfast. Four months earlier, during the first hunger strike, there had been a crowd of 10,000.[3] Only the prisoners inside the Maze seemed to realize that this hunger strike was deadly serious. Outside, people were more sceptical. At the time I remember thinking that it was almost inconceivable that Sands would die. I thought his hunger strike would be brought to the brink and then the compromise that that had almost worked after the first hunger strike would be successfully applied. Since the women prisoners in Armagh already had their own clothes, and as, some time previously, the Government had already gone a long way down the road with 'civilian-type' clothes, it did not seem beyond the wit of British officials and the IRA to sort the thing out. All of us underestimated Mrs Thatcher. She calculated that *she* would have public support, not the prisoners, and no doubt considered seeing out the hunger strike as dealing the IRA a blow from which it might never recover. It was no accident that she later declared, during a visit to Belfast, that the men of violence had played 'their last card'. Outside the prison, concern mounted amongst the Provisionals as the new campaign stubbornly refused to set the world alight, let alone West Belfast. Then one of those rare accidents of history happened that was to transform the hunger strike and the future of the whole Republican Movement. Five days after Bobby Sands first refused food, Frank Maguire, the Independent republican MP for Fermanagh–South Tyrone died. Initially, it was a matter of little concern to the Provisionals. Sinn Fein was, after all, an abstentionist party, and did not fight elections to take seats. The matter of who contested the by-election was a local matter for local people. Because the nationalist and unionist vote in the constituency was finely balanced, the only way a nationalist candidate could win was for one nationalist candidate to stand who was acceptable to all the rival nationalist parties and personalities and thus avoid splitting the vote. More than one nationalist candidate meant losing the seat. Frank Maguire's brother, Noel, said he would stand as did Bernadette McAliskey (formerly Bernadette Devlin). She was lucky to be alive, having narrowly escaped death in a loyalist assassination attack on 16 January 1981 in which she had been shot seven times. The next fortnight saw intense trading in Irish horses. The SDLP saw it as their natural right to run but others had different ideas.

If failure is an orphan, success has many parents. But this does not apply to the Republican Movement where the leadership makes collective decisions. No Provisional rushes forward to claim credit for being the first to suggest that Bobby Sands should contest the election, but Gerry Adams records it was Jim Gibney's idea.[4] Nevertheless, the true instigator appears to have been David O'Connell. Bernadette McAliskey said she would withdraw in favour of a prisoner and the SDLP's candidate, Austin Currie, another veteran civil-rights campaigner, said he would not stand against Bobby Sands. That only left Noel Maguire. Arms were gently twisted. With ten minutes to go the before the deadline for nominations, Maguire had still not indicated his intention to withdraw. If he did not do so, Sands faced defeat and the British would have enjoyed a propaganda bonanza. Outside the electoral office, Adams, Gibney and Francie Molloy watched Noel Maguire go in. Would he hand over his nomination papers or announce his withdrawal? Maguire came out and said he had withdrawn. There was jubilation.

The by-election was held on 9 April 1981. It was to be a straight fight between Bobby Sands, the 'H-Block/Armagh' candidate and the unionist candidate, Harry West, a dour Fermanagh farmer. Sands was into the fortieth day of his hunger strike and had already lost two stone in weight. In the H-Blocks, the prisoners waited for the result. The tension was unbearable. The concealed crystal set, known as 'Mrs Dale', was their only source of information. News was rattled down the heating pipes. The danger was that if cheering erupted, the prison officers would detect the radio and deprive the prisoners of their only contact with the outside world. Then news came through. Bobby Sands had won. Laurence McKeown will never forget the moment 'Mrs Dale' was put at risk.

I remember in our particular wing when we heard it, there was like a suppressed cry, like someone who was yelping or something. The next minute someone banged the pipes and then I heard somebody saying, 'He's won!' Then the place just went mad. Doors were banged, pipes were banged, everything was banged. People danced around their cells. It was without doubt the highest point of my existence and I've no doubt every other prisoner's existence during that period.

Bobby Sands beat Harry West by almost 1,500 votes. He received 30,492 votes to West's 29,046. There had been a massive turnout of 86.9 per cent.

The Government responded by amending the Representation of the People Act so that prisoners could not stand for parliament. Sands' campaign had been run on the issue of the prisoners' Five Demands. A vote for Bobby Sands, his campaign managers and canvassers insisted, was a humanitarian vote, *not* a vote for the IRA. But inside the prison, the Provisionals' OC, 'Bik' McFarlane, knew that the reverse was true.

The IRA had been anything but quiescent in the closing days of the campaign. By coincidence, the election had coincided with a census that was being conducted throughout Northern Ireland to establish, amongst other things, the religious affiliations of its citizens. Republicans and many nationalists boycotted the census and destroyed their forms in protest against the Government's refusal to bend on the hunger strike. There were ritual burnings of the forms. On 7 April 1981, two days before the Fermanagh–South Tyrone by-election, a young Protestant woman, Joanne Mathers, was collecting census forms on a nationalist estate in Derry. She had been handing them out, helping people fill them in and then picking them up again. It was only a part-time job. At half past six, she was standing on a doorstep helping a man with his form when a man ran up and shot her through the neck. She was dead on arrival at hospital. She had been married, with a two and a half year-old son, Shane. Her husband was devastated.

I told Shane that his mummy wasn't coming back because she was in heaven. He thought this was a great place for her, even at that early age. I think he was very sensible and knew his mummy wasn't coming back. He sort of grew up more or less overnight. He has never, ever complained that he hadn't got a mummy. He's always been like that.

I see it as a complete waste of a good life, someone who's gone out of this world who had the right to be here as much as anyone else. It's very sad that she can't be here to see Shane grow up, to see him starting school for the first time or going to get his driving licence for his car. It's all these wee things that people never think of. It's just so unfair.

I don't think the 'Troubles' are worth one single person's life. I don't really think people understand what it's like unless they get caught up in it themselves.

But however much Joanne's death shocked the community, it did not stop Bobby Sands being elected. No organization ever claimed responsibility for her death. The security forces had no doubt it was the Provisionals, who were possibly too embarrassed to claim it.

The murder of Joanne Mathers no doubt confirmed Mrs Thatcher's determination not to give in. There were to be no concessions. 'We are not prepared to consider special category status for certain groups of people serving sentences for crime,' she said. 'Crime is crime. It is not political.'[5] A stream of potential intermediaries visited Sands, who, by this time, was dying. Among them were de Valera's granddaughter, the Pope's personal envoy and officials from the European Commission for Human Rights. But the Government remained unmoved. 'If Mr Sands persisted in his wish to commit suicide, that was his choice,' said Secretary of State, Humphrey Atkins. 'The Government would not force medical treatment upon him.'[6] Sands now only had hours to live. Jim Gibney, who had run his election campaign, was one of the last people to see him alive. Sands' parents and his sister, Marcella, were also at his side.

I knew that Bobby Sands was close to death. I'd visited him four or five times while he was on the hunger strike. I knew I wasn't supposed to do this because the prison authorities would have banned me from the prison. But I just decided that I was going to go in and say goodbye to him for what I knew was going to be the last time. When I went into his cell, it was one of the saddest scenes that I can recall in my time in the struggle. He was lying there, obviously, gaunt. His mum and his sister were standing by his bedside. He had a pair of rosary beads around his neck which had been sent to him by the Pope, through his envoy. He sensed my presence in the room. He didn't know who I was because at that stage he was blind, but he said 'Is that you Jim?' And I said 'Yes it is, Bobby'. And he held his hand out. I took his hand and he said 'Tell the lads I'm hanging in there'. And I wished him goodbye. He died shortly afterwards.

After he was elected, I never thought Margaret Thatcher would let him die. I thought that she had run her campaign on the basis that the prisoners didn't have support. Here was a test of that support. He won yet she let him die. For me anyway that was a very hard and bitter lesson. I carry Bobby's death personally with me every day of my life.

Bobby Sands died on 5 May 1981 on the sixty-sixth day of his hunger strike. Humphrey Atkins issued a statement declaring that he had committed suicide, 'under the instructions of those who felt it useful to their cause that he should die'.[7] It was a turning point in the history of the Republican Movement. 100,000 people streamed behind his coffin. The funeral was conducted with full IRA military honours. The media poured into Belfast from all over the world. Nevertheless, Mrs Thatcher showed no sign of regret. 'Mr Sands was a convicted criminal,' she told the House of Commons. 'He chose to take his own life. It was a choice his organization did not allow to many of its victims.'[8] She was perhaps thinking of Joanne Mathers. The day after the funeral, Joe McDonnell from Belfast, who had been arrested with Sands after the bombing of the furniture showroom, joined the hunger strike. In the following two weeks, the three other hunger strikers died. Francis Hughes on 12 May after fifty-nine days, and Raymond McCreesh and Patsy O'Hara on 21 May after sixty-one days. It was on a visit to Belfast at the end of May, the month that had seen four hunger-strike deaths, that Mrs Thatcher made her famous 'last card' remark. 'Faced with the failure of their discredited cause,' she said scornfully, 'the men of violence have chosen in recent months to play what may well be their last card.'[9]

Not only was there high emotion within the prison, there was also tension between the prisoners and the IRA leadership outside who had not been enthusiastic about the hunger strike in the first place. According to McFarlane, after Bobby Sands died, 'everything seemed to freeze. Nothing moved – not even a hint of an opening for dialogue – no offers from the British that would go some way to negotiating a settlement. It was like living in a vacuum.'[10] It was what the leadership had feared. Before Sands died, a 'comm', presumably from the Army Council, had come into the prison saying that if Sands or any of the other three died, no one was to replace them. Laurence McKeown was furious. He was desperate to go on hunger strike himself and was enraged by the suggestion that they should call it a day. If there was a death and no replacement, he argued, the 'Brits' would know they had won. Many prisoners shared his view. 'We were steeled for the conflict,' he said. The tactical differences were resolved but it was to be almost three weeks after Sands' death before the next prisoner, Kieran Doherty from Belfast, joined the hunger strike on 22 May. The following day, Kevin Lynch, an INLA prisoner from County Derry, did the same. The strategy was now that prisoners should join at regular intervals so there would be no more lengthy gaps but a continuous stream of hunger strikers joining and, failing a settlement, dying one after the other.[11] As OC, 'Bik' McFarlane had the lonely task of selecting the candidates. Three days after Kevin Lynch first refused food, Martin Hurson from Cappagh joined the hunger strike on 26 May. He was followed by Tom McIlwee from County Derry on 8 June; Paddy Quinn from South Armagh on 15 June; Michael Devine (INLA) from Derry City on 22 June; and Laurence McKeown from County Antrim on 29 June. McKeown had finally got his chance.

> I remember when it came to the time to actually join the hunger strike, a 'comm' came from the Army Council which, if anybody had any doubts or romantic notions, it would have certainly knocked them out of their heads. It said, 'Comrade, you have put your name forward to embark upon the hunger strike. Do you realize the full implications? What it means, comrade, is that in a short time you will be dead. Rethink your decision.'

In June circumstances intervened once again to provide the prisoners with a much-needed boost to morale. The Taoiseach, Charles Haughey, called a general election for 11 June in the Irish Republic. The Provisionals decided to run nine prisoners, including four hunger strikers, as candidates. Two of them, Kieran Doherty and Paddy Agnew, won and became members, *in absentia*, of Dail Eireann. The nine H-Block prisoners won a combined total of 40,000 votes.[12] Charles Haughey lost and Dr Garret Fitzgerald became Taoiseach. By the end of June, there appeared to be a marginal softening in the British position, encouraged by the intervention of the Dublin-based Irish Commission for Justice and Peace (ICJP). One of its members, Father Oliver Crilly, was a cousin of Tom McIlwee and, during a visit, had offered the Commission's services as mediator. Father Crilly had assured McIlwee that he believed the Five Demands were reasonable and that he personally supported them. McIlwee had told him that, during the course of the hunger strike, the brutality on the wings had stopped. It was like interposing his body to stop the suffering. Father Crilly had gone into the Maze under the impression that the hunger strike was being manipulated by the IRA leadership outside but he soon revised his view. McFarlane and the prisoners cautiously agreed to Crilly's proposition and the Commission entered into discussions with Michael Alison, the Minister of State at the NIO with responsibility for prisons. The NIO stressed that these meetings were for 'clarification' not 'negotiation'. The Commission's members were working along the lines of the formula they had outlined in the hiatus after the deaths of the first four hunger strikers: that 'own clothes' could be extended to all prisoners as the women in Armagh already wore them; that there could be greater freedom of association without the kind of military training and parades that had been such a feature of the compounds; and that the definition of prison work could be broadened to include cultural and educational pursuits.[13] But 'Bik' McFarlane was deeply suspicious, trusting the 'Brits' even less after the collapse of the first hunger strike. He saw the Commission's mediation efforts as an attempt, supported by the Dublin establishment, to undermine the prisoners.

On 4 July, the prisoners issued an important statement, intended to show that it was not they but the Government who was being intransigent. Perhaps, they suggested, the authorities had misunderstood their position. The statement was conciliatory in tone. It said the prisoners were not looking for any 'differential' treatment. 'We would warmly welcome the introduction of the Five Demands for all prisoners. Therefore, on this major point of British policy, there is no sacrifice of principle involved.' The granting of the demands 'would not in any way mean that the administration would be forfeiting control of the prison, nor would their say on prison activities be greatly diminished.' On 'free association', they said, the Secretary of State was misinformed or greatly exaggerating the demand. 'Supervision need not be restricted,' they reassured the Government. 'There would be no interference with prison officers, who would maintain their supervisory role.'[14] The statement appears to have had some effect. Given the violence triggered by the deaths of four hunger strikers, the Government had no wish to see more prisoners die, thus triggering more deaths outside. And Joe McDonnell was near death. The Government wanted a settlement but was not prepared to sacrifice any principle. That same day, members of the Commission were allowed into the Maze to meet the hunger strikers. McFarlane wanted to be there but permission was refused as the NIO would have seen his presence as a recognition of the IRA's command structure within the prison. 'Criminals' do not have 'OCs'. The following day, the Commission met McFarlane as his 'visitors'. They claimed that for the Government to accept the Five Demands would entail a huge loss of face and there was no way that it was going to do that. They suggested, therefore, that the prisoners compromise and concentrate on three demands: own clothes, work and association, which represented the substance of the Five Demands, they argued. They intimated that their conversations with Michael Alison had indicated that such a compromise might be acceptable. McFarlane refused to budge. Joe McDonnell had not long to live and McFarlane felt the 'Brits' were simply applying the pressure again. That may have been why, he suspected, the Commission had been allowed into the prison in the first place. Sean McKenna's last-minute transfer to Musgrave Park hospital at the end of the first hunger strike was painfully emblazoned on his memory. As McFarlane scathingly and unfairly put it, with the emotion of the time, the 'self-appointed mediators' were fast becoming 'frantic salesmen with a deadline to get rid of some cheap product'. He refused to agree to 'isolating any of our demands'.[15] But, unbeknown to the ICJP delegation, other moves were afoot that were being conducted in the utmost secrecy. The 'Mountain Climber' channel had been opened again. The Contact, either on his own initiative or through the IRA leadership, had once again been in touch with London. The prisoners' conciliatory statement of 4 July no doubt played its part in creating the atmosphere in which it was possible to open the channel. The Contact presumably dealt with another British official as it seems that Michael Oatley was out of the country. The IRA did not blame the 'Mountain Climber' for the failure of the initiative leading to the end of the first hunger strike. The document Oatley had brought over to Belfast had been genuine enough. To the IRA, it was the British who had refused to work it and not the prisoners. From now on, Gerry Adams was to deal directly with the British through the Contact. The immediate result was that Danny Morrison, who was part of the leadership, was allowed into the prison despite the fact he had been banned from it after the first hunger strike. As he walked in, a prison officer spat out the word 'bastard'. Morrison naturally assumed it was a reference to him until he discovered the PO meant Mrs Thatcher, suspecting her to have given in to the prisoners' demands. Why else would Danny Morrison be allowed into the prison? Morrison met McFarlane and the other hunger strikers. Joe McDonnell, who had now been on hunger strike for sixty days, was in a wheelchair and very ill. 'Don't worry,' he said. 'I might only last a few days but I'll hang on as long as I can and buy all the time we need.'[16] Morrison repeated what Adams had been told via the Contact. The Government was prepared to issue a public statement outlining agreed concessions, on the understanding that it would bring an immediate end to the hunger strike: all prisoners in the North would be allowed to wear their own clothes, regardless of the nature of their offences; visits and other such privileges would be agreed; prison 'work' would be fudged; and there was a vague offer to restore a proportion of lost remission. The important thing for the prisoners, apart from the concessions, was that the Government was prepared to put it in writing and make a public statement. Remarkably, neither Michael Alison nor the ICJP knew anything about this secret initiative. Adams was told that if word leaked out the deal was off. Presumably fearing that the confusion arising from two separate strands might end in disaster, Adams took the risk of telling the ICJP about the 'Mountain Climber' initiative and asked them to withdraw to leave the field clear and unconfused. The Contact probably expressed the anger felt in London at this unauthorized revelation but indicated that the initiative would carry on. Word came that an NIO official would come into the prison and confirm directly what was on offer with the hunger strikers. It looked as if a settlement was finally on the cards. Word came that the official had not been able to make it on the evening of 7 July, but was planning to come the following morning at 8.30am. But it was too late. At 4.50am that morning, Joe McDonnell died. Surprisingly, the IRA did not see it as brinkmanship but a genuine miscalculation by the British.[17] Five days later, Martin Hurson died unexpectedly, after a series of frantic convulsions, on the forty-fifth day of his hunger strike. Six men were now dead. The final phase began.

Already there were signs of what the IRA leadership feared most, cracks in the families' readiness to stand by their sons. Joe McDonnell's parents, worried that the prisoners were being manipulated by the IRA, had to be steadied and Kieran Doherty's girlfriend had to be encouraged to stand firm. The architect of the families' revolt was Father Denis Faul, who had already had fierce exchanges within the prison with McFarlane, accusing him of being responsible for Martin Hurson's death through his unwillingness to compromise. McFarlane, tempted to hit him but restrained by his colleagues, was convinced that Faul wanted to end the hunger strike not by supporting the prisoners' demands but by driving a wedge between the hunger strikers and their families. His assessment was right.[18] On 17 July, one last attempt was made to resuscitate the 'Mountain Climber' initiative. The IRA leadership was sent a lengthy message with a statement which the Government proposed to publish as a *quid pro quo* if the hunger strike was ended. There was very little new on offer but the tone was conciliatory. In the wake of the ending of the hunger strike, it intimated that a genuinely 'new' regime would be on offer and that Stanley Hilditch's days as Governor would be numbered. The messages relayed back over the telephone were in code: the prisoners were 'the workers', the leadership of the IRA were 'the shop stewards' and the Government was 'the management.' But the offer still fell short of what 'the workers' demanded: work and association were still problems. There was a limit, the messages said, to how far 'the management' could go for political reasons. 'The shop stewards' replied that although they appreciated the 'frankness' of the Mountain Climber, they too had to operate within their own Movement's constraints: the prisoners were comrades and friends and they could not let them down; if 'the shop stewards' agreed to something less than 'the workers' would accept, they would be rejected by them and this they could not afford; anything agreed had to be in writing as prison officers interpreted prison rules to the letter; goodwill and verbal assurances were not enough. 'The shop stewards' claimed that they genuinely wanted the hunger strike to end – they had not wanted it in the first place and any political advantage that accrued from it had been neither anticipated nor planned.[19] The parties to the dispute still remained too far apart, each constrained by their own political and domestic pressures. The Contact regretted it had to end like this. So too did the IRA leadership. Gerry Adams conveyed the details of the Contact's 'frank statement' to 'Bik' McFarlane, telling him that there were only two options: to accept it and end the hunger strike or carry on with more men dying. There was no room for half measures, it was all or nothing. McFarlane agreed and said that they were in the front line and should fight on.

Meanwhile, Father Denis Faul had been at work. On 28 July, he had called some of the families together for a meeting at a hotel in Toomebridge, readily accessible from all parts of the province. He told them how bleak the situation was and that he did not believe that the hunger strikers and the prisoners really knew the score. Some of the families had become increasingly frustrated and angry as they saw more men dying and no sign of a settlement. Was the IRA leadership really doing all it could to end the strike? Faul believed that Adams, were he so minded, could call it off. A decision was made to go and see Adams that night. It was, said Adams, a 'very difficult discussion'. He explained to the families that for him to undermine the hunger strikers 'would have been disastrous'. He knew what the strikers mood was from his 'comms' with McFarlane and that they were set on a final showdown with Mrs Thatcher. Had the IRA given the order to end the strike, which constitutionally it could have done, it was virtually certain that the order would not have been obeyed. Faul found Adams a formidable debater.

> Adams was the one that did all the talking. No one else spoke. He did come round gradually. Mrs Quinn [Paddy Quinn's mother], from South Armagh, was very insistent. She said she wasn't going to let her son die. The families were pretty well equipped with the arguments which we'd discussed at Toomebridge. Then Mr Adams agreed to ask the IRA to order the men off the hunger strike. We thought at that stage that was the only way we could get them off.

Arrangements were made through Cardinal O'Fiaich for Adams to visit the Maze the following day when he met the hunger strikers in the canteen of the prison hospital. By now there were eight: Laurence McKeown, Paddy Quinn, Matt Devlin, Tom McIlwee, Pat McGeown and Mickey Devine (INLA), known to his comrades as 'Red Mickey'. Kieran Doherty and Kevin Lynch were too ill to attend. Adams outlined the position in blunt, stark terms.[20] The hunger stikers knew the situation well enough but it was something they preferred not to face. Hope had kept them going.

They were told that if they chose to end the strike now, the Movement and their supporters outside would understand and respect the decision. Had not they and their comrades endured enough? There would be no shame in ending it. The group did not want to know. There was no basis for a settlement. They would carry on to the death.

But why was the hunger strike not settled once six men had died and the substance of the Five Demands seemed to be on offer? The simple explanation is that the IRA wanted to extract the maximum propaganda advantage from what was becoming a conveyor belt of death, and did not wish to do anything that would impede its progress. However, this is a mistaken analysis and a misunderstanding of the prisoners' mood and the IRA's relationship with them. They had been on protest for five years, they had been brutalized and had seen six of their comrades waste away to painful deaths. To accept anything less than what their comrades had died for would be betrayal. The sheer intensity of what had happened and the bonds that had been forged between the prisoners meant that there could be no compromise. Although some doubts were expressed, there was no manipulation of the hunger strikers either by the IRA outside the prison or the leadership within. Laurence McKeown put it succinctly.

We were committed to something. Unless someone was coming in and saying 'Right, you have your own clothes, you won't do prison work, you have all your demands', short of that we wouldn't have entertained it. It was all or nothing at that stage. The fact that so many people had died made us even more determined.

Before he left the meeting with the hunger strikers, Adams asked if they had any questions. 'Have we got any heavy gear [armaments] yet?' one of them asked. Adams did not record his reply.

Two days later, on 31 July, Mrs Quinn intervened to save her son's life. She was a determined woman and was not going to let her son die. She directed medical intervention, which a family was entitled to do. Paddy Quinn was rushed to hospital and remained in a coma for two days. When he came round, his mother was at his bedside. 'Mummy,' he said. 'I'm sorry if I upset you. It is good to be alive.' It was the beginning of the end of the hunger strike although it was to be another two months before it finally ended. Father Faul had located its Achilles' heel, and the final, dreadful phase had begun. There were to be no more attempts at resolution. The Government had made its final offer through the 'Mountain Climber' initiative and the prisoners had given their response. Kevin Lynch died on 1 August after seventy-one days. Kieran Doherty died the following day after seventy-three days. His girlfriend, Geraldine, was heartbroken. She had been desperate to save his life but, as she was not family, was unable to do so. A week later, on 8 August, Tom McIlwee died after sixty-five days, and on 20 August, Mickey Devine died after sixty-six days of refusing food. He was the last hunger striker to die. I remember going to a council house on Derry's Creggan estate and seeing his body lying in the coffin in the living room. Masked men stood around it as the INLA honour guard. Men and women trooped by, crossing themselves and silently saying prayers. A knot of people hung around outside. More than three months earlier, an estimated 100,000 people had come to Bobby Sands' funeral. In comparison, a handful came to 'Red Mickey's. The day of the funeral, Sinn Fein's Owen Carron defeated his unionist opponent, Ken Maginnis, in the Fermanagh–South Tyrone by-election and succeeded Bobby Sands as the Member of Parliament. Carron exceeded Sands' vote by 786 on an increased turnout of 88.6 per cent.

Despite the stalemate and continuing deaths, prisoners continued to join the hunger strike, a measure of their commitment and determination not to be beaten, although few had any illusion that in so doing they were likely to die. To the incomprehending world outside, they seemed like lemmings. But as prisoners joined, others were being taken off by their families. It was as if the wheel was spinning both ways. On 6 September, Laurence McKeown's family authorized medical intervention on the seventieth day of his hunger strike. They were the fourth family to intervene. He has only a vague recollection of what happened.

You're very sleepy and very, very tired and you're sort of nodding off to sleep but something's telling you to keep waking up. This was the thing that kept everybody going through the hunger strike in trying to live or last out as long as possible. I knew death was close but I wasn't afraid to die – and it wasn't any sort of courageous or glorious thing. I think death would have been a release. You can never feel that way again. It's not like tiredness. It's an absolute, total, mental and physical exhaustion. It's literally like slipping into death.

How did you feel about your mother after she'd taken you off?

I didn't feel any way different about her because I just knew that she had stood by me all that time anyway. I could understand her point of view. A number of people had made interventions. She wasn't politically committed to my ideas but she was committed to me as a son. I certainly didn't ever say anything to her that would have been hurtful. I think much was left unspoken.

A week later, on 13 September, there was a significant change in the implementation of British Government policy. Humphrey Atkins departed and James Prior became Secretary of State for Northern Ireland. The following day, Gerard Hodgkins joined the hunger strike. Prior had not wanted the job which he knew had few compensations but, after a series of differences with Mrs Thatcher, he reckoned there was not much else on offer and reluctantly, he packed his bags for Belfast. Why did he think Mrs Thatcher had given him the job?

> She wanted to get rid of me from London, I think, more than anything. I think she thought perhaps that I had some of the qualities that could be useful in Northern Ireland but I suspect it was much more that she wanted me out of the way. I saw the hunger strike as a great obstacle to making progress on anything else and I didn't think I could begin to make political progress with the hunger strike still in operation and therefore I wanted it ended.

I asked Lord Prior what advice Mrs Thatcher had given him on how to handle the hunger strike. Remarkably, he said that she had given him none.

One of the first things the new Secretary of State did was to visit the Maze prison. He looked through a window of a cell and saw one of the hunger strikers lying there. It was the INLA prisoner, Liam McCloskey, who was on the forty-fifth day of his hunger strike. 'It had a profound effect on me,' Prior recalls. 'I expected to find someone who was very uptight and struggling and very uncomfortable. But this man seemed to be serenely quiet and content with himself and not in any particular pain.' The following day, McCloskey's mother asked to see him. Prior was advised that he should leave it to his Deputy, Lord Gowrie, who then reported back to Prior. Mrs McCloskey had said that she did not want her son to die and that when he lapsed into a coma she would take him off. 'I would like you to know that my son is not a criminal,' she said. 'He was a bad boy and he should not have shot that person. But if I thought he was a criminal I would never allow him to come inside my house again.' Prior learned fast. 'That told me a great deal about the attitude and the mentality of the Republican community.' Mrs McCloskey was true to her word, and on 26 September, she intervened and took Liam off hunger strike.

It was now virtually all over. Liam McCloskey was the fifth prisoner to be taken off by his family. A week later, on 3 October, the hunger strike was finally called off completely. The families of the remaining six men had indicated that they too would intervene. The hunger strike had collapsed. Gerard Hodgkins, who at its end had been fasting for twenty days, had mixed emotions.

> The hunger strike had started out as a prison struggle for political status but it came to encapsulate the whole struggle for us. We believed that if we lost out on this one, we'd lost the war and everything that went with it. Everything we had sacrificed to date would have been in vain. We genuinely believed that we had to hold out. We hoped to salvage something.
>
> On one hand you felt relieved that it was over, that you weren't going to die. You were relieved for your family. On the other hand, you felt guilty: that you'd actually ended the hunger strike and you hadn't achieved what you set out to achieve. Although you were going to live, you had to live in the knowledge that there were ten men dead who had set out on the same journey. You wonder, 'Have I betrayed them? Have I betrayed their families?' I would still think about it even to this day.

Three days later, Jim Prior announced a series of partial concessions: prisoners would be allowed to wear their own clothes at all times; there would be fifty per cent remission of time lost through the protests; greater freedom of association between adjacent wings of the H-Blocks; more visits; and the definition of prison 'work' would be reviewed. The Secretary of State was far too sensible to claim victory. The tragedy was that much the same had been on offer almost three months before, when only six men had died. In the interim, four more had gone to their graves.

The Hunger Strike is a watershed in the history of the Republican Movement. Although the deaths of ten men made it clear to the British Government that the IRA was determined to see its 'struggle' through to the end, regardless of the cost, its real historical significance lies in the election of Bobby Sands and Owen Carron to Westminster. Their victories laid the foundation for the political base that Gerry Adams knew had to be built if the 'struggle' were to progress. Sinn Fein's electoral successes through the next two decades are the hunger strike's political legacy. Many years on, a senior NIO prison official told me he thought the hunger strike was 'a magnificent achievement'.

Three years after the hunger strike, on 16 October 1984, the Provisionals took their revenge. The IRA planted a twenty-pound bomb with a delayed timer in the Grand Hotel, Brighton, where Mrs Thatcher and most of her Cabinet were staying for the Conservative Party's annual conference. The bomb exploded at 2.54am, collapsing the building like a pack of cards.

Five members of the Conservative Party were killed. Mrs Thatcher narrowly escaped. The IRA declared that she would have to be lucky all of the time: they only had to be lucky once. The prisoners shed no tears.

Chapter Eighteen

Counterstrike

Warrenpoint and Mountbatten's death were disasters for the security forces but Warrenpoint was by far the bigger of the two. The British Intelligence agencies may not have been expected to know about the attack on Mountbatten, which was carried out well across the border, but Warrenpoint was a different matter. The attack had been carried out with meticulous planning by the South Armagh Brigade under the direction of Northern Command which operationally covered the counties on both sides of the border. It indicated a serious deficiency in British Intelligence. The problem was twofold: there was clearly a shortage of 'humint' (human intelligence), the informers and agents who provide the RUC's Special Branch, army intelligence and MI5 with the inside information that is critical in countering the IRA; and there was a lack of co-ordination between the police and army in gathering and sharing intelligence. The first problem was rectified in the eighties with sometimes spectacular results; the second problem was addressed and improved but nevertheless remained endemic.

The army did not like 'The Way Forward', the change in security policy which gave the RUC the lead role in countering republican and loyalist terrorism. The army believed that its vast experience in counter-insurgency operations from Kenya to Malaya gave it the right to take the initiative in security policy. In the late seventies, the problem was compounded by temperamental differences between the Chief Constable, Sir Kenneth Newman, and the GOC, Lieutenant-General Sir Timothy Creasey. Newman was a systems man, cerebral and clinical. Creasey was an action man, a veteran of Kenya, Oman and Aden. The General did not like playing second fiddle to the Chief Constable. Sir John Hermon, Deputy Chief Constable in charge of Operations at the time, recalls the incompatibility. 'Creasey was used to forceful action on the field. He was a military man and I don't think his temperament was entirely suited to the Northern Ireland scene in discretion and tact.' In the aftermath of Warrenpoint, Mrs Thatcher had flown over to Northern Ireland to make her own assessment of what needed to be done by talking to the police and army commanders on the ground. She told Hermon she was not sending 'her boys' over to be slaughtered by the IRA. She talked to the army and got one story, then talked to the police and got another. One of the army commanders she met was General Glover. He had no doubt where the problem lay. Intelligence needed to be properly co-ordinated as a matter of urgency. 'It was a very difficult situation to control throughout the province, from top to bottom, in particular within the intelligence community,' he said. 'People tended to be at sixes and sevens with each other and it needed to be sorted out.' The Generals told the Prime Minister that what they needed was a Security Co-ordinator to fulfil the role that Field-Marshal Sir Gerald Templer had so successfully carried out against terrorists in Malaya in the 1950s. It was Templer who had originally coined the phrase, 'hearts and minds'.[1] Glover knew that this idea was 'politically naive and totally unacceptable' given the policy of 'police primacy' but he believes it sowed the necessary seed in the Prime Minister's mind. On her return to London, Mrs Thatcher announced that she was appointing Maurice Oldfield, the former head of MI6, as her Security Co-ordinator in Northern Ireland. Sir Maurice, who is widely believed to have been the model for John Le Carré's 'George Smiley', had been brought out of gentle retirement at Oxford, where he was a Fellow at All Souls, and thrust into the bloody maelstrom of Northern Ireland. To the Provisionals, he became known as 'Morris the Mole'. He was not sent over to bang heads together. That was not his style. His job was to iron out differences and co-ordinate the whole intelligence operation so no Warrenpoint could slip down the middle. Oldfield had no executive authority: he was there only to advise and not direct. 'He was a referee. He was a catalyst. He was a Solomon,' says Glover. 'He made a very substantial contribution towards drawing us all together by being prepared to hear both sides of the case, by getting us together, talking together and producing a solution based on logic rather than on emotion.' But the RUC was not enthusiastic about Mrs Thatcher's 'George Smiley'. Senior officers were dismissive. 'I must say I paid scant attention to him,' says Sir John Hermon, who became RUC Chief Constable in 1980. 'Quite frankly, I didn't consider his role was necessary or that it contributed very much. Maurice Oldfield very quickly became superficial. Not because of his inabilities or anything else, but because he wasn't needed.'

Oldfield did make a significant contribution in oiling the wheels but the problem largely solved itself when there was a change in management at the top of the RUC and army headquarters, Lisburn. The new Chief Constable, Sir John Hermon, and the new GOC, Lieutenant-General Sir Richard Lawson, were soul mates, as close together as their predecessors had been far apart. This new, much warmer relationship at the top filtered down through the ranks of both organizations. 'There was a considerable transformation,' says Hermon. 'It was a happy meeting of two people who could relate.' The relationship bore fruit to the detriment of the IRA. By the mid-eighties, the RUC's Special Branch and military intelligence were not only sharing information but running some agents together. Maurice Oldfield, meanwhile, had a tragic end. On 16 June 1980, he resigned because of ill health. He was dying of cancer. What was not known at the time was that he was a homosexual and the fact only became public knowledge after his death when Mrs Thatcher informed the House of Commons in 1986. She assured Parliament that security had not been compromised. He was said to have had a penchant for young men but Mrs Thatcher never gave the details.

Oldfield had known, from his vast experience of running agents behind the Iron Curtain and elsewhere during the Cold War, that intelligence was the key to undermining the IRA. Nothing was more lethal than an agent recruited from within the enemy's ranks. In Northern Ireland, agents were not trained by the security services and then infiltrated into the IRA's structure. That was the stuff of thrillers. The reality of close-knit republican areas and the IRA's cellular structure made such a task almost impossible or suicidal. The risks were too great. IRA Volunteers and loyalist paramilitaries were propositioned and 'turned' from within their own organizations. One of the most fertile recruiting grounds was Castlereagh (see chapter fourteen). Working for Special Branch, with protection and money on offer, was in some cases a more attractive option than spending years in gaol 'on the blanket' or otherwise. No doubt Castlereagh is where many agents, informers and 'sources' were recruited.

Gradually, throughout the late seventies and eighties, a complex intelligence network was built up by the police, army and MI5. Resources were made available and the system of recruiting and operating 'sources' throughout Northern Ireland was extended and refined. It was one of the most important contributions in the post-Oldfield era that the security services made in their battle against the IRA. If the Provisionals were fighting a 'Long War', British Intelligence was gearing up to fight it too. Some agents were exposed and ended up with an IRA bullet through the back of the head, their hands tied and bodies dumped on lonely border roads. Others were 'exfiltrated' when their cover was at risk, and given new identities outside the province. But the vast majority stayed in place for years. I asked Sir James Glover, who had experience of running agents behind the Iron Curtain and in Northern Ireland, why they did it.

There are a variety of reasons. They do it for the excitement, for political motivation, jealousy, cash, women, the good life, working off old scores. There is a huge range of ways in which you can appeal to someone to become a source. Every man, and I suppose every woman, has their price.

In the wake of Castlereagh and the restructuring it had forced on the IRA, Volunteers were under strict orders not to do anything that would jeopardize the security of their cell. They were ordered to keep a low profile, not to be seen in each other's company or in the company of known republicans and not to do anything that would draw attention to themselves or other members of the cell. But the hunger strikes changed all that. IRA Volunteers broke cover and broke the basic rules. They were seen talking together, marching together and rioting together. The intense emotion of the time and the need to organize massive street protests in support of the Five Demands made Volunteers come out into the open and drop their guard. British Intelligence had a field day. The IRA's Derry Brigade became especially vulnerable as Hugh McMonagle and many others found out to their cost.

Everybody was meeting everybody again. All the different units were congregating around the Creggan shops. In our normal time, we would never have met anybody. Now we're all meeting together and seeing faces and handing over gear and whatever.

British Intelligence had the resources and the money and they put a lot of effort into recruiting agents to infiltrate the IRA to try and break down the cells. The cell structure was working effectively and they were getting nowhere cracking them. There were operations getting done in the town, and probably getting done throughout the Six Counties, and they hadn't a clue who was doing it, or who was involved. The cells were that effective. But at the time of the hunger strike, they became vulnerable. Our security was not tight because of the emotion of the time and the mobilization of the people. You wanted to back up the prisoners as much as possible, and you wanted to be effective outside as well as being effective inside to help them try and gain their political status.

The IRA threw caution to the wind. I saw it myself. Nobody would have known who was who but because Derry became a 'no go' area, Volunteers were walking about openly about the street, carrying out operations or whatever and giving 'touts' [informers] the opportunity to gather as much information and as many names as possible and convey all that back to their handlers.

But the infiltration of the IRA and its Derry stronghold was not carried out only by informers. British army undercover teams took advantage of the hunger strike to move in even closer. Such covert operations had long been a feature of intelligence gathering and had become perfected by 14 Intelligence Company, the specialist unit that, along with the Special Air Service (SAS) and Special Boat Service (SBS), make up the British army's 'Special Forces'. On 28 May 1980, after Bobby Sands, Francis Hughes, Raymond McCreesh, Patsy O'Hara and Kevin Lynch had died, an officer from 14 Intelligence Company was carrying out surveillance in the heart of Derry's Creggan estate. It was the day Mrs Thatcher visited Belfast and made her famous remark about the IRA playing its 'last card'. The fact that a plain-clothes army officer was driving around the IRA's territory was, in itself, nothing new and was unlikely to have escaped the IRA's own intelligence network. RUC stations and army bases were regularly watched and the make and number plates of the cars that emerged were 'clocked'. The IRA also had its own scanners in the Creggan where it listened in to the army and police radio 'net'. It worked both ways: the IRA could pick up army presence in their area and could ascertain whether their own vehicles had been 'pinged' (identified) by the army and police. That day it appears that either the scanner or the IRA's own watchers had 'pinged' the presence of a suspicious 'Brit' vehicle – an Opel Ascona. This information was passed on to an IRA unit that was driving around Creggan in a Ford Escort. The unit consisted of George McBrearty, Charlie 'Pop' Maguire, Eamon 'Peggy' McCourt and a fourth man, the driver, whose identity is not revealed for legal reasons. They were allegedly armed with an Armalite, a Woodmaster and an M16 rifle. They decided to intercept the Opel Ascona. McBrearty got out of the Escort and made his way over with his weapon to the driver's side of the Ascona. The undercover soldier reacted with lightening speed, drew his Browning 9mm semi-automatic pistol and shot McBrearty dead. He got his retaliation in first. McCourt had also got out of the Escort.

> I was just walking towards it and the next thing, there's all hell let loose, a mad sort of shooting. It just blew up. It lasted seconds but it seemed like an eternity. I remember just spinning round. I knew I was hurt bad. I was hit in the stomach, my chest, the arm and the back. Five times. But I said to myself that I wasn't gonna die, I was just gonna keep fighting on 'cos I had a family to get back to like everyone else.

Charlie Maguire was shot dead in the front seat of the Escort but the driver survived and escaped. The undercover soldier escaped. He had taken no chances. Eamon McCourt was sentenced to five years for possession of two rifles. It was a severe blow to IRA morale as McBrearty and Maguire were two experienced and popular IRA Volunteers. Hugh McMonagle was a friend.

> When there's a death, it always saps your morale. You feel down. George [McBrearty] and 'Pop' [Maguire] had been well-respected IRA men. I remember the Brigade Staff once describing George, who'd been involved for a long time, as 'the cream of the IRA'. Two good Volunteers were lost that day. For two or three days, morale was very low. There's this sick feeling of loss and grief, because the boys were your comrades and you've been among them on numerous occasions. It's just a sickener. But you pull yourself up from it and continue on. Strive on for what they died for.

Hugh McMonagle and his comrades strove on, not knowing that they were soon to be hit by a devastating blow, leading to the arrest of dozens of IRA suspects in Derry. A process was about to begin which would inflict severe damage on the IRA not only in Derry but in Belfast too. The INLA and the loyalist paramilitaries were also badly hit. On 21 November 1981 began the era of the 'supergrasses'. That day an IRA Volunteer from Belfast's Ardoyne, Christopher Black, was arrested during an IRA 'propaganda exercise', which invariably meant providing the media with a 'photo opportunity' featuring men with masks and guns.[2] During his interrogation at Castlereagh, Black remained silent for two days before asking the police, 'If I help yous [sic], will yous help me?'[3] Black indicated that he would be prepared to name names and give evidence in court against his former comrades. Three days into his interrogation, he was promised immunity from prosecution. He was also to receive a new identity and new life outside Northern Ireland. The deal was struck and Black named thirty-eight people. On 5 August 1983, after a six-month trial that cost the taxpayer £600,000, thirty-five IRA suspects were convicted and sentenced to a total of more than 4,000 years.[4] The majority of the charges related to the period of the hunger strikes. In eighteen of the cases, there was no corroborating evidence.[5] The only evidence was the word of Christopher Black. The trial judge, Mr Justice Kelly, said that he was 'one of the best witnesses I have ever heard . . . very, very many situations, conversations and comments he described in language and manner which suggested only truth.'[6] Christopher Black was the first of many.

The IRA's Derry Brigade thought it would be immune since its Volunteers sprung from a tightly-knit community and informers were a rarity. They also felt a sense of superiority over their looser-tongued brethren in Belfast. But they proved to have a false sense of security. Early one August morning in 1982, the police and army raided republican houses in Derry in the biggest anti-terrorist operation since 'Operation Motorman' a decade earlier. Creggan and the Bogside swarmed with troops and around forty IRA suspects were arrested. Hugh McMonagle was not at home. His mother gave the milkman a message and asked him to drop it off at the house where her son was staying. Having received the tip-off, McMonagle went down to Creggan shops which was the Provisionals' usual meeting place. Others, having also received the warning, were there too. Someone said that a furniture van had been seen outside the house of one of their comrades, Raymond Gilmour. The Gilmours had told neighbours they were going on a caravan holiday in Donegal.[7] The Provisionals needed no further intelligence. A removal van had been seen outside Christopher Black's house in Belfast the year before. Raymond Gilmour had turned 'supergrass'. 'We were taken aback,' recalls McMonagle. 'We never expected it in Derry. We never expected it from Raymond Gilmour. I had no suspicions of him. Never, ever.' McMonagle and half a dozen other IRA suspects headed across the border into Donegal and 'got offside'. He remained there for four years and escaped the 'supergrass' net. Slogans appeared on walls in Derry, 'I knew Raymond Gilmour. Thank God he didn't know me!' When the Chief Constable, Sir John Hermon, heard the news at RUC Headquarters, he was delighted.

Here was a man prepared to reveal everything that he knew about the IRA. Indeed, I visited the detectives who were handling the case and was astounded at the mass of paper. One room was stacked high in every direction. Copies of statements, copies of files. Everything had to be prepared. The amount of paperwork shocked me, but it was necessary. The detectives told me about the quality of the information they were obtaining and how they were trying to get it processed in a way which would be evidential and would lead to the prosecution of those people who had committed very serious crimes.

To the Chief Constable, Christopher Black and Raymond Gilmour were not 'supergrasses' but 'converted terrorists', a name coined by Hermon because of the stigma attached to the word 'informer', although the change did nothing to change its perception in the community from which these men came.

In his statements, Gilmour named dozens of names, linking them with bombs, shootings, 'punishments', hijackings and every other conceivable type of IRA operation. He ripped apart the IRA structure in Derry from top to bottom. Amongst the dozens of allegations he made were that Hugh McMonagle was an IRA section leader in Creggan and that Cathal Crumley and Gary Fleming were members of the IRA's Derry Brigade Staff. Crumley, he alleged, was Quartermaster, in charge of the IRA's weapons and explosives, and Fleming, he alleged, was the Brigade's Explosives' Officer. All three denied Gilmour's allegations. The RUC hoped that Raymond Gilmour would do to the Bogside and Creggan what Christopher Black had done to Ardoyne.

Gilmour was married with two children. His wife, Lorraine, had no idea that her husband had been leading a double life for four years. Unlike Christopher Black, Gilmour had been a paid Special Branch agent since September 1978 when he was just seventeen. Whilst on bail for the armed robbery of a post office, the police made him an offer he was not inclined to refuse. He was probably given the choice of serving a lengthy prison sentence or changing sides. He chose the latter. At the time, he was not a member of any illegal organization because he was too young. But, coming up to eighteen, he was ripe for joining and just the sort of potential informant Special Branch was looking for. Gilmour was ideal 'agent' material. He was from Creggan, knew people, and his 'street cred' had been notably enhanced following the armed robbery. He was given a personal Special Branch handler known as 'Pete'.[8] Gilmour afforded Special Branch a rare opportunity. Because of his connections in Derry, he could be infiltrated into INLA or the Provisional IRA and directed what to find out and what to do. Not least, he could provide his handlers with information about forthcoming operations that would save lives. In November 1978, he was directed by his handlers to join INLA. His cover story, which again had local credibility, was that a friend and neighbour of his, Colm McNutt from Creggan, a member of INLA, had been shot dead by undercover British soldiers on 12 December the previous year (1977). Gilmour claimed that he was out for revenge. Joining INLA was much more straightforward than joining the Provisionals. He knew where to go and who to contact. He discussed it with certain individuals, went to a house, said 'hello' and was told he was now a member. 'I wasn't sworn in or anything like that,' he said.[9]

He was told that he would be doing any 'jobs' that came up with the other boys who were there in the room. His first 'job' was a punishment shooting of an INLA member who had stolen money that did not belong to him. The victim was shot in the thigh with a .38 revolver. Gilmour stayed with INLA until he finally helped engineer the collapse of the cell he had joined through information he was feeding back to 'Pete'. In the summer of 1980, as the prison protest was approaching its climax and the first hunger strike loomed, Gilmour was told to infiltrate the Provisional

IRA. This was not as easy as joining INLA. He knew some Provisionals from the contact he had had with them when he was with INLA and told them he was fed up with INLA because of the way it was run and now wanted to join the 'Provies'. At first they turned him down. He then approached a prominent member of Sinn Fein and asked again. He was told that if he joined, he would have stay away from marches and keep himself to himself. The Sinn Fein person then took him to the house of a man who was thought to be the Provisional IRA's Commanding Officer in Derry.

> He questioned me as to why I wanted to join the Provisional Irish Republican Army. I told him about the time I was in the INLA and in my view the 'Provies' were a much better outfit. I also told him about my best friend being shot . . . and I wanted to avenge his death. The INLA had done nothing about it and I thought that I could avenge his death better if I was in the 'Provies'.[10]

Gilmour was finally accepted and began studying the IRA's 'Green Book' under the Provisionals' Education Officer. He actually did the studying in a school building for five or six nights between 6.30 and 9.00pm. 'I was always put in this same science store and made to read this Green Book over and over again'.[11] His study over, the instructor told him that he would have to go away on training camps and take part in ambushes. 'He also asked me how I felt about killing people on behalf of the organization. I told him if I had to do it, I would do it.' Again he was told to 'keep away from republican marches and protests so that I wouldn't become known to the security forces.'[12] The homework done, Gilmour was then taken back to see the IRA's Commanding Officer.

> We were told to stand to attention. He told me to raise my right hand and then repeat after him an obligation to Oglaigh Na Eireann [IRA] which I did. When this was over, he shook hands with me and welcomed me into the Provisional Irish Republican Army. He told me I would be put in a cell with a number of other Volunteers.[13]

Gilmour was then introduced to the three men and a woman who would make up his 'cell'. Gilmour was sworn in at the end of October 1980 just as the first hunger strike was beginning. For his handlers, the timing could not have been better. Gilmour continued working with his cell as the unit's driver which meant he came into contact with a whole range of IRA men and women in Derry. For almost two years, Gilmour was involved in a series of hijackings, shootings and bombings. He lived as close to the edge as it was possible to do – both as an IRA Volunteer and as a British agent. Every action in which he took part increased his credibility with his cell and the Derry Brigade and made him ever more valuable to his handlers. Although agents walk the thinnest and most dangerous of fine lines, they are not permitted to engage in criminal activity, least of all murder. Astonishingly, Gilmour crossed the line and became involved in killing. On 20 January 1981, his unit ambushed soldiers as they were closing Castle Gate on Derry's city walls. They were armed with two high-velocity Armalites and a Woodmaster rifle. Wanning appears to have been given of some such attack but it was some considerable time before, and the details were imprecise. Gilmour had the Woodmaster. Eleven armour-piercing Armalite rounds went through the steel gate, killing twenty-one-year-old Private Christopher Shenton of the First Battalion, Staffordshire Regiment. He was hit in the back and died almost immediately. Gilmour kept the safety catch on his Woodmaster and did not open fire. It was the agent's awful dilemma: to refuse to take part in such an operation would arouse suspicion and possible exposure, resulting in death; to participate would mean being involved in murder. After the killing, the Derry OC congratulated the unit and said it was a job well done. Gilmour was asked why he had not opened fire. He replied that he thought the rifle had jammed and his explanation was accepted. The key question is, did Gilmour's handlers know about the attack and, if so, why was nothing done to stop the killing? When Gilmour gave evidence in court at the trial of those he named, he said he had given his handlers full details of the plan but had not known the precise date. He also said that none of those involved were ever arrested or questioned by the police. When cross-examined by defence counsel, Desmond Boal QC, and asked why the police had done nothing, Gilmour replied that 'Pete' might be able to explain better than he could.[14] 'Pete' has never done so. No explanation has ever been given as to why the killing was not prevented. No doubt the RUC wished to draw a veil over an affair which raises so many questions. Was the life of an agent more important than the life of a soldier? Why was no one arrested afterwards, although Special Branch would have known who did it? Would Gilmour have been exposed had the unit been lifted, given that he had not fired his weapon? Or was it, as Gilmour said, simply that he was not able to tell his handlers the precise time and place of the attack? These questions have never been answered and probably never will be. Such are the perils of agent running.

The IRA in Derry was devastated by Gilmour's treachery and in November 1982 took hostage Raymond's father, Patrick Gilmour, saying that he would be killed unless his son retracted his evidence. He refused to do so. After ten months, Patrick Gilmour was released unharmed. By this time, Raymond and Lorraine Gilmour and their two children had been moved from pillar to post, always under police protection, to ensure that the IRA did not catch up with them and silence Raymond Gilmour for good. Lorraine Gilmour said the police had told her that they could go to any country in the world and that they would never have to work: they would have a brand-new house, a car, a new identity and a gun for Raymond.[15] At one stage the family were accommodated for six weeks in a five-star hotel in Cyprus from where an increasingly unhappy Lorraine Gilmour frequently telephoned home. Six days later, her husband spotted an IRA man from Derry in the vicinity of the hotel. His minders were taking no chances and promptly put the family on a flight back to England. But after nine months in hiding, Lorraine had had enough of life on the run. She said she wanted to leave Raymond and go home to Derry. She spoke on the telephone to Martin McGuinness who said she was free to return.[16]

On 18 December 1984, at the close of a six-month trial, the Gilmour case ended as spectacularly as it had begun when the Lord Chief Justice of Northern Ireland, Lord Lowry, acquitted the thirty-five suspects who had been charged with 180 terrorist offences on Gilmour's uncorroborated testimony. Lord Lowry was not impressed with Gilmour as a witness whom he described as 'a selfish and self-regarding man to whose lips a lie invariably came more naturally than the truth'. In acquitting the accused, however, he did not dispel the suspicion that they were indeed members of the IRA in Derry. Lord Lowry told the court there was more than a trace of probability that many were members of a proscribed organization and were 'no doubt people police believe to be guilty of terrorist acts and plans, but the necessary evidence was only through the mouth of a witness whom I condemn.'[17]

Sinn Fein and other concerned bodies bitterly attacked the 'supergrass' system, saying that those who gave evidence were 'paid perjurers' whose testimony was totally unreliable. Sometimes the judges agreed, sometimes they did not. They weighed each case on its merits and did not dismiss charges just because the evidence was uncorroborated. In the end, they judged each charge – and there were scores of them – according to the credibility of the evidence given by the 'supergrass' concerned in each particular instance. Jim Gibney, for example, one of ten republicans charged in 1983 on the evidence of Kevin McGrady, was found not guilty of murdering a Protestant in October 1975. Lord Lowry described McGrady's evidence in this respect as 'contradictory, bizarre and in some respects incredible' and his manner of giving it 'devious and deliberately evasive'.[18] Nevertheless, Lord Lowry did accept some parts of McGrady's evidence and sentenced Gibney to twelve years for wounding with intent,

Jim Gibney, late 1970s.

Snapshot: Declan Arthurs, Dermot Quinn, Martin McCaughey, Seamus Donnelly, Tony Gormley and Eugene Kelly (left to right) at the Cappagh memorial to Martin Hurson, 1986.

Bodies in the street following the IRA's bomb on Remembrance Day in Enniskillen, 1987.

Loyalist Michael Stone carrying out a grenade and gun attack at Milltown Cemetery, 1988.

British army corporals being attacked during a funeral at Andersonstown, 1988.

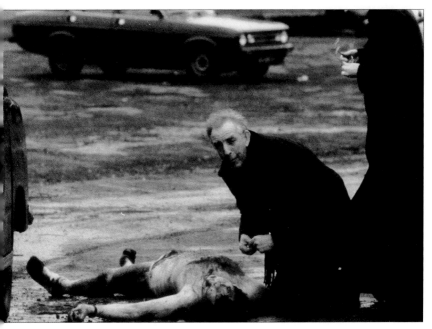

Father Alec Reid giving last rights to a British army corporal killed at Andersonstown, 1988.

IRA bomb devastation at the Baltic Exchange, City of London, 1992.

The aftermath of the IRA bomb at Docklands, 1996.

Gerry Adams, Albert Reynolds and John Hume meeting in Dublin, 1994.

Bill Clinton meeting Gerry Adams in Belfast, 1995.

Martin Meehan, 1997.

Michael Oatley.

Seán MacStiofáin, 1997.

Brendan Hughes, 1997

possession of guns and IRA membership.[19] At his trial, McGrady had said that Gibney was 'high on the list of people the RUC wished to convict'.[20] Three of the ten charged with Gibney were acquitted. Two more, whose convictions were based purely on McGrady's uncorroborated testimony, were later released on appeal. Gibney stayed in gaol. Kevin McGrady was a 'supergrass' with a difference. He was a born-again Christian who had returned from Amsterdam in 1982 where he had been on the run, living with a religious group. He had given himself up, confessed to three sectarian murders in 1975 and received a life sentence. After surrendering to the RUC in Belfast, he had turned 'supergrass'. McGrady was released in April 1988 having served only six years of his life sentence. Gerry Adams said it proved that 'there is no British justice in Ireland'.[21]

But the biggest blow to the 'supergrass' system came on 17 July 1986 when, after a sixty-day hearing, the Northern Ireland Court of Appeal quashed the convictions of eighteen republicans who had been sentenced on the uncorroborated testimony of Christopher Black in what had been the biggest 'supergrass' trial of all. The Appeal Court declared that 'the learned trial judge . . . has greatly overestimated the honesty as a witness . . . of the accomplice Black'.[22] With the Crown's star 'supergrass' thus discredited, the system was finished. But by this time, as we shall see in the next chapter, other ways had been developed to counter the Provisional IRA.

Chapter Nineteen

Snapshot

If ever any place deserves the name 'IRA stronghold', it is the village of Cappagh. Surrounded by the rolling hills of County Tyrone, whose beauty and tranquillity belie the violence they have seen, Cappagh scarcely seems big enough to be a stronghold for anything. It has one main street with Boyle's Bar at one end and a parade of shops at the other. A faded Tricolour always flys there. Cappagh has seen it all, in this and every other campaign. Eighty-eight-year-old Tommy O'Neill, one of the village's oldest inhabitants, remembers joining the IRA in 1938 and carrying messages on his bicycle sixty miles across the mountains from Dungannon to Strabane; and on the hill at the top of the main street is the memorial to Cappagh's most famous son, Martin Hurson of the IRA's Tyrone Brigade, who died on hunger strike after forty-five days. His death had a profound effect on the young people of an already militant republican village. Francie Molloy, the local Sinn Fein leader, watched his remains being brought home to Cappagh.

> It was unbelievable. There were people everywhere. The village was black with them. It was the first sign in Tyrone of thousands and thousands of people all assembling to honour the remains of a native son coming home. Martin was young when he went to gaol and young when he died on hunger strike. His death just made young people more determined that they were actually going to replace him. They saw ten men dead as the British Government taking people out of the struggle. I think the young people of Cappagh and the surrounding areas decided then that they were going to replace every one of them and replace them tenfold. And that is what they did. The number of young people who joined up in response was massive.

One the new recruits to the IRA's Tyrone Brigade was Declan Arthurs whose family ran a small farm just outside Cappagh, rearing pigs, cattle and hens. At the time of the hunger strike Declan was sixteen and, according to his mother, Amelia Arthurs, the quietest of five brothers. They were not a republican family and politics played little part in their lives. There was no television in the house and the boys used to play games and chess at nights to keep themselves amused. Homework was not popular but they did what they had to. The five brothers were very close and were deeply affected by the death of Martin Hurson who had been a good friend. They went to his wake to pay their last respects and were shocked by the sight of their friend, emaciated and lying in a coffin. As soon as he was seventeen, Declan joined the IRA without telling his mother. Gradually she began to worry where he was and what he was doing, first becoming concerned one winter's evening at about half past eight when she received a phone call saying that Declan had been stopped at a checkpoint on the border with Donegal and given a hiding. The caller said he was bleeding from the nose and face. She called a doctor and a solicitor, drove over to pick up her son and took him to hospital. 'Nothing was ever done to that soldier who struck the blow, you know,' she told me bitterly. Her worst fears were confirmed when the security forces started coming to the house looking for Declan. It was not the first visit Mrs Arthurs had had from the police as, by then, her eldest son, Brian, had already joined the IRA and the family home had become a target. She desperately wanted Declan to stay out of trouble and told him she did not want him joining the IRA.

What was his future? Life imprisonment? On the run? Or was he going to be killed? I knew his future wasn't going to be any good. I said to him, 'For God's sake, Declan, please think of us because we love you so much.' And he'd just look at me and say, 'I'm sorry mum, there's nothing else I can do. I have to fight for my country.' I begged him, often I begged him, but to no avail.

In 1986, Declan Arthurs and five of his friends attended a commemoration in Cappagh to mark the fifth anniversary of Martin Hurson's death. A memorial had been erected in his name and the six young men had a group snapshot taken by it as a souvenir (see photograph). They were Declan Arthurs, Seamus Donnelly, Tony Gormley, Eugene Kelly, Martin McCaughey and Dermot Quinn. Following their friend's death all six joined the IRA. Within five years, five of them were dead, ambushed by the SAS in different incidents. Only one of them is alive today.

The SAS was the most deadly and feared weapon in the Government's arsenal against the Provisional IRA, carrying out its operations with clinical efficiency. Although sometimes it made arrests without a shot being fired, these encounters were few. SAS operations that grabbed the headlines were the ones in which there were dead bodies at the end which inevitably gave rise to allegations that the Governement was pursuing, through its most specialized soldiers, a 'shoot to kill' policy – meaning, in its most extreme form, selective assassinations. This has always been vehemently denied by its political and military masters who insist that the SAS operates under the same rules of engagement as any other soldiers: opening fire is only permitted if the soldier believes that his own life – or anyone else's – is threatened, and he need not give a warning if he believes doing so would put life at risk.[1] What is often forgotten, or simply not known, is that when the SAS do open fire, they shoot to kill, not wound. Guns are not shot out of hands. Questions only tend to be asked when the victims transpire to have been unarmed or not to be 'terrorists'. This is what happened in the three cases John Stalker, the Deputy Chief Constable of Manchester, was tasked to investigate in which an élite RUC anti-terrorist unit, trained by the SAS, shot dead three members of the Provisional IRA, two members of the INLA and one person with no paramilitary affiliations, in three separate incidents at the end of 1982.[2] These shootings sharpened the RUC's response to the Provisionals' campaign in the early eighties, but after the controversy they provoked – because in two of the three cases, the victims were unarmed – a decision may have been made to leave such operations to those best trained to carry them out. That meant the SAS. Between November 1978 and December 1983, the SAS was not responsible for the deaths of any republicans in Northern Ireland.[3] This was to change dramatically. Furthermore, by the mid-eighties, the intelligence on which such interceptions and ambushes were mounted was far more precise, with sophisticated electronic surveillance supplementing the information supplied by agents and informers within the IRA's ranks. The SAS went for, and largely achieved, 'clean kills' – the victims were armed – with the notable exception of the shooting of the three unarmed IRA Volunteers in Gibraltar in 1988 (see chapter twenty-one).

Through the second half of the eighties and early nineties, the SAS devastated the Provisional IRA in Tyrone in a manner unlike anywhere else in the province. Such operations were, on the whole, difficult to carry out in urban areas like Belfast and Derry because of the risk to civilians and extremely difficult in South Armagh where the locals knew every suspicious-looking hedge, barn and ditch. Under the right circumstances rural areas like Tyrone offered a perfect killing field. By the mid-eighties, the area had again become 'hot' as the IRA raised its campaign to a new level, energized by the mass break-out of senior IRA prisoners from the Maze on 25 September 1983. The escape was important, not just to fulfil an IRA prisoner's first duty, but to provide experienced men to regenerate the campaign outside. Amongst them was Padraig McKearney, brother of

Tommy McKearney and one of the architects of a new strategy in which police and army bases were to be attacked and destroyed in order to deny the 'enemy' the ground, thus forcing them to retreat ever further north. The Vietcong had pursued a similar policy in Vietnam. As a local man, Francie Molloy understood the strategy and the reasons behind it.

> The Tyrone IRA would have been trying to do in Tyrone what Tom Barry's 'Flying Columns' did [in Cork] in 1920–21. They were typical republican guerrilla politics. I think what they were trying to do in a pretty targeted way was to remove what the British and unionists would see as the second line of defence, like the second border.

RUC stations became the target. The IRA's assault began on 28 February 1985 with a devastating mortar attack on Newry police station in County Down. It was tea-break time on a wet Monday evening. 'Gerry' was sitting in the sergeant's office when he remembers hearing the loudest explosions he had ever heard, right above the station. He dived under the table as more explosions thundered all around him. 'It seemed to go on for an eternity but it was obviously all over in seconds,' he told me, still visibly shaken by the experience. As he emerged from the dust, he heard somebody say the canteen had been hit and he rushed to give help.

> Nothing that I had ever been trained for or experienced could ever describe the scene I saw there. There were people dead and people in the process of dying. We tried to help one young woman who was lapsing in and out of consciousness. She lay there crying and saying nothing. We did our best to keep her alert and awake by sticking a pin in her palm. The ambulance crew arrived very quickly after that and took her away. She died soon afterwards.

Her name was Rosemary McGookin, aged twenty-seven. Eight police officers died with her.

> It was a scene of utter devastation, like a war-time bombing. The darkness and the bleakness and the gore will be with me for the rest of my days. They died a terrible death in a lonely place. They were my comrades and they were just snuffed out on a bleak Monday's night.

Ten months later, on 7 December 1985, the IRA struck again with a full-frontal attack on the RUC station in Ballygawley, County Tyrone. It was just before seven o'clock and the handful of police officers who were manning the station were just getting ready to hand over to the next shift and go home. One of them, 'Alan', was at the back of the station getting changed whilst his two colleagues, Billy Clements and George Gilliland were already on their way out. 'It was just a normal day,' 'Alan' recalled, standing in the yard where it happened. 'I had been out all day dealing with the sort of cases that the average English bobby would deal with.' Suddenly, as he was putting on his T-shirt, he heard the continuous sound of automatic gunfire raking the front of the building, which seemed to go on forever. It stopped as suddenly as it had begun, to be followed by the sound of two cars roaring away. 'Alan' emerged to be confronted by a beer keg in front of the station yard. Immediately recognizing what it was, he yelled to his remaining colleagues to 'Run for it!' They ran to take shelter round the back where they hoped the walls might provide some protection. 'Alan' remembers the bomb exploding.

> The whole place just erupted. The blast lifted me and threw me into a wall about fifteen feet in front. I had great difficulty trying to breathe because all the air had been sucked out of me. I was gasping for breath and couldn't hear anything. The explosion had deafened me. The explosion had taken out the electricity supply so the whole place – and the whole of Ballygawley – was in darkness. I climbed out of the rubble and made my way up to the front gate. Lying there was Billy Clements. I lifted his head up to see if I could feel a pulse in his neck but he was dead. Then we found George, covered in rubble. He was dead too. Both of them must have been cut down by the automatic fire in the early stages of the attack. I tried to hold myself together so that I wasn't physically sick and tried not to break down because I knew there was still work to do. You've just got to keep going.

What 'Alan' probably did not notice was that Constable Clements' Ruger revolver was missing, taken by his killers. Padraig McKearney is thought to have led the attack.

The following summer, on 11 August 1986, the IRA attacked the RUC station at the Birches in County Tyrone, which was unmanned at the time. Here the unit employed a new tactic. A two-hundred-pound bomb was loaded into the bucket of a mechanical digger which was driven through the perimeter fence where it exploded and destroyed most of the station. The driver was probably Declan Arthurs, used to driving the digger on his family's farm. As the unit left, they raked the building with gunfire. Declan Arthurs was now a marked man. In January 1987 he was arrested three times and taken for questioning to Gough Barracks, Armagh, where, according to his mother, he was held for seven, five and three days respectively.

> I was very afraid he was going to be killed. That's what they often told him when they stopped him at checkpoints. One night they made him lie down on the road and measured him and told him they were going to kill him.

Mrs Arthurs had no doubt her son was telling the truth.

The IRA intensified its campaign in the spring of 1987, killing Harold Henry, a member of the Henry Brothers construction business that carried out repairs on RUC stations. As part of its strategy of denying the ground to the enemy, the Provisionals had warned contractors and their employees of the consequences of repairing the damage caused by the IRA. Those who ignored the warning were declared 'legitimate targets' and killed. At eleven o'clock on the night of 21 April 1987, Harold Henry was taken from his home in front of his family, put up against the wall of his backyard and shot dead with two rifles and a shotgun. He left a widow and six children. Members of the IRA's East Tyrone Brigade were responsible. He was the first of more than twenty such 'collaborators' to be 'executed' for 'assisting the British war machine'.[4]

Four days after Henry's death, the IRA struck again, carrying out one of its most spectacular operations since the assassination of Lord Mountbatten. The target was Lord Justice Gibson, a Lord Justice of Appeal and Northern Ireland's second most senior judge, who had been high on the IRA's hit list since acquitting three RUC officers in 1984 for the killing of three IRA Volunteers in 1982, and his commendation of the policemen for their 'courage and determination' in bringing the Volunteers to 'the final court of justice'.[5] The case was one of those investigated by John Stalker. On 25 April 1987, Lord and Lady Gibson were returning from holiday and driving north from Dublin to Belfast. They left their Gárdái escort on the southern side of the border and drove across the short stretch of 'no man's land' to meet the RUC escort that would accompany them for the rest of their journey. A car packed with five hundred pounds of explosives was parked by the side of the road. As they drove by, the bomb exploded, killing Lord and Lady Gibson instantly. The tabloids demanded blood. 'Unleash SAS on the killer squads' announced the *Daily Mail*. 'SAS set to Swoop – Undercover army is briefed for battle', revealed the *Daily Mirror*.[6] The Secretary of State, Tom King, never mentioned the word 'SAS' when he announced to an outraged House of Commons that there would be 'additional support' to combat the IRA, but his audience and the British media read between the lines and felt they knew – and hoped

– what he meant. King himself had visited the scene of the killing and had been determined to act.

> It was obviously my duty after that appalling outrage to give reassurance to the law-abiding people of Northern Ireland that they would be protected from being terrorized and murdered in that way . . . We were conscious that we were facing an enhanced threat and we took enhanced measures to meet them.

On Friday 8 May 1987, a fortnight after the killing of Lord and Lady Gibson, the IRA's East Tyrone unit, which by now had become known as the 'A' team, went into action for the last time. With Declan Arthurs were three of the friends with whom he had been photographed at Martin Hurson's memorial in Cappagh the previous year: Seamus Donnelly, Tony Gormley and Eugene Kelly. The other older and more experienced Volunteers were the OC Patrick Kelly, Padraig McKearney, Gerard O'Callaghan, and Jim Lynagh. Patrick Kelly had previously been arrested in 1982 and charged with terrorist offences on the word of 'supergrass', Patrick McGurk, but, like most IRA suspects convicted on uncorroborated testimony, he had subsequently been released. Jim Lynagh, who lived across the border in Monaghan, was one of the security forces' prime suspects and had fought the Republican Movement's battles on both fronts, having been elected as a Sinn Fein councillor for Monaghan Urban District Council in 1979 and having been a highly active IRA Volunteer before and afterwards. Known as 'The Executioner', Lynagh was suspected of having led the IRA unit in January 1981 that shot dead Sir Norman Stronge, former speaker of the Stormont parliament, and his son James, at their stately home near the border, Tynan Abbey, which was then set on fire. In May 1987, the 'A' team's target was to be the RUC station in Loughgall, a quiet Protestant village in County Armagh, close to the border with Tyrone. Historically, Loughgall has a special place in the Protestant tradition, being the village where the Orange Order was founded in 1795. The RUC station was hardly a military garrison, being open for only four hours a day and manned by a token force. The attack was to be a exact copy of the attack on the Birches. With the benefit of hindsight, it seems strange that the IRA thought they could get away with it, but Sir John Hermon, RUC Chief Constable at the time, did not see it like that.

> If they had two successes they could see no reason why they wouldn't have a third – or a fourth or a fifth. The only thing that would stabilize that would be if they were caught. Then they might decide such operations weren't very fruitful. This is their thinking.

Why use the SAS?

The SAS are used in any situation where we believe that there's going to be a level of fire power which could transcend that which the RUC are capable of dealing with and that the army are trained to respond to. That's why they are in Northern Ireland, available to the RUC and available to the military. That's the best instrument you've got and you use it.

The attack was planned for the Friday evening. Just after lunchtime, a blue Toyota Hiace van was hijacked in Dungannon and at around tea-time, a mechanical digger was taken from a farm five miles from Loughgall. Declan Arthurs was again to drive the digger. The operation was a disaster from every point of view and the movements and actions of the 'A' Team suggest that there may well have been last-minute differences of opinion about the wisdom of proceeding with the operation. Arthurs drove the digger to where the explosives were located in the form of a two-hundred-pound bomb. It is highly likely that the location where the bomb was concealed had been under electronic and human surveillance for some time.

With Declan Arthurs at the wheel and the bomb in the bucket, the digger trundled into Loughall about 7.15pm, drove past the police station, turned and drove back again. The blue Toyota van driven by Eugene Kelly, with Patrick Kelly in the passenger seat and the rest of the unit in the back, did the same, both presumably to scout out the target and check the coast was clear. Tony Gormley and Gerard O'Callaghan then got out of the van and joined Arthurs on the digger, literally riding shotgun, with weapons in one hand and one of them carrying a lighter in the other to light the forty-second fuse for the bomb. The sequence of events that followed tends to confirm the suspicion that some members of the unit felt that all was not right. Inexplicably, Patrick Kelly – followed by others – appears to have jumped down from the passenger seat of the Toyota and opened fire on the station, perhaps to encourage the others, perhaps to resolve some dispute as to whether the operation should go ahead or perhaps because that was the way the attack on Ballygawley had also been launched – in a blaze of gunfire. The SAS soldiers lying in wait – an estimated two dozen – opened up with heavy weaponry including belt-fed General Purpose Machine Guns (GPMGs). Immediately before or after the gunfire Declan Arthurs smashed the digger through the station's protective fence. The fuse was lit and the bomb exploded, blowing off the roof, almost destroying the building and injuring the handful of specialist RUC men who had volunteered to stay inside, presumably, as 'bait' for the attackers. The commander of the SAS unit was also inside. The SAS cut the IRA unit to pieces with its GPMGs, Heckler and Koch high-velocity rifles and Browning pistols. Declan Arthurs died with the lighter in his hand. The photographs taken at the scene of the eight men are gruesome, their bodies – all dressed in blue boiler suits and some with masked faces – riddled by the 200 rounds fired by the SAS. The Toyota van was shot through like a sieve. It was a shattering blow for the IRA. The security forces and unionists were jubilant: the IRA had been given a taste of its own medicine and some of its most experienced killers had been removed from the scene forever. The RUC carried forensic tests on the eight weapons with which the unit had been armed and linked them to thirty-three incidents, including eight murders.[7] I put it to Sir John Hermon that once the decision had been taken to use the SAS, it was inevitable that the IRA unit ended up dead.

> I can't agree with that. I would go no further than to say that they fired first. If the SAS are on the ground and there's firing taking place to kill people with weapons of that fire power, what are they [the weapons] for? The people are using the weapons for terrorism and that's a risk they've got to take.

In the euphoria generated by the biggest loss suffered by the IRA since the Anglo-Irish war of 1920–21, the fact that a totally innocent civilian, Anthony Hughes, was also shot dead by the SAS, was in danger of being overlooked. He had been travelling in a car with his brother, Oliver, unaware of the ambush they were about to run into. Unfortunately, both brothers were wearing overalls. As the car tried to reverse out of the line of fire, SAS troopers positioned elsewhere mistook them for part of the IRA unit and opened fire. Forty shots were aimed at the Hughes' car, killing Anthony and wounding his brother. Hughes' widow lates received compensation from the British Government for the death of her husband. A few miles away in the operations room of the Tasking and Co-ordinating Group (TCG) at Gough Barracks, Armagh, a group of SAS men were reported to have gathered, waiting to hear the outcome from their officer who was listening to the radio. When the news came through, the officer turned to his men and said, 'Eight'. 'Eight arrested?', asked one. The officer shook his head and gave the thumbs down sign.[8]

To republicans and many others, the burning question is why was the IRA unit not arrested? The intelligence services had known of the plan, they knew the blue Toyota Hiace van had been hijacked, they probably had the cache of explosives under surveillance and, given the precedent of the attack on the Birches, probably calculated that a digger would be used.

Intercepting a digger trundling along a country lane would not have been difficult; intercepting the Hiace van bristling with armed IRA Volunteers would have been a far riskier, impromptu operation as it is unlikely that the precise route would have been known. Given its track record, the IRA unit would not have come out with hands in the air. There would almost certainly have been a shoot-out and lives of the interceptors might well have been lost. By lying in wait at Loughgall RUC station, the SAS maintained the element of surprise and sprang the ambush on its terms. Under the circumstances, it is difficult to imagine that arresting the IRA unit before they reached Loughgall was ever seriously contemplated. Sir John Hermon believes it was never a realistic possibility.

> If you start trying to do those things on country roads, setting up hiding places behind hedges and ditches on a route, you've got to make sure that your possibility of success is greater. Nothing else is moving. People see every movement. I cannot see that putting up road blocks is going to help. You know the way the IRA work. They've got vehicles going ahead, people looking at the scene and radioing back. In operational terms it doesn't make sense, unless you're 100 per cent certain that it would work.

Mrs Arthurs did not hear about the death of her son Declan and his friends until early the following morning. Her husband had come home late from work that evening at about half past ten with the news that, 'something has happened at Loughgall.' They turned on the radio and heard that men had been killed. No names were given. They said their prayers and went to bed. In the early hours of the morning cars drew up and neighbours came to tell the family that Declan was dead, killed in a hail of thirty-six bullets. He had the lighter in his hands. The bitterness has never left Amelia Arthurs.

> He was mowed down. He could have been taken prisoner. They knew that the 'boys' were coming and they lay in wait. The SAS never gave them a chance. Declan died for his country and I'm very proud of him. He was caught up in a war and he died.

The leadership of the IRA and Sinn Fein turned out in force for the eight funerals, delivering some of the most bitter graveside orations of the 'Troubles'. A special loss required special words; eloquence mingled with anger. Addressing 5,000 mourners in Monaghan at the funeral of Jim Lynagh, the most senior IRA Volunteer to be killed, Gerry Adams declared that Loughgall would become 'a tombstone for British policy

in Ireland and a bloody milestone in the struggle for freedom, justice
and peace', charging that the British Government did not understand
'republican activists'.

> It thinks it can defeat them. It will never defeat them. If Jim Lynagh
> could speak today, he would tell me to simply ask you to involve
> yourselves in the struggle which he fought in . . . Each Volunteer
> was riddled scores of times. Each had at least one bullet wound to
> the head. Their executions were the pound of flesh demanded by
> the British colonial murder machine.

To the IRA and its community, the most traumatic question posed by
Loughgall was, had they been betrayed by an informer? Certainly, the
intelligence in the hands of the security forces was of a very high grade
and likely to have been compiled from more than one source. Not
only had the cache of explosives probably been kept under electronic
surveillance – a bug installed by MI5's technical division – but it had
also been targeted by physical line-of-sight surveillance carried out by the
RUC's own covert squad, E4A, and the army's own undercover teams
from 14 Intelligence Company and other specialist units. It is also likely,
given the sophisticated web of electronic intelligence gathering being put
in place, that the homes and haunts of leading IRA suspects were being
bugged as well as their telephones being tapped. One former officer with
14 Intelligence Company who served in Northern Ireland around this
time told me that bugs placed in houses could transmit for months on end
and the material they recorded be downloaded from a helicopter directly
above the location so the intelligence could be processed and studied at
leisure. But despite the awesome technical capabilities now on hand, the
most valuable resource to the intelligence services at this time remained
human intelligence, provided from within the IRA's own ranks. There
were rumours that there *had* been an informer and that he had been killed
at Loughgall. Whether this was true, no one knew. There were suspects
and the IRA conducted its own internal inquiry but nothing was ever
proved and no one was ever 'executed'. The rumour could have been
'disinformation' designed to sow dissent and suspicion within the IRA.
I did hear from one very senior and well-informed security force source
that the informer had died with his comrades at Loughgall. I remember
the chill I felt when I heard this. Although that is what he remembered
hearing from someone else, my source could not be absolutely sure so I
subsequently checked with another highly placed security force source
who would have been in a position to know. This source was very
guarded but said 'the informer' – if indeed there had been one – was

not killed at Loughgall although he did not rule out the possibility that 'an informer' had been killed in the operation. I knew I was not going to get any further. Understandably, this is one of the most difficult areas in which to establish the truth and, as a result, this most sensitive of matters remains unresolved.

The Provisionals would prefer to forget the year 1987 as Loughgall was followed by yet more disasters for the IRA. On 27 October, a foreign-registered freighter, the *Eksund*, was seized off the coast of France. Above deck were three IRA men travelling on false passports: below deck were at least twenty surface-to-air-missiles; a thousand Czech-made AK 47 high-velocity rifles; two cases of RPG7 rocket launchers; two tons of Semtex high explosive; and a huge quantity of machine guns, mortars and grenades. They were a gift to the Provisional IRA from Colonel Khaddhafi of Libya. It was the biggest arms haul ever and the British and Irish authorities were jubilant. Not only, they thought, had the FBI cut off arms supplies from America – confirmed by the seizure of the *Marita Ann* off the coast of Kerry on 29 September 1984 with seven tons of American arms on board – but a new supply route from Libya had been nipped in the bud. They were wrong. In fact, four other shipments had already got through, in a staggering indictment of British and Irish Intelligence, which had been blind for over two years whilst the IRA got under the wire. In August 1985, a converted fishing boat, the *Kula*, had landed seven tons of arms at Clogga Strand off the coast of County Wexford, brought ashore in 'Zodiac' inflatable dinghies, and including seventy AK 47s and a consignment of Taurus pistols. The *Kula* had made a second trip in October 1985, off-loading at the same location ten tons of Libyan arms, including 100 AK 47s, ten machine guns and seventy boxes of ammunition. But it was the *Kula*'s third consignment in July 1986 that the IRA had been waiting for – a fourteen-ton consignment that now included four surface-to-air missiles (SAMs). There was more to come. In April 1986 Margaret Thatcher permitted American F111 jets to bomb Tripoli from bases in England. On the basis that my enemy's enemy is my friend, the Libyan leader was now even more enthusiastic to help the IRA, so much so that a bigger vessel was needed. The *Villa*, a boat twice the size of the *Kula*, was purchased, filled with 105 tons of arms, including an unknown number of SAMs, and arrived in Ireland in October 1986. It is staggering that this huge tonnage of weaponry was smuggled from Libya to Ireland, unloaded and conveyed for storage in underground bunkers right across the country without apparently arousing the slightest suspicion.[9] Consequently, when the *Eksund* was seized a year later, however great the triumph seemed, in fact the damage has already been done. The IRA now had an arsenal of almost 150 tons of weaponry with which to prosecute its 'Long War' almost indefinitely. It appears that only one of the SAMs has been fired – unsuccessfully since it seems to have been deflected by the helicopter's Electronic Counter Measures (ECM). Why the rest have not been used remains a mystery: it is suggested that parts may have been missing or that the batteries are dead. Sir John Hermon told me at the time that 'neither the South nor the North can rest until those arms have been recovered'. Some have been seized but most have not and still lie hidden in bunkers across Ireland. When the unionists talk about 'decommissioning' the IRA's arsenal, this is what they have in mind.

A week after the seizure of the *Eksund*, the IRA suffered a further catastrophic reverse. On 8 November 1987, as people gathered at the Enniskillen war memorial to commemorate Remembrance Sunday, a bomb exploded killing eleven people and injuring sixty-three. It had been meant for the security forces but, for whatever reason, was triggered prematurely, slaughtering civilians and Protestants saw it as a direct assault on their community. One of the lasting, agonizing memories of the day is Gordon Wilson's description of trying to rescue his dying daughter, Marie, from the rubble and his astonishing lack of bitterness in the wake of such a loss. The IRA issued a statement of 'deep regret' and Gerry Adams declared that the Republican Movement could not withstand another Enniskillen.

In the year since Declan Arthurs and his five friends had been photographed by Martin Hurson's memorial in Cappagh, much had happened. Four were now dead and one, Martin McCaughey, was to live for another three years before meeting an equally violent death at the hands of the SAS. Martin McCaughey illustrates in a way that few other cases do – not because they do not exist but because they are seldom brought to light – the interchangeability between the IRA and Sinn Fein. Martin McCaughey, whose IRA gloves and beret proudly adorn the walls of the family smallholding just outside Cappagh, became a Sinn Fein councillor on Dungannon District Council in the local elections of May 1989, when Gerry Adams spoke in support of his campaign. I asked Francie Molloy if Martin McCaughey was a reluctant Sinn Fein candidate given that his activities were more IRA than Sinn Fein.

> I would think so, yes. I don't think it would have been his natural line, although he had a natural ability as a leader within the area. He slotted into those roles because he knew his community and he knew its needs. I don't think it was any real problem for him to be a councillor but certainly it wouldn't have been the role he would have chosen himself.

McCaughey's role as a Sinn Fein councillor was short-lived. He was clearly on the security forces' most-wanted list and narrowly escaped being killed in a shoot-out allegedly involving army undercover soldiers in Cappagh's main street. McCaughey was wounded and went on the run, making no more appearances in Dungannon's Council Chamber. One night, 9 October 1990, twenty-three-year-old McCaughey and another senior IRA Volunteer, Dessie Grew from Armagh (whose brother Seamus had been shot dead by the RUC in another of the incidents John Stalker had investigated), were ambushed by the SAS whilst they were allegedly moving weapons from a mushroom shed near Loughgall.[10]

Dessie Grew was suspected of involvement in the IRA's European campaign and, according to the security forces, was linked to the killing of an off-duty Royal Air Force Corporal, Maheshkumar Islania, and his six-month-old baby on 26 October 1989 at a filling station in Wildenrath, West Germany. The precise circumstances of the shooting that led to the deaths of McCaughey and Grew remain unclear as, almost seven years after the event, at the time of going to press, the inquest had still not been held. I visited the sight of what was assumed to be an SAS ambush. It was a lonely, secluded spot. The inside of the large shed, coated with a polystyrene-type material, had been riddled with scores of bullet marks, each one circled with chalk by the forensic experts. As the two bodies were found lying on the concrete apron outside the shed, with two weapons lying nearby, it was a mystery how the *inside* of the shed had been peppered with gunshots. I could only assume that some of the soldiers had been lying in wait inside at the back of the shed. Given the topography of the shed and the bullet marks on its walls, most of the bullets could not have been fired from outside because of the angle at which they hit the walls. The only non-security force witness to the aftermath of the shooting was Monseigneur Raymond Murray who had received a phone call in the middle of the night from the RUC simply saying that there had been a shooting and that a priest was needed. Father Murray arrived at the scene at about three in the morning and was told the two men had been shot at around midnight.

He described to me what he saw.

The bodies were quite close to each other, maybe four or five yards apart. They were sprawled out, lying face down with legs and arms scattered. I anointed the two men whilst the RUC Inspector at the scene shone his light on the bodies. I remember one of them especially – I think it was Dessie Grew. There was a lot of congealed blood around his head, almost looking like black oil, with a slight sheen of red on it. The brain material out of the head was all mixed up with it. I can't remember Martin McCaughey's wounds but I got the impression that both had been badly shot up.

Did you see any weapons?

As far as I remember, there were two what I thought were Kalashnikov AK47s, lying two to three yards from the heads of the men, and I noticed that there was a pistol butt jutting out of Martin McCaughey's pocket.

Francie Molloy provided an epitaph for his friend. 'I think Martin McCaughey was very much an image of this entire struggle, with all aspects of it, and he died as part of that struggle.' Sinn Fein councillor and IRA Volunteer – Martin McCaughey had been both.

A by-election was held to fill McCaughey's dramatically vacated seat. Francie Molloy stood for Sinn Fein against the united opposition of the SDLP and the unionists on the Council and won by six votes. For a representative of any other party to have been elected would, he says, have been 'a discourteous act' and a betrayal of Martin Hurson's memory, whose death on hunger strike it was that had driven Martin McCaughey and his five friends to join the IRA.

Only one person in the snapshot survived: Dermot Quinn, who was sentenced to twenty-five years for the attempted murder of two policemen in April 1988. At least he is still alive.

Chapter Twenty

Armalite and Ballot Box

Throughout the late seventies and eighties, the critical period when the Republican Movement was redefining its strategy, Danny Morrison would have been regarded as one of the 'leadership'. In public relations and propaganda terms, he was a gift – bright, articulate, witty and devoted to the cause fought for by his family down the years. I met him in a hotel room in the mid-seventies and he arrived out of breath and grinning following some escapade that I preferred not to ask about. His uncle, a legendary IRA veteran called Harry White who was born in 1916, joined the IRA after the family had been burned out by loyalists in the twenties and thirties, and had then risen to become OC of the IRA's Northern Command during the forties campaign. Morrison remembers his uncle showing him a pistol during the loyalist attacks in Belfast in August 1969, when Harry White and his close friend, Billy McKee, had been amongst the handful of IRA veterans around to defend the nationalist population. The fact that Morrison's two sisters went on to marry British soldiers would not have pleased Uncle Harry.

Morrison's name will be associated forever with the history of the IRA and Sinn Fein because of his momentous phrase – the 'Armalite and Ballot Box' – used whilst addressing the Sinn Fein Ard Fheis at the Mansion House in Dublin on 31 October 1981, the month the hunger strike ended. Bobby Sands' remarkable victory in Fermanagh–South Tyrone and Owen Carron's success in holding the seat after Sands' death, had confirmed the leadership's belief that the Provisionals had to pursue an electoral strategy in parallel with their 'armed struggle'. It was perhaps not the kind of news that IRA Volunteers wished to hear following the collapse of the hunger strike only four weeks earlier. Morrison was scheduled to make a keynote speech to reassure the faithful that, despite the setbacks, the Movement was still strong and undefeated. Morrison's delivery of his address and the alacrity with which the media seized upon 'the Armalite and Ballot Box' phrase suggest that he had thought long and hard about what he was to say and had discussed the concept and phraseology with Adams, McGuinness and the other members of the leadership. However, the truth was that Morrison thought up the phrase literally a minute before he rose to his feet. The words did not come out quite as neatly as history records. 'Who here really believes we can win the war through the ballot box? But will anyone here object if, with a ballot paper in one hand and the Armalite in the other, we take power in Ireland?'[1] Nevertheless, the words were there. Martin McGuinness who was sitting beside him is said to have looked up and asked 'what the fuck's going on?' Morrison seemed to be articulating policy on the hoof. The 'Armalite and Ballot Box' is the twin strategy pursued by the IRA and Sinn Fein from that time to the declaration of the IRA's second ceasefire in 1997.

Initially, however, it did produce tensions within the Movement, in particular amongst the older Provisionals like Ruairí Ó'Brádaigh and David O'Connell who had helped to form the Provisionals and steered them through more than a decade of 'war' and, on two occasions, negotiations with the British Government. The policy the Movement now embarked upon was not that of the old IRA leadership. The veterans, who had never wholeheartedly embraced the Northerners' notion of the 'long war', asked why Volunteers would join if they knew they had to fight for ever, but Morrison replied that they were exactly the kind of Volunteers the Movement needed. There was no doubt that by the early eighties, the Adams axis of the Republican Movement was in the ascendancy. A year later, on 20 October 1982, the 'Ballot Box' element of the strategy passed its first test, to the surprise and concern of those outside the Republican Movement. Like most of his predecessors, the Secretary of State at the time, James Prior, tried his own political initiative by holding elections for an assembly. The elections for this were the first province-wide elections in Northern Ireland contested by Sinn Fein since the outbreak of the 'Troubles' in 1969 – the party won five of the seventy-eight seats with 10.1 per cent of the vote. The SDLP took 18.8 per cent. Adams and McGuinness both won seats in what appeared to be a comprehensive vindication of their strategy. Concerned mutterings began to emerge from the political undergrowth that one day Sinn Fein might eclipse the SDLP as the main nationalist party in Northern Ireland. A week later, on 27 October 1982, a thousand-pound bomb exploded on the Kinnego embankment near Lurgan, killing three policemen. As Morrison had promised, the Armalite and Ballot Box were advancing together. The following year saw even more spectacular gains for Sinn Fein. On 22 March 1983, another bright, articulate young Sinn Fein activist, Seamus Kerr, won a seat on Omagh District Council in a by-election. It was the first time in half a century that Sinn Fein had contested a council election in the North. Although to outsiders it was only a by-election seat on a remote District Council, Seamus Kerr was well aware of its significance.

> The councillor who had resigned actually had done so in protest at the stance of the SDLP on the hunger strike and other issues. The void was created. And through a well-planned and cohesive effort, we secured, I think, fifty-five per cent of the votes. It was a milestone.

But the most spectacular justification of the leadership's new policy came nearly three months later on 9 June 1983 when Gerry Adams was elected as the Member of Parliament for West Belfast. Throughout the province, Sinn Fein won 13.4 per cent of the nationalist vote and the SDLP 17.9 per cent. Adams, in accordance with republican tradition, refused to take up his seat at Westminster. James Prior was deeply depressed by Adams' election.

> I think my reaction was almost one of despair, that they were going to elect someone whom we considered to be a terrorist and who was not going to play any part at Westminster. I had no doubts at all that he belonged to the Provisional IRA. I think he encapsulated the Armalite and the Ballot Box completely. What a waste the whole thing was.

Gerry Adams' triumph was crowned on 13 November 1983 when he was elected President of Sinn Fein in succession to Ruairí Ó'Brádaigh. For the old Southern leadership, the writing was on the walls of Belfast and Derry as Adams, McGuinness and those around them gradually began jettisoning much of what they regarded as historical baggage which they now felt hindered, not advanced, the cause. Nevertheless, 'armed struggle' was to remain the cutting edge of the Republican Movement whose centrality was never in any doubt, as Adams emphasized in his first address as President to Sinn Fein's annual conference.

> I would like to elaborate on Sinn Fein's attitude to armed struggle. Armed struggle is a necessary and morally correct form of resistance in the Six Counties against a Government whose presence is rejected by the vast majority of the Irish people . . . There are those who tell us that the British Government will not be moved by armed struggle. As has been said before, the history of Ireland and of British colonial

involvement throughout the world tells us that they will not be moved by anything else. I am glad therefore to pay tribute to the freedom fighters – the men and women Volunteers of the IRA.

Adams' message was clear: Sinn Fein was pursuing an electoral strategy but not at the expense of the IRA. Sinn Fein was no longer just a 'paper seller', which was how it had been seen for years by many Volunteers, but was now in the process of becoming an equal partner to the IRA. For this strategy to work, the leadership had to show political results whilst at the same time allowing the IRA freedom to operate. Inevitably there were times, like at Enniskillen, when it became clear that the IRA's military campaign was in danger of jeopardizing all the political support that Sinn Fein had so assiduously built up, but such mistakes were seen as temporary, not terminal setbacks. By the end of 1983, the IRA was filled with a new confidence, boosted by Adams' endorsement of its central role in the 'struggle' and the mass break-out of many of its most experienced Volunteers from the Maze prison in September 1983. The Army Council issued a defiant New Year message.

This war is to the end. There will be no interval . . . when we put away our guns, Britain will be out of Ireland and an Irish democracy will be established in the Thirty Two Counties with a national Government.

1984 was to be the year of the Brighton bomb, but the IRA's campaign was matched by the equally determined loyalists who also stepped up their efforts. On 14 March 1984, a UDA unit, under its *nom de guerre* the Ulster Freedom Fighters (UFF), launched a gun attack on Gerry Adams as he was being driven away from Belfast City Hall. He was lucky to survive the ambush, his life saved by the body armour he wore. His assailants were found and gaoled for attempted murder. I later met one of them, who had pulled the trigger, inside the Maze prison and asked if he had any regrets – I meant given the length of his sentence. His only regret was that he had not succeeded.

Sinn Fein's seemingly meteoric political rise caused alarm bells to ring not just amongst their political opponents who continued to insist that a vote for Sinn Fein was a vote for violence, but also in the political corridors of the Northern Ireland Office and Number Ten Downing Street. Something had to be done. Sinn Fein had to be stopped. The British Government's new strategy was to try to marginalize Sinn Fein, boost the SDLP – the representatives of constitutional nationalism – and hit the IRA hard on both sides of the border by enlisting the support of the

Dublin Government. This was to be done by changing the historical axis of the problem. Since partition, Westminster had seen Northern Ireland as an exclusively British concern and its neighbour, the Irish Republic, as a foreign Government with no right to interfere in what was regarded as a British domestic affair. Geographically and historically, that approach became increasingly removed from reality as the conflict intensified and, as events affected its security too, Dublin came to have more than a passing interest in what happened in the North. The British also recognized the necessity of involving Dublin due to the IRA's use of the Republic as a logistical and operational base. As the British Government later found out, all the Libyan arms had been landed on the Republic's eastern seaboard. Gradually and reluctantly, Mrs Thatcher was persuaded of the necessity to lock Dublin into any solution of the problem. The political axis was redirected from London–Belfast to London–Dublin, the historic change becoming formalized in the Anglo-Irish Agreement signed at Hillsborough Castle, County Down, on 15 November 1985 by the British and Irish Prime Ministers, Margaret Thatcher and Garret Fitzgerald. The British Cabinet Secretary, Sir Robert Armstrong, who had metaphorically dragged a reluctant Mrs Thatcher to the table and put the pen in her hand, once told me that he felt the Anglo-Irish Agreement was the greatest achievement of his lifetime in politics. The Agreement basically gave Dublin a direct say in Northern Ireland affairs through a permanent representative's office at Maryfield just outside Belfast and regular meetings of British and Irish Ministers in what became known as the Anglo-Irish Conference. The two Governments were no longer conducting often acrimonious megaphone diplomacy but talking in a civilized way across a table and attempting to sort out the endless problems that affected both states. From that day to this, all political initiatives and developments have flowed from the relationship between the two Governments institutionalized in the Anglo-Irish Agreement.

Despite the fact that the very first words of Article One of the Agreement were a confirmation by both Governments that 'any change in the status of Northern Ireland would only come about with the consent of the majority of the people of Northern Ireland,' unionists screamed betrayal.[2] To them, it was the final step on the road to a united Ireland that had begun with the abolition of 'their' parliament at Stormont in 1972 and ended with their Government in bed with the enemy. There were violent loyalist street protests that Sir John Hermon's RUC heroically withstood despite intimidation, injury and the burning of some of their homes by loyalist mobs. One of the most bizarre images was the sight of a 'loyalist' protestor beating a member of the Royal Ulster Constabulary with a Union Jack. Mrs Thatcher knew the lesson of the UWC strike of 1974 when loyalist protests had brought down the last Conservative Government's power-sharing initiative and she was not prepared to see it happen again. Nor, as the hunger strike had shown to republicans, was she prepared to give in to threats, from whatever quarter they came. Tom King, who had succeeded James Prior as Northern Ireland Secretary, and who was perhaps never as enthusiastic about the Agreement as the Cabinet Secretary, apppreciated the depth of feeling it provoked amongst unionists and partly blamed their mistrust on the secrecy with which the Agreement had been drawn up by British and Irish officials under Sir Robert Armstrong and his Irish opposite number, Dermot Nally. Armstrong and Nally even commissioned a tie to commemorate the partnership. Neither unionists nor the Northern Ireland civil service were ever consulted or made aware of the detail of what was going on. As Tom King recognized, this inevitably caused great offence.

> I don't think it was the best way to go about it with a very secret committee from the mainland and the Cabinet Office. I don't think there was sufficient Northern Ireland input into the negotiations and the exclusion of Northern Ireland civil service was, I think, a mistake. Somebody as wise as Ken Bloomfield [the head of the the province's civil service] could have played, I think, a very useful role at an earlier stage in it.

The first that people outside this tight circle of Whitehall mandarins knew about the detail of the Agreement was when they saw it for themselves. For the Dublin Government it was a great breakthrough, the momentum driven by the need to counter the rise of Sinn Fein, as Garret Fitzgerald recognized.

> That was the driving force. It was the rise of Sinn Fein that led me to contemplate and work towards an agreement with Britain as the only way, it seemed to me, of blocking the rise of Sinn Fein and showing that it didn't have the backing of the majority of people in Ireland.
>
> **In your discussions with Mrs Thatcher and her officials prior to the signing of the agreement, did you spell out to her the reasons why you thought the agreement was necessary?**
>
> I'm not sure she ever emotionally grasped the idea of conciliating nationalism, providing them with hope that would make them go back to the constitutional nationalism. Intellectually she realized and accepted what I was doing but emotionally she was really always orientated towards security measures and she always kept going back

to security. But I think her officials understood both emotionally and conventionally what I was trying to do.

The Provisionals knew precisely what the Anglo-Irish Agreement was designed to achieve but they were not unduly dismayed. It was simply the latest in a long line of British initiatives to undermine and destroy them and they had no reason to believe that this latest strategy would succeed where others had failed. Sinn Fein was confident because of its electoral successes and the IRA was confident for a number of reasons. By the beginning of 1986, the Army Council knew that nearly twenty tons of Libyan arms were stored away in its underground bunkers following the *Kula*'s first two landings in 1985 and also that there were more arms in the pipeline from closer to home. The thirty-eight Volunteers who had escaped from the Maze prison had been specially selected, not just for their operational expertise, like that of Padraig McKearney, but also for their organizational abilities and skills. The IRA prisoners in the Maze had skilfully engineered their presence in one block so key personnel would be in position for the break-out. Two of the most valued escapees were Brendan 'Bik' McFarlane, who had played such a prominent role in the hunger strikes, and Gerry Kelly, who had been one of the team that had planted the Provisionals' first bombs in London in 1973. Kelly had finally been transferred from England to the Maze prison as part of the 1975 truce negotiations after a prolonged hunger strike in which he had been painfully force fed. On 16 January 1986, following a tip-off from British Intelligence, McFarlane and Kelly were arrested by Dutch police after a raid on an apartment in a modern, middle-class estate outside Amsterdam. In the flat was £3,000 in assorted European currencies, seventeen fake passports and maps of various European cities. The apartment was thought to be a base for the next phase of the IRA's campaign in Europe. Keys to a container parked nearby were also found. Inside were fourteen rifles, 100,000 rounds of ammunition and four huge drums of nitro-benzine, the basic ingredient of many IRA bombs. The two escapees fought extradition on the grounds that their offences were political, with Kelly likening their position to that of Nelson Mandela. 'As a prisoner of war,' he told the Dutch court, 'I have always looked on it as my duty to escape and rejoin the organization.' Both were extradited and returned to serve their sentences in the Maze, with McFarlane being returned to the same cell he had left on the day of the escape.

It is probable that the arrest of Kelly and McFarlane was the result of inside information although no doubt surveillance would have played its part once the targets had been identified – informers were always the biggest danger the IRA faced. Anti-terrorist co-operation, like anti-drugs co-operation, between the British and Dutch authorities was close, both being seen as similar evils. Intelligence co-operation between the police and army had improved a great deal after the disasters of the seventies, and by the eighties they were actually running some informers as a joint operation. One agent was Frank Hegarty from Derry, thought to have been recruited in 1979 and instructed, like his contemporary, Raymond Gilmour, to work his way up within the IRA. By the mid-eighties, the Derry Brigade had already been devastated by Gilmour and those in charge could not risk further betrayals. The hunt for informers was intensified. Frank Hegarty, attached to the Derry Brigade's Quartermaster's Department and therefore in a position to know where many of the arms dumps were, was invaluable to his handlers. In January 1986 he is thought to have pinpointed two of the caches in Roscommon and Sligo which had been used to store some of the first consignments of Libyan weapons from the *Kula*'s two trips the previous year, including eighty-seven AK 47s and a box of Taurus pistols. No doubt the British hoped that such an important discovery in the Irish Republic would prove to loyalists the security benefits of the Anglo-Irish Agreement. One of the boxes was faintly marked, 'Libyan Armed Forces'.[3] The find may have been the Intelligence services' first clue – North and South of the border – that there might be traffic between Libya and Ireland, which makes even more remarkable that two additional huge consignments were landed undetected. Hegarty may have known where the weapons were being stored but would have had no idea how they had come into Ireland, due to strict compartmentalization within the IRA's operations, to maximize security. The evening before the arms were seized, Hegarty took his partner, Dorothy Robb, out for a drink. 'You know I'm going away tomorrow,' he said. 'If I don't make it tomorrow, you may not see me for a long time.' Puzzled, Dorothy asked him what he was doing. He said he could not tell her. The next morning, as the arms were uncovered, Frank Hegarty had vanished. He is believed to have gone to the Foyle Bridge in Derry where he was met by British Intelligence officers and spirited away to England. He spent the next three months in protective custody at a Ministry of Defence house in Sittingbourne, Kent, from where he was allowed to telephone Dorothy and offer her a visit. She was flown to Gatwick where she met Frank and his minders at the nearby Copthorne Hotel. He and Dorothy were allowed to spend some time alone. 'When he closed the door, I asked him who the men were. He said they were MI5 – Maggie Thatcher's men,' she said. Dorothy told me she was offered £100,000 to include a house, a car and a trust fund for the children if she would 'vanish' with her partner. She refused and returned to Derry.

Somewhat surprisingly, a month later Frank Hegarty returned to Derry and explained that he wished to clear his name and prove his innocence. He said he had been set up to protect another highly placed informer within the IRA's ranks. Perhaps he thought he could bluff his way out of danger. He did not. On 25 May 1986 his body was found on a lonely border road near Castlederg, County Tyrone. His eyes were taped and his hands tied. Frank Hegarty had been interrogated, 'confessed' and shot through the head with a single bullet. In a statement the IRA said:

> We have now executed Frank Hegarty. Responsibility for the danger in which he finally placed himself rests not just with his handlers, or the British Government, but with the Dublin Government, now a partner with Britain in the recruiting of agents and spies.

It was the IRA's defiance of the Anglo-Irish Agreement.

As the autumn of 1986 approached, Adams had refined and put in writing the Provisionals' new strategy. A critical moment in the history of the 'Provos' was fast approaching and the President of Sinn Fein wanted people both inside and outside the Movement to know where he stood. In *The Politics of Irish Freedom*[4] he wrote:

> The tactic of armed struggle is of primary importance because it provides a vital cutting edge. Without it, the issue of Ireland would not even be an issue ... armed struggle has been an agent of bringing about change ... At the same time, there is a realization in republican circles that armed struggle on its own is inadequate and that non-armed forms of political struggle are as at least as important ...

Adams was preparing the ground for what historically was to be a seismic change in the Republican Movement. In 1969 the IRA had split over the issue of abstentionism – the refusal to take seats in any British or Irish parliament – and this was the issue on which, once again, internal battle was to be joined fifteen years later in the autumn of 1986. The Provisionals were about to jettison the principle which had been their birthright. But the issue was much more than one of principle. In effect it was a showdown between the old Southern leadership of Ruairí Ó'Brádaigh and David O'Connell, who had been amongst the founding fathers of the Provisionals, and the Northern leadership that had emerged before and after the hunger strike. Fortunately it was a bloodless coup. A working party – on which Ó'Brádaigh sat – was set up to examine the issue and a clear majority emerged in favour of taking seats in the Irish parliament, Dail Eireann, breaking with what had been the cardinal tenet of republican policy since the Treaty and partition. Jim Gibney, who had been one of the architects of the notion that Bobby Sands should run for election, knew that abstentionism had no place in republican politics at the end of the twentieth century.

> I think that abstentionism was a millstone round Sinn Fein's neck. [Ending it] brought Sinn Fein and republicans a dose of reality. The idea that in 1986 you could put on the mantle of republicanism and say that we do not recognize Leinster House [the seat of the Irish parliament] because it emerged from the Treaty is not a credible position. Not only is it not credible, you cannot build a political party without recognizing and accepting the institutions of that state.

But such a dramatic policy change could not be cleared by Sinn Fein alone. As with the split in 1969, the new direction had first to be given the IRA's imprimatur through a secret meeting of the Army Convention representing IRA units from all over Ireland. Only then could the motion be put to Sinn Fein. The special Army Convention is thought to have been held in County Navan in the Irish Republic in September 1986 when the IRA agreed that seats could be taken up in Leinster House. But, in the process, the IRA itself came extremely close to splitting. One of the Provisionals' most senior leaders was bitterly opposed to the policy change and is said to have gathered a small group of 'dissidents' around him to resist it. Such action verged on treason and there was even talk of a coup. He was summoned to face an IRA disciplinary inquiry and was lucky to escape with his life. It is thought that only his long and close friendship with Gerry Adams saved him from a bullet in the head. On several occasions I visited his home in West Belfast to see if he would throw light on an episode that has always been shrouded in secrecy. He was never at home and I was told that even if he was, he did not wish to talk. Perhaps silence was a condition of his survival.

Adams knew that a split was inevitable but wished the parting of the ways to be bloodless. Much lobbying was done in the Ó'Brádaigh camp, not least by younger veterans like Brendan Hughes, highly respected by both factions.

> I went round asking them not to walk out. A lot of them were friends and comrades of mine and I had a lot of respect for them. Everything was done to try and avoid a split but at least, for the first time in Irish history, they didn't split by shooting each other. It didn't mean the end of the involvement of Southern people in

the leadership but it certainly meant the end of the domination of the Republican Movement by people from the South.

Ó'Brádaigh was defeated in the vote and walked out of the Mansion House in Dublin with around twenty of his colleagues. Fifteen years earlier, he had walked out to form the Provisionals. Now he walked out to form a rival group, Republican Sinn Fein (RSF), committed to the maintenance of abstentionism and truly 'republican' policies. An armed wing, known as the 'Continuity IRA', later became associated with it. It was, if ever needed, a bolt hole for disaffected Provisionals although few actually made the transition.

Election results in 1987 showed that in political as well as security terms, the Anglo-Irish Agreement was beginning to work. Sinn Fein's performance in the Irish general election of 19 February was nothing short of disastrous with the party winning no seats and capturing only 1.7 per cent of the vote. The prime movers of the vote to end abstentionism and build a political base in the Republic argued that the process would take time. At the General Election on 11 June 1987, Sinn Fein suffered a further blow, seeing its vote fall by two per cent on its General Election performance in 1983. In contrast, the SDLP's vote increased by three per cent. To the British and Irish Governments, it was a triumph for the Anglo-Irish Agreement. So far, in a run-off between the Agreement and the ending of abstentionism, it seemed the British were winning two-nil.

Although only a handful of supporters left the Mansion House with Ruairí Ó'Brádaigh, there were still those amongst the Provisionals who were unhappy with the turn of events, yet not unhappy enough to step out into the cold. One such was Stephen Lambert from Derry who had been one of those named by Raymond Gilmour. Lambert had joined the Provisionals in the late seventies and been sentenced to six years imprisonment for acting as look-out during the attempted murder of a UDR man in the Protestant Waterside district of the city. He was released in late 1984 and returned home to find the Derry Brigade in disarray following the damage caused by Gilmour. Lambert decided to confine himself to Sinn Fein political activities by trying to build up the party's support on the huge, nationalist Shantallow estate and worked hard for the party during the 1987 June election.

I first met Stephen Lambert later that year and was astonished by his story of how he had been propositioned by a British Intelligence officer. He told me, in great detail, what had happened only a short time before.

I was sceptical at the time but now, ten years later and being myself more familiar with the recruitment and running of agents, I have little doubt that his account is essentially true.[5] Lambert provided me with copies of the handwritten documents he had given to the leadership in Derry to keep himself straight with the Republican Movement in the city. Frank Hegarty's fate the previous year was lesson enough to any potential British Intelligence recruit. Responding to criticism of Frank Hegarty's 'execution', Martin McGuinness had said, 'the only way out that I can offer people who find themselves being recruited and wish to get out of it would be to contact me or any member of Sinn Fein who would only be too willing to provide assistance'.[6] That is precisely what Stephen Lambert did, documenting everything that happened and passing it on to the leadership.

Lambert was ripe for recruitment since British Intelligence would have known that he was disillusioned with the direction the Republican Movement was taking after the vote at the 1986 Ard Fheis. The first approach was made to him on 19 September 1988 when he received a mysterious letter marked 'personal' with £50 inside, made up of one ten-pound and two twenty-pound notes. He had no idea where it came from but was worried that someone might be trying to set him up. Three days later, another letter arrived with a map of part of Donegal inside, leading him to believe that it might be an approach from the Gárdái Special Branch. Lambert was taking no chances and reported his unsolicited mail to Martin McGuinness.

Plenty of others had been killed because they were accused of 'touting' or who were 'touting' and in ninety per cent of these cases, the initial approach had come in a manner similar to the way I was approached.

Were you disillusioned with the Movement at the time and is that why you would be approached?

They seemed to think that I was. There were certain things that were happening that I wasn't entirely in agreement with, but how did they know? What's more, how could they have imagined that the differences could be so big that they could approach me?

In fact, although Lambert himself was opposed to the ending of abstentionism, when the vote was taken at the Ard Fheis he voted in favour because he was the representative of the Sinn Fein members in Shantallow, who supported abolition.

A fortnight later, Lambert says he was getting into his car near the Magazine Gate in Derry city centre when a man walked up to him, thrust an envelope under his arm and told him in an English accent, 'Look after it, kid. Take care of yourself.' He then ran away and was picked up by a passing car. Inside the envelope was £200 – in ten-pound notes – and a note roughly saying 'We believe you are being set up by the Republican Movement. Our organization can help you', with the instruction to go to Belfast's Aldergrove airport at six o'clock the following evening and indicating the route he was to take, along the A6 via Antrim. He immediately informed Sinn Fein and it was agreed that he should go to the airport on the appointed day, Tuesday 6 October, to find out more. Lambert was fifteen minutes late and it was pouring with rain as he left his Fiat Panda in the car park. As he was walking to the Arrivals terminal, he heard a voice behind him saying, 'Stephen'. He ignored it and walked on. The voice repeated his name. Lambert turned round to be confronted by a man in his late thirties wearing a cap, about five foot eight, with 'a kind of puffy, baby face and fairish hair going scarce' and an English accent. He said, 'Hello, I'm the man you're to meet,' told Lambert to go back to his car and said he would follow. The stranger said his name was 'Steve'. He got into the passenger seat of Lambert's car and they sat there for about an hour an a half with 'Steve' doing 'ninety per cent of the talking' whilst Lambert chain-smoked to calm his nerves.

'Steve' apologized for the way the approach had been made and asked Lambert if he had told anybody about the money. He said he had told a certain person in Sinn Fein about it to which 'Steve' remarked 'that person couldn't fart but they knew about it'. 'Why me?' asked Lambert. 'Steve' said they had been watching him for over a year and admired his 'commitment, honesty and organizational ability'. Even Martin McGuinness had remarked to certain people, 'Steve' said, that he had been impressed at the way the last election campaign had been organized in Shantallow. Lambert asked which organization he worked for. He said he was not 'police, Special Branch or Military Intelligence' but represented a body 'far higher than any of that' – which one, he was not prepared to say at this stage. There was only one intelligence agency left – the Security Service, MI5. MI6 no longer operated in Northern Ireland. The following details of the conversation are based on the eight-page, highly detailed account of the meeting, written in capital letters in Lambert's hand, which he compiled and handed to Sinn Fein.

'Steve' described Lambert as having a more 'romantic vision of the IRA than it really was – along the lines of the "Tan" war, flying columns, full-time soldiers and Connolly and Pearse' and stressed that he was not asking Lambert to turn or change his ideals. Far from it, he said, he was instead offering him a chance to achieve some of the things he believed in – such as 'a united thirty-two county state'. According to Lambert's testimony, he then outlined the incredible 'Plan'. Certain individuals in Sinn Fein, said 'Steve', believed by his organization to have 'potential' or to perhaps be of 'use', would be 'worked into key positions within Sinn Fein'. The purpose of this strategy would be that the 'new' Sinn Fein leadership would eventually disavow the armed struggle before any British declaration of intent to withdraw. This, he added, was to be 'a long-term operation spanning ten to fifteen years' at the end of which there would be a British withdrawal. The Anglo-Irish Agreement was 'the first step along this road' and British 'hyping of the security aspects of the Agreement at this stage is to appease the loyalists', he claimed. 'Steve' went on to explain the British rationale behind the 'Plan'.

1. No side is willing or able to appear to have been defeated.
2. Britain wants to withdraw from Ireland but will not do so at the point of a gun.
3. Neither of the above two aims are possible until the armed struggle is over but the 'right' Sinn Fein leadership could end the armed struggle without appearing to be defeated.
4. The British do not believe such a Plan is possible while the present leadership is in control of the Movement.

'Steve' noted that Martin McGuinness was 'more military minded' and was therefore a 'no hoper' but that Gerry Adams was 'very political' and 'would do almost anything to further his political career'. It is important to note that the account of this remarkable 'Plan' was written by Stephen Lambert who took it for granted that Martin McGuinness would himself read it.

'Steve' also outlined the 'Method' of implementing the 'Plan'. It was equally astonishing. 'Steve' explained that as far as Lambert was concerned, he ('Steve') was the leader of 'a small group of operatives' who would 'manage' whatever 'plants' they had 'sowed'. This would include the security of the 'plants', their promotion and development and the transfer of information and instructions between 'Steve', the 'plants' and 'Steve's bosses. He said that the Prime Minister, Mrs Thatcher, was aware of the operation and its progress without knowing the name of the 'plants'. The 'plants' were to 'rise', 'mainly by eliminating opposition', which would be done by 'discrediting and lifting'. Lambert also assumed that 'killing' would be another method. The fact that this was not mentioned lends credence to his account. The 'plants' were to be aided by freeing them from financial worries so they could work 'full-time' for the parties or organizations. Finally, 'Steve' indicated to Lambert what his role would be: 'to pass on information of the mood within the party, attitudes . . .

of particular individuals to particular policies and to implement and push policies' originating from 'Steve'.

No wonder Lambert chain-smoked through the encounter. As 'Steve' left, he took out 'a ton' (£100) and gave it to Lambert saying it was only the start. Lambert was given time to think about the proposition and was to report back at a meeting with 'Steve' the following day, Wednesday, 7 October 1987. Lambert drove back to Derry where he met a senior member of the IRA in the city and recounted what had happened. He was told to put everything in writing, with as much detail as he could remember. He started writing about one o'clock that morning and finished five and a half hours later. The Movement asked Lambert if he was prepared to go ahead with the second meeting that day. He said he was. It was suggested that he should be wired for sound so that this time the meeting could be recorded. Lambert, recognizing the risk, said no, at first, but then agreed to it. He told me how it was done.

> A small tape recorder was secured with surgical tape down my trousers, inside my underpants, and the mike was fed up through to my chest. As I left Derry, the tape recorder was left on pause and just as I came towards the forest [where the meeting was planned], I pressed the pause button so the tape actually started probably two or three minutes before I actually met 'Steve'.

Lambert had been given specific questions to ask in order to record on tape much of what he had heard in the car at Aldergrove the night before. The quality of the tape is variable and the sound of rain can be heard incessantly hitting the car roof. At one stage, there is a metallic noise – Lambert rattling his car keys in his pocket in the hope that it would deaden the 'click' as the tape came to its end. The tape is a remarkable record of the encounter, and having listened to it several times and compared it with Lambert's handwritten account of the previous evening's encounter at Aldergrove, I have no doubt it is genuine. 'Steve' starts by saying how glad he is that Lambert turned up and that he is now under his protection. 'Your security is the major consideration and that goes above anything else,' says 'Steve'. 'You're safe as houses.' Lambert then puts the key question he has been instructed to ask. Which organization does 'Steve' work for?

> Let's say we work for the Government. We're not restricted by anything – like the [Special] Branch, army or anything like that. You'll get a really good service from us. We go to the highest, let's put it that way. I know the question that's burning in your mind – 'am I going to be a Branch "tout" or anything like that?'

It's nothing like that ... We run professional agents all over the world, usually fighting terrorism. You'll work with us, not for us. That's the really important thing I really want to get to you. You're part of us now. It's going to be a whole change of your way of life. It's definitely a step up-market for you.

Lambert then says he does not want to be like Raymond Gilmour, going into the [RUC] Barracks and 'shopping' everybody. 'Steve' assures him that will not happen.

Gilmour was just a normal Branch 'gouger' and they used him until he was burned out completely and then they pressurized him into becoming 'supergrass'. I'm not interested in collecting evidence so that I can put someone in court – so that I can stand you up in court [to give evidence against them]. I get information which is useful to us so that we can actually use it to defeat terrorism, so that we can put people away ... just get them off the scene, whether it's to discredit them ... [or] set them up.

The most difficult moment for Lambert comes when 'Steve' asks him about Martin McGuinness, as Lambert knows that McGuinness will hear what he says. Yet he has to maintain credibility with 'Steve'.

'Steve' So, if we start with Martin McGuinnness, good ol' Martin, what position do you reckon he would hold in the great sway of things?

Lambert Well, I know for a fact he's Vice-President of Sinn Fein.

'Steve' What about on the military side?

Lambert Well, as you said last night, Army Council. But I mean there's no way I could ever know.

The meeting ended with Lambert and his tape intact, many more cigarette ends in the ashtray, and a third rendezvous arranged for a week later. Lambert reported back to the Republican Movement in Derry who listened to the tape. The day before the next meeting was due, Sinn Fein held a press conference to announce what had happened. To Lambert's surprise, he received another telephone call from 'Steve' a couple of weeks later. Lambert thought the revelation of the tape would have put paid to 'Steve's recruitment attempts but he was wrong. He was told to come to a meeting in ten minutes. Lambert consulted the Republican Movement on the spot and made off, with no tape recorder tucked down his underpants. The meeting, which was short, was held in Ness Woods outside Derry. 'Steve', far from being angry about the press conference, was over the moon.

> From his point of view, he thought that the press conference was a brilliant idea. If ever they wanted a secure cover for an agent, that was it. Just brilliant! That was just perfect! He still claimed he wanted me to work for him.

Lambert was instructed never to see 'Steve' again. The tape had served its purpose. However, 'Steve' was nothing if not persistent and appeared again a month later while Lambert was filling his car at a petrol station. 'Steve' said he wanted to meet. Lambert told him to 'get stuffed'. At this, according to Lambert, 'Steve's tone changed and he started to make threats. It appeared that the tables had been turned and 'Steve' had made his own recording of their last meeting in Ness Woods. What would happen, he wondered, if *his* tape fell into the hands of the Movement. Lambert said he did not care – the Movement already knew of the meeting – and told 'Steve' he wanted nothing more to do with him. Allegedly, 'Steve' again threatened Lambert with the tape, suggesting that if information was passed on to the Movement that Stephen Lambert was working for them, he would at least have to be put out of Derry or might even be found with a hood over his head. He claimed he was giving Lambert 'one last chance', named a time and a place and said that if Lambert turned up, he would hand over the tape. For the last time, Lambert told him to 'get stuffed'.

Stephen Lambert is lucky to be alive today. Frank Hegarty and several other IRA Volunteers from Derry are not.

Chapter Twenty-one

Stalemate

It was perhaps the biggest funeral in Belfast's Milltown cemetery since republicans had flocked in their tens of thousands to bury Bobby Sands. The cortège had wound its way from Dublin, the route lined with mourners. In the coffins lay the bodies of three IRA Volunteers from Belfast, shot dead by the SAS in Gibraltar on 6 March 1988 – Mairead Farrell, Danny McCann and Sean Savage, who was a nephew of Billy McKee. Their names joined the pantheon of IRA martyrs alongside the hunger strikers and the dead of Loughgall. At Loughgall, the IRA Volunteers had been carrying weapons. In Gibraltar they were unarmed. To republicans and many others, they had been shot down in cold blood, a powerful vindication of the belief that for years the British Government had operated a 'shoot to kill' policy, a conviction borne out by eye-witnesses in Gibraltar who said no warnings had been given by the men in plain clothes who opened fire. The SAS killings became the subject of fierce controversy between Mrs Thatcher's Government and the media, in particular Thames Television's *This Week* programme, *Death on the Rock* which investigated the Gibraltar incident and interviewed the eye-witnesses. The IRA admitted that its three Volunteers had been on active service at the time although it did not specify for what reason. British Intelligence said the unit was planning to blow up the Royal Anglian Regiment's band at a guard-changing ceremony and the SAS had intercepted them as, it was believed, they were about to detonate the explosives by remote control. In fact, the vehicle that was suspected of containing the explosives was subsequently found to be empty. Two days later a car containing 140 pounds of plastic explosure was found in Marbella and traced to the members of the IRA unit.[1] The Intelligence services had the right targets but the wrong timing and approach.

The Gibraltar killings triggered an astonishing series of events. As the coffins were being lowered into the graves in Milltown's Republican plot ten days after the shooting, a lone figure was seen heading towards the mourners from the motorway that runs along the bottom of the cemetery. The mourners could not believe what was happening. The man started

shooting and throwing grenades. Almost the entire Provisional leadership
was gathered around the graveside, a unique target for a loyalist gunman
apparently prepared to commit suicide. Richard McCauley watched
incredulously.

> The next thing I remember is this dull thud and not being quite
> sure what it was. Then a second dull thud and seeing the smoke and
> realizing that a bomb had gone off. There was an initial concern that
> we could be standing on top of a bomb and that people were going
> to be killed. Then I became aware that it was actually somebody
> throwing things. We could see this guy had at least two guns and
> grenades.

Terence 'Cleeky' Clarke was equally astonished.

> It was pandemonium. I actually thought mortars were being fired in
> Milltown. I couldn't believe what was happening. Here we were in
> a cemetery burying the dead and people were being attacked. Hand
> grenades were being thrown and shots fired. People screaming. Just
> unbelievable.
>   The leadership of the Movement started to calm people, telling
> them to get down. He was firing into the crowd and wasn't looking
> for a specific target. He just wanted to kill Catholics – if they were
> republicans, then it was a bonus. If he hit the leadership people, then
> it was ten free points. There was no sense of who he wanted. He
> just fired into the massive crowd and just wanted to kill people.

The attacker was a loyalist called Michael Stone. Both the UDA and UVF
disclaimed association. Stone was lucky to escape with his life after being
caught by a group of republicans who pursued him along the motorway
whilst he was still armed. Only the police saved Stone's life. He claimed
three victims, killing one IRA Volunteer, Kevin Brady, and two civilian
mourners. More than fifty others were injured.

Three days later, as Stone's IRA victim, Kevin Brady, was being buried,
another astonishing confrontation took place that was just as sudden and
unexpected. As the funeral cortège wound its way through Andersontown,
a silver Volkswagen car suddenly drove towards the procession at high
speed and then tried to reverse, only to find its line of retreat blocked
by a black taxi. In remarkable scenes, the crowd surrounded the car and
tried to apprehend its occupants, not knowing who they were but fearing
loyalists and a repetition of Michael Stone's Milltown attack. Their worst
fears were confirmed when one of the men produced a Browning pistol

and fired a shot in the air. In the charged atmosphere of the time, the crowd was convinced it was a Milltown situation all over again. 'Cleeky' Clarke, the chief steward at Kevin Brady's funeral at the family's request, took immediate action.

> Here people were once again faced with the same threat. The car came from nowhere. They thought they were the same type of people [as Michael Stone] only this time there were two of them – armed and dangerous men. They fired a shot and the people again reacted in the only way they knew how.
>
> **What do you think the men in the car were?**
> I thought they were loyalists, I really did. They had no uniforms and were in civilian clothes. They looked scruffy and it was an unmarked, ordinary civilian car.
>
> The man actually pointed the gun at me and I said, 'Don't be firing! Don't be firing! Who are you? Who are you?' No answer. No talk whatsoever. He turned round and I thought at that time, he's looking for a specific target. He's looking for Gerry Adams. He's looking for Martin McGuinness. He's looking for some of the leadership. Instantaneously that's what I thought. I jumped on him then, brought him to the ground, struggled with him with others and eventually disarmed him and left the scene.

What 'Cleeky' Clarke did not know – as nobody did at the time – was that the men were two army corporals called Derek Wood and David Howes of the Signals Regiment. Corporal Howes had only recently arrived in Northern Ireland. Despite the conspiracy theories that tend to surround such dramatic events, it appears that the soldiers were not on some undercover surveillance mission, nor were they members of the SAS as republicans had initially believed: they were ordinary soldiers on their way back to Army Headquarters at Lisburn from an army barracks in the city. How they came to be there and stumble across the funeral procession remains a mystery. One theory was that Corporal Wood was showing the new arrival, Corporal Howes, the sights of West Belfast and thought the funeral of an IRA man was something worth seeing. We shall never know. The corporals were bundled into a black taxi, driven away, stripped and shot dead by the IRA with their own gun. The photograph of Father Alec Reid, a priest from the nearby Clonard monastery, kneeling by the naked and bloodied body of one of the corporals, administering the last rites, shocked the British – and Irish – public when they opened their newspapers the following morning. 'Savages' was the most common word used by the British tabloids to describe not only the soldiers' killers but also the 'mob' that had surrounded their car and dragged them out to certain death. Was 'Cleeky' Clarke – a Catholic who would always repeat 'God have mercy on us' whenever he mentioned the dead – not ashamed when he saw the fate of the soldiers?

> Not ashamed. I had no part in that [their killing]. I had part in the capture of them. I didn't know they were soldiers then but I was sad. It shouldn't happen to anyone. I don't want people to think, 'here's another IRA hypocrite'. That's not the case. What happened was wrong. Why the soldiers were there was wrong. That isn't to justify their death, right. Death's wrong.
> **People saw those responsible for their deaths and the crowd who had attacked the soldiers – for whatever reason – as savages.**
> I'm not sorry for my actions but we were only savages after the act, after it was found out that they were soldiers. Before then, we were heroes [for stopping another loyalist attack].

Clarke was subsequently gaoled for his part in the apprehension of the soldiers.

The dreadful events of March 1988 that began with Gibraltar and ended with the killing of the corporals was, like the hunger strike, a historical watershed in the conflict although few may have realized it at the time. In that bloody fortnight, the SAS had killed three IRA Volunteers, the loyalist Michael Stone had killed one IRA man and two civilians, and the IRA had killed two soldiers. Memories of Enniskillen the previous November were also still fresh in people's minds. All three parties to the conflict – the British army, the IRA and the loyalist paramilitaries – had blood on their hands. People cried out for it to stop. If one tries to identify the point where what became known as the 'peace process' began, then this is probably it.

The impetus behind the process came from the republican and nationalist side, each initially working separately and then joining forces. A year earlier, in May 1987, Sinn Fein had published the first of a series of discussion documents called 'A Scenario for Peace' which marked some advance from the position the Provisionals had adopted at Cheyne Walk in 1972 and during the Truce of 1975. Critically, it began to address the problem of the majority unionist population in Northern Ireland without whose agreement no lasting settlement can be reached. In the unlikely event of any unionists bothering to read its slim eight pages, they would have found little comfort in the section headed 'Loyalists'.

> We do not intend to turn back the pages of history, or to dispossess the loyalists and foolishly attempt to reverse the Plantation. We offer them a settlement based on their throwing in their lot with the rest of the Irish people and ending sectarianism. We offer them peace. We offer them equality.
>
> Britain must take the initiative and declare its intention to withdraw. That is the first step on the road to peace. Republicans will respond quickly and positively.

In other words, unionists had to go along with the Provisionals' analysis. As so often before, there was a total absence of realism in the Movement's political thinking. In addition, 'A Scenario for Peace' said that Britain not only had to disengage but had to set a definite date 'within the lifetime of a British Government . . . for the completion of this withdrawal'. That meant 'Brits Out' in five years! In effect, it gave the British two years more than Séan MacStiofáin had offered William Whitelaw at Cheyne Walk fifteen years earlier.

> The ending of partition, a British disengagement from Ireland and the restoration to the Irish people of the right to exercise self-sovereignty, independence and national self-determination remain the only solution to the British colonial conflict in Ireland.

The language may have been different, with reference to 'national self-determination' instead of 'Brits Out', but the message was exactly the same. 'A Scenario for Peace' hardly marked a giant leap forward. Apparently, the original draft was even worse with the suggestion that resettlement grants should be offered to unionists if they did not like the solution. Wiser counsels prevailed and the reference was omitted. Tom Hartley, one of the architects of Sinn Fein's peace strategy, accepts that the document had obvious limitations. But at least, he argued, it marked a beginning from which the Provisionals began to inform a wider audience outside the republican 'family' precisely where the Movement stood.

> Republicans wanted to strengthen their view of what peace meant. It was really what the republican struggle was about, that you put in place political conditions that lead to a lasting peace in this country. What we were doing was to define our views on how we thought the conflict could be ended and how you could have a lasting, peaceful settlement.
>
> The weakness of 'A Scenario for Peace' is that we had produced

a document which I suppose in republican terms is a 'ground' document. But only republicans read it. So we went back to the drawing board after that to figure that one out. What we wanted to do was to develop a politic in which we would engage with all the political forces on this island so that it wasn't just republicans talking to republicans. We could do that day in, day out. What we wanted was to engage with everyone on the island and indeed with the British too.

Tom Hartley's definition formed the basis of the 'peace strategy' that Sinn Fein continued to refine over the next ten years. The strategy evolved towards recognition of the unionist position, as republicans made further contacts with members of its community. It was an eye-opening experience for both and, as Hartley accepts, had a profound influence on republican thinking.

What we have now said is that you can't have an accommodation without the unionists. You can't have peace in Ireland if the unionists don't have their fingerprints on a settlement. So our thought processes have changed more this last number of years because of that dialogue.

Adams, Hartley and the group around them knew there was much work to be done. Richard McAuley, another of Sinn Fein's leading political thinkers, endorsed the need for a new peace strategy that would look forwards not backwards and confront the political realities faced by the Republican Movement and which were also common to all parties to the conflict. McAuley also recognized the shortcomings of 'A Scenario for Peace'.

Looking back on it now, it was quite a naive document and quite a short document. It was in many ways quite traditionalist in its approach but I think that was understandable. Republicans had long accepted that this was a war that nobody could win and in that context what do you do? The obvious answer is to try to find some way of bringing the different enemies together, preferably around a table, and work out some way of negotiating a settlement. I'm not sure how focused or how clear-headed we were about all of that back in the mid-1980s.

But if the new strategy was to work, the IRA had to go along with it. That meant that it had to produce tangible results which would indicate the strategy was working and that it genuinely offered an alternative way forward. In other words, the peace strategy finally had to lead to talks with the British Government and negotiations with all the other parties and, most critically and difficult of all, with the unionists. Only when the Army Council and its Volunteers were convinced that movement towards a final settlement was under way, would the Armalite be put away. The process was to take many years before it appeared to approach fruition with the IRA ceasefires of 1994 and 1997.

The cardinal weakness of Sinn Fein's position at this critical period in the late eighties was that Sinn Fein, true to its name which means 'Ourselves Alone', still stood alone. Although it had made impressive electoral gains since its embrace of the 'Armalite and Ballot Box' at the beginning of the decade, it remained a minority nationalist party – the SDLP were still way out in front – with between ten and twelve per cent of the total Northern Ireland vote. Three months before the publication of 'A Scenario for Peace', Sinn Fein had almost been wiped out in the Irish Republic, winning no seats and taking less than two per cent of the vote. So much for ending abstentionism, said the critics. Sinn Fein realized that if it was to progress its policies and move forward it had to build strategic alliances with others. This was to become the key to Sinn Fein's peace strategy. The building of this 'nationalist coalition' – which unionists simply saw as a republican front – started at the beginning of 1988 and, despite almost terminal ups and downs, went on to become the most powerful nationalist coalition Ireland has ever seen, embracing Sinn Fein, the SDLP, the Dublin Government, Irish America and the White House. For Sinn Fein and the others like John Hume and Albert Reynolds, the Irish Taoiseach, who also worked tirelessly to build it, it was a remarkable political achievement which began to produce remarkable political results.

The process began on 11 January 1988, two months after Enniskillen, when the President of Sinn Fein, Gerry Adams, met John Hume, the leader of the SDLP. Both had been appalled by the Remembrance Day bomb. Adams had remarked that another atrocity would 'undermine the validity of the armed struggle' and added tellingly, 'there is no military solution. Military solutions by either of the two main protagonists only mean more tragedies.' Significantly, he concluded by saying that he was now prepared 'to consider an alternative unarmed form of struggle to achieve Irish independence. If someone would outline such a course, I would not only be prepared to listen but I would be prepared to work in that direction.'[2] John Hume, whose mind had long been working along similar lines, heard and acted. He knew that the key to peace lay in persuading the IRA to give up 'armed struggle' and, through its political wing, Sinn Fein, to become exclusively involved in politics. But Hume was also aware that to give rise to a situation in which the IRA would be prepared to put its guns away, the British Government would have to create circumstances that would enable the IRA to do so. The creation of these circumstances initially took over six years. Hume knew that the concept would only work if two things happened: the Republican Movement's recognition of unionist consent to any settlement and the British Government's acceptance of the principle of Irish self-determination. The question of how self-determination was to be exercised engaged all those involved for months on end. Hume was experienced enough to realize that the British would never give the IRA the declaration of intent it required because of its responsibilities to the Protestant majority in the province, but he thought that the British Government might ultimately be persuaded to declare that it had no self-interest in remaining in Northern Ireland and did so only because of the wishes of its majority population. The onus would then lie with nationalists and the republicans to persuade their Protestant fellow Irishmen and women that their interests would be best served by a new constitutional arrangement, which Hume broadly referred to as 'A New Ireland', to be agreed by all people and traditions on the island. In such a settlement, as Hume declared, 'nothing would be agreed until everything is agreed'. Britain would create the framework for such a process but would not interfere in it.

Hume was taking great personal and political risks in opening up a dialogue with Gerry Adams and Sinn Fein. As loyalists saw it, he was supping with the perpetrators of Enniskillen and other IRA atrocities far too numerous to mention. Loyalists did not make the distinction between the IRA and Sinn Fein which, to the intense irritation of Sinn Fein, led to the expressions 'IRA/Sinn Fein' or 'Sinn Fein/IRA' entering political currency. There was indeed a distinction. Although both were part of the same organization, the difference was one of emphasis and means. Sections of Hume's party were also unhappy at the dialogue as they saw it boosting the standing of Sinn Fein to the detriment of the SDLP. Three years earlier, on 23 February 1985, John Hume had met members of the Army Council to try and persuade them 'to end their campaign of terror'.[3] He had been driven across the border, blindfolded and taken to a secret location where he met one of the leaders of the Maze escape, Brendan McFarlane, who was still on the run, and two other senior IRA figures. The meeting had lasted seven minutes but came to an abrupt end when McFarlane insisted on video-taping the encounter. Hume had refused, suspicious of the purposes for which such a recording might be used.[4] In 1988, however, Hume and Adams came together on a very different footing. Both were Westminster MPs and both recognized the benefits of trying to build a broad nationalist coalition. The initial approach to the two leaders had been made almost a year earlier in the spring of 1987 by Father Alec Reid from the Clonard monastery in Belfast, who was to play a pivotal role as the intermediary who made the building of the coalition possible.[5] Father Reid's administration of the last rites to the two army corporals came in the midst of what became known as the Hume–Adams talks and only increased the priest's determination to see that they came to fruition. The meetings became formalized when delegations from the two parties met, although their deliberations were initially kept secret, thereby fuelling loyalist suspicions. Sinn Fein was represented by Gerry Adams, Tom Hartley, Danny Morrison from Belfast and Mitchel McLaughlin from Derry. The SDLP delegation consisted of John Hume, Seamus Mallon, Sean Farren and Austin Currie, none of whom were from Belfast. Each side produced discussion papers in a process that lasted for most of 1988. At one stage they exchanged documents in the three days between Michael Stone's attack at Milltown and the IRA's killing of the corporals, the violent backdrop to their talks underlining the importance of what Sinn Fein and the SDLP were trying to do. Four days after the killing of the corporals, the delegations met again. Sinn Fein had largely based its position on 'A Scenario for Peace' that demanded the setting of a date for withdrawal within the lifetime of a British Government. John Hume had always taken issue with what he believed was a naive and dangerous position that disregarded the political realities of Northern Ireland. The savagery of the past few days made Hume even more determined to get his point across and he sent the following letter to Adams and the Sinn Fein delegation.

It is not enough to suggest that the British presence is the primary source of our problems and therefore the cause of all the violence . . .

Does anyone in Ireland, even among supporters of the IRA, believe that the present British Government will accede to the demands of the IRA made by force? Does that not mean that the whole country and the members and families of the IRA face at least another decade of what we have just been through with all the suffering and without any guarantees of achieving their objectives at the end of it?

Is it not time for the IRA and members of the Provisional Republican Movement to seriously reconsider the methods that they have chosen to achieve their objectives or are they in danger of moving to a situation – or are they already in it – where the methods have become more sacred than the cause?

Hume argued that the Anglo-Irish Agreement provided a basis for a settlement when it stated that if a majority of the people of Northern Ireland at some future date 'wish for and formally consent to the establishment of a united Ireland' the British Government would introduce legislation to make it possible. In other words, Hume said, unionists had to be persuaded and not forced at the point of a gun. The way out, he concluded, was a conference convened by the Irish Government.

> . . . to try and reach agreement on the exercise of self-determination in Ireland and on how the people of our diverse traditions can live together in peace, harmony and agreement. It would be understood that if this conference were to happen that the IRA would have ceased its campaign.

The meetings survived the continuing violence of 1988 and the increasingly vociferous demands from unionists to call them off. The Sinn Fein/SDLP talks finally came to an end on 5 September 1988 without any agreement on an 'overall strategy'. Both sides made public the positions they had reached, in words that were to become increasingly familiar as the 'peace process' gathered momentum over the following decade. The SDLP concluded:

> . . . the search for agreement on the *exercise of that right [for self-determination]* . . . is the real search for peace in this island . . . it is self evident it cannot be pursued by armed force and cannot be won by armed force. The agreement of the unionist people is essential. Such agreement is obviously a task of persuasion, not a task of coercion . . . The SDLP hopes and expects that the debate . . . will continue in the public and private arena . . .

Sinn Fein announced that it was:

> . . . somewhat perplexed that the SDLP continues to maintain that the British Government is now a neutral party to the conflict in Ireland . . .
> If Irish nationalist parties and the Dublin Government are genuine about ending the British presence then they must be involved in concerted political action nationally and internationally to bring about conditions in which the right to national self-determination can be exercised . . . we look forward to further debate and discussion.[6]

Although the dialogue ended without agreement, Hume and Adams kept in contact with each other privately. Whilst the talks had been going on, parallel approaches were being made, through the auspices of Father Reid, to politicians and officials in Dublin. Similar messages had also been sent to the White House through John Hume's long-standing connections with the Kennedy family and others in America. Sinn Fein, too, now began to develop its own political network in the United States. Gradually, through 1988 and beyond, the foundations of the peace process were laid. The Anglo-Irish Agreement had failed to isolate Sinn Fein and now the party was gradually being brought in from the cold. But there was still a long road ahead with more death and suffering in store for all sides.

In accordance with its strategy, the IRA carried on killing during the Sinn Fein/SDLP talks. On 20th August 1988, a bus full of soldiers from the First Battalion, Light Infantry returning from leave was driving along the main A5 trunk road back to their barracks in Omagh. The driver had been warned not to take that route as there was intelligence of 'a threat' along that particular stretch of road. Just outside the village of Ballygawley, County Tyrone, a two-hundred-pound bomb hidden in a car trailer exploded, throwing the bus off the road and onto its side, killing eight young soldiers and injuring twenty-eight. It is not known why the driver ignored the warning. One of the first civilians to arrive at the horrific scene was a part-time UDR soldier from Ballygawley and local unionist councillor, Sammy Brush. During the hunger strike Brush had miraculously survived an IRA assassination attempt and seriously wounded one of his attackers in the process. Gerry McGeough, the IRA man later convicted of trying to buy surface-to-air missiles in America, was suspected of the attack on Brush. Standing by the memorial at the scene of the explosion, Sammy Brush described what he had found on the pitch-black night when at first only torches had revealed the scene of devastation.

> There was glass, blood and bodies, and young soldiers badly mutilated but still alive. It was a scene of carnage that I would never want to witness in my life again. It was probably the worst night of my life. All you could do was to try and comfort them and give them words of encouragement and comfort and do your best for them. One soldier had actually crawled through the mud towards a little house and died because no one found him in time to save him. The story is he bled to death. It was a terrible incident, terrible to think that another human being could blow up other human beings.

Ten days later, the SAS shot dead three IRA men near Drumnakilly, a spot not far from where the bus had been blown up. The dead IRA Volunteers were two brothers, Gerard and Martin Harte, and Brian Mullin from the Provisionals' Tyrone Brigade, who had helped to carry the coffin of one of the IRA men killed at Loughgall. The three men were believed to have carried out the bombing of the bus. It was a carefully laid ambush as the IRA had been under surveillance for some time, including, it is thought, electronic surveillance carried out by 14 Intelligence Company. The person the intelligence services had identified as the IRA unit's target was a known UDR man who drove an easily recognized lorry around the area. The UDR man was used as bait to lure the IRA into a trap. On 30 August 1988, the lorry faked a breakdown on a lonely road outside Drumnakilly but, unknown to the IRA unit that planned to kill him, the driver was an SAS soldier posing as the UDR man. The IRA were meant to believe that the UDR man was attending to his broken vehicle. Mullin and the Harte brothers, armed with two AK 47s and a Webley .38 revolver, drove past, intent on killing their target, unaware that the SAS were lying in wait. As often happens in such incidents, both sides give different accounts of what happened. The army claimed the IRA opened fire first. Republicans say it was the SAS who started shooting. At the inquest into their deaths almost five years later, it was revealed that the SAS had fired 220 rounds and the IRA sixteen. The tabloid press were jubilant. The *Sun* proclaimed, 'SAS rub out IRA rats' whilst the *Star* was more specific, 'Revenge! SAS kill three bus bombers'. Whether or not the three were responsible for the bus bomb, the SAS had struck yet another blow against the IRA's Tyrone Brigade. Six weeks later, on 19 October 1988, the Government introduced restrictions which forbade all broadcasting organizations to transmit the actual voices of those believed to be involved in 'terrorism' or organizations that were deemed to support it. The restrictions covered both republican and loyalist groups and meant that Sinn Fein members and their loyalist counterparts could be seen but not heard. Actors' voices were used and the thespian who perfected Gerry Adams' intonations is reputed to have made a small fortune. The restrictions were reduced to near farce when broadcasters started to synchronize the actor's words to the movement of the 'banned' person's lips. The restrictions did have some effect on Sinn Fein: in the four months before the ban, the party had 471 enquiries for interviews, whereas in the four months immediately afterwards it had only 110. Television producers were also inclined to run even briefer 'sync-bites' if they involved using an actor's voice. The restrictions themselves were more cosmetic than real but were a demonstration of the British public's abhorrence of what it saw as the IRA's mass murder of its soldiers at Ballygawley and the hypocrisy of the IRA's Sinn Fein apologists.

Mrs Thatcher's Government continued to hit back at the IRA in more devastating ways. On 3 June 1991, three members of the East Tyrone Brigade, Tony Doris, Laurence McNally and Michael 'Pete' Ryan, were ambushed by the SAS in the Protestant village of Coagh and 200 rounds were fired at the car they were in. The petrol tank exploded and the car ended up a charred wreck. Two weapons were found nearby, one of which was shown forensically to have been used in the killing of three Protestants in Coagh two years earlier.[7] Almost a year later, on 16 February 1992, four IRA Volunteers – again from the East Tyrone Brigade –- Sean O'Farrell, Kevin Barry O'Donnell, Patrick Vincent and Peter Clancy were shot dead by the SAS. The IRA unit had mounted a heavy Russian DHSK machine gun – believed to have been part of the Libyan arms shipments – on the back of a lorry and opened fire on Coalisland RUC station. They then withdrew to the nearby St Patrick's church at Clonoe just over a mile away to abandon the lorry and make for their getaway from the church's car park. The SAS was lying in wait, again no doubt working on very high-grade intelligence either from a source within the IRA or electronic surveillance – or both. The British press said the unit was given the opportunity to surrender but chose to fight its way out. Three AK 47 rifles were found at the scene. Kevin Barry O'Donnell had been acquitted at the Old Bailey in London the previous year after his arrest following a car chase through North London. Two AK 47s had been found in his car. O'Donnell's defence was that he had been horrified to find that the IRA had used his vehicle and he was trying to dump the weapons at the time. The jury found him guilty on minor charges but acquitted him of the serious offence and O'Donnell soon returned to Tyrone to carry on the 'war'. The SAS delivered a different verdict. Patrick Vincent's mother asked the IRA and Sinn Fein to stay away from her son's funeral as the family did not believe he had been a Volunteer. Patrick had been driving the lorry. 'As far as we are concerned,' she said 'our son was not involved with the IRA, but they are claiming him. We are sure he was pressurized.' All four men were barely twenty and from the generation that followed Declan Arthurs and his friends who had been photographed at Martin Hurson's memorial and later killed by the SAS at Loughgall. Kevin Barry O'Donnell had joined the IRA the year after Loughgall. At O'Donnell's funeral the priest, Father MacLarnon, no doubt echoed the feelings of a large section of the community in Tyrone when he urged that 'the politics of co-operation' must replace 'the politics of confrontation' before there could be peace. 'So many families in this and other areas have been affected,' he said. 'There have been so many bereavements, so much sorrow and mourning.'[8]

The IRA was being attacked from another front too. The loyalist paramilitaries, who had for a long time satisfied themselves by killing innocent Catholics as a way of putting pressure on the nationalist community to tell the IRA to stop, refined their tactics and began targeting and killing known republicans. In February 1989, the lawyer Pat Finucane who had defended many IRA members, and a Sinn Fein councillor, John Davy, were both shot dead by loyalists in killings only two days apart. The Provisionals cried 'collusion' as they refused to believe that loyalists could carry out such precise operations without the connivance of the security forces – mainly, they alleged, the UDR – and there was indeed evidence that this had happened. Two UDR soldiers were convicted of aiding and abetting the murder of a republican, Loughlin Maginn, in August 1989, by the loyalist Ulster Freedom Fighters, the *nom de guerre* of the UDA. Members of the UDR tended to live in the areas from which the Provisionals came and they knew who the suspects were. Although there were attacks on republicans from all over the province – Loughlin Maginn was shot dead at his home in County Down – Tyrone suffered disproportionately. On 29 November 1989, an American IRA Volunteer called Liam Ryan and a civilian were shot dead in a loyalist attack on the Battery Bar in Ardboe, East Tyrone, by the shore of Lough Neagh. Ryan was convicted in America in 1985 of using forged documents to buy three Armalite rifles and received a suspended sentence. It was thought that the gunmen had made their approach and getaway by boat. But the loyalists' biggest 'success' against the IRA in Tyrone came on 3 March 1991 when a unit, thought to be from the UVF's mid-Ulster Brigade, hit Boyle's Bar at the end of Cappagh High Street. The loyalists attacked Boyle's Bar at 10.30pm on a Sunday evening and shot dead three IRA Volunteers in the pub car park – John Quinn, Dwayne O'Donnell and Malcolm Nugent. Their car was riddled with bullets. A civilian, Thomas Armstrong, was also found shot dead outside the Gentlemen's toilet. Whether the loyalist hit team were acting on precise intelligence that told them that the three IRA men would be in the car park at a certain time or whether they just 'struck lucky', nobody knows. Local republicans have no doubt that the attack could not have been carried out without the help of the security forces whose presence, they said, had been heavy on the ground that day. The loyalist paramilitaries kept up their offensive over the next eighteen months and shot dead five members of Sinn Fein.

These lethal attacks on both wings of the Republican Movement by the SAS and loyalist paramilitaries, as well as conventional attrition by the police and army through the courts, were no doubt an important contributory factor in the IRA's decision to call its ceasefire in 1994. The IRA had recognized that it could not win a purely military victory and the British had long since realized that they could not inflict a military defeat on the Provisionals. Stalemate was the result. By the beginning of the third decade of the 'Troubles', everyone was crying out for peace. The Republican Movement wanted it too, but only on terms it could accept. John Hume and Gerry adams had begun the process. Now others had to respond.

Chapter Twenty-two

Endgame

It was one of those glorious early summer days with which Belfast is sometimes blessed. In the cool, marbled corridors of City Hall, history was about
to be made. Sinn Fein supporters were everywhere, giving the appearance
that no other party was contesting the British general election of 1 May
1997. By lunch time the excitement was high. Word came from inside
the count that Gerry Adams looked set for victory. The cheering and the
chanting began. Unionist supporters kept their distance, angry and resentful
that what had always been 'their' City Hall had been, as they saw it, taken
over by the IRA. Joe Hendron of the SDLP, the moderate nationalist and
sitting MP for West Belfast who had defeated Adams at the 1992 election,
came out of the count, not looking happy. (Hendron had defeated Adams
because large numbers of protestants in the Shankhill Road area of the West
Belfast constituency had voted tactically for the catholic, Joe Hendron, to
keep Adams out.) Hendron was the man Adams had to beat. His appearance
was greeted by boos and insults – an undeserved response of which Adams
himself would not have approved. In contrast, a huge cheer erupted as
the President of Sinn Fein himself emerged, to be immediately swamped
by the mob. They expected a victory speech but Adams was only on his
way to the Gents, and afterwards disappeared back inside the count.

The news everyone had been waiting for finally came. Adams had won,
having defeated Joe Hendron by 8,000 votes. City Hall erupted and, after
Hendron's graceful speech conceding defeat, Adams and his entourage
pushed their way through the jubilant throng and repaired to the Sinn Fein
office in the bowels of the building to relax, reflect and take incoming calls
of congratulation. Adams' security men, led by Terence 'Cleeky' Clarke,
stayed on guard outside the door, very aware that Adams had once escaped
an assassination attempt in the vicinity of City Hall. Although Adams was
able to relax there was still no news from the count in West Tyrone where
Martin McGuinness, Sinn Fein's Chief Negotiator, was a candidate.

As he left the room to face more cameras and talk about 'peace', Adams
told 'Cleeky' his shirt was hanging out. 'Cleeky' promptly tucked it in –

a brief indication of the respectable front of Sinn Fein. Collars and ties and suits are now the order of the day. As Adams descended the ornate City Hall staircase, word came through that McGuinness had made it. A magnum of sparkling wine was produced, tied with red ribbon, and the crowd cheered Martin and Gerry to the roof. Not only were Adams and McGuinness Westminster MPs, but Sinn Fein was now the third largest party in Northern Ireland. History had been made that afternoon. For republicans, there seemed no end to the good news. Tony Blair was now installed in Downing Street with a colossal majority of 169 seats, banishing the nightmare of a wafer-thin parliamentary majority which had haunted his predecessor, John Major. But the good news did not stop there as, on 20 July 1997, the IRA declared a renewed ceasefire and prepared to enter all-party talks on 15 September. It looked as if, almost a decade after the 'peace process' had started with the Hume–Adams talks way back in 1988, it might be about to come to fruition. How had it happened?

Ironically, it was the driving force of politicians on all sides – British and Irish, republican and loyalist, nationalist and unionist – all determined to end the violence, that drove the process forward, encouraged by the Clinton administration. For almost the first time in nearly thirty years, individuals drove events rather than being driven by them. The endgame seemed to have begun, however long it might take to reach a conclusion. It was a remarkable period in which so many took risks for peace – including the IRA's Army Council itself and its loyalist counterpart, the Combined Loyalist Military Command (CLMC). Mitchel McLaughlin was one of the Sinn Fein leadership who made a realistic assessment of the situation in which the Republican Movement found itself as the last decade of the century began, and he put it to the IRA.

> The British Army had 100,000 men, and helicopters and armoured cars and tanks and guns whilst the IRA at its most active presumably had somewhere, according to the estimates, of between five and six hundred people. For me that posed an obvious conundrum – how do we resolve this situation and how will it actually end?
>
> **Did you actually say that to the IRA – that they weren't going to drive the British out of Ireland?**
>
> I probably didn't use that language but certainly I used that rationale on more than one occasion, yes.
>
> **What response did you get?**
>
> On occasions quite a dusty response. I think people maybe believed it would be deviation or distraction from the issues ['armed struggle'] but at the same time you always inevitably got someone who was prepared to engage in that discussion and as a result you learned and

as a result they learned and as a result I think the political arguments developed.

Isn't the irony that in the end you are trying to do away with the IRA?

Yes, that is an irony but I also think that it's extremely important that the IRA are actually supporting that process. They know quite clearly that a successful outcome means that the IRA has to disappear from the equation.

The world had been undergoing change elsewhere. On 9 November 1989, the Berlin Wall came down, heralding the end of the Cold War era. World leaders somewhat optimistically proclaimed a new dawn but there was no doubt that the world was changing. There was movement towards resolving the seemingly intractable conflicts in the Middle East and South Africa. Nelson Mandela and Yasser Arafat, once 'terrorists', were becoming 'statesmen'. Was Ireland to remain locked in its ancient conflict?

The first politician on the scene at the beginning of this new era was Peter Brooke, who succeeded Tom King as Northern Ireland Secretary on 24 July 1989. Branches of Brooke's family had lived in Ireland for over 200 years, firmly rooted in the unionist tradition. One of his ancestors was the eighteenth-century poet, Charlotte Brooke, who had been the first writer to use the word 'Fenian'.[1] Nationalists, who had not been enamoured of Tom King, were less than rapturous about Brooke's arrival – he was simply one unionist following another, they thought. They could not have been more wrong. In tackling the Irish problem Brooke displayed a sensitivity and boldness that few other British politicians had shown. He knew he was coming into office at a potentially historic moment and was determined to do all he could to encourage the IRA to end its military campaign. The Intelligence briefings Brooke received from Special Branch and MI5 were encouraging, indicating that a debate had begun 'on the other side of the hill' – amongst the IRA leadership – on the direction the Republican Movement should take. Given the political movement in conflicts elsewhere, Brooke observed that 'there were people who said that the IRA were beginning to become worried that they were going to be the last unsolved problem.'

Sections of the Republican Movement had already started to think in a different direction when the new Secretary of State came into office, and Brooke knew he had to encourage them still further. He did this by sending a series of clear messages to the Provisionals, to the consternation of his critics, openly and not in code. The first message was sent, almost inadvertently, on 1 November 1989 in interviews with journalists during Brooke's first One Hundred Days in office. One journalist, Derek Henderson of the Press Association, asked whether, given 'a Mexican stand-off [a military stalemate], he could ever envisage a British Government talking to Sinn Fein. The normal reaction of British Ministers was to express horror, say 'no' and repeat the mantra about not 'talking to terrorists'. Brooke broke all the unwritten rules and said what he genuinely believed.

> . . . it is difficult to envisage a military defeat [of the IRA] . . . if, in fact, the terrorists were to decide that the moment had come when they wished to withdraw from their activities, then I think the Government would need to be imaginative in those circumstances as to how that process should be managed.
>
> Let me remind you of the move towards independence in Cyprus. A British minister stood up in the House of Commons and used the word 'never'. Within two years there had been a retreat from that word.

The combination of the word 'Cyprus' with its images of colonial withdrawal and the implication that HMG might at some stage consider dialogue with the 'terrorists' provoked a reaction of horror, astonishment and interest depending on the political dispositions of those who heard the speech.[2] Barely five weeks prior to Brooke's comments the IRA had bombed the barracks of the Royal Marines School of Music in Deal, killing ten bandsmen and injuring twenty-two. To many unionists and Conservative backbenchers, the thought that a British Secretary of State would ever contemplate talking to representatives of those responsible for such an atrocity was obscene. However, despite the storm they provoked, Peter Brooke told me he had no regrets about his remarks.

> As the troubles had by then been going on for twenty years and there was no particular reason at that moment to think the security forces were going to make a sudden breakthrough which would lead to their defeat, I gave an honest answer to an honest question. I was arguing that if you reach this kind of impasse, it was sensible to explore other ways of resolving matters.

Republicans were intrigued by what Brooke had said, not being used to such startlingly forthright admissions by British Secretaries of State, but as yet they were unsure what to do. The IRA, as ever, had no doubt: keep up the pressure on the 'Brits' on all three fronts; Northern Ireland, England and Europe. In 1990 in Northern Ireland, the IRA killed eleven civilians, eleven policemen and seventeen soldiers – five of them on 24 October when their van was booby-trapped during a charity 'Fun Run'. In England, they bombed the Stock Exchange, shot dead a soldier sitting at a railway station and killed Ian Gow MP, one of Mrs Thatcher's closest political confidants and friends, by booby-trapping his car. In Holland they shot dead two Australian tourists whom they mistook for off-duty British soldiers and in Germany they killed a British army officer. But the incident in Northern Ireland that shocked a community which was by now almost immune to shock involved the killing of five soldiers and a civilian at a border crossing army checkpoint in Derry. The IRA took hostage the family of Patsy Gillespie, strapped him into a car loaded with a thousand pounds of explosives and told him to drive to the checkpoint. The IRA told his family he would be released when he had carried out their orders. Patsy Gillespie became a 'human bomb' and when he arrived at the checkpoint the IRA detonated the explosives by remote control, killing him and five soldiers. The IRA claimed Gillespie was a 'legitimate target' because he worked at an army base. In fact, he worked in the canteen. The vast majority of Catholics in Derry were sickened by the attack and no doubt let the IRA know what they thought. The revulsion caused by this use of a 'human bomb' increased a groundswell for peace that the IRA could not ignore. After twenty years of 'war', it was becoming increasingly clear that a considerable section of the community on which the Provisionals relied for their support, and whom they had originally come into existence to defend, had had enough. By actions such as this and the revulsion they provoked within the community, the IRA inadvertently strengthened the hand of those within the Republican Movement who argued that an alternative route to 'armed struggle' had to be found. Martin McGuinness, whose military credentials, track record and powerful personality made him hugely influential with the most militant sections of the Movement, became its strongest supporter. He had never agreed with killing for killing's sake, believing instead that the 'war' had to be just and supported by the people on whose behalf it was being fought. McGuinness could see that the situation and the world was changing. As he told a huge crowd gathered in Derry in 1997 to commemorate the twenty-fifth anniversary of 'Bloody Sunday', there was nowhere else to go other than the negotiating table.

It was almost inconceivable given the murder of her close friends and political colleagues, Ian Gow and Airey Neave, who had been killed by INLA in 1979, as well as the recent 'human bomb' attack in Derry, that Mrs Thatcher would ever entertain any dialogue with the Provisionals. Nevertheless, Peter Brooke continued to send out messages. On 9 November 1990, a fortnight after the death of Patsy Gillespie, he made a landmark speech to the unlikely audience of the British Association of Canned Food Importers and Distributors at the Whitbread Restaurant in London. The assembled guests must have been surprised to be treated to a seminal discourse on 'The British Presence' which became known as 'The Whitbread Speech'.

> An Irish Republicanism seen to have finally renounced violence would be able, like other parties, to seek a role in the peaceful political life of the community. In Northern Ireland, it is not the aspiration to a sovereign, united Ireland against which we set our face, but its violent expression . . .
>
> The British Government has no selfish or strategic or economic interest in Northern Ireland: our role is to help, enable and encourage. Britain's purpose . . . is not to occupy, oppress or exploit but to ensure democratic debate and free democratic choice.
>
> Partition is an acknowledgement of reality, not an assertion of national self-interest.

At last, John Hume had got the British Government to say publicly what he believed was the key to the peace process, not a declaration by the British that they intended to withdraw from Northern Ireland, but an assurance that their interest in remaining was neither, 'selfish, strategic or economic'. This was the foundation of his ongoing dialogue with Gerry Adams from which everything else was to flow.

Unforeseen circumstances were to further the process when Mrs Thatcher stepped down as Prime Minister following a coup by disillusioned Conservatives who believed that the party was unlikely to be returned to power at the next election under her increasingly unpopular leadership. Mrs Thatcher resigned, having occupied Number Ten Downing Street for over eleven years, and John Major took over as Prime Minister. Although Mrs Thatcher had supported Peter Brooke in his endeavours, it was doubtful, given the intensity of her feelings about the IRA, that she would have had the determination to further the peace process in the way that was required. On John Major's first visit to Belfast as Prime Minister, there was obvious relief amongst some of the senior people he met that he came fresh to the problem without Mrs Thatcher's personal inheritance, stretching from the hunger strike to the Brighton bomb, Airey Neave and Ian Gow. John Major was seen as the man able to start with a clean sheet: the man and the circumstances seemed to match. Major was, above all, a pragmatist but one with a genuine desire to bring a permanent end to the violence that had scarred relationships between Britain and Ireland for over twenty-five years – or four or eight hundred depending upon the perspective. Major was aware of changes going on in the world, and in Europe in particular. The United Kingdom and the Irish Republic were partners within the European Community and economically the border between North and South had effectively ceased to exist. Given the direction in which Europe was moving, with the passing of time, that border was likely to become even more faded politically. The Provisionals also recognized that the geopolitical map of Europe and, by definition, of Ireland was changing. They knew too, as did the British Government, that the population balance within Northern Ireland was gradually shifting and that the Catholic/nationalist minority was moving up through the forty per cent mark to the point where it would, in the fullness of time, become the majority population. Predictions varied on when this would happen – and statisticians and sociologists pointed out that a natural majority and a *voting* majority were two different things – but there was no doubt that change was unavoidable although it might be as much as forty years down the road. All those involved in the peace process knew that this shifting scenario was the key to moving the relationship between the two communities – the two parts of the island and the British and Irish Governments – onto a different level altogether. They recognized that a permanent peace might be built but only if the IRA abandoned its 'armed struggle'. The fact that Peter Brooke had now declared that Britain had no selfish, strategic or economic interest in remaining in Northern Ireland and only did so because that was the wish of the majority of its population, was the vital starting point.

It was at this juncture that the Contact, who had played such a vital role in the truce of 1975 and the ending of the first hunger strike in 1980, returned once more to play a crucial role in the shadows. Although the MI6 officer, Michael Oatley, had departed from Northern Ireland more than fifteen years before and had become the head of MI6 operations in Europe, he and the Contact had vaguely kept in touch with each other over the years in case either side should wish to send a message. The Contact had also been in touch occasionally with Martin McGuinness.[3] Given the circumstances at the beginning of the 1990s, perhaps it was time for the Contact to become active once again as the secret channel of communication between the Provisionals and HMG. Significantly, probably through the Contact, a copy of 'The Whitbread Speech' was sent to the Provisionals. The Secretary of State was a regular reader of their weekly paper *Republican News* and, as he admitted, it would have been foolish not to have ensured that its editor and readers were alerted to the speech. However remarkable it may have appeared at the time that an advance copy was being sent to the 'enemy', it was in fact part of a string of strategic 'confidence-building measures' designed to draw the Republican Movement in from the cold. I asked Martin McGuinness what his reaction was to the Whitbread speech.

> I thought it was an interesting statement at the time, but like all statements coming from British Ministers, and given the history between us over the course of many, many years, I treat all such statements with a considerable degree of scepticism. I think that many more people would have been interested, or even more interested, if Peter Brooke had included the word 'political' in that statement.
>
> **But you took that as a positive sign, did you not?**
>
> Well I took it as an indication that there were people within the British establishment and the British Government who may want to or wish to grapple with new realities.[4]

The IRA responded to 'The Whitbread Speech' by declaring a three-day ceasefire over Christmas 1990 – the first of its kind in fifteen years. Three days before it came into operation however, the IRA shot dead an off-duty policeman in County Down. Christmas came and went and the IRA's campaign was resumed although at a relatively low level for the next few weeks, perhaps to allow the British Government space in which to respond. During this period, Peter Brooke was, as always, in regular contact with the Head of MI5 in Northern Ireland, John Deverell, who was also the Director and Controller of Intelligence (DCI) in the province.

> John and I saw each other with very great regularity. We would see each other once a week and it would be an entirely private occasion. Although we had a particular agenda that we were pursuing on those occasions, there was ample opportunity for the conversation to range much more widely. We had bilateral discussions which went on every week for two and three-quarter years and we therefore had ample opportunity for testing this sort of subject [secret contacts with the IRA] . . . It was a continuing process.
>
> **Did you know anything about the Contact through whom that channel was activated?**
>
> I made it my business to know as little as I needed to in the whole of this area . . . the need to know principle is, in my view, extremely important. Although I knew enough to know what I was doing, it was in my view much better that I did not know every last dotted 'I' and every crossed 'T'.

In January 1991 Michael Oatley visited Derry and, through the Contact, met Martin McGuinness. Oatley was about to retire from MI6 and wanted to talk with McGuinness before he did so. I asked Peter Brooke whether he had authorized the meeting. He said it had been mentioned and he had been asked whether he would be 'content for it to occur'. He said he was. Oatley and McGuinness, with the Contact present, talked for three hours about the general situation, the current state of British policy, Anglo-Irish relations and the prospects for peace, with Oatley pointing out that the Government's private position was the same as its public position – that it would not give in to the IRA's campaign of violence.[5] McGuinness described the meeting as 'low key' and said very little in accordance with his listening brief and was 'non-committal on all aspects of republican policy'. According to McGuinness, Oatley suggested that another British Government Representative should be appointed to 'reactivate the line of communication'. Again, McGuinness says he was 'non-committal' but felt that should the British wish to do so, the Republican Movement was 'morally and tactically obliged not to reject their offer'.[6]

The following month, the IRA launched one of the most spectacular attacks of its campaign. On 7 February 1991, with British troops engaged in the Gulf War, Peter Gurney, the head of the Explosives Section of the Metropolitan Police Anti-Terrorist Branch, was drinking his morning coffee in his office in Cannon Row police station, a couple of hundred yards from Downing Street. It had been snowing outside and a white blanket covered the grass around the Ministry of Defence and St James' Park beyond. Suddenly he heard a very heavy 'crump', so powerful that it knocked a picture off his wall. Gurney immediately assumed it was an IRA bomb, having dealt with many over the years since he defused the IRA's first car bomb outside Scotland Yard in 1973. He rushed into Whitehall and saw a white Ford transit van in flames further up the road opposite Horse Guards Parade. The heat was too great for him to get too close but he saw three tubes in the van. They were the IRA's lethal Mark Ten mortars, previously used to devastating effect in Northern Ireland but never before used in Britain. It was the IRA's first mortar attack in England. Gurney looked at the direction in which the tubes were pointed to work out the intended target. Number Ten Downing Street was in the line of fire. Informed by a policeman that a mortar had landed in the garden, Gurney rushed into Number Ten, through the halls, down the stairs and through a passage into the back garden where, at the far end, he saw a smoking cherry tree and a small crater in the ground. He assumed that the mortar had hit the tree during its angled descent and exploded before landing. John Major and the Gulf War Cabinet were sitting in the Cabinet briefing room on the first floor of Downing Street only thirty yards away. Two more mortars had landed just outside the garden, across the road from St James' Park, but had not exploded. Each was about four foot six inches long, six and a half inches in diameter, weighing around 140 pounds and carrying forty pounds of semtex high explosive. The IRA had almost succeeded in wiping out the Prime Minister and his entire Cabinet. I stood in the garden of Number Ten with Peter Gurney as he pointed out the geography and explained how lucky the Cabinet had been to survive. He was astonished at the IRA's technical ability.

It was a remarkably good aim if you consider that the bomb was fired 250 yards [across Whitehall] with no direct line of sight. Technically, it was quite brilliant and I'm quite sure that many army crews, if given a similar task, would be very pleased to drop a bomb this close. You've got to park the launch vehicle in an area which is guarded by armed men and you've got less than a minute to do it. I was very, very surprised at how good it was. If the angle of fire had been moved about five or ten degrees, then those bombs would actually have impacted on Number Ten.

Once he had discovered the exploded bomb, Gurney proceeded to defuse one of the other two bombs which had fallen outside the garden. He borrowed a large, adjustable spanner from Number Ten, sat astride the casing and started to defuse the bomb. 'The fuse is held on by four great big bolts rather similar to wheel nuts on a car', he explained. 'To keep the bomb steady, I sat astride it and locked it with my knees.' The casing was red hot and he had to stuff snow down his fireproof trousers to 'damp it down a bit' and complete the job. Some time later, he met Mrs Thatcher and was introduced as the person who had defused the mortars. 'Oh yes,' she said, 'weren't they the ones that destroyed that poor cherry tree?'

The violence in Northern Ireland continued throughout 1991 as Peter Brooke endeavoured to get the talks process under way with the Northern Ireland political parties to the exclusion of Sinn Fein, since he had made it clear that it could only become involved once the IRA had declared 'a cessation of violence'. 'Temporary ceasefires' were not enough. During this time the Contact remained active, passing messages from HMG to the Provisionals and informing them that a new 'British Government Representative' would be taking over now that Michael Oatley had retired. Oatley's successor (who I shall refer to as 'BGR'), introduced himself to the Contact and, according to Martin McGuinness, produced a letter from Peter Brooke authenticating his status which was in turn verified by Oatley. Unlike Oatley, 'BGR' was working for MI5 under John Deverell. It appears that both the British Government and the Republican Movement wanted to reactivate the secret dialogue that had taken place during 1974–5, and through the same channel. Through 1991 and 1992, McGuinness and the Provisionals' leadership were briefed through the Contact on British Government policy and given advance notice of key speeches and moves.[7]

In February 1992, Sinn Fein maintained the political momentum by publishing its latest discussion document, 'Towards a Lasting Peace in Ireland', designed not just to promote debate amongst republicans but also amongst a wider public on how best 'to develop a strategy for peace in Ireland'. Although the document was underpinned, as ever, by the requirement for an eventual 'peaceful and orderly British political and military withdrawal from Ireland', it was now to be 'within a specified period'. In 1972 it had been within three years, in 1987 'within the lifetime of a British Government' – normally five years – but now no time frame was being placed upon it. The period had to be 'specified' but the precise specification was never stated. In addition to this degree of flexibility which seemed to be entering republican policy, there was the recognition that unionists would have to be involved in the process and that the 'historic changes in Europe' might provide the framework within which this could happen.

> We recognize that peace in Ireland requires a settlement of the long-standing conflict between Irish Nationalism and Irish Unionism. We would like to see that conflict, often bloody, replaced by a process of national reconciliation, a constructive dialogue and debate.
>
> Unionists have democratic rights which not only can be upheld but must be upheld in an independent Ireland . . . Those democratic rights, however, must not extend to a veto over the national rights of the Irish people as a whole.[8]

The document also made it clear that 'armed struggle' was likely to be 'sustained for the foreseeable future' and that it was up to those who proclaimed that it was counter-productive 'to advance a credible alternative'. That was what Gerry Adams, Martin McGuinness and the Republican Movement were looking for and that was what the British and Irish Governments, guided by John Hume, now sought to provide. It was the *raison d'être* of the peace process.

Meanwhile, the secret dialogue between the British Government and the IRA leadership was maintained despite the ever-escalating violence. On Friday evening, 17 January 1992, the IRA bombed a minibus carrying Protestant workmen home from the RUC station in Tyrone where they had been working. Triggered by a command wire, the huge bomb exploded at the Teebane crossroads just outside Cookstown, killing seven Protestants and the driver. It was the IRA's biggest attack on Protestant workers since the Kingsmills massacre in 1976. To the IRA, the workers were 'legitimate' targets because they had been working for the security forces, whilst to Protestants and most other people it was a nakedly sectarian act. In a statement for which he received almost universal disgust, Gerry Adams did not blame the IRA but 'the failure of British policy in Ireland'.[9] Peter Brooke condemned the killings in the strongest possible words but, as for both his predecessors and successors, the language of condemnation seemed almost exhausted.

That same Friday evening, the Secretary of State had been invited to appear on the Gay Byrne Show, Ireland's most popular television programme. Astonishingly, given the carnage of Teebane earlier that same evening, he ended up singing 'My Darling Clementine' in the television studio and horrified Northern Ireland with what appeared to be such an uncharacteristic display of insensitivity. Unionists demanded his head. Deeply regretting what he had done, Brooke publicly apologized and offered his resignation to the Prime Minister. I had often wondered how he had been drawn into doing what he did with the result that his tenure in Northern Ireland might be more famously remembered for 'Clementine' than for the remarkable work he did in helping to end the IRA violence. For the first time, he explained the circumstances.

> Mr Byrne's researcher came to see me on the Thursday before the programme and she asked me a number of questions which included references to the death of my first wife. I told her after I'd answered the questions I did not wish to discuss my first wife on the television programme, particularly as my present wife, whom I'd recently married, was actually going to be sitting in the studio. And Mr Byrne *did* ask me questions about my first wife. While I had concentrated entirely on Teebane up to the moment that that entered the conversation, once he had actually, in my view, broken the rules that I thought had been agreed in advance of the programme, I'm afraid my mind went more to protecting my second wife than to what was going on round me. I was in a sense totally preoccupied on another subject and I did not actually realize the enormity of what I had done until I came off the programme.

The Prime Minister refused Peter Brooke's resignation.

Nearly three weeks later, on 5 February 1992, the loyalist Ulster Freedom Fighters (the UDA's military wing) took revenge for the massacre at Teebane by walking into Sean Graham's bookmaker's shop on Belfast's Lower Ormeau Road, opening fire with assault rifles and shooting dead five Catholics including a sixteen-year-old boy and a pensioner. The UDA commander who is said to have ordered the attack was later shot dead by the IRA.[10] By the end of 1992, for the first time in the history of the current 'Troubles', the loyalist paramilitaries had claimed as many victims as the IRA, both having killed thirty-four. Three of the loyalists' victims were members of Sinn Fein.

The day after the killings in the bookmaker's, Albert Reynolds was elected leader of Fianna Fail and became Taoiseach. The slaughter made him even more determined to act in concert with John Major to end the killing for good. The two leaders had built up a good personal relationship through European Community meetings and were not dissimilar in character. Whereas Reynolds' predecessor, Charles Haughey, saw himself as a Soldier of Destiny (the meaning of 'Fianna Fail'), Reynolds was more a Soldier of Fortune. He was known, with some affection, as the 'Rhinestone Taoiseach' because he loved country-and-western music and had made his money out of dance halls, bingo and pet food.[11] John Major did not have the same colourful past but shared the can-do pragmatism of his Dublin counterpart. Both were totally without affectation and spoke their minds, often being brutally frank with each other in the private head-to-head meetings they would hold, without officials and minute takers, to try to resolve the apparently unsurmountable differences frequently arising between London and Dublin. They would invariably emerge with a deal, to the astonishment of their civil servants. However candid these private exchanges, they never appeared to damage their personal relationship which in the end made the evolution of the peace process possible.

When Reynolds took over the reins of government Haughey told him that he had been talking to John Hume who had in turn been talking to Gerry Adams about the possibility of bringing about a cessation of IRA violence and that it was up to Reynolds to make his own judgement as to whether there was anything in it. The party's principal adviser on Northern Ireland, Dr Martin Mansergh, was to fill him in with the details. During the Hume–Adams talks of 1988 Dr Mansergh had held two clandestine meetings with senior Sinn Fein figures at a discreet location in Dundalk on the Irish side of the border and had subsequently drawn up a draft document or 'working paper' that became contentiously known as 'Hume–Adams' because, whatever the changes, the ideas developed during their dialogue of 1988 remained at its core. Its foundation was the statement that Britain no longer had any selfish, strategic, political or economic interest in Northern Ireland. The insertion of the word 'political' was wishful thinking on the part of those involved in drawing it up since it had never come from Peter Brooke's lips. It was the word that Martin McGuinness wanted in there but for the British and unionists it was a word too far. Some of the ideas and words were rejected or refined as the months and years went by but their essence remained the same. Albert Reynolds gave me the impression that Haughey had given him only the most general of briefings.

> I decided to talk to John Hume myself first and to make an assessment as to whether there were opportunities to go ahead and he strongly advised me that in his view there was a window of opportunity there. He said that from his off-and-on talks with Adams there had been a change of mood within the Republican leadership and that it could be exploited and possibly win out in the end. But even if he and Gerry Adams kept speaking, as he said, until the cows came home, it wasn't going to go anywhere if the two Governments didn't embrace it. In other words, they had to take up the ball and run with it. Basically he was saying to me, 'you have a good relationship with John Major. Here's the result of our work. You can input your own work and see if you can take it further down the line with John Major because if the two Governments don't get involved, there will be no end result.'

> **Did you believe that the Republican leadership was serious?**

> Not at that point I didn't. I decided later on to open up indirect communications, with Dr Martin Mansergh representing me on a personal basis. There was certainly an internal debate going on within the Movement itself, and there were people there who were trying to create a new strategy and a new policy away from violence and towards peace. A new language appeared talking about an 'agreed Ireland' and an 'accommodation', these sort of words. I felt, yes, this was a situation in which I would certainly become involved and take the risks for peace and hopefully we might get a result at the end of the day.

Dealings through Martin Mansergh were kept so tight that in the early stages not even Reynolds' own Cabinet knew about them. There was much speculation, fed by the total secrecy surrounding the operation, as to what the so-called 'Hume–Adams' document contained and this was fuelled by John Hume's insistence that no such document existed. Reynolds clarified the situation:

> I can't identify any document in the process that could be exclusively labelled 'Hume–Adams'. In my view, Hume–Adams was the result of bringing together the various statements made by Hume and

Adams over a period. It was a combination of those statements that represented what Hume–Adams meant to me and to those of us who were working on it.

In the early stages of the peace process, the British Government was not involved; although Reynolds had mentioned to Major what was afoot, it was only in the most general terms. The British Government had other things on its mind. On 10 April 1992, the IRA had launched another devastating attack on the financial institutions of the City of London by bombing the Baltic Exchange with a huge bomb made out of home-made explosives. The IRA's warning was inadequate and three people were killed, one of them a fifteen-year-old boy. The bomb caused damage amounting to a staggering £800 million. Up until then, the total damage in Northern Ireland since the outbreak of the 'Troubles' in 1969 had amounted to just over £600 million. The IRA was jubilant. The British government was worried and, by the beginning of 1993, had embarked upon its own top-secret dialogue with the IRA at what it regarded as Provisional Army Council level. Once again the Contact was closely involved. Now there were two tracks running towards what both Governments hoped would be peace. The difference was that Dublin knew nothing of what London was up to. Nor did anyone else.

Chapter Twenty-three

Expectations

The day after the IRA bombed the Baltic Exchange and sent insurance companies reeling, Sir Patrick Mayhew took over from Peter Brooke as Northern Ireland Secretary in John Major's post-election Cabinet reshuffle. Mayhew and Brooke could not have been more different – although both were patrician in their ways and unionist by inclination, to republicans and many nationalists Sir Patrick, with his patronizing manner and plummy voice, seemed a caricature of a British colonial governor. But the manner did not reflect the man. Civil servants at Stormont spoke of 'Paddy' Mayhew with affection: 'a real gentleman', they said, and there was more to Mayhew than met the eye or ear. He, too, recognized that the only way to end the violence was to give every encouragement to those within the Republican Movement who wanted to lead the IRA away from 'armed struggle'. Sir Patrick, like his predecessor, continued to send messages to the Republican leadership.

On 16 December 1992, he made a keynote speech at Coleraine on 'Culture and Identity', anticipating that the Provisionals would be listening.

> Unity cannot be brought nearer, let alone achieved, by dealing out death and destruction, It is not sensible to suppose that any British Government will yield to an agenda for Ireland prosecuted by violent means . . . provided it is advocated constitutionally, there can be no proper reason for excluding any political objective from discussion. Certainly not the objective of a united Ireland through broad agreement fairly and freely agreed . . .
>   . . . in the event of a genuine and established cessation of violence, the whole range of responses that we have had to make to that violence could, and would, inevitably be looked at afresh . . .[1]

In other words, a united Ireland could be on the negotiating table, but not at the point of a gun. It was almost as if Sir Patrick had dusted down and slightly rephrased what Merlyn Rees had said in the run-up to the 1975 truce. What was to follow had much in common with that process.

Although the secret contacts had been going on intermittently since January 1991, when Michael Oatley met Martin McGuinness, the dialogue began in earnest at the beginning of 1993, carried on through the intelligence officer who had succeeded Oatley after he had retired, known as the BGR – the British Government Representative. The dialogue was, as in the past, facilitated by the Contact. The 'BGR' would pass messages either verbally or in writing to the Contact, sometimes face to face, sometimes over a safe phone or fax, and the Contact would pass them on to the Provisionals' leadership, which now included Gerry Kelly, who had been convicted for his part in the 1973 London bombs and who had also been a Maze escapee. After his release from the Maze prison, Kelly had emerged to become a prominent figure in Sinn Fein and stood in several elections as a Belfast candidate, setting myriad female hearts a-flutter with his good looks and charm. Kelly was an unlikely-looking former 'terrorist' and slipped easily and elegantly into the politician's suit. Because of his long and colourful IRA history, Kelly, like McGuinness, had great 'street cred'. Downing Street had no doubt that when it was dealing with McGuinness and Kelly, it was talking directly to the Provisionals' Army Council. Number Ten believed, as had its predecessors in 1975, that there was not much point in talking to anyone else. The main obstacle to be overcome in translating the secret dialogue into a ceasefire or 'cessation' of violence – which was always the object – was the Provisionals' massive distrust of the British Government, not of the Contact who played his difficult and dangerous role with consummate skill. Adams and McGuinness still remembered the 1975 Truce and what they regarded as the duplicity of the British Government in promising much in the meetings with Ruairí Ó 'Brádaigh and Billy McKee but delivering very little. In the wake of 1975 the IRA had said it would never again declare a cessation without a declaration of intent to withdraw by the British Government. Adams and McGuinness knew that in the world of the 1990s such a declaration would not be forthcoming and, if the 'peace process' was to work, other ways and words had to be found which would enable the IRA to wind up its campaign. The problem was how to do it with honour, as the IRA had not been defeated but it had not won. The secret exchanges of 1993 became so sensitive not just because, whatever the British said, they amounted to talking to the IRA, but because the position of both sides as undefeated parties to an almost twenty-five year 'war' had to be preserved.

Ironically, when knowledge of the secret dialogue exploded into the open at the end of 1993, one of the most delicate areas of all was how and when it had begun. The Provisionals said it had started two years earlier – which was true given Oatley's visit and the appointment of his successor – but the British insisted that it had only been undertaken when it received a message from Martin McGuinness and 'the leadership of the Provisional Movement' on 22nd February 1993. According to the British, the message said:

> The conflict is over but we need your advice on how to bring it to an end. We wish to have an unannounced ceasefire in order to hold dialogue leading to peace. We cannot announce such a move as it will lead to confusion for the Volunteers because the press will interpret it as surrender. We cannot meet the Secretary of State's public renunciation of violence, but it would be given privately as long as we were sure that we were not being tricked.[2]

I subsequently asked Sir Patrick Mayhew whether he regarded the 'message' as a signal from the trenches that amounted to a flag of surrender. He said he most certainly did not and also insisted that the message was genuine and had been received from Martin McGuinness. McGuinness, however, emphatically denied he had ever sent such a communication. The publication of the words themselves, which did indeed smack of 'surrender', caused McGuinness enormous embarrassment and anger. I understand that no such message was ever given to the Contact to pass on to the British – the procedure for such 'official' communications had been formalised over the years – but that what the British probably received from the 'BGR' was his assessment of the Provisionals' position. The assessment was broadly true – the IRA leadership was looking for a way to bring the conflict to an end – but the precise wording caused great offence. The most probable explanation is that during these critical exchanges of 1993, the 'BGR' was rather freer with his assessments and words than he should have been, at times suggesting that he had almost 'gone native'. This was to cause further difficulties as the months went by and an almost terminal problem at the end of the year. Michael Oatley's MI6 successor in 1975, 'HM', had also been prone to giving similar, over-generous interpretations. It would be surprising if both were not subsequently reprimanded when what they had been saying emerged.

According to Sinn Fein's account of the exchanges of 1993, the first significant meeting came on 12 January, presumably between the Contact and the 'BGR', after which the Contact reported back to the Provisionals. This meeting set the scene for what was to follow. As in 1975, the Republican Movement took minutes of the proceedings – at points there are remarkable similarities. The Sinn Fein minute of what the 'BGR' said, based on a debriefing by the Contact, is as follows.

[The meeting] began with an outline of the political risks being taken by the British government. Republicans should be in no doubt this [approach] indicates their seriousness in the whole thing. The conflict has been going on for too long. He [the 'BGR'] said the British Government were not serious in 1974/75 but they were now. There was a conviction by senior civil servants that talks had to start. The politicians were slower but they were moving to this position.

It could not be done without a major gesture from republicans. They realized that an IRA ceasefire was a non starter. He voiced his view that a suspension – an easing off – would start the ball rolling in a significant way. *The republicans would be convinced in that time that armed struggle was not necessary any longer* [author's emphasis].[3]

The British strategy was to argue that 'armed struggle' was no longer relevant in the changing world of the last decade of the century, and that if the Republican Movement wished to achieve its goal, it was far more likely to do so by getting involved in politics than by carrying on with its military campaign. The following month, on 20 February, Martin McGuinness responded publicly when he told Sinn Fein's Ard Fheis that the British Government privately believed in the need for 'inclusive dialogue' and should now say so openly.

The concept of inclusive dialogue as the way forward is gathering momentum . . . If both governments [in London and Dublin] have the courage of their private convictions, they should now finally meet with Sinn Fein . . . Republicans are willing to engage in the search for a democratic settlement with courage and flexibility.[4]

Significantly, McGuinness also informed his audience that Irish republicans would have to apply 'new and radical thinking to the predicament unionists find themselves in'. He said this would require 'particular consideration to guarantee and protect their interests in any new arrangements which will be needed to resolve the conflict'. Compromise was in the air. The British got the message and responded four days later when the 'BGR' held a meeting with the Contact. Things now appeared to be moving. The BGR said he was 'very upbeat' about the possibility of delegation meetings as the politicians were serious but republicans would have to 'grasp the opportunity while it exists'. According to the minutes, the 'BGR' went on to outline the conditions in which such a delegation meeting could take place.

> Events on the ground will bring an enormous influence to bear. The IRA needs to provide the space to turn the possibility of meetings into reality. A suspension is all that is being required of them.
>
> The British believed that two or three weeks was a sufficient period to convince republicans [that 'armed struggle' was no longer necessary]. There would be an intensive round of talks . . . Reciprocation would be immediate. Troops withdrawn to barracks. Checkpoints removed. Security levels determined by loyalist threat.[5]

McGuinness and Adams went to the IRA and the IRA agreed in principle to call an unannounced suspension of operations to facilitate the meetings, which were to be attended by McGuinness and Gerry Kelly. The British had suggested that if the initial talks seemed fruitful, they could continue elsewhere, for example in Sweden, Norway, Denmark, Scotland or, even closer to home, in the Isle of Man.[6] Progress was slow, not least because of continuing IRA violence. For the IRA the explanation was simple: they were at 'war' and were only prepared to stop at an agreed point for an agreed reason. The reason had been agreed but the point had not, so the campaign continued. By 19 March, however, the British Government had passed on a paper on its position to the IRA. It said that all those involved shared a responsibility to end the conflict and there was need for 'a healing process' but, in an echo of 1975, both sides had to have 'a clear and realistic understanding of what it is possible to achieve so that neither side can in the future claim that it has been tricked'. The Government said it had 'no blueprint' for a political solution but wanted 'an agreed accommodation, not an imposed settlement, arrived at through an inclusive process in which the parties are free agents'. It also spelled out its position on a united Ireland.

> The British Government does not have, and will not adopt, any prior objective of 'ending of partition' . . . It has to be accepted that the outcome of such a process could be a united Ireland, but this can only be on the basis of *the consent of the people of Northern Ireland* [author's emphasis]. Should this be the eventual outcome of a peaceful, democratic process, the British government would bring forward legislation to implement the will of the people here.[7]

The Provisionals received HMG's position paper on 19 March 1993 and gave it a swift and positive response. It was agreed that Martin McGuinness and Gerry Kelly should, for the first time, hold a formal face-to-face meeting with the 'BGR' and more importantly his boss, John Deverell, the head of MI5 in Northern Ireland. McGuinness and Adams may not have known Deverell's precise position but they had their suspicions. From their experience over the years, they assumed the dialogue was being conducted from the London end by British intelligence agents. Then tragedy struck. On the following day, 20 March, the IRA planted two bombs in litter bins in Warrington on a busy Saturday when the town centre was full of shoppers. The bombs killed three-year-old Johnathan Ball and twelve-year-old Tim Parry and injured fifty-one people. Warrington was one of those atrocities, like Enniskillen and 'Bloody Friday', that remains in people's minds. It was remembered, too, for the dignified and passionate plea for peace made by Tim Parry's father, which was similar to that made by Gordon Wilson after Enniskillen.

The meeting between McGuinness and Kelly representing the PAC, and the 'BGR' and John Deverell on behalf of the British Government, had been scheduled to take place on 23 March 1993. In the immediate aftermath of Warrington, it seemed that the meeting would have to be called off. If it ever came to light that British representatives had met the Provisionals three days after the bombing that had shocked the nation, Ministerial heads would have been called for. But remarkably, the meeting went ahead due, it appears, to the persistence of the Contact in his role as facilitator. Warrington seemed to make the meeting even more urgent if the violence was ever to stop. However, John Deverell did not materialize and the 'BGR' went to the meeting on his own.[8] What was said at this meeting was even more surprising than the fact that it had taken place. According to Sinn Fein's minute, taken in shorthand language, which I believe to be broadly accurate, the 'BGR' made the following remarkable statement.

Any settlement not involving the people of North and South won't work. A North/South settlement that won't frighten Unionists. The final solution is union. It is going to happen anyway. The historical train – Europe – determines that. We are committed to Europe. Unionists will have to change. This island will be as one.[9]

Again, the words had overtones of those spoken by Michael Oatley's successor, 'HM' in 1975. I questioned Martin McGuinness closely about that astonishing meeting. Could he be fabricating the account to suit his own political purposes?

I could be, yes. But I'm not.

Couldn't it be that what the 'BGR' said was simply his own personal view and not necessarily the view of the British Government?

It could be, but he was there representing the British Government and whatever he told me on that occasion I took to be a message from the British Government. Likewise, whatever I told him, he was reporting back to the Government as a message from Sinn Fein.

Did you believe him?

At that stage, no.

Why not?

Because I totally distrust the British Government. I've had too many experiences in the past to be so naive as to trust the British Government.[10]

British Ministers and officials steadfastly refuse to make any comment on the secret contacts beyond what Parliament has been told. On several occasions I have asked questions about that meeting of those in a position to know. They would say nothing. I did, however, ask Sir Patrick Mayhew about it and, whilst not confirming or denying what had been said, he did tell me that he had known nothing about it until the following autumn. Like Merlyn Rees and Peter Brooke, Secretaries of State were not always in the intelligence 'loop' and preferred it to be that way. They could not comment or get into hot water about something of which they had no knowledge.

On 3 April, the Provisionals responded and sent a message to the British Government saying that whilst disappointed that 'only one of your representatives was in attendance', the discussion was 'most useful' and a response was being considered.[11] The following week, on 7 April, the Prime Minister, John Major, underlined HMG's position in a speech to police officers in Strabane.

Those who use violence for political aims exclude themselves by their own actions, and if they wish to be taken into account, the choice lies entirely in their own hands. They must demonstrate to the satisfaction of people who are rightly sceptical, that they turn their backs on violence, clearly, unequivocally and irrevocably . . . only they can do that and I hope that they will.[12]

Three weeks later, the IRA gave its response with a further devastating attack on the City of London. On 24 April, it detonated a ton of fertilizer-based explosives outside the NatWest Tower, killing one person, injuring over thirty and causing a staggering one billion pounds worth of damage.[13] The same day, Gerry Adams and John Hume, who had started meeting again, issued the first of several statements on the state of what was now referred to as the 'Irish Peace Initiative'. Adams, of course, knew what was going on behind the scenes in the secret dialogue with the British but very few others did. Although the peace process was now operating on twin tracks, very few people were aware of the fact, and furthermore, the two tracks operated entirely independently of each other.

Hume and Adams set out what they believed was the basis for 'a lasting peace'. They said an 'internal settlement' within Northern Ireland was not a solution: that the Irish people as a whole had the right to 'national self-determination'; its exercise was 'a matter for the people of Ireland'; and any new agreement was only 'achievable and viable' if it enjoyed the allegiance of the different traditions on the island, by 'accommodating diversity and providing for national reconciliation'.[14] Hume and Adams had also been working secretly with the new Taoiseach, Albert Reynolds, who had made it clear that the process would only work if the British Government was brought onside, and that would only happen if the unionists were not written out of the equation. After much discussion, Reynolds decided to give John Major what he called a 'peace document', which he had drawn up, broadly based on his conversations with Hume and Adams. He initially proposed to fly to London and give it to Major on a 'take it or leave it' basis, a proposition that horrified his coalition partner, Dick Spring, the leader of the Labour Party and Irish Foreign Minister. Spring told Reynolds that if he did that, he was on his own.[15] The original 'peace document' that Reynolds and his political adviser, Martin Mansergh, had drawn up was something both knew that John Major could never accept as it was essentially a republican/nationalist document with no unionist input. From the beginning, Reynolds had to convince John Major that any documentation he received from Dublin was from Reynolds himself and from not Adams and Hume. Reynolds knew that if their fingerprints were on a document, the British Government would not touch it and the unionists would not go anywhere near it. I asked Reynolds what was in that original document which he planned to give to Major.

First of all there was a timeframe for withdrawal, which was a repetition to some extent of the old republican slogan. 'Brits Out'.
But that's pure republican-speak. It's going to make the British and the unionists run a mile.
That's right. Well, I started with it. I was into negotiations believing

that people take the ultimate and the extreme in their starting points and that somewhere down the line there will be a point where we can converge. And if people don't go into negotiations on that basis, well, I think those negotiations are going to fail and they'll be futile. Nobody can get out of negotiations everything they want. There has to be give on both sides. I knew it wouldn't run with the British and I knew it wouldn't run with the unionists. I expressed that view but said I was prepared to start with that document with those things in it and take it from there. But from the very start I made it clear that the principle of consent would have to be paramount, and that was not in the document.

What time frame was the document thinking of?

It wasn't really stated but if I remember rightly maybe something between 15 and 40 years or something like that.

Reynolds also recollected that it recommended that the British Government should 'persuade' the unionist community that it was in their interests to sit down and work out new arrangements for the future. The mechanism would be referenda, North and South, held on the same day, that would collectively add up to self-determination. This was fundamentally different from the Republican Movement's insistence that self-determination could only be exercised in a single referendum of the whole of the Irish people acting as a unit. The Provisionals' position was little different from that which Seán MacStíofáin had spelt out to William Whitelaw at Cheyne Walk in 1972.

Reynolds rang Major and told him he had completed a 'peace' document with which he was not totally satisfied but nevertheless would provide a starting point for discussion. On reflection the two Prime Ministers decided that it would not be a good idea for Reynolds to fly to London as his sudden arrival would be bound to provoke intense speculation amongst the British and Irish media as to what the Taoiseach was up to. John Major suggested that the Cabinet Secretary, Sir Robin Butler, should fly over to Dublin and take personal delivery of it. Reynolds agreed and in early June 1993 met Sir Robin at Baldonnel military airport near Dublin. They had tea and coffee in the airport offices and Reynolds handed the Cabinet Secretary the document in a sealed envelope.

I told him that I felt the document could put us on the road to a ceasefire and peace but there was a lot of work to be done and a lot of views would have to converge. Nevertheless I said it was a very important document in that respect and I felt we were starting on to something new.

At the time, the Reynolds document probably seemed like a distraction to the British Government which was trying to involve the Northern Ireland parties in a 'three strand' process, covering political relationships within Northern Ireland, between London and Belfast and between London and Dublin. John Major was also extremely wary of having anything to do with 'Hume–Adams'. Nevertheless, the Prime Minister rang the Taoiseach 'in a matter of days' and said it was 'an interesting document' but did not see that it would 'run'. Reynolds explained it was only a starting point.

> I asked him to open discussions on it to see how far we could get and what we could make of it. I didn't expect he was going to accept it in totality. There was no balance in it. But nevertheless the principles were there. It was the first time we had a document on the table where we knew what the thinking of the republican leadership was and what might bring about a ceasefire. The prize was big and so I persuaded the Prime Minister to get involved in discussion and see where it would lead us.

But John Major had other problems which were to dog the rest of the premiership. His parliamentary majority at Westminster became increasingly slim as each by-election resulted in an ominous Labour landslide, and therefore his own and his Government's survival came to rely increasingly on the votes of the nine Ulster Unionists MPs and their uncharismatic but politically astute leader, James Molyneaux. In the critical vote on 22 July 1993, involving Britain's opting out of the Social Chapter of the Maastricht Treaty, the Government's survival was ensured by the support of the Ulster Unionists. Although Number Ten denies that the parliamentary arithmetic governed the rest of John Major's policy towards Ireland, there is no doubt that it was an important factor. Major was a realist. He knew there was only so much the unionists would accept and that without them the peace process would get nowhere. The evolution of his Irish policy was probably as much governed by that as by more domestic political considerations.

By the summer of 1993, the secret dialogue between the Government and the IRA had run into the sand, not least because of the intensity with which the IRA had carried on its campaign both before and after the bombing of the NatWest Tower. The British sent a clear message: 'Events on the ground are crucial, as we have consistently made clear. We cannot conceivably disregard them. We gave advice in good faith, taking what we were told at face value. It is difficult to reconcile that with recent events.'[16] Sinn Fein wished the dialogue to continue, whilst expressing caution as a result of its previous experience of secret talks with the British. It said the IRA had agreed to the two week suspension that had been sought 'which underlines the sincerity of those involved and their faith in us'. It hoped that the delegation meetings previously discussed could now proceed and outlined its position in response to that given by the British on 19 March, the day before the Warrington bomb.

1. We do not seek to impose pre-conditions nor should pre-conditions be imposed on us.
2. The restoration to the Irish people of our right to self-determination – in the free exercise of that right without impediment of any kind.
3. The British Government should play a crucial and constructive role in persuading the unionist community to reach an accommodation with the rest of the Irish people.
4. The process of national reconciliation must secure the political, religious and democratic rights of the Northern unionist population.[17]

These were broadly some of the 'principles' that Albert Reynolds reflected in the 'peace' document he sent to John Major.

Summer turned to autumn and no progress was made. The 'BGR' and the Contact kept on talking, as did Hume and Adams, and the IRA kept on bombing. Suddenly, the province once more was pushed to the brink. On 23 October 1993, the IRA planted a bomb in a fish shop on the Protestant Shankill Road. Their intended target was a meeting of the loyalist UFF thought to be going on in the UDA office that had been above the shop – the IRA did not know the meeting was over. The bomb exploded prematurely, killing ten people, including the owner and his daughter, and one of the IRA bombers, twenty-three-year-old Thomas Begley. There was universal outrage. The Government asked how the IRA could be talking peace and slaughtering civilians. The question became even more controversial when the media showed Gerry Adams carrying Thomas Begley's coffin. In fact it would have been disastrous for the peace process had Adams *not* carried the coffin as the RUC Chief Constable, Sir Hugh Annesley, recognised.[18]

I think a lot of people found that abhorrent and I think they found difficulty in reconciling that with some of the comments of Gerry Adams about peace. If, on the other hand, one looks at it from his point of view, it's difficult to see what else he could have done. In a pragmatic way, I don't think he had much option.

Albert Reynolds also knew that Adams had no choice.

> If he was going to have the influence and status to carry through the change in the organization's policy and strategy, in my view he had to.
> **And it would have been pointless talking to somebody who had lost that influence.**
> There's no point if people can't deliver. It's like in a trade union dispute. I prefer to deal with the hard-line trade union negotiator who at the end of the day, when you have finished your negotiations, can deliver on the deal, rather than somebody who will agree with you for the sake of argument but can't deliver.

The loyalist paramilitaries took dreadful revenge. In the following week, the UVF shot dead two Catholics and the UFF two more. But the bloody climax came exactly one week after the Shankill bomb when on Halloween night – 30 October 1993 – UFF gunmen walked into the Rising Sun bar in the village of Greysteel just outside Derry. They said 'Trick or Treat' and opened up on the customers, killing six Catholics, including an eighty-one-year-old pensioner and one Protestant. They wounded thirteen. The UFF claimed it had attacked the 'nationalist electorate' in revenge for the Shankill bombing.[19] In that one month – October 1993 – as the province struggled towards peace, twenty-seven people were killed. It was the greatest death toll in any single month since October 1976, when twenty-eight people had died. On the eve of the Greysteel massacre, John Major and Albert Reynolds had a stormy meeting in Brussels on the margins of a European summit. Reynolds has a vivid recollection of it.

> John Major was not an easy man to discuss things with at that stage and I could understand that. He said 'Here is the front page of every British newspaper with a photograph of Gerry Adams carrying the coffin of the Shankill bomber. Realistically, you know as well as I do that I can't live with that situation. The British public wouldn't accept for a moment that I would have anything to do with, or even dream about, talking to the people who would perpetrate that heineous crime.'
> He really believed that continuing talks with Sinn Fein was a waste of time and that nothing would be delivered. It was difficult getting him to agree to even a communiqué at that stage or to hold the talks together.

Reynolds and Major adjourned to another room for forty-five minutes and hammered out their differences. No one else was present. They emerged with their friendship still intact and agreed a communiqué that said there could be no talks with those who used, threatened or supported political violence and the principle of consent had to be enshrined in any settlement. If, however, it said there was to be a renunciation of violence, 'new doors could open' and both Governments would wish to respond 'imaginatively' to the situation. In other words, the Republican Movement could still come in from the cold. The communiqué was a triumph of wording by the team of British and Irish officials, watched over by the two Prime Ministers. What Reynolds did not know was that all that year, the British Government had been involved in a secret dialogue with the IRA. How did Albert Reynolds feel when he found out?

> Initially I felt a bit let down. There was I putting all my cards on the table and I felt at the time a bit disappointed that I wasn't getting the full facts, the full story. But if the British Government decided to go their road, they'd every entitlement to make that decision.

In November 1993, many genuinely feared that Northern Ireland was on the brink of civil war as the main players in the drama on all sides desperately tried to regain control of events and seize the initiative before the province plunged into total disaster. In the House of Commons on 1 November 1993, John Major and John Hume had a heated exchange as Hume vented his frustration at the lack of political progress. Television had showed him in tears at the Greysteel funerals. The Prime Minister said that if Hume was implying that the Government should sit down and talk with Gerry Adams, he would not do it. 'The thought would turn my stomach,' he said. 'I will not talk to people who murder indiscriminately.'[20] The Prime Minister was almost forced to eat his words four weeks later when the journalist Eamonn Mallie reported in the *Observer* of 28 November that the Government had been involved in secret talks with the IRA. However skilfully Government spin doctors played with semantics, there was no fooling the public. Far from turning on Sir Patrick Mayhew, the House of Commons gave the Secretary of State its full support and sympathy for the roasting the media had given him. Sir Patrick appeared astonished, relieved and delighted in equal measure.

During the week of the Shankill bombing and Greysteel massacre, the Contact had been abroad and, realizing how critical the situation back home had become, had arranged to meet the 'BGR' when returning through London on Tuesday, 2 November 1993. It is not clear what happened at the meeting but it appears that the Contact expressed strong feelings at the way in which he believed the British Government had squandered the opportunity for peace. No message from McGuinness or the Republican Movement was handed over to the 'BGR', not least because the Contact had been out of the country and this was a hastily arranged face-to-face. Martin McGuinness was therefore astonished when, three days later, he received a copy of a message purporting to have been sent from 'the leadership of the Provisional Movement' to the British Government the previous Tuesday. The message said:

> You appear to have rejected the Hume–Adams situation . . . Now we can't even have a dialogue to work out how a *total end to violence* [author's emphasis] can come about. We believe that the country could be at the point of no return. In plain language please tell us as a matter of urgency when you will open dialogue in the event of *a total end to hostilities* [author's emphasis]. We believe that if all the documents [ie our respective position papers] are put on the table – we have the basis of an understanding.[21]

Attached to the copy of the message was the British Government's 'substantive response' welcoming the 'message' as being 'of the greatest importance and significance' and offering a first meeting for 'exploratory dialogue' within weeks 'if a genuine [and permanent] end to violence is brought about within the next few days'. McGuinness was furious. No such message had been sent and moreover, at this stage, there had been no mention by the Provisionals of a 'total' end to violence. That, of course, was why the Government's response was so fulsome. HMG thought the IRA had finally agreed to end its campaign for good, but the IRA had done nothing of the kind. McGuinness consulted Adams and they agreed to send a disclaimer to the Government which said that the message was 'entirely bogus' and that Sinn Fein had not sent this or any other message on that Tuesday. The Contact was embarrassed and upset. McGuinness told him his role was over. I asked McGuinness what had happened.

> The British Government have effectively abused the Contact to destruction. They have destroyed it.
> **How did the Contact feel about it?**
> I'm sure he's disgusted, disgusted with the British government and the way in which they abused him. Absolutely. How else could he feel.
> **Was the dialogue then over?**
> For now, it's over.[22]

After risking his life for twenty years acting as the intermediary between the IRA and the British Government, the Contact was finished.

So what happened at the meeting in London? The most probable explanation is that the 'BGR' embellished what the Contact in his anger and frustration had told him and presented it to the Government as the message it had been waiting so long to hear – that the IRA was prepared to declare a total and permanent end to violence. This was not true, and it caused McGuinness such embarrassment because the Army Council might think that things were being said which had not yet been agreed. No wonder McGuinness was furious. Bogus or not, the 'message' probably encouraged John Major to make the speech on Ireland he had planned for the Lord Mayor's Banquet on 15 November 1993 far more upbeat than it would have been otherwise. 'There may now be a better opportunity for peace in Northern Ireland than for many years,' he announced. At the time he did not know how shaky that foundation was from the Provisionals' point of view.

The dialogue with Albert Reynolds on the 'peace' document was speeded up to give the province some hope after the recent shedding of so much blood, but it was still not easy. The document the Taoiseach had given to Sir Robin Butler back in June had been considerably modified, and it now contained input from the Protestant clergy that included the Northern Presbyterian minister, the Reverend Roy Magee, and Dr Robin Eames, the (Protestant) Primate of All Ireland. But there was still not the balance the British wanted. There was another crisis meeting between Major and Reynolds, this time in Dublin, when Sir Robin Butler brought over an alternative document which Reynolds thought undermined all they had worked on 'long and hard for many, many months'. Then, according to Reynolds, to make matters worse, the British introduced yet another document. The two Prime Ministers left the room for another private head to head. Reynolds was furious, and said that he 'regarded it as a total breakdown in personal relationships'. This time, there was no resolution when they rejoined their officials. The meeting was on the point of collapse and Major broke his pencil in frustration. Tempers cooled over lunch and the conversation turned to rugby which helped relieve the tension. In the end, agreement was reached and what became known as the 'Joint Declaration' was born. At last, the peace process that had begun way back in 1988 with those first meetings between Hume and Adams had borne fruit. It was a breakthrough.

On 15 December 1993, John Major and Albert Reynolds stood side by side in Downing Street, smiling, their differences forgotten and their friendship intact. 'I felt history was in the making,' said Reynolds, 'at least the risks were well worth taking up to that point.' Although the

Joint Declaration – or the Downing Street Declaration as it became better known – contained many words and phrases from Hume–Adams, it was far less nationalist than both would have liked. Unionist concerns, or at least some of them, were addressed by the repetition *five times* that nothing would be done against the wishes of a majority of the people of Northern Ireland. It was a carefully worded and meticulously balanced document, the result of hours of work and painful negotiation. The principles enshrined in the Declaration were to underpin any final settlement that might be agreed. For unionists, the principle of consent was almost written in neon lights. For nationalists the principle of self-determination was established for the people of Ireland, but on the basis of consent, with separate referenda ultimately being held North and South. Whitehall and Dublin mandarins had spent months agreeing the tortuous wording.

> The Prime Minister, on behalf of the British Government, reaffirms . . . that they have no selfish, strategic or economic interest in Northern Ireland.
>
> The role of the British Government will be to encourage, facilitate and enable the achievement of . . . agreement . . . They accept that such agreement may, as of right, take the form of agreed structures for the island as a whole, including a united Ireland achieved by peaceful means on the following basis.
>
> The British Government agree that it is for the people of the island of Ireland alone, by agreement between the two parts respectively, to exercise their right of self-determination on the basis of consent, freely and concurrently given, North and South, to bring about a united Ireland, if that is their wish.[23]

Although on the face of it, the Joint Declaration was a nationalist green in colour, it was essentially a unionist document effectively enshrining the unionist veto that the Provisionals had spent years fighting to destroy. It was not surprising that republicans were not jumping for joy. I spent some time visiting the Maze prison a few weeks later and found that IRA prisoners were almost unanimous in their rejection of the Joint Declaration. The weeks and the months went by and there was no word of a ceasefire. The omens did not look good.

Chapter Twenty-four

Breakthrough

In America, President Bill Clinton gave the Joint Declaration the warmest of welcomes and hinted that the visa that Gerry Adams had sought and been refused earlier in the year 'because he was involved in terrorist activity' might be up for review 'as the developing situation warrants'.[1] On 29 January 1994, President Clinton relented despite continuing opposition from the State Department and Department of Justice and granted Adams a 'limited duration' visa. Adams' strongest backer in the White House was the President's Foreign Policy Adviser and Staff Director of the National Security Council (NSC), Nancy Soderberg. Her brief included Northern Ireland and for many years she had been close to John Hume, who had told her that he thought the IRA was moving towards a ceasefire. Soderberg was an experienced operator and close to the President.

> There was a natural disinclination to deal with someone like Adams, and the NSC opposed his visa for a long time. The visa became the test for who was right and who was wrong. If Adams delivered the ceasefire, great. If not, we could tell Irish America [that had been lobbying for the visa] that it was 'no-go'. News of the visa leaked on the wires before the announcement. It was the first time America had ever gone against Britain on the Irish question. There was not an opposing voice in the White House. The Department of Justice was not happy. The visa was only for two days and there was to be no official comment. It wasn't a particularly risky move.

Adams was given the visa in order to attend a one-day Peace Conference in New York organized by the National Committee on American Foreign Policy. It was also to be addressed by John Hume and John Alderdice of the Alliance Party. Unionists boycotted the event because of Adams' presence. The Conference, held at the Waldorf Astoria hotel, was organised by the multi-millionaire William (Bill) Flynn, Chairman of United Mutual Life Insurance Company. As a result of careful lobbying by Sinn Fein supporters in America, Flynn was one of a group of wealthy Irish Americans who had been persuaded to put their weight and money behind the peace process, which effectively meant behind Sinn Fein's version of it. Flynn had already been to Belfast and had a long talk with Gerry Adams, and had also made contact with the political representatives of the loyalist paramilitaries. Some of the group had powerful connections in the White House, as they had helped finance Bill Clinton's election campaign, and they had put their considerable weight behind the application for Adams' visa. To the astonishment of Bill Flynn, the Sinn Fein President took the Peace Conference and America by storm.

> He was a tremendous hit. It confirmed the suspicions of most Americans of Irish heritage – and really of both traditions – that this was a thoughtful, reasonable, thinking person. What he had to say and the way he acted, seemed to belie the label of 'terrorist'. But curiously, what made the thing a public relations success of the first order was the fact that he had been drowned out by the British rules and regulations [that did not allow his voice to be heard on the media]. He became the darling of the press and the darling of the TV and everyone wanted to see him.

The British Government was disgusted by the adulation Adams received and furious that the White House had granted the visa without Adams delivering a ceasefire or even endorsing the Joint Declaration. Downing Street thought Clinton was being naive. Relations between Number Ten and the White House began to deteriorate as the months went by and Clinton gave Adams more visas and lifted the ban on fundraising for Sinn Fein. At one stage, it was said that John Major refused to return the President's calls. I remember watching television news coverage of Adams' first visit to America with IRA prisoners whilst I was visiting the republican wings of the Maze prison. They were ecstatic and could not believe the reception the man they regarded as their leader was getting. To the IRA, Adams was delivering, and the remarkable television pictures were proof of his success.

Despite republican euphoria, for months there was no sign of movement towards the long-anticipated ceasefire. The IRA carried on killing policemen, whilst the UVF and UFF carried on slaughtering Catholics in ever greater numbers. It was a pattern that had become familiar over the years: the closer the Government appeared to be getting to the Provisionals, the more active the loyalist paramilitaries became. It had happened in 1972, 1975 and was happening now. The most horrific attack was carried out by the UVF on 18 June 1994 when gunmen opened fire on Catholics in a bar in Loughinisland as they were watching the Republic of Ireland play in the football World Cup in America. Six men were shot dead. One of them was eighty-seven years old. As the summer of 1994 approached, rumours of an IRA ceasefire were rife but still nothing happened. Albert Reynolds became more and more frustrated, having staked so much upon the assurance that a ceasefire would be delivered. He thought he had an agreement with Adams and Adams was letting him down. In the wonderfully indiscreet and colourful diaries of Reynolds' Press Secretary, Sean Duignan, an Irish Alan Clark, Duignan recounts Reynolds' anger on 12 August 1994 when there was still no confirmation of a ceasefire and the IRA was saying that it still wished to reserve the right to defend nationalist communities. 'I've told them if they don't do this right, they can shag off. I don't want to hear anything about a six month or six year ceasefire. No temporary, indefinite or conditional stuff. No defending or retaliating against anyone. Just that it's over . . . period . . . full stop. Otherwise, I'll walk away.'[2]

On 31 August 1994, it finally happened. The IRA announced its cessation. Its statement said:

> Recognizing the potential of the current situation and in order to enhance the democratic peace process and underline our commitment to its success, the leadership of Oglaigh na Eireann have decided that as of midnight, Wednesday, 31 August, there will be a complete cessation of military operations. All of our units have been instructed accordingly . . .
>
> We believe that an opportunity to create a just and lasting peace has been created . . . We note that the Downing Street Declaration is not a solution, nor was it presented as such by its authors. A solution can only be found as a result of inclusive negotiations.[3]

The news was greeted with jubilation in Belfast although few IRA supporters thought they had won – the word 'victory' was never mentioned; instead, 'undefeated' was the expression used. The celebrations were more a sign of relief that now at last the 'war' might be over. Soon, the British Government started to complain that the word 'permanent' was not in the statement, thus erecting the first of the hurdles that were to stand in the way of progress over the next seventeen months. But the RUC's Chief Constable, Sir Hugh Annesley, had no doubt about the significance of the IRA's announcement.

> I had the head of Special Branch camping in my office in the preceding two weeks and we were well tuned in to the fact that

a statement was going to be made and we had some idea of its general content. When it did come, it was vastly in excess in its wording of what I had expected. It was open ended and it talked of 'a complete cessation of military operations'. We had expected a ceasefire but we had expected it would have parameters like three months or something of that nature or would be largely caveated. It wasn't. I felt like many others at that stage that at long last there was the potential breakthrough for which we'd all hoped.

Did you think it was genuine?

I thought at that time and for a considerable period afterwards that republicans meant what they said and that was the view that I and the intelligence community conveyed to the Prime Minister.

Did it matter that the cessation did not include the word 'permanent'?

It would have been better had it used the word 'permanent' but those who were close to it did not expect them to use the word because the Provisional Army Council could not declare a permanent end to the campaign. That would have required a decision by a General Army Convention which would have run into a meeting of some 500 members. I think they were unlikely to go for the word 'permanent' at that stage without knowing the response by the Government. The key issue was did they intend it to be permanent? Did they intend it to hold? The unanimous view of the intelligence community at that stage was 'yes'.

The wrangle over the absence of the word 'permanent' continued and was seized upon by unionists as a sign that the Provisionals were not sincere. In the end, on the advice of the 'intelligence community', the Prime Minister decided to make a 'working assumption' that the cessation was indeed 'permanent'.

But behind the scenes, Albert Reynolds and others, either directly or through intermediaries like Dr Robin Eames and the Reverend Roy Magee, had been working to persuade the loyalist paramilitaries to declare a ceasefire to complete the scenario for a potential peace. When I had been in the Maze prison earlier in the year, I had talked to the leaders of the UDA/UFF and UVF prisoners and asked them what their reaction would be to a possible IRA ceasefire. 'If they stop, we'll stop,' they said, pointing out that their campaign was only a reaction to the IRA's. The loyalist paramilitaries had also been courted from America by Bill Flynn, who knew that they too would have to be included if there was to be a genuine end to all violence. The emergence of their political parties, the Ulster Democratic Party (UDP) – linked to the UDA – led by Gary

McMichael and the Progressive Unionist Party (PUP) – linked to the UVF – led by David Ervine had been one of the more encouraging recent features to emerge on the bleak political landscape of Northern Ireland. Ervine, McMichael and their colleagues have shown themselves to be articulate and unbigoted spokesmen for their cause, refreshingly free of slogans like 'no surrender' and 'not an inch' with which loyalist vocabulary was traditionally laced. In terms of social class, they had much more in common with the Provisionals than they had with the Unionist parties. In October, Bill Flynn flew over to Belfast and spent some time with the leaders of the loyalist paramilitaries as they were putting the final touches to their announcement of a loyalist ceasefire.

> The night before I sat with the leadership of the loyalist paramilitary organizations and we reviewed the statement they were going to make the next morning. We did that for about two or three hours. The one thing I told them was that they should never even think of taking out was the genuine statement of remorse over the harm they had done to people in the North by their military actions.
>
> In their statement, they apologized and asked forgiveness. I thought that was a marvellous statement to have made and I wished I had been with Adams six weeks earlier and had had the foresight to suggest that they [the Provisionals] might consider doing the same thing.

On 13 October 1994, six weeks after the announcement of the IRA cessation, the loyalists followed suit. They stressed that their ceasefire was conditional on the Provisionals maintaining theirs. In a remarkable scene, Gusty Spence, who almost thirty years earlier had been convicted of one of the first murders of the current 'Troubles', read the statement of apology.

> In all sincerity, we offer to the loved ones of all innocent victims over the past twenty-five years abject and true remorse. No words of ours will compensate for the intolerable suffering they have undergone during the conflict. Let us firmly resolve to respect our differing views of freedom, culture and aspiration and never again permit our political circumstances to degenerate into bloody warfare . . . so that together we can bring forth a wholesome society in which our children, and their children, will know the meaning of peace.[4]

Perhaps a new dawn really was beginning – as long as the IRA cessation held. That was the problem. Despite what the IRA said, the cessation was always contingent on progress to the all-party talks that they had been led to believe would be the prize for their cessation.

Within weeks another and far more serious hurdle had been erected on the road to those talks by the British Government and the unionists. It became known as 'decommissioning' or disarmament of the IRA and loyalist arsenals. Both argued that if the IRA was serious about having given up its 'armed struggle' it would have no problem in handing in its weapons. The very thought was anathema to the Provisionals. Not only had 'decommissioning' never happened before in Ireland – the IRA had always 'dumped' its weapons after previous campaigns – but in what republicans referred to as 'conflict resolution situations' all over the world, arms had not been handed over until a final settlement was reached. For the IRA to hand over any weapons before such a settlement would be taken as a sign of surrender. The IRA might not have won but it certainly was not defeated. Symbolism was everything in Ireland. The most pressing demands for decommissioning came from the unionists, many of whom would have treasured the sight of the IRA 'surrendering' itself and its weapons, and they were backed by the Prime Minister, despite the advice he had received from his security and intelligence chiefs. Sir Hugh Annesley was astonished that decommissioning became such an issue.

> Everybody who was close to what was going on wanted to see the guns out of circulation but there was a difference between what was achievable and what wasn't achievable. It was perfectly clear from all of the intelligence assessments that the Provisionals were not going to hand in their arms. Indeed, some individual reports made it clear that some prominent players said they wouldn't hand in as much as a single rifle. In pragmatic terms, the issue of decommissioning was less important for the security forces – because of the build up of home-made equipment [mortars and home made explosives] – than it was on the political front. What I wanted to see was clear evidence that the Provisional IRA was demobilizing its whole system. I believe that whilst decommissioning was important politically, it was not as important operationally and in security force terms as some people have attempted to make out.

Decommissioning was the issue on which the IRA's cessation fell apart. The Provisionals were adamant that they would not give up 'one bullet' until a final settlement had been agreed. They pointed out that it had never been raised as an issue during the secret dialogue of 1993, and it had not been raised in the discussions between Albert Reynolds and John Major. Decommissioning had come out of the blue and unionists seized on the issue, knowing the discomfort it caused their enemy. Albert Reynolds had warned John Major at Chequers in October 1994 that decommissioning was an extremely sensitive issue for both republicans and loyalists.

> There's no way the IRA would give up its arms in advance. That's a symbol of surrender. I was the leader of a party, Fianna Fail, who'd come out of a civil war situation ourselves and refused to give up our own arms at the time. We even went to the Houses of Parliament [to negotiate the Treaty of 1921] without giving them up and I couldn't have any credibility asking others to do what we weren't prepared to do ourselves in our own time.
>
> When I looked around the world, it wasn't a precondition in Bosnia, in the Middle East or indeed in South Africa. But I felt that I had got a clear understanding from the IRA that decommissioning was necessary and that there couldn't be any final settlement without full decommissioning and that we would have decommissioning as part of the process. I thought that I had convinced John [Major] of that in October at Chequers. It wasn't being forgotten but it was never a pre-condition.

Mistrust between the Provisionals and the Government was intensified when Sir Patrick Mayhew made a speech in Washington on 8 March 1995 in which he set out three conditions for decommissioning that would finally allow Sinn Fein into all-party talks. First, the IRA had to be willing in principle 'to disarm progressively'; second, it had to agree on how in practice decommissioning would be carried out; and third, and most controversially, it had to decommission some of its weaponry at the *beginning* of the talks as 'a tangible, confidence-building measure'. This third condition became known as 'Washington Three' and was, for the Provisionals, an insuperable hurdle. In 1995, spring, summer and autumn passed and more than a year into the IRA cessation, Sinn Fein seemed no nearer to entering all-party talks. I remember being in Dublin that autumn and being told by senior Provisionals that the media had no idea of just how serious the situation was. Adams and McGuinness had staked their reputations on getting the IRA to deliver the ceasefire and now they were being left to twist in the wind. The ledge on which they were standing, I was told, was getting ever narrower. I understood their frustration and concern.

On 30 November 1995, President Clinton made a triumphant visit to Northern Ireland, basked in the acclaim of his role as the American Peacemaker, heard Van Morrison sing 'Days Like This' and 'bumped into' Gerry Adams during a 'walkabout' on the Falls Road and shook hands. Belfast had never felt so good. Peace, people thought, was here to stay. But the Chief Constable, Sir Hugh Annesley, saw the intelligence reports and read the warning signs.

> I would have thought it was relatively easy in the initial stages for the PIRA/Sinn Fein to control others who were against the peace process – and clearly a number were – while there was development and activity was taking place. But when the stalemate about decommissioning became more intense and more rigid, then I think it became progressively more difficult for the leadership of the Provisional IRA to hold in check those who wanted to go back to violence, and there were significant bodies of opinion in South Armagh, in East Tyrone, in South Derry and in West Belfast who wanted to go back. I think also at that stage there was the potential spectre of a split in the Movement. I have no doubt that the preparations for Canary Wharf [the IRA bomb that was to end the ceasefire] were made in the latter part of 1995.

Recognizing the gravity of the looming crisis and the imminent arrival of President Clinton, Major and Bruton (he had succeeded Reynolds as Taoiseach on 15 November 1994) at Downing Street on 28 November 1995 and agreed on a 'twin track' approach to resolve the question of decommissioning. An 'international body' was to be set up to report on the problem, chaired by former US Senator George Mitchell and accompanied by Harri Holkeri, a former Finnish Prime Minister, and General John de Chastelain, the Canadian Chief of the Defence Staff. They published their report on 22 January 1996, setting out principles to which all those seeking to engage in all-party talks must commit themselves. They famously became known as 'The Mitchell Principles'. They included a commitment to 'democratic and exclusively peaceful means of resolving political issues'; the total disarmament of all paramilitary organizations; a renunciation of the use of force to influence the outcome of all-party negotiations; and an end to 'punishment' killings and dealings. Sinn Fein said it would meet them. On decommissioning, the issue it was primarily set up to address, their report concluded:

> ... there is a clear commitment on the part of those in possession of such arms to work constructively to achieve full and verifiable decommissioning *as part of the process* [author's emphasis] of all-party negotiations; but that commitment does not include decommissioning prior to such negotiations ... we have concluded that the paramilitary organizations will not decommission any arms prior to all-party negotiations.[5]

The phrase 'as part of the process of all-party negotiations' was suitably vague and seemed to provide the basis for progress. But far from seizing the opportunity to use the report as a way of finally getting the Provisionals into all-party talks, John Major pushed Sinn Fein further away by announcing that elections would be held for a Forum that would sit to accompany the talks. This gave the unionists what they wanted, since the result would reflect their majority in the province. Both Sinn Fein and the SDLP were appalled. Elections had only been mentioned in paragraph fifty-six of the sixty-two paragraph report, and then almost by way of an afterthought. Sir Hugh Annesley, who had watched the IRA cessation being born now saw it being thrown away.

> I was disappointed at the response. I was disappointed that the Government decided to go for elections. I thought there was an opportunity there to accept the Mitchell principles – as Sinn Fein did – but also to accept the Mitchell thrust of a compromise [on decommissioning]. Had that been pushed fair and square to Sinn Fein, it would have caused them to go one way or the other.

At 7.01pm on 9 February 1996, the IRA gave its response. A huge bomb that had been placed in the car park of a building near Canary Wharf in London's Docklands exploded. It killed two men, injured more than a hundred and caused £85 million worth damage. The scene in Docklands was one of utter devastation. I asked Martin McGuinness if he had known the bomb was coming. He said he did not and warned that because of the attitude of the British Government, there was 'considerable danger that the authority of people like himself and Gerry Adams has been to some degree seriously undermined'. Once again, the Provisionals felt let down and betrayed. Despite the punishment beatings and killing of alleged drug dealers, the IRA cessation had held for seventeen months. The Republican Movement had got nothing in return, and the promised all-party talks were a mirage that seemed to get ever further away. Had the IRA not bombed Docklands, it would have probably split.

Three weeks later, on 28 February 1996, the British and Irish Governments issued a joint communiqué announcing a firm date for all-party talks – 10 June 1996. Many thought the announcement of the long-awaited date was Downing Street's response to the Docklands' bomb. The bomb was certainly a warning but the Prime Minister also knew he had to move the process on. Sinn Fein would only be allowed to take part in those talks if the IRA declared another ceasefire – and there was no sign of that. The campaign continued, but this time it was largely restricted to operations in England. The most devastating was the IRA's attack on Manchester city centre on 17 June 1996. A van containing a massive, one and a half ton bomb, exploded, injuring 200 people and causing an estimated £100 million worth of damage.

Although Northern Ireland was, for the most part, spared the familiar horror of an IRA campaign and the bloody loyalist response, sectarianism flared across the province. For three consecutive years an Orangemen's march from a church at Drumcree along the Catholic Garvaghy Road in Portadown resulted in widespread violence. 'Parity of esteem' became the new republican slogan. In July 1996 violence engulfed the province when the Chief Constable, Sir Hugh Annesley, who had decided to reroute the march away from the Catholic area, reversed his decision and let the march through. He judged it to be the lesser of two evils, calculating that more lives would be lost had he stuck to his original decision. A year later, his successor Ronnie Flanagan had the same unenviable decision to make. Flanagan let the march through for the same reason. By the early summer of 1997, Northern Ireland had settled back to the pattern of killing that it had lived with for almost thirty years, but, with a difference. For the first time, the killing was largely one-sided as, remarkably, the loyalist ceasefire held despite intense provocation. The political leaders of the loyalist paramilitaries recognized the benefits of inclusion in the political process and did not want to throw them away. Again, there were harrowing incidents that touched both communities and both islands and made people cry out for peace. On 13 February 1997, an IRA sniper shot dead Lance-Bombadier Stephen Restorick as he was manning a checkpoint outside the huge army base in Bessbrook, South Armagh. He was leaning over and handing back a driving licence to Lorraine McElroy, who had been out buying ice cream for her children. 'He smiled and thanked me,' she said:

> Then there was a crack and a flash and I then heard the soldier groaning. He was on the ground beside my car and my first thought was to try and help him but there was nothing I could do. There was just no regard for what lives were going to be taken as long as they killed the poor soldier, no matter who went with him. I just feel so very, very angry about it. And it's awful to think, is this the start of it all again?[6]

Stephen Restorick was cremated on his twenty-fourth birthday. There were few military trappings. At the funeral, his mother, Mrs Rita Restorick, said she hoped that Stephen's death would be 'a catalyst to restart the peace process and bring both sides together to talk.'[7]

Five months later, her plea was answered. The IRA renewed its ceasefire, announcing 'a complete cessation of military operations' from midday on Sunday 20 July. It did so, it said, 'having assessed the current political situation'. By the summer of 1997, the political landscape in Britain and Northern Ireland had changed literally overnight. At the general election of 1 May, Tony Blair, the leader of the Labour Party, had swept to victory with a stunning majority of 179 seats. The Conservatives' day had passed, and with it went John Major. The Ulster Unionists were no longer a factor in the Westminster political equation. Sinn Fein's Gerry Adams and Martin McGuinness were also elected to Westminster, although, as tradition demanded, they declined to take their seats. The new Secretary of State for Northern Ireland, Dr Maureen 'Mo' Mowlam, stunned everyone with her energy and determination to get the peace process back on the road. Within weeks, she had given the Republican Movement the assurances it needed: that, given an IRA ceasefire, Sinn Fein would be admitted to all-party talks and decommissioning would not become an obstacle at the beginning of negotiations. She also managed to persuade the Ulster Unionists under David Trimble, James Molyneux's successor, to participate in the talks, despite profound reservations. Nevertheless, Trimble made his position clear. 'If we sit down with Sinn Fein, they will be under pressure to start decommissioning straight away,' he said, 'and Sinn Fein will not have any excuse not to do so'.[8] But to the Reverend Ian Paisley, it was immaterial. He declared that his Democratic Unionist Party would not attend as the talks were a sell-out to the IRA. A date was set for the first meeting – 15 September 1997.

Chapter Twenty-five

Dissidents

The overriding concern of Gerry Adams and Martin McGuinness through the years in which they and the leadership of the Republican Movement had endeavoured to steer the Provos from war to peace was to avoid a split. They knew that such divisions, which had haunted the IRA through the century, were potentially disastrous for the organization and played into the hands of the enemy. There was nothing the 'Brits' would like to see more, they reasoned, than the Irish Republican Army rent asunder. Hence the caution and political skill with which they moved, always making sure that the right individuals were in the right places at the right time and that the rank and file IRA Volunteers were brought along with them. They knew that to leave the membership in the dark would breed dissent, mistrust and potentially dangerous opposition. Although the strategy was carried through with remarkable success – a tribute to the dexterity with which it had been handled – a split was inevitable given the astonishing turnaround the Provisionals were eventually to make: virtually accepting partition by deciding to take seats in the new Northern Ireland Assembly which was the lynchpin of the historic Good Friday Agreement of April 1998. This chapter investigates how that split came about and how a handful of defectors from the Provos, whose military experience far outweighed their numbers, endeavoured to carry on the campaign under the name of the 'true' IRA. And they were not the only republican splinter group in the field. The Irish National Liberation Army (INLA) had not declared a ceasefire and the Continuity IRA, of which little had been heard since the split in the Republican Movement in 1986 (see Chapter Twenty), now became increasingly active. These three groups, whose actions triggered a bloody response from the loyalist paramilitaries, provided the violent backdrop to the momentous events in the year that followed Sinn Fein's entry into all-party talks in September 1997. But of the three, it was the 'true' IRA that posed the most serious threat due to the proficiency and expertise of its bomb-makers and engineers who had defected from the Provos. It was only vigilance and the high-grade intelligence in the possession of the RUC and its Irish counterpart, the Garda Síochana, that prevented a series of major disasters in the course of 1998. So what was the 'true' IRA and who was behind it and why?

Within a month of Sinn Fein entering the talks in September 1997, the internal dissension that had been growing within the Provos came to a head. It had been evident since the ending of the 1994 ceasefire at Canary Wharf but in an organization run with iron discipline it had been kept within bounds. Now, with Sinn Fein in the talks, it had reached the point where it had to be confronted by the leadership. The dissident group was led by the IRA's Quarter Master General (QMG), a powerful individual because of his rank, track record and personal standing. For legal reasons, he cannot be named. The QMG is a critical figure at the top of the IRA's command structure with a senior position on the IRA's General Headquarters Staff (GHQ), which is responsible for assembling and maintaining every aspect of the IRA's 'war' machine. His role is vital because he is responsible for organizing the procurement, storage and distribution of the tons of IRA weapons that have been smuggled in and stashed away over the years. The QMG drew powerful support from within his own department – including his second in command – and from the Engineer's department with whom he and his men worked closely. Most of his supporters either lived in the South or were on the run across the border. His strategy, it appears, was to engineer a coup from within, waiting until Adams and McGuinness signed up to a partitionist agreement that would trigger their demise, as they would be perceived to have sold out. The QMG anticipated that a special Army Convention would then be called at which the discredited leadership of the Provos would be kicked out and his faction voted in. But the scenario did not work out as planned.

The drama was played out an an IRA Extraordinary Army Convention. The Army Convention, made up of delegates representing IRA units from all over Ireland, is the supreme authority from which all power flows. It elects the twelve person Army Executive which, in turn, elects the seven man Army Council which then elects the GHQ Staff. According to the IRA's constitution, an Extraordinary Army Convention can only be summoned when a majority of the Executive so decides. The leadership was concerned because not only were four members of the Executive already siding with the QMG but there was a fifth potential defector in the person of a powerful IRA leader from Belfast. If he were to defect to the dissidents, then the Executive would become delicately balanced with five members supporting the QMG and only seven supporting current policy. Such a margin would be dangerously narrow for the leadership. The dissidents had requested the Convention as the proper forum in which to air their dissatisfaction but, unknown to them, the leadership had a strategy in place to confront and outflank them. It began by not only acceding to their request for a Convention but by bringing forward the date in order to catch the dissidents on the wrong foot.

The Extraordinary Army Convention was held on 10 October 1997 at a community centre near Falcarragh in the stunningly beautiful Gweedore area of north-west Donegal. As always, it was held in secret and meticulously organized to avoid the attention of the security forces North and South of the border. Around 80–100 delegates attended. The Convention began on a Friday evening and lasted through the night until the following morning. There were two motions: that the Mitchell principles of non-violence – to which Sinn Fein had tactically signed up to enter the talks – should be rejected; and that the IRA's second ceasefire of July 1997, which had made Sinn Fein's entry possible, should be ended. The debate was long and heated, with the leadership of Gerry Adams and Martin McGuinness on the line. Both men were present and vigorously defended their strategy and the progress it had brought. They won the day with around 80 per cent of the delegates voting against the motions. Critically, the IRA's Army Council supported Adams and McGuinness to a man. New elections to the Army Council and Army Executive followed. The Belfast IRA leader on the Army Executive who was a potential defector to the QMG's camp was elected to the Army Council, thereby assuring his loyalty. The man who had been the IRA's Chief of Staff for many years and who was now in ill-health was not re-elected to the Army Council but voted onto the Army Executive. In effect, he and the Belfast leader swopped places. Four of the seven members of the new PAC are thought to be senior members of the Sinn Fein leadership. The QMG suffered a further blow to his plans when one of his key supporters on the Executive was not re-elected. This meant that the dissidents now only numbered three. With nine to three support on the Executive instead of the seven to five it had feared, the leadership was home and dry.

The QMG had miscalculated and been politically outmanoeuvred. After the Convention, a leading Provisional told me with a mixture of bitterness and satisfaction that he had tried to take over the IRA and failed. But he also made a further mistake. Angry at the loss of his key supporter's seat on the Executive, he suddenly resigned about a week after the Convention. At an allegedly stormy meeting with some members of the Army Council, he is believed to have given an assurance that he would not interfere with the arms dumps he once controlled. He is thought to have done so to avoid a court martial which would have led to dismissal with ignominy and possibly death. Perhaps his thinking was that he had to stay 'clean' if he was ever to return to the IRA and take over should the current leadership fail. His error was to resign so suddenly, without first alerting his supporters. This again enabled the leadership to seize the initiative, steady the doubters and critically keep another key potential defector – the QMG's second in command – onside. The person was in America at the time and taken completely unawares by his leader's precipitous action. He subsequently withdrew his support and reaffirmed his commitment to the leadership. Nevertheless, the QMG's hard-core adherents, including, critically, those in the Engineer's department, subsequently resigned and joined him, providing the dissidents with a small but highly experienced nucleus prepared to carry on the 'war'.

Two months later, on 7 December 1997, an organization called the 32 County Sovereignty Committee was set up in the Fingal area of Co. Dublin. The Sovereignty Committee reflected the views of the IRA dissidents and declared its adherence to the principle it believed the Republican Movement had now abandoned. Its founding document called for Ireland's right to national sovereignty in accordance with the declaration by Dail Eireann in 1919 (see Chapter 1): total British disengagement from Ireland, opposition to any internal or partitionist settlement, and opposition to the Mitchell principles of non-violence. Ominously, the Committee re-affirmed 'the right of the Irish people to armed struggle in pursuit of national sovereignty'. The most prominent member of the Committee was its Vice-Chairperson, Bernadette Sands-McKevitt, sister of the dead hunger striker and republican icon, Bobby Sands (see Chapter 17). She told me that the course on which the current leadership of the Republican Movement was embarked was not what her brother had died for.

> In his own words, he clearly stated what he believed he was dying for, and that was the sovereign independence of his country. It wasn't just simply a prison issue. He recognized that it was much more than that. I feel that is not what is going to come out of these talks. It's not what he died for and it's not what most of the Volunteers in the Irish Republican Army would have gone out and given their lives for – the freedom of their country.[1]

She insisted that the Committee was a single issue pressure group with no military wing or military connections. I asked that if that was the case, why had two members of the Committee's Executive been recently charged with explosives offences concerning the seizure of materials with the potential for making a bomb. The discovery of 1.5 tons of fertilizer was made on 8 January 1998 in Howth, a small fishing port to the north of Dublin. Ms Sands-McKevitt said, quite rightly, that her colleagues were innocent until proven guilty. But in the following months, there were several bombings and finds of explosives that the security forces on both sides of the border linked with individuals 'close to the 32 County Sovereignty Committee'. Among the most significant were bombs in Moira (20 February) and Portadown (23 February); a sophisticated mortar attack on the RUC station in Armagh (10 March); the discovery of a 1,200-lb car bomb in Dundalk (22 March) – presumably awaiting delivery to the North; the interception by the Garda's Emergency Response Unit of a 1,000-lb car bomb at the port in Dun Laoghaire near Dublin on its way to England; and the defusing of a 700-lb car bomb near Armagh RUC station (17 May). Some of the above, notably the bombs in Portadown and Moira, were also suspected to have been carried out by – or in tandem with – the Continuity IRA, whose background I will cover later in the chapter. The difficulty in attributing responsibility for the above is that none of them were ever claimed by either dissident republican group. Nevertheless, the RUC's Chief Constable, Ronnie Flanagan, told me he had no doubt what was happening.

We believe that there is a coalescence of a number of dissident groups. We think there are some contacts between the Continuity IRA and the 32 County Sovereignty Committee and we think they have had assistance from some dissident elements of the Provisional IRA acting on an individual basis without organization or sanction.

Do you believe that these operations are co-ordinated by the various dissident groups?

I do. We are now seeing a pattern of co-ordination. Largely these attacks emanate from the Republic. We are in daily contact with our colleagues in the Garda and I would like to pay tribute to the tremendous success they have had in thwarting quite a number of these proposed attacks. But there is evidence of co-ordination in relation to the various attempted attacks.

What sort of a threat do you believe the 32 County Sovereignty Committee poses?

Undoubtedly people close to that Committee have knowledge and expertise and experience in the terrorist field and probably have access to materials to allow that expertise and experience to be brought to bear in the carrying out of attacks. So I think people close to that Committee pose a very significant threat indeed.

Would the IRA's former Quarter Master General be close to that Committee?

I think that that is the case and I think there is a knowledge and expertise there that could be brought to bear in terrorist attacks.[2]

So far only one member of the QMG's dissident republican group has been killed. Rónán Mac Lochlainn was shot dead by the Gardaí during an attempted robbery in County Wicklow on 1 May 1998 and was claimed as a member by the dissident Provos who broke away after the IRA Convention at Gweedore. The robbery was to raise funds for the dissidents' war chest. Leading figures from the 32 County Sovereignty Committee were at the graveside at his funeral. The main oration was delivered by one of its Executive members, Francie Mackey, a former Sinn Fein Councillor from Omagh, who had been expelled from the party following his espousal of the Sovereignty Committee's cause. In his oration, Mackey declared:

> Rónán Mac Lochlainn remained loyal and true to the IRA constitution when others have used and usurped it. Rónán was proud to stand by it, take the risks and give everything to the cause he cherished.

He concluded by saying that republicans would make the 'right decision' and 'develop the struggle against British rule in Ireland' and do 'whatever is necessary' to prevent the dilution of Irish national sovereignty.[3] Shortly after the funeral of their first martyr, the dissident Provos for the first time gave their group an identity. In a statement, it claimed it was the authentic – or true – IRA and said 'the war machine is once again being directed against the British Cabinet'.[4] The irony that was one of the other republican splinter groups in the field, the Continuity IRA, also claimed by virtue of its name that it was the authentic IRA. Apart from sporadic incidents – most notably the bomb it planted on 14 July 1996 that destroyed the Killyhevlin hotel just outside Enniskillen – little had been heard of the group. In the wake of this attack which came at the height of the Drumcree crisis (see Chapter 24), the Continuity IRA issued a statement warning that 'military action will continue to be taken against British occupation in Ireland until such time as the British Government withdraws finally from our country.'[5] But as Sinn Fein entered the talks, the Continuity IRA seized the headlines again. On 16 September 1997, a 400-lb car bomb devastated the small County Armagh village of Markethill. A warning was given and no lives were lost but the damage amounted to around £3,000,000. The Continuity IRA claimed responsibility. Immediately, the unionists falsely accused the Provisional IRA – arguing that the two groups were effectively the same. In fact this was the real purpose of the Continuity IRA attack – to destabilize the talks by provoking the unionists to walk out. Nevertheless, even more remarkably given the circumstances, David Trimble's Ulster Unionists went ahead and joined the talks, despite the provocation.

But what was the Continuity IRA? Who were its leaders and where did they come from? Surprisingly, the security forces in the North seemed to have little intelligence on the group, since to date the Continuity IRA had not been deemed a significant 'player' and most resources had been concentrated on countering the Provisionals. I was fascinated by its origins as its history shed light on the road the Provos had travelled down the years and the ideological departures that others had made on the way. Given the defection of the dissidents who formed the 'true' IRA, it was instructive to see what had happened in 1986 when the Republican Movement last split (see Chapter Twenty). Then, the former President of Sinn Fein, Ruairí Ó'Brádaigh, had led his supporters out of Sinn Fein's annual conference, the Ard Fheis, because they were ideologically opposed to the decision to end abstentionism – to allow Sinn Fein to take seats in the Irish Parliament, Dail Eireann. Ruairí Ó'Brádaigh and his group subsequently formed a rival organization called Republican Sinn Fein (RSF), committed to the principle of asbstentionism. Ó'Brádaigh became President. The Continuity IRA was formed shortly afterwards and became to RSF what the IRA was to Sinn Fein.

Making contact with those able to provide insight into the thinking and activities of any paramilitary group is never easy, and the Continuity IRA is no exception. All exist in the shadows and any public pronouncement is usually limited to a statement issued to the media through recognized channels and accompanied by a recognized code word to establish its authenticity. It took several months before I was finally able to make contact with sources close to the Continuity IRA. As the following interview clearly indicates, its supporters have no love for the current leadership of the Provos. Bitterness over the split at the IRA Convention and subsequent Sinn Fein Ard Fheis of 1986 is still tangible.

After the disastrous IRA Convention of 1986, the majority of the Army Executive who were opposed to the move [to end abstentionism], met a couple of months later and decided to reorganize the IRA. Three or four months after the Sinn Fein Ard Fheis, a [Continuity] Army Convention was called.

Prior to 1986, the conspirators [mainly the Northern leadership of the Provos] did their homework and secured all the dumps. The [Continuity] Army still called itself the IRA. A sizeable number came to the Army Convention. Sixty-five per cent of them came from the South and the remainder from the North. The majority had joined in the seventies.

We acquired new avenues and roads for fundraising and weapons which took some time. Some areas had nothing, although a few weapons that had been stashed away came out. There was a period of inactivity from 1986 to 1991, when we were acquiring finance, expertise and weapons. There was no hurry to get into operations.

The Killyhevlin bomb was the first big operation. It was a political statement. Markethill was a political statement too. Our aim was to avoid civilian casualties at all costs and avoid the mistakes of the past.

The number of defectors has increased over the past two years – it started with a trickle and has built up. As disillusionment with the peace process increases, so does the number of Volunteers defecting to the Continuity IRA. We reject more than we accept at the moment to avoid spies and fifth columnists.

Currently, there is an inexplicable blind loyalty to the Provo leadership and a lot of people are war weary. They've chosen the easier of two roads. This is particularly the case in Belfast. We've a feeling there'll be a return to Stormont and the Provos will take a sizeable proportion of their current supporters with them. Some defectors will come to us.

The Continuity IRA's long term strategy is to end British rule in this country – however long it takes. The leadership of the Provos is on a road leading to a cul-de-sac. The Provos have decided to cash in their chips and take what they can. The notion of collusion with the Provisional IRA is ridiculous. It would make nonsense of our stand. Our severance from them was a straight cut.

Our operational potential has greatly increased. We will arrive at a situation where we can sustain a military campaign for as long as required – and at whatever level.

Whether the Continuity IRA's prediction becomes a reality depends on two considerations: whether what the sources told me is based on fact and not wishful thinking; and the evolution of the political situation over the next few years following the implementation of the Good Friday Agreement. Inevitably, given the road the Provos have now chosen, there are likely to be more defections to one splinter group or another, although most of those who were likely to go have perhaps already gone. But with the future far from clear, it would be unwise to rule out the possibility of an amalgamation of three splinter groups – the 'true' IRA, the Continuity IRA and the INLA – which would be likely to pose a far greater threat. Nor should we rule out the possibility of the Provisional IRA itself returning to 'war'. Everything depends on the future of the Good Friday Agreement.

Chapter Twenty-six

Agreement

I looked at my watch as Martin McGuinness and the Sinn Fein delegation entered the room. It was 9.58pm on Thursday 9 April 1998 and there were just over two hours to go before the midnight deadline for reaching a final peace agreement expired. The world's press sat crammed into a large Portakabin outside Government Buildings at Stormont, where the all-party talks had ground on since the previous September with little outward sign of real progress. The British and Irish Governments and the talks' Chairman, the endlessly patient Senator George Mitchell, had given no indication that the deadline was flexible, reasoning that there was not much point in having one if it was. Outside it was freezing and inside it was not much warmer. The only hot drinks machine in the press area had broken down. It seemed a fitting metaphor for the mood of the hour.

McGuinness looked exhausted. The years that had seen him rise from the IRA's young Commander in Derry to Sinn Fein's Chief Negotiator had been kind to him but now suddenly they seemed to have taken their toll. In the glare of the television lights, he looked tired and much older. McGuinness was angry and spoke with a passion that reflected his frustration. 'As I speak to you now,' he said, 'there is no agreement. The unionists are blocking it. There can be no agreement that will work without Sinn Fein.' Most of us knew he was right. Of course there could be a deal without the Provos, but that would negate the decade of tireless endeavour by John Hume, the British and Irish Governments and the Sinn Fein leadership itself. Sitting there, I felt this was no mere negotiating ploy. McGuinness talked of the history of the past thirty years, speaking eloquently of the injustice of discrimination and what he saw as his community's legitimate demands. 'We have worked for years and hope to conclude an agreement that will consign to history the mistakes of the past,' he said. The mistakes, he implied, were not all one-sided. Everyone had taken risks for peace but 'Gerry Adams and I have taken the greatest risks of all'. Few realized how potentially suicidal these risks were given the fate of Michael Collins (see Chapter One). As midnight approached, the omens did not look good.

Suddenly, they looked even worse. With impeccable timing the Reverend Ian Paisley, who had boycotted the talks because they involved Sinn Fein, burst into the press Portakabin with a handful of devoted followers. He condemned the negotiations, denounced Sinn Fein as the IRA and lashed the Ulster Unionists and their leader, David Trimble, for negotiating with 'terrorists' and selling out the union. The press woke up. Ironically, sitting in their midst was Danny Morrison, the legendary architect of the Provisionals' strategy of the Armalite and Ballot Box which had brought Sinn Fein to its present position. Morrison had become a member of the press corps, now preferring pen to sword, but at that particular moment was anxious not to be reminded of his past by catching Dr Paisley's eye. The intrusion was soon over and the Reverend and his followers disappeared into the cold night as suddenly as they had arrived. The hours dragged by as journalists snatched what sleep they could, stretched out on chairs or sprawled full length on the floor, now littered with discarded newspapers and paper cups. At irregular intervals the silence and the snoring would be broken by delegations from the different parties who would come in, even more bleary eyed than the press, and give the latest update. By 3am it was snowing outside. Gradually, the mood became more upbeat. The Prime Minister's press secretary, Alastair Campbell, told us that Tony Blair was taking a shower, eating bananas and pushing the process forward.

The sign that a historic breakthrough appeared close came at around 6am on Good Friday morning when Sinn Fein's Mitchel McLaughlin announced that real progress had been made, and said it as if he meant it. Gone were the references to unionist intransigence. I walked out into the chill morning and could sense the mood of optimism. I watched two senior Provisionals, Gerry Kelly and Pat Doherty, walking round the compound outside Government Buildings, perfectly in step. Adams and McGuinness emerged and went for a leisurely stroll, smiling and waving to the press, brushing aside the shouted questions. 'What ministerial job are you going for, Martin?' cried one. 'Fly Fishing!' came the reply. Through one of the windows, a television cameraman captured the silhouette of the SDLP's Brid Rodgers embracing one of her colleagues. The memorable image summed up the moment. As the day brightened, so did the hopes on both sides of the barrier that separated press and politicians. By mid-afternoon, it seemed to be all over bar the signing. By now everyone was demob happy. Then suddenly faces fell and pieces were hastily rewritten – the word was that the deal was off. The Ulster Unionists had dug their heels in over the possibility of Sinn Fein taking part in the proposed Executive without the IRA decommissioning its arms. The issue that had derailed John Major's endeavours and was to haunt Tony Blair's well beyond that afternoon, refused to go away. The Prime Minister hastily drafted a letter giving David Trimble some assurance, although it was less than categoric. Harmony was restored and the deal was finally done, announced on the steps of Government Buildings by the beaming British and Irish Prime Ministers, Tony Blair and Bertie Aherne, who had laboured so long and hard to make it possible. For once the overworked word 'historic' was not out of place. I asked one Government official why the Secretary of State, Mo Mowlam, was not there to share the triumph she had done so much to achieve. 'That's not the way Presidential politics work,' he said.

It was an astonishing climax to a dramatic seven months that had begun the previous September when Sinn Fein had first entered the all-party talks. Although the IRA was on ceasefire as were the loyalist paramilitaries, the UDA and UVF – whose respective political representatives, the Ulster Democratic Party (UDP) and the Progressive Unionist Party (PUP) were also a critical part of the talks – the dissident republican splinter groups continued bombing and killing. They, along with a new loyalist splinter group, the Loyalist Volunteer Force (LVF) – whose leader, Billy Wright, had recently split from the UVF – were bent on destroying the peace process as it entered its final phase.

Suddenly, in December 1997, as the talks continued through the winter, making little headway, two incidents in the Maze prison became the focus of events. The first was merely an embarrassment for the Government. The second was catalytic. On 10 December 1997, it was party time in the gaol. Christmas was approaching and in keeping with a privilege first granted in the summer of 1995, parties were arranged 'to help prisoners maintain family ties' in which initially children, and then wives and partners, were allowed into the Maze to celebrate birthdays and special occasions.[1]

Provisional IRA prisoners were to have three such children's parties – one for each PIRA H-Block – in the prison gymnasium in the run-up to Christmas. Around 9.30am on 10 December, 51 IRA prisoners left H Block 8 to join 47 women and 103 children for the Christmas celebrations. Although all the visitors were searched, it appears that no hand-held metal detectors were used. One of the prisoners was Liam Averill, who had been to a party two days before to meet his own family and was now attending as a 'helper'. This time Liam Averill did not return to his cell. During the party, with over 200 people milling around, Averill changed into women's clothes, put on make-up and walked out of the gaol with visitors. No one noticed the IRA man in drag and at 6pm that evening the Provisionals' OC approached the Senior Officer on H–Block 8 and informed him that Liam

Averill, a life-sentence prisoner, had escaped. Officials had red faces. The Provos had a good laugh. The embarrassment was all the greater given the discovery of a sophisticated and well-advanced tunnel from a Provisional IRA H-Block the previous month. Questioned by the media, Gerry Adams repeated the traditional republican position: that IRA prisoners of war had a duty to escape. At the time of writing, Liam Averill is still at liberty. On 11 December, the day after the escape, a Sinn Fein delegation walked through by Gerry Adams and Martin McGuinness, met Tony Blair at 10 Downing Street. Despite fears and loud unionist objections, Averill's escape did not torpedo the historic encounter. It was the first time republicans had entered Downing Street since Michael Collins and his Sinn Fein delegation walked through the doors of Number 10 to negotiate the Treaty in 1921 (see Chapter One). Senior Provisionals had previously told me that they wanted to be 'friends' with the British Prime Minister.

The second incident in the Maze was far more serious and provoked a series of killings which almost derailed the peace process. It involved one of the loyalists' most notorious prisoners, the LVF leader, Billy Wright. Wright, or 'King Rat' to the media and his many enemies, was a charismatic paramilitary leader from Portadown at whose door popular myth had laid many atrocities, most reputedly committed while he was still a member of the UVF, although no proof was ever forthcoming. Wright was feared and reviled by Catholics and worshipped by many of his own community in Portadown and elsewhere. I met him at the time of the Drumcree crisis of 1996 and remember watching hushed groups of loyalists part as the slight muscular figure, immaculate in pressed jeans, white T-shirt, and gold earring, walked through with his minders. Wright himself was a renegade, having left the UVF after personal and policy differences. The UVF had publicly stated that they intended to kill him unless he left the country but Wright ostentatiously ignored the threat and continued to live in Portadown. In the end, the law caught up with him and he was gaoled for menacing behaviour. Once in the Maze, he demanded – and got – a separate wing for the prisoners who had defected from the other loyalist paramilitary organizations to join the LVF. The only available wing at the time was one leg of H-Block 6. The other leg was occupied by republican prisoners of the Irish National Liberation Army (INLA). Neither group was on ceasefire. There was no other space available at the time due to refurbishment, in particular of H-Block 8 from which the recent IRA tunnel had been built, and the refusal of the other loyalist prisoners to have anything to do with Wright and his LVF. Not surprisingly, antagonism grew between the deadly enemies in H-Block 6. Although they were physically separated, they were within earshot and sight of each other and occasionally met face to face when separate vans would arrive to take them to visits. Prison officers were not happy and warned of the growing tension between the rival wings and the difficulty of providing the full cover and surveillance necessary to ensure that the lid on the powder keg did not blow off. These difficulties were largely due to staff shortages.

At 9.15am on 27 December 1997, as prisoners prepared to take their visits, a decision was made to stand down the prison officer manning the watchtower that overlooked the INLA exercise yard adjacent to its wing. At the time there was a shortfall of eight staff involved in prison visits.[2] A few minutes later, a prison officer shouted Billy Wright's name down the wing, indicating that transport for his visit was ready. The call would have been clearly audible to the INLA prisoners on the other wing and his departure would have been equally visible from their cells. Wright and another LVF prisoner got into the van and waited as it prepared to leave the forecourt of the H-Block 6. Suddenly, the sliding door was pushed open and an INLA gunman fired several rounds at Wright hitting him in the chest. He died 54 minutes later. At a prearranged signal, the gunman and two other INLA prisoners had climbed onto the roof of their exercise yard, leaped down into the forecourt and assassinated Billy Wright. Within minutes they had returned whence they had come. There was no attempt to hide what they had done. Wright's assailants voluntarily gave themselves up and handed over two firearms and a pair of wirecutters that presumably had been used to cut through the yard fence – probably at some earlier stage. The question of how two guns got into the prison was never answered.

The killing of Billy Wright provoked a bloody cycle of tit-for-tat killings that threatened once more to plunge Northern Ireland into the abyss. The INLA, whose day was erroneously thought to have gone, gained enormous kudos for eliminating Wright and in the process staked its claim to be the true defender of the nationalist community by killing the man perceived to be its deadliest enemy. Privately, senior Provisionals admitted that with the IRA on ceasefire it was a serious challenge to their prestige. Within hours, the LVF gave its response, shooting dead that same evening Seamus Dillon, a former republican prisoner who was working as a doorman at the Glengannon Hotel just outside Dungannon in County Tyrone. Over the following three weeks, the cycle of killing intensified as six more Catholics and Protestants were shot dead by LVF and INLA gunmen. The pressure on the IRA and the loyalist paramilitaries on ceasefire to retaliate was enormous, lest their respective positions be usurped by their rivals. Loyalist gunmen of the UDA broke ranks first. On 19 January 1998, the INLA shot dead the South Belfast UDA commander, Jim Guiney, at his carpet shop in Dunmurry. The UDA took their revenge hours later by killing a Catholic taxi driver, Larry Brennan, as he was sitting in his car outside Enterprise Taxis in Belfast's Ormeau Road. He was the fifth Catholic to be shot dead by loyalists since the killing of Billy Wright.

The continuing violence fuelled the concerns of unionist politicians who pointed the finger at the IRA, claiming – erroneously – that all republican attacks, be they by bullet or bomb, were part of some great IRA conspiracy. Other republican groups not on ceasefire, they argued, could not carry out their operations without the tacit consent of IRA leaders. Nothing could have been further than the truth. Unionist anxieties were increased even more by the string of concessions they believed the British Government was making to the Provos to keep Sinn Fein in the talks and the IRA on ceasefire. They were known as 'confidence building measures' but to Northern Ireland's majority community, they were capitulation to the demands of the IRA and Sinn Fein. The most controversial was Tony Blair's announcement on 21 January 1998 that there would be a judicial inquiry into the events of 'Bloody Sunday' (see Chapter Nine). The Tribunal would be presided over by three judges, two of them from the Commonwealth, with Lord Saville of Newdigate in the chair. It was what nationalists and the relatives of the thirteen unarmed Catholics shot dead by paratroopers in 1972 had been demanding for years. Their campaign, now taken to the highest levels of Government in both London and Dublin, had finally paid off. As the twenty-sixth anniversary of the killings approached, Tony Blair told the House of Commons.

> 'Bloody Sunday' was a tragic day for all concerned. We must all wish it had never happened. Our concern now is simply to establish the truth, and close this painful chapter once and for all . . . It is also the way forward to the necessary reconciliation which will be such an important part of building a secure future for the people of Northern Ireland.[3]

Nationalists were overjoyed. Unionists were dismayed and demanded a parallel inquiry into how the Dublin government had covertly financed the IRA in the autumn of 1969. (see Chapter Five).

In an attempt to inject some life into the negotiations which by January 1998 appeared to be going nowhere, the all-party talks were moved to London for three days. The two Governments hoped that the London air and the splendid location, Lancaster House, might at last produce some progress. The symbolism of the venue, where in 1979 Mrs Thatcher and her Foreign Secretary, Lord Carrington, had negotiated the independence of Zimbabwe with its 'terrorist' leaders, was not lost on either side. Compared with the Spartan conditions of Government

Buildings in Belfast, the location and facilities were sumptuous. To the astonishment of the Northern Ireland press corps which had stoically covered the talks in Belfast for so many long and dreary months, caterers were brought in to create gourmet food for the world's media. But despite all the luxuries, the atmosphere inside the talks was charged. The issue that dominated the agenda for almost two of the three days was the future of the Ulster Democratic Party (UDP) that represented the loyalist paramilitary Ulster Defence Association (UDA), some of whose members, under the banner of the UFF, had been involved in the recent sectarian killing. The UDA, although technically on ceasefire, admitted responsibility and that its actions were in clear breach of the Mitchell Principles that underpinned the talks. The governments had a dilemma: to kick the UDP out of the talks for good would risk bringing down the whole carefully constructed negotiating structure; to ignore its paramilitary wing's culpability would be to make a nonsense of the Mitchell Principles. In the end, as ever, a compromise was reached and on 26 January, the UDP was excluded for a month on the grounds that 'the UDP's commitment to the Mitchell Principles had been demonstrably dishonoured'.[4] Nevertheless, despite the wrangling, by the end of the Lancaster House leg of the talks, there were signs that some progress was being made.

In February, the talks moved to Dublin where Sinn Fein became involved in a new crisis which threatened to be terminal for the Republican Movement's involvement in the peace process that had begun a decade before. The violence did not abate as the negotiations continued and the IRA became increasingly concerned, as Catholics were being killed and it was doing nothing to defend its community. The Provisionals' deadly rival, the INLA, now seemed to be seizing the Provisionals' role of defender of the nationalist population. They were dangerous days for the Provos. It seems that the IRA Army Council made a decision to take its guns out again without claiming responsibility for actions on the principle of 'no claim, no blame'. It carried out two killings, one of a drug dealer, Brendan Campbell and the other of a prominent UDA figure, Robert Dougan from South Belfast. Both were thought to have been on the IRA's target list and both killings were thought to have been authorized by the Army Council. The Chief Constable, Ronnie Flanagan, blew the whistle and publicly stated that he believed that the Provisional IRA was involved in both of the killings. Significantly, the IRA did not specifically deny them but made a statement on 12 February that 'contrary to speculation surrounding recent killings in Belfast, the IRA cessation of military operations remains intact.'[5] Sinn Fein, predictably, said it was not involved as it was not the IRA and therefore should not suffer any consequences. Faced with the Chief Constable's analysis, the governments had no choice. Sinn Fein was suspended from the negotiations – but for only two weeks. The talks at Dublin Castle were dominated by the issue and in a brilliant example of turning a public relations defeat into victory, Sinn Fein seized the initiative by claiming that the British Government was excluding the 120,000 voters whom the party democratically represented. Much of the media consequently turned the heat on the British Government and not the Republican Movement.

By March, Sinn Fein was back in the talks as if nothing had happened. By the middle of the month, its leaders, along with those of most of the other parties, were on the way to America to celebrate St Patrick's Day on 17 March and meet President Clinton. It was an offer none of them could refuse, with the opportunity to make their respective cases to the most powerful man in the world and enjoy a social round of glittering parties and banquets that most would never have dreamed of. Their hosts, the White House and various affluent Irish American organizations, also hoped that the informality of such occasions would encourage private dialogue over the canapés and Guinness. Their greatest hope was that David Trimble would finally engage with Gerry Adams, perhaps in some corner out of the glare of the media, as they were certainly under the same chandeliers often enough. But it was not to be. At one reception I asked David Trimble who was standing a matter of feet away from the Sinn Fein President, if he would be talking to him.

> I don't expect to, not on this occasion, nor do I expect to be talking to him seriously in the future unless he commits himself to the democratic process and to peaceful means and in that democratic process the crucial thing there is the consent principle.
> **You could go and ask him. He's just over there.**
> He's already declared his position that many times. It is for him.[6]

David Trimble was true to his word. At function after function, it was as if Mr Adams did not exist. For Trimble to have engaged directly with the Sinn Fein President in America – or anywhere else for that matter – would have jeopardized support in his already deeply troubled party.

The trip to America also afforded Adams and McGuinness a vital opportunity to convince their supporters there, who throughout the years had provided the IRA with money and guns, that the leadership was not about to sell out the Republican Movement. The message got through. I talked again to Gabriel Megahey who had gone to gaol for trying to buy surface to air missiles for the IRA (see Prologue) and he had no doubt that the Provisionals were on the right track.

Everybody is hopeful because we feel it's the best chance we have ever had to solve the problem. Anybody who doesn't want this solved – God! Do they really know what that's going to cause in the future? It's only going to condemn our people to more deaths, more prisons. We've got to solve it this time. It's got to be solved.

Do you think that Sinn Fein can accept an agreement which in reality is a partionist settlement?

If anyone thinks that we're going to get a united Ireland in May [1998] or shortly thereafter would be living in dreamland. But I think that there has to be in this agreement some light that shows our people that we can move forward to a united Ireland and this has got to be the stepping stone. Everybody is going to have to give a little and take a little and there has to be a meeting of minds. It's like a fire burning. We have the flames out at the moment but it's still smouldering underneath. Now it's going to take time to put that smouldering out so that it doesn't flare up again.

You played your part in the IRA's campaign and spent years in prison as a result. What are you prepared to settle for?

I'm prepared as a republican to settle. My aspirations are for the unification of our country but I have to accept in the long run that it's not going to happen. The Brits are not going to sail away in the sunlight. Go back to war? What are we going to do? It would only cause more misery, more suffering and mostly to our own people and to ourselves.[7]

Gabriel Megahey spoke for the vast majority of members of the Republican Movement whom I met, although he was more candid than most were prepared to be. Adams, McGuinness and their colleagues in the leadership had done a remarkable job in preparing the rank and file for the deal they were finally likely to reach. As we will see, unionist leaders had not done the same.

At the end of the American interlude, the White House was confident, convinced that Sinn Fein would not only sign up to an agreement but would also take its seats in any new Assembly. Adams and McGuinness must have given that assurance to the President who had done so much to support them and played such a vital role in bringing Sinn Fein into the political mainstream.

Although on the surface, there were little signs of political progress, the word was that behind the scenes things were moving. The Government set a deadline for the parties to reach agreement in the hope that the cut-off point – midnight on Thursday 9 April, the day before Good Friday –

would concentrate minds. Without such a deadline, the Government reasoned, the talks could drag on indefinitely. Although Sinn Fein had only joined the negotiations the previous September, the talks themselves were already almost two years old. But the road to agreement still proved bloody. The LVF committed one of those atrocities which, like La Mon, Enniskillen, Warrington and Loughinisland, remained etched in people's minds. On 3 March two masked men burst into the Railway Bar in the tiny village of Poyntzpass, County Armagh, and shouted, 'On the floor, you bastards!' They then opened fire, killing two lifelong friends, Philip Allen (34) and Damien Trainor (25). Philip was a Protestant and Damien a Catholic and their friendship was typical in a village which the Troubles seemed to have passed by. 'We don't need any Agreement here,' one of its inhabitants told me, 'We have agreement already.' The grief that engulfed the village over the apparently motiveless killings seemed to be shared by the rest of the nation which identified with the families in their grief. Mrs Allen was at Philip's side as life slowly left him. 'He was just lying on the floor of the pub,' she told me. 'I just kept talking to him. I asked him was he all right and he just said, "I'm dying, I'm dying," and they were the last words he spoke.' Both families made a moving plea for peace which was not lost on the politicians. LVF suspects from the nearby town of Banbridge were swiftly arrested and four men were charged with murder. A fortnight after the killings, one of them, David Keys (26) was found hanging in his cell in the LVF wing of the Maze prison. He'd been first tortured by his 'comrades' who thought Keys had 'grassed' to the RUC. In prison he paid the price.

At tea-time on Good Friday 10 April, after a nail-biting, final thirty-six hours, the climax of twenty-two months of negotiation, agreement between the parties was finally reached. The seemingly impossible had been done, although the Agreement still had to be ratified on 22 May by simultaneous referenda held both North and South. Standing in a mixture of hailstones and sleet on the steps of Government Buildings, an exhausted Tony Blair, who had finally pushed the parties to lengths few thought they would ever go, had words to fit the moment. 'When I arrived on Wednesday, I said I felt the hand of history on our shoulders. Today I hope that the burden of history can at long last be lifted from them.' The images were flashed round the world with the astonishing sight of the parties inside the building laughing and joking with each other in a mixture of disbelief, relief and sheer exhaustion. But, as the Prime Minister warned, this was only the beginning. 'I want to say this to the politicians and people of Northern Ireland with all the force I can muster. Even now, this will not work unless, in your will and in your mind, you make it work.' Even the most hard-bitten members of the press could scarcely believe that the deed was done. The prophets of doom were confounded, at least for the moment. The Good Friday Agreement – which was only signed by the two Prime Ministers and not by the parties – was a carefully constructed compromise that contained something for everyone as had been outlined by John Major and Albert Reynolds in the Downing Street Declaration of December 1993 (see Chapter Twenty-Three). Unionists were able to say with justification that the union was secure whilst republicans were able to claim, more in hope, that it was a stepping stone on the road to a united Ireland. In essence, it gave unionists the guarantee that the constitutional status of Northern Ireland would not be changed without the consent of the majority of its people, a principle recognized for the first time by the Irish Government whose own constitution written by the President Eamon de Valera in 1937 had laid territorial claim to the North. As part of the Agreement, Dublin agreed to reword its constitution, thus recognising the principle of consent. Remarkably (but quietly) Sinn Fein also accepted the principle, which was tantamount to recognizing the unionist veto the IRA had fought for more than a quarter of century to destroy. Unionists also got a British–Irish Council 'to promote the harmonious and mutually beneficial development of the totality of relationships among the peoples of these islands'.[8] The Council, made up of representatives from the British and Irish Governments and the newly devolved Scottish and Welsh Parliaments, was designed to underpin unionists' continuing linkage with the rest of the United Kingdom.

But the cornerstone of the Agreement was to be a new devolved Assembly for Northern Ireland in which unionists and loyalists would share power with nationalists and republicans – although the word 'power sharing' was never used because of its emotional connotations (to unionists) with the fall of the power sharing Executive in 1974 (see Chapter Twelve). The new Assembly would assume most of the powers exercised by the Northern Ireland Office since direct rule was introduced in 1972. Again, Sinn Fein had consistently opposed the setting up of such a body but was now prepared to go along with it in yet another reversal of its traditional position. To both nationalists and republicans, the most important part of the Agreement was the establishment of a North/South Ministerial Council 'to bring together those with executive responsibilities in Northern Ireland and the Irish Government, to develop consultation, co-operation and action within the island of Ireland'. The Council would oversee a series of cross border bodies with power to implement agreed policies on issues ranging from Agriculture, Education, Transport and Social Security to Health, Environment, Tourism and Urban and Rural Development. To Sinn Fein this Ministerial Council and the cross border bodies were the stepping stone to a united Ireland. Unionists opposed to the Agreement, led by the Reverend Ian Paisley, loudly proclaimed that Sinn Fein was right.

The most contentious areas of all had nothing to do with complex constitutional issues but concerned gut issues that every single person in Northern Ireland could understand and had passionate feelings about: the decommissioning of terrorist weapons and the release of prisoners. The Agreement's commitment to reform the RUC also caused unionists grave concern. Decommissioning had been the hurdle at which John Major had stumbled (see Chapter 24) and had been conveniently sidelined by the Blair administration to move the process forward. But despite the best efforts to wish it away, the issue refused to die. The most effective way of decommissioning, some wise heads observed, was 'rust'. It was certainly mentioned in the Agreement but only in general terms with the parties (notably Sinn Fein and those representing the loyalist paramilitaries) agreeing 'to use any influence they may have, to achieve the decommissioning of all paramilitary arms within two years'. There was no clause that said that the IRA had to decommission, or at least begin to do so, *before* Sinn Fein would be allowed to take any seat in the new Executive. The British and Irish Governments knew that any such precise wording would have delighted the unionists but would have driven Sinn Fein out. The closest the Agreement came to the sentiment was in the following sentence in paragraph 25 of the section concerning the Assembly and Executive. 'Those who hold office should only use democratic, non-violent means, and those who do not should be excluded or removed from office under these provisions.'9 The problem of course was that Sinn Fein would simply say the condition would not apply to its members as Sinn Fein was not the IRA. To avoid an eleventh hour walkout by the unionists on Good Friday afternoon, Tony Blair had given David Trimble a hastily written assurance that if by the end of the year the intention of paragraph 25 had not been realized, then the Government would introduce legislation to make it more effective. Again, the statement was suitably vague but the unionist delegation accepted it – with the exception of Jeffrey Donaldson MP, who had ostentatiously torn up the Framwork Document at Lancaster House. At that point, Donaldson left the talks, no doubt putting down a leadership marker. In a statement of 30 April, the IRA repeated its oft-stated position. 'Let us make it clear that there will be no decommissioning by the IRA. This issue, as with any other matter affecting the IRA, its functions and objectives, is a matter only for the IRA, to be decided upon and pronounced upon by us.' Nevertheless, the statement gave a guarded welcome to the Agreement as 'a significant development' and commended Sinn Fein for its efforts.

In the wave of euphoria and expectation that followed the signing of the Agreement, it was almost taken for granted that the dual referenda to be held on 22 May would produce a thundering majority in favour. But as the weeks went by and the Yes and No campaigns got underway, alarm spread through the government and pro-Agreement ranks. From the beginning, David Trimble had an uphill task to secure widespread unionist support for what he had done and his problems were made even greater by the fact that six of his ten Ulster Unionist parliamentary colleagues were opposed to the Agreement. The opposition was led by Ian Paisley who, yet again, defied all predictions that he was yesterday's man and galvanized unionist opposition in a way that few others could. His campaign for a No vote, supported by the UK Unionist, Robert McCartney, was given added impetus by the presence of dissident Ulster Unionist MPs who shared the same platform. One issue above all seemed to provoke mass unionist defections from the Yes camp – the release of prisoners. It was without doubt the most contentious part of the Agreement and the one that perhaps swung it for Sinn Fein. If the Provos were not getting a united Ireland, at least they were getting their comrades out within a stipulated two years. Despite what many unionists thought, it was not a case of opening the gates of the Maze prison and releasing hordes of convicted terrorists onto the streets of Northern Ireland but simply bringing forward the prisoners' release dates, most of which were due soon anyway. Even then they were only released on licence which meant that they could be locked up again should they transgress. Furthermore, it only applied to those whose organizations were on ceasefire, which is perhaps why the LVF declared a ceasefire the week before the referendum was held.

The issue of the prisoners exploded in the full glare of the media on Sunday 10 May at the Sinn Fein special Ard Fheis in Dublin. It was convened to ratify the Agreement and change the party's constitution so that party members could take seats in the new Assembly. The critical motion permitting this constitutional change was passed by a staggering 331 votes to 19 following emotional speeches by revered IRA veterans like Joe Cahill, John Kelly and Martin Meehan all of whom had been founder members of the Provos almost thirty years earlier. I sat and listened to Joe Cahill, commander of the Belfast Brigade at the time of internment in 1971, as he spoke to those who attacked the Agreement as a sell-out. Cahill was the veteran of veterans, having escaped the gallows during the IRA's Forties campaign. 'It hurts me when I hear republicans say "that's not what previous generations died for",' he said. 'In 1942, I could have died a martyr's death and been hanged and people could have said that's not what I died for. This is the only way forward.' Shortly before Cahill spoke, the hall erupted as the four members of the Balcombe Street 'gang'

– Hugh Doherty, Martin O'Connell, Edward Butler and Harry Duggan – were led down the aisle to the platform. All had been given life sentences for murder and had served twenty-two years in English gaols for their notorious campaign of killing and mayhem on mainland Britain in 1975 (see Chapter Thirteen). They had just been transferred to an Irish prison where they were due to serve the rest of their sentences and had been released temporarily by the Dublin Government to attend the Ard Fheis and boost the chances of an overwhelming vote for the Agreement. I watched them mount the platform amidst scenes of wild rejoicing and the thunder of stamping feet. McGuiness and Adams embraced them as tears came to many hardened eyes. 'We said there could be no political settlement until all the prisoners were free,' choked Adams. 'And we meant it!' There was more deafening applause as they were hailed as 'our Mandelas'. As I watched the astonishing scenes, I thought the 'war' might really be over but I also thought of the impact such theatre might have on an already beleagured David Trimble. The effect was disastrous. To many doubting unionists, the spectacle seemed to confirm their worst fears: that the prisoners were out and Adams and McGuinness would soon be in Government without a single weapon being handed in. In other words, the IRA had won. The No campaign was jubilant.

The problem was compounded the following week when one of the loyalists' most infamous prisoners, Michael Stone, who had launched the gun and grenade attack on republicans at Milltown cemetery in 1988 (see Chapter Twenty-One) was released on four days' parole and attended a packed rally at Belfast's Ulster Hall organized by the loyalist UDP. Although the UDA's high command seated on the platform did not applaud his entry and pointedly sat on their hands (Stone was not the image they wished to portray), the crowd went wild and once again the cameras turned. Again, the No campaign could not believe their luck as Michael Stone and the Balcombe Street Four gave Paisley a field day.

As polling day approached, Tony Blair made his third visit to the province since the Agreement to try and shore up the Yes vote in the unionist ranks. Despite the encouragement of Bill Clinton and the intervention of John Major and his successor, William Hague, the Yes campaign failed to catch fire. Prisoners and decommissioning – or lack of it – seemed to have lost them the battle. With three days to go, the Agreement seemed in deep trouble. Then suddenly the tide turned. Around 2,000 young people turned out for a free pop concert at Belfast's new Waterfront Hall, headlined by the supergroup U2 and the hugely popular Northern Ireland band, Ash. To a tumultuous welcome, U2's lead singer, Bono, welcomed John Hume and David Trimble onto the stage and into the spotlight. They had made a concession to the occasion by removing their jackets but not their ties. One commentator noted that at least they could have invested in a pair of chinos. That was not their style. The Hall erupted as the leaders of nationalism and unionism shook hands and waved to the crowd. The emotional scenes were a graphic illustration of what so many people on the streets of both communities had said: that however imperfect, the Agreement should be supported for the sake of the children. Hume was almost moved to tears. Many wondered why it had not happened before. If this was the future, why had we not been given a glimpse of it earlier in the campaign? The reason, as ever, was political, with Trimble fighting a war not only with the No campaign but with more than half his parliamentary party. Sinn Fein, whose support was assured, coasted through the campaign, not unduly upset at the discord within the unionist ranks. Sensing the changing tide, Tony Blair barnstormed the province, giving endless interviews designed to reassure the large percentage of 'don't knows' that the Agreement was not a sell out and that the issue of decommissioning would not be fudged. It was a remarkable period, with politicians returning to the kind of electioneering that television appeared to have consigned to history. Night after night, they would hold rallies or descend on pubs and clubs, explaining the Agreement with slides and endless patience and encouraging their audience to vote Yes or No. For countless unionists, the question was not about the constitution but about how they could vote Yes for something Gerry Adams had signed up to.

On referendum day, there was a record turn out in Northern Ireland with 81 per cent of the electorate casting their votes. Ironically, it was 200 years to the day since the United Irishmen, a unique alliance of Roman Catholics and Presbyterians, first took up arms against British rule. The returning officer, whose microphone let him down but whose booming voice did not, declared that the Yes vote was 71 per cent and the No vote 29 per cent. Supporters of the Yes campaign broke into the football chant, 'Here we go, here we go,' followed by cries of 'easy, easy'. But the mood in the victors' camp was more relief than ecstasy. Most had been expecting a percentage in the mid-sixties whilst desperately hoping for 70 per cent plus. In the end, they just made it. John Hume, whose dialogue with Gerry Adams to seek 'agreement between our divided peoples' had begun ten years earlier amidst the carnage of 1988 (see Chapter 21), movingly thanked the people of Northern Ireland for voting Yes by more than two to one. A slightly subdued David Trimble, no doubt aware of the huge problems ahead, said he now wanted to see 'the squalid little terrorist campaign and the IRA dismantled'. He knew that both issues were far from resolved. Within hours of the result, the Garda intercepted two cars containing bomb-making materials near Dundalk. It was probably the work of the 'true' IRA, and seemed an ominous warning of what may be to come.

In the Republic, the turn out was considerably less but the vote in support of the Agreement and the change in the Irish constitution was a massive 94 per cent. Although the parallel was not quite exact, it was the first time the people of Ireland had spoken as a unit – although in separate parts – since the general election of 1918 when Sinn Fein had swept the board (see Chapter 1). Gerry Adams and Sinn Fein denied it was the self-determination that they and the IRA had fought for, but it was pretty close to it. Paisley and his supporters refused to admit defeat with the claim that as the total unionist vote amounts to 52 per cent, more than half the unionist population had voted No. The fact that some republicans and others had voted No made the claim questionable. The referendum, he announced, was only round one. The real battle would now begin as, without drawing breath, the parties began their campaign for the Assembly elections to be held on 25 June 1998. The concern now was that the No campaign might win enough seats to wreck the Assembly or make it unworkable. Paisley had done it before and was determined to do it again.

But whatever happens in the immediate future, the Provos seem to win most ways: in a remarkable transformation, Sinn Fein has entered the mainstream of Irish politics and is now poised to challenge the SDLP as the main representative of Northern nationalists and make serious political inroads in the south; the Republican Movement remains in the main united whilst unionism is split; and the IRA and its arsenal remain intact. Although for the moment it may seem like game and set to the Provos, the match is not yet over.

In the wake of the result, Gerry Adams was repeatedly asked if the 'war' was over. He refused to say that it was.

A month after the referendum, Northern Ireland wearily went to the polls again to elect the Assembly that was the cornerstone of the Good Friday Agreement. Politicians in favour of the Agreement, exhausted by the referendum campaign, feared that many of those who had come out in their tens of thousands and voted Yes might stay at home feeling that their duty had been done. Such fears scarcely affected Sinn Fein whose electorate needed no reminder of how critical the election was to the Republican Movement and the leaders who had so precariously steered it down the constitutional path. The day before the poll, there was a violent reminder from republicans opposed to that path in the form of a 200-lb bomb that devastated the centre of the South Armagh village of Newtownhamilton. Responsibility was claimed by the INLA but there were strong suspicions that the attack was a combined effort involving the other republican splinter groups, the Continuity IRA and 'true' IRA. It was an ominous warning of what might lie ahead.

On 25 June 1998, the new 108 member Assembly was elected by a complex system of proportional representation designed to be fair to all parties, especially the minority ones. To the relief of the British government which had gambled so much on the outcome, the result was an endorsement of the referendum with around 75 per cent of the electorate voting for pro-Agreement candidates. No one could have been more relieved than David Trimble whose party narrowly won the greatest number of seats in the Assembly – twenty-eight – thereby making him effectively the first Prime Minister of Northern Ireland for more than a quarter of a century. But as Trimble surveyed the disarray within unionist ranks, his only consolation was that Ian Paisley and his anti-Agreement supporters in other parties with a combined total of twenty-seven seats, failed to reach their target of thirty which would potentially have enabled them to deadlock and perhaps destroy the Assembly and the Agreement with it. David Trimble was further discomforted by the sight of the SDLP winning the target number of first preference votes which was an event unprecedented in Northern Ireland's history. His unionist opponents were unlikely to let him forget the humiliation – although when it came to actual seats, the SDLP ended up in second place with twenty-four because of transferred votes under the system of proportional representation. But the party that made the greatest advance was Sinn Fein receiving its highest ever percentage of the vote at 17.6 per cent and winning eighteen seats, many held by those leading Provos who had played such a prominent part in the 'war': Gerry Adams, Martin McGuinness, Pat Doherty, Gerry Kelly, Mitchel McLaughlin, Alex Maskey and the veteran of the IRA's 1956–62 campaign, John Kelly. But for the Republican Movement, the past and the future are inseparable. Another successful candidate was Dana O'Hagan, daughter of the legendary Joe 'J.B.' O'Hagan, the former Army Council member and onetime helicopter escapee from Dublin's Mountjoy gaol. But the historic importance of Sinn Fein's success was that the party's representation in the Assembly entitled it to two seats in the Executive – the new government of Northern Ireland. It was the nightmare that unionists had feared and a situation destined to cause the beleaguered David Trimble even more problems with the prospect of Gerry Adams and Martin McGuinness in the new Cabinet without the IRA agreeing to decommission its arms. For the Provos this was but another stop on the road to the united Ireland for which they had fought, killed and died for almost thirty years. By the summer of 1998, the Provos were convinced they were winning. History will tell if they were right.

Notes

Chapter One: Origins

1. Whereas I use the Republican Movement as the generic term for the 'Provos' – the Provisional IRA and Sinn Fein – the term the 'Movement' is used by republicans to mean the IRA. They do not go to gaol for saying they belong to the 'Movement': they do if they say they belong to the IRA. In fact, to the Provisionals, the term the Republican Movement means the IRA – not the IRA and Sinn Fein.

2. Most of the time I use the non-denominational terms nationalists (for Catholics) and unionists (for Protestants) as the conflict is essentially about identity and allegiance. Loyalist is the term generally used for the more extreme unionists. The fact that these identities coincide with the religion of those who wish to maintain the union with Great Britain (unionists) and those who aspire to a united Ireland (nationalists) is the legacy of history. Republicans support the use of force to achieve a united Ireland, while nationalists do not. John Hume is a nationalist. Gerry Adams and the 'Provos' are republicans.

3. *Pearse. The Triumph of Failure*, Ruth Dudley Edwards, Victor Gollancz Ltd, 1977. p. 291.

4. Ibid., p. 318.

5. Ibid., p. 319.

6. *The Irish Uprising 1916–22*, CBS Legacy Collection, 1966. p. 27. 'The Coming Revolution' by Patrick Pearse. Reprinted from *Collected Works of Padraic H Pearse: Political Writings and Speeches*, London and Dublin, 1922.

7. *The Treaty*, Thames Television and Radio Telefis Eireann, 1991. p. 8.

8. *The IRA. The Secret Army*, J. Bowyer Bell, Academy Press, Dublin, 1983. p. 19.

9. *Peace by Ordeal. The Negotiation of the Anglo-Irish Treaty, 1921*, Lord Longford (Frank Pakenham), Sidgwick & Jackson Ltd, 1972. p. 49. This is the classic account of the Anglo-Irish War and Treaty negotiations, initially published in 1935 and compiled from first-hand sources.

10. *The Black and Tans*, Richard Bennet, Barnes and Noble, reprinted 1995. p. 121.

11. *The Troubles. The background to the question of Northern Ireland*, Richard Broad, Taylor Downing, Ian Stuttard and team, Thames Futura, 1980. p. 87.

12. *Ireland 1912–85. Politics and Society*, J J Lee, Cambridge University Press, 1993. p. 47. The IRA figure is from *The IRA*, op. cit., p. 26.

13. Ibid., p. 91.

14. *The Troubles. The background to the question of Northern Ireland*, op. cit., p. 72.

15. Both names for Londonderry are in use. Protestants and unionists call the city and

county Londonderry, the title that refers to its founding by merchants from the City of London in the seventeenth century. Catholics and nationalists refer to it as Derry, from the Gaelic name 'Doire'. But it is not a universal rule. Many Protestants in the city itself traditionally refer to Derry.

16. *Irish Historical Documents 1172–1922*, T C Curtis and R B McDowell, Methuen and Co Ltd, reprinted 1977. Government of Ireland Act, 1920. p. 298.

17. *Peace by Ordeal*, op. cit., p. 248.

18. *The Northern Ireland Peace Process 1993–96. A Chronology*, Paul Bew and Gordon Gillespie, Serif, London, 1996. p. 25. John Major's answer to remarks by Dennis Skinner MP in the House of Commons on 1 November 1993.

19. *The Troubles. The background to the question of Northern Ireland*, op. cit., p. 95.

20. *Irish Historical Documents*, op. cit., Articles of Agreement for a Treaty between Great Britain and Ireland, dated the sixth day of December 1921. p. 324.

21. *Michael Collins*, Tim Pat Coogan, Arrow Books, 1991. p. 301.

22. *The IRA*, op. cit., pp. 30–1.

23. *The Troubles. The background to the question of Northern Ireland*, op. cit., p. 105.

24. *The Green Flag. A History of Irish Nationalism*, Robert Kee, Weidenfeld & Nicolson Ltd, 1972. p. 744.

25. Ibid., p. 740.

26. Ibid., p. 741.

27. Ibid., p. 744.

28. *The Troubles. The background to the question of Northern Ireland*, op. cit., p. 105.

29. Ibid., p. 97.

30. *The Green Flag*, op. cit., p. 747.

31. Ibid., p. 744.

32. Ibid., p. 748.

33. Ibid., p. 749.

Chapter Two: Commemoration

1. *States of Terror. Democracy and Political Violence*, Peter Taylor, Penguin, 1993. p. 192.

2. Ibid.

3. Ibid., p. 194.

4. *The Irish Cabinet Papers: 1966*, quoted extensively in the *Irish Times*, 1–2 January 1997. p. 6.

5. Ibid., p. 6.

6. *The Irish Cabinet Papers*, op. cit., p. 6.

7. *The British Cabinet Papers*, quoted in the *Irish Times*, 1–2 January 1997. p. 7.

8. Ibid., p. 7.

9. *Paisley. Man of Wrath*, Patrick Marrinan, Anvil Books, Tralee, 1973. pp. 82–4.

10. *Northern Ireland: the Orange State*, Michael Farrell, Pluto Press, 1976. p. 234.

11. *Before the Dawn. An Autobiography*, Gerry Adams, William Heinemann, 1996. p. 51.

12. *Paisley. Man of Wrath*, op. cit., p. 90.

13. *The Troubles. The background to the question of Northern Ireland*, op. cit., p. 79.

14. *Paisley. Man of Wrath*, op. cit., p. 92.

15. *Before the Dawn*, op. cit., p. 59.

16. *Seeking a Political Accommodation. The Ulster Volunteer Force. Negotiating History*, Roy Garland, A Shankill Community Publication, 1997. p. 7.

17. Ibid.

18. *The UVF 1966–73. An anatomy of loyalist rebellion*, David Boulton, Torc Books published by Gill and Macmillan, Dublin, 1973. pp. 40–1.

19. Ibid., p. 50.

20. Ibid., p. 51.

21. *States of Terror*, op. cit., p. 198.

22. Ibid., p. 199.

23. The 'mainland' is a term only used by unionist and British politicians who regard Northern Ireland as being part of the United Kingdom. It is not an expression used by nationalists who regard Ireland as being one island with no mainland.

24. *States of Terror*, op. cit., p. 203.

Chapter Three: Escalation

1. For a detailed history of the McKearney family see *Families at War. Voices from the Troubles*, Peter Taylor, BBC Books, 1989. Chapter eleven, 'Sons and Guns'.

2. *Violence and Civil Disturbances in Northern Ireland in 1969. Report of Tribunal of Inquiry*, Chairman the Hon. Mr Justice Scarman, Vol. II (Appendices), HMSO, Cmd. 566, April 1972, pp. 21–2. This is better known as the Scarman Report after Mr Justice Scarman (later Lord Scarman) who chaired the Committee. The details of the Caledon incident are taken from Lord Cameron's Report.

3. *Northern Ireland 1968–73. A Chronology of Events. Vol I. 1968–71*, Richard Deutsch and Vivien Magowan, Blackstaff Press Ltd, 1973. pp. 8–9.

4. *Violence and Civil Disturbances in Northern Ireland in 1969*, op. cit., p. 22.

5. *Violence and Civil Disturbances in Northern Ireland in 1969*, op. cit., p. 53.

6. Ibid. p. 22.

7. *Violence and Civil Disturbances in Northern Ireland in 1969*, op. cit., p. 39.

8. Ibid., p. 40.

9. Ibid., p. 41.

10. Ibid. p. 45.

11. Ibid. p. 46.

12. *Paisley. Man of Wrath*, op. cit., pp. 167–8.

13. *Violence and Civil Disturbances in Northern Ireland in 1969*, op. cit., p. 73.

Chapter Four: Explosion

1. *Belfast Graves*, The National Graves Association, AP/RN Print, Dublin, 1985. pp. 57–8.

2. *Violence and Civil Disturbances in Northern Ireland in 1969*, op. cit., pp. 27–8.

3. *Violence and Civil Disturbances in Northern Ireland in 1969*, op. cit., p. 65. I draw extensively on Scarman for the description of the Battle of the Bogside.

4. Bernadette Devlin had been elected as MP for Mid Ulster in the by-election of 17 August 1969. The turn-out was a remarkable ninety-two per cent. At twenty-one, she was the youngest woman ever elected to Westminster.

5. *Violence and Civil Disturbances in Northern Ireland in 1969*, op. cit., p. 44.

6. Myth has it that Lynch said that his government would not stand 'idly by' but the word 'idly' was in fact never used. Its use, however, was contemplated in his

Fianna Fail Cabinet where Lynch was under pressure from the more republican members of his government.

7. *Violence and Civil Disturbances in Northern Ireland in 1969*, op. cit., p. 84.
8. Ibid., p. 84.
9. Ibid., pp. 84–5.
10. The account of the disturbances in Belfast on 13/14 August 1969 is based on Scarman's detailed analysis on pages 114–221 of the Scarman Report.
11. *Violence and Civil Disturbances in Northern Ireland in 1969*, op. cit., p. 131.
12. BBC television's *Timewatch. The Sparks that lit the Bonfire*, 27 January 1992.

Chapter Five: Provos

1. *A Soldier's Tale*, BBC television, August 1994.
2. Ibid.
3. *Memoirs of a Revolutionary. Seán MacStiofáin*, Gordon Cremonesi, 1975. p. 99.
4. *States of Terror*, op. cit., p. 228.
5. The account of the Convention is based on *Memoirs of a Revolutionary*, op. cit., chapter nine.
6. *Memoirs of a Revolutionary*, op. cit., pp. 142–3.

Chapter Six: Defence

1. *Northern Ireland. A Chronology of the Troubles 1968–93*, op. cit.
2. *Memoirs of a Revolutionary*, op. cit., p. 146.
3. *Northern Ireland. A Chronology of the Troubles*, op. cit.
4. *In Holy Terror*, Simon Winchester, Faber, 1974. p. 30.
5. *Northern Ireland 1968–73. A Chronology of Events. Vol I. 1968–71*, op. cit., p. 63.
6. *In Holy Terror*, op. cit., p. 59.
7. *Ulster, The Sunday Times* Insight Team, Penguin Special, 1972. p. 212.
8. Ibid., p. 213.
9. *In Holy Terror*, op. cit., p. 68.
10. Ibid., p. 69.
11. *Ulster*, op. cit., p. 217.
12. *Memoirs of a Revolutionary*, op. cit., p. 155.
13. *A Soldier's Tale*, op. cit.
14. Ibid.
15. *Before the Dawn*, op. cit., p. 141.
16. *An Index of Deaths from the Conflict in Northern Ireland 1969–1993*, Malcolm Sutton, Beyond the Pale Publications, 1994. p. 3.
17. *Before the Dawn*, op. cit., p. 142.

Chapter Seven: Attack

1. *Memoirs of a Revolutionary*, op. cit., p. 160.
2. Ibid.
3. *Before the Dawn*, op. cit., p. 149.
4. *Survivors*, Uinseann MacEoin, Argenta Publications, Dublin, 1980. p. 278.
5. *Northern Ireland 1968–73. A Chronology of Events. Vol I*, op. cit., p. 92.

6. *In Holy Terror*, op. cit., p. 127.
7. *The Provisional IRA*, Patrick Bishop and Eamonn Mallie, Corgi Books, reprinted 1993. p. 178
8. *Law and the State. The Case of Northern Ireland*, Kevin Boyle, Tom Hadden and Paddy Hillyard, Martin Robertson, London, 1975. p. 58.
9. *Before the Dawn*, op. cit., p. 166.
10. *Memoirs of a Statesman*, Brian Faulkner, Weidenfeld & Nicolson Ltd, 1978. p. 124.
11. *Torture and Emergency Powers under the European Convention on Human Rights: Ireland v the United Kingdom*, Michael O'Boyle, reprinted from the *American Journal of International Law*, vol 71, No. 4, October 1977. p.677.
12. *Report of the enquiry into allegations against the security forces of physical brutality in Northern Ireland arising out of events on the 9th August, 1971*, Chaired by Sir Edmund Compton, GCB, KBE, HMSO, Cmnd. 4823, November 1971. p. 12.

Chapter Eight: Enemies

1. *Families at War*, Peter Taylor, BBC Publications, 1989. p. 152. This is part of a full chapter on the McKearney family.
2. Author's own calculations.
3. *An Index of Deaths from the Conflict in Northern Ireland 1969–1993*, op. cit., p. 42. Also *Northern Ireland 1968–73. A Chronology of Events. Vol. II. 1972–3*, op. cit. p. 277.

Chapter Nine: Bloody Sunday

1. *In Holy Terror*, op. cit., pp. 150–1.
2. *Ulster*, op. cit., p. 257. This account is based largely on the contemporary account of the *Sunday Times* Insight Team.
3. *Northern Ireland 1968–73. A Chronology of Events. Vol I*, op. cit., p. 114.
4. Some of these interviews were conducted for the documentary we made, *Remember Bloody Sunday*, transmitted on BBC1 television on 28 January 1992.
5. 'Stickies': the nickname for the Official IRA is based on the fact that at Easter, its supporters 'stick' Easter lilies on their lapels.
6. *Report of the Tribunal appointed to inquire into the events of Sunday, 30th January 1972, which led to loss of life in connection with the procession in Londonderry on that day*, by The Rt Hon Lord Widgery, OBE, TD, HMSO, HL 101, HC 220, 1972. pp. 35 and 37.
7. *Bloody Sunday: An Open Wound, Sunday Times* Magazine, 26 January 1992, Peter Taylor. The five were Bernard McGuigan, John Young, Michael McDaid, William Nash and Kevin McElhinney. The two were Patrick Doherty and Michael Kelly. The other two were John ('Jackie') Duddy and Hugh Gilmore. The four were James Wray, William McKinney, Gerald McKinney and Gerald Donaghy.
8. *Remember Bloody Sunday*, BBC1, 28 January 1992.

Chapter Ten: Ceasefire

1. *Memoirs of a Revolutionary*, op. cit., pp. 237–8.
2. *Fortnight*, 'Tom Caldwell's Initiative', 23 March 1972.

3. *The Provisional IRA*, op. cit., p. 215.
4. *The Politics of Power*, Joe Haines, Cape, 1977. p. 128.
5. *The Last Post. The details and stories of Republican dead 1913–75*, National Graves Association, Dublin, 1976. p. 61.
6. *Memoirs of a Revolutionary*, op. cit., p. 243.
7. *Memoirs of a Statesman*, op. cit., p. 158.
8. *INLA. Deadly Divisions*, Jack Holland and Henry McDonald, Torc, 1994. p. 18.

Chapter Eleven: Setbacks

1. *Beating the Terrorists? Interrogation in Omagh, Gough and Castlereagh*, Peter Taylor, Penguin, 1980. pp. 195–6.
2. *Belfast Telegraph*, 4 November 1988.
3. *Newsletter*, 28 October 1974.
4. *The Future of Northern Ireland. A Paper for Discussion*, HMSO, 1972. Paras 76–8.
5. *Irish Independent*, 2 January 1973.
6. *Northern Ireland 1968–73. A Chronology of Events. Vol II*, op. cit., p. 255ff.
7. *Irish Times*, 30 January 1973.
8. *25 Years of Terror. The IRA's war against the British*, Martin Dillon, Bantam Books, 1994. p. 166ff.
9. *The IRA*, op. cit., p. 434.
10. *Northern Ireland 1968–73. A Chronology of Events. Vol. II*, op. cit., p. 315.
11. Ibid., p. 345.
12. Ibid., p. 357.
13. Checked through *An Index of Deaths from the Conflict in Ireland. 1969–93*, Malcom Sutton, Beyond the Pale Publications, Belfast, 1994. Years 1972–3.
14. *Northern Ireland 1968–73. A Chronology of Events. Vol II*, op cit., pp. 356–7.
15. Ibid., p. 362.
16. *Daily Telegraph*, 23 March 1974.
17. *Sun*, 23 March 1974.
18. *Daily Telegraph*, 11 May 1974.

Chapter Twelve: Contact

1. *Northern Ireland. A Chronology of the Troubles*, op. cit., p. 84.
2. In 1968, the Russian army invaded Czechoslovakia to put down the reforming government of Alexander Dubcek following the popular, peaceful uprising known as the 'Prague Spring'.
3. John Major faced the same problem 1993–6 when his dependency on unionist votes in the House of Commons inhibited his room for political manoeuvre with Sinn Fein.
4. *Northern Ireland. A Personal Perspective*, Merlyn Rees, Methuen, 1985. p. 157.
5. *Northern Ireland. A Chronology of Events. Vol. III. 1974*, op. cit., p. 13.
6. *Northern Ireland. A Chronology of the Troubles*, op. cit., p. 263.
7. *Northern Ireland. A Chronology of Events. Vol. III*, op. cit., p, 164.
8. *Error of Judgement. The Truth about the Birmingham Bombings*, Chris Mullin, Poolbeg Press, 1987. p. 207.
9. *Northern Ireland. A Chronology of the Troubles*, op. cit., p. 243.
10. *Irish Times*, 13 December 1974.

11. *The Provisional IRA*, op. cit., pp. 269–71.
12. *Northern Ireland. A Personal Perspective*, op. cit., pp. 150–3.

Chapter Thirteen: Truce

1. *Republican Movement Minutes.*
2. *Fortnight*, 7 February 1975. p. 12.
3. *Report of a Committee to consider, in the context of civil liberties and human rights, measures to deal with terrorism in Northern Ireland*, Chairman Lord Gardiner, HMSO Cmnd. 5847. p. 33ff.
4. *Fortnight*, op. cit., p. 10.
5. *Northern Ireland. A Chronology of the Troubles*, op. cit., p. 131.
6. *RM Minutes*, op. cit.
7. Ibid.
8. *Fortnight*, 11 April 1975. pp. 9–10.
9. Ibid., p. 10.
10. When Belgium withdrew from the Belgian Congo in 1960, a bloodbath followed.
11. *RM Minutes*, op. cit.
12. *An Index of Deaths from the Conflict in Northern Ireland 1969–1993*, op. cit., p. 73.
13. *The Volunteer. A Former IRA Man's Story*, Shane O'Doherty, Fount Paperbacks, 1993. p. 181. In 1989, I made a BBC documentary about Shane Paul O'Doherty, called *The Volunteer*.
14. *An Index of Deaths from the Conflict in Ireland 1969–1993*, op. cit., p. 77.
15. *Northern Ireland. A Chronology of the Troubles*, op. cit., p. 106.
16. *Fortnight*, 6 February 1976.

Chapter Fourteen: Counteroffensive

1. *Before the Dawn*, op. cit., pp. 249–50.
2. Overall, 1,981 were detained between August 1971 and December 1975. Only 107 were loyalists. The rest were republicans. *Northern Ireland. A Chronology of the Troubles*, op. cit., p. 107.
3. *Republican News*, 1 May 1976.
4. Ibid., 8 May 1976. On 3 October 1997, following transmission of the television programme in which I referred to this quotation, I received a letter from the Sinn Fein Press Centre in Belfast, saying that Mr Adams rejected the allegation that he wrote the article.
5. *Before the Dawn*, op. cit., p. 256.
6. *War and Words. The Northern Ireland Media Reader*, Bill Rolston and David Miller, Beyond the Pale Publications, 1996. p. 77.
7. *Beating the Terrorists? Interrogation in Omagh, Gough and Castlereagh*, op. cit., p. 63.
8. *Report of the Commission to consider legal procedures to deal with terrorist activities in Northern Ireland*, Chairman Lord Diplock, HMSO, Cmnd. 5185, December 1972. p. 32.
9. *Beating the Terrorists*, op. cit., p. 77.
10. Between July 1976 and November 1979, over 5,000 suspects were questioned at Castlereagh. 1,964 were charged. At Gough, between October 1977 and October 1979, nearly a thousand suspects were questioned and 197 were charged. *Beating the Terrorists*, op. cit., p. 194.
11. *Beating the Terrorists*, op. cit., pp. 218–19.

Chapter Fifteen: Reassessment

1. *Northern Ireland. A Chronology of the Troubles*, op. cit., p. 125.
2. Ibid., p. 118.
3. *Beating the Terrorists*, op. cit., p. 345.
4. 'Northern Ireland: Future Terrorist Trends', leaked to press in May 1979.
5. *This Week: Life Behind the Wire*, Thames Television, September 1977.
6. *An Index of Deaths from the Conflict in Ireland 1969–93*, op. cit, p. 107.
7. *Nor Meekly Serve My Time. The H-Block Struggle 1976–81*, compiled by Brian Campbell, Beyond the Pale Publications, 1994. p. 70. This is a series of first-hand testimonies by the H-Block prisoners.
8. *Ten Men Dead. The Story of the 1981 Irish Hunger Strike*, David Beresford, Grafton Books, 1987. p. 29. This is the classic account of the 1981 hunger strike based on the 'comms' (communications) between the prisoners and the leadership outside.
9. *Nor Meekly Serve My Time*, op. cit., p. 29.

Chapter Sixteen: Hunger Strike: Fighting

1. *Northern Ireland. A Chronology of the Troubles*, op. cit., p. 133.
2. *The British Army in Northern Ireland*, Lt-Colonel Michael Dewar, RGJ, Arms and Armour Press, 1985. p. 160.
3. *Nor Meekly Serve My Time*, op. cit., p. 104
4. In the end, the Army Council had ordered MacStiofáin off his hunger strike. It is alleged that he asked them to issue a statement that would let him off the hook. The wounding joke at the time was that his phone number was Curragh 888. *The IRA*, op. cit., p. 415.
5. *Nor Meekly Serve My Time*, op. cit., p. 128.
6. Ibid., p. 121.
7. *The Troubles*, op. cit., pp. 231–2.
8. *Nor Meekly Serve My Time*, op. cit., p. 130.
9. Ibid., p. 135.
10. *Ten Men Dead*, op. cit., p. 47.
11. *Nor Meekly Serve My Time*, op. cit., p. 137.
12. Ibid, p. 137.
13. *Ten Men Dead*, op. cit, p. 54.
14. Author's own calculations.
15. *The Troubles*, op. cit., p. 234.

Chapter Seventeen: Hunger Strike: Dying

1. *Ten Men Dead*, op. cit., p. 55.
2. Ibid., p. 56.
3. Ibid., p. 83.
4. *Before the Dawn*, op. cit., p. 292.
5. *Northern Ireland. A Chronology of the Troubles*, op. cit., p. 146.
6. Ibid., p. 147.
7. *The Provisional IRA*, op. cit., p. 371.
8. Ibid., p. 148.

9. Ibid.
10. *Nor Meekly Serve My Time*, op. cit., p. 178.
11. Ibid.
12. *The Provisional IRA*, op. cit., p. 371.
13. Ibid., p. 268.
14. *Nor Meekly Serve My Time*, op. cit., pp. 196–7.
15. Ibid., p. 205.
16. Ibid., p. 208.
17. *Ten Men Dead*, op. cit., p. 302.
18. *Nor Meekly Serve My Time*, op. cit., p. 224.
19. The above account of the final 'Mountain Climber' initiative is based on David Beresford's detailed account in *Ten Men Dead*, op. cit., pp. 324–7.
20. *Before the Dawn*, op. cit., p. 308.

Chapter Eighteen: Counterstrike

1. *British Special Forces*, William Seymour, Grafton Books, 1985. p. 411.
2. *Supergrasses. The use of accomplice evidence in Northern Ireland*, Tony Gifford QC, The Cobden Trust, 1984, p. 19.
3. Ibid.
4. *Northern Ireland. A Chronology of the Troubles*, op. cit., p. 171.
5. *Northern Ireland. Killings by Security Forces and 'Supergrass' Trials*, Amnesty International, United Kingdom, 1988.
6. *Supergrasses. The use of accomplice evidence in Northern Ireland*, op. cit., p. 20.
7. *Guardian*, 19 November 1982.
8. *Daily Telegraph*, 22 May 1984. The details concerning Gilmour's Special Branch activities were outlined by Crown counsel when the case of those named by Gilmour came to trial in 1984.
9. Statement to RUC of Raymond Gilmour, 18 August 1982.
10. Ibid., 22 November 1982.
11. Ibid., 26 November 1982.
12. Ibid.
13. Ibid.
14. *The Times*, 8 November 1984.
15. *Supergrasses. The use of accomplice evidence in Northern Ireland*, op. cit., p. 30.
16. *Belfast Telegraph*, 19 April 1983.
17. *Irish Times*, 19 December 1984.
18. *Supergrasses. The use of accomplice evidence in Northern Ireland*, op. cit., p. 22.
19. *Irish Independent*, 27 October 1983.
20. *Northern Ireland. Killings by Security Forces and 'Supergrass' Trials*, op. cit., p. 73.
21. *Irish News*, 16 May 1988.
22. *Northern Ireland. Killings by Security Forces and 'Supergrass' Trials*, op. cit., pp. 71–2.

Chapter Nineteen: Snapshot

1. *Ambush. The war between the SAS and the IRA*, James Adams, Robin Morgan and Anthony Bambridge, Pan, 1988. p. 194. These were the rules of engagement for 'Operation Flavius' in Gibraltar in which the SAS shot dead three IRA Volunteers. They are not a departure from the normal rules of engagement.

2. *Stalker. The Search for the Truth*, Peter Taylor, Faber and Faber, 1987. *Stalker*, John Stalker, Harrap, 1988. I do not propose to go into any detail about the incidents and the subsequent controversy surrounding John Stalker and his suspension from his Northern Ireland inquiry as John Stalker and I have written about the subject extensively in our respective books. Suffice it to say that Mr Stalker believes there was a conspiracy to remove him from the inquiry as he was getting close to the truth. I believe that, although he was getting close to highly sensitive material, there was no conspiracy as such to remove him.

3. *Policing the Shadows. The Secret War Against Terrorism in Northern Ireland*, Jack Holland and Susan Phoenix, Hodder and Stoughton, 1996. p. 130.

4. *Rebel Hearts*, op. cit., p. 54.

5. *Stalker. The Search for the Truth*, op. cit., p. 71.

6. *Daily Mail* and *Daily Mirror*, 28 April 1987. Quoted in *The SAS in Ireland*, Raymond Murray, Mercier Press, 1990, p. 378.

7. The sources I use for Loughall are: *The SAS in Ireland*, op. cit.; *Big Boys' Rules. The Secret Struggle against the IRA*, Mark Urban, Faber and Faber, 1992; *Who Dares Wins*, Tony Geraghty, Warner, 1995; *Phoenix*, op. cit.

8. *Phoenix*, ibid., p. 145.

9. The details concerning the Libyan Arms shipments are based on my investigation for *Panorama: The IRA – The Long War*, BBC1, 29 February 1988.

10. Seamus Grew and Roddie Carroll, both members of the INLA, were shot dead in Armagh on 12 December 1982 by RUC Constable John Robinson, a member of the RUC's specialist anti-terrorist unit. Neither of them was armed. Constable Robinson was acquitted of their murder.

Chapter Twenty: Armalite and Ballot Box.

1. *An Phoblacht/Republican News*, 5 November 1981.

2. *The Anglo-Irish Agreement. Commentary, Text and Official Review*, Tom Hadden and Kevin Boyle, Edwin Higel Ltd, Sweet & Maxwell Ltd, 1989. p. 18.

3. The account of Frank Hegarty is based on my BBC investigation, *Panorama: The Long War*, op. cit., as well as more recent research.

4. *The Politics of Irish Freedom*, Brandon Books, 1986, p. 64.

5. In *States of Terror*, op. cit., I wrote a chapter, 'The Agent', around a former MI5 agent I had met.

6. *Irish Times*, 28 May 1988

Chapter Twenty-one: Stalemate

1. *Northern Ireland. A Chronology of the Troubles*, op. cit., pp. 211–12.

2. *John Hume. Peacemaker*, op. cit. p. 132.

3. Ibid., p. 117.

4. Ibid., p. 118.

5. *The Fight for Peace. The Secret Story Behind the Irish Peace Process*, Eamonn Mallie and David McKittrick, Heinemann, 1996, p. 73.

6. *The Sinn Fein/SDLP Talks. January–September 1988*, Sinn Fein Publicity Department, Dublin, January 1989.

7. *Northern Ireland. A Chronology of the Troubles*, op. cit., p. 247.

8. Account of Clonoe taken from newspapers of the time: *Daily Mirror*, *Irish News*, *An Phoblacht/Republican News* and (Tyrone) *Courier and News*.

Chapter Twenty-two: Endgame

1. *The Fight for Peace. The Secret Story Behind the Irish Peace Process*, op. cit., p. 98.
2. Cyprus was the British colony given its independence in 1959 after a 'terrorist' military and political campaign.
3. *Setting the Record Straight. A record of communications between Sinn Fein and the British Government October 1990–November 1993*, Sinn Fein, 2 December 1993.
4. Interview for *Panorama: A Mountain to Climb*, BBC TV, 21 February 1994.
5. *States of Terror*, op. cit., p. 325.
6. *Setting the Record Straight*, op. cit., p. 12.
7. Ibid.
8. *Towards a Lasting Peace in Ireland*, Sinn Fein, Dublin and Belfast, 1992.
9. *Northern Ireland. A Chronology of the Troubles*, op. cit., p. 255.
10. *UVF*, Jim Cusack and Henry McDonald, Poolbeg, 1997. pp. 285, 313.
11. *The Fight for Peace*, op. cit., p. 132.

Chapter Twenty-three: Expectations

1. Northern Ireland Office.
2. *Messages passed between HMG and the Provisional Movement, February and November 1993*, Northern Ireland Office.
3. *Setting the Record Straight*, op. cit., Sinn Fein. p. 22.
4. Ibid., pp. 23–4.
5. Ibid., p. 25.
6. Ibid., p. 25.
7. Ibid., p. 27.
8. John Deverell never lived to see the IRA ceasefire he had worked so hard to achieve as he died on 2 June 1994 on board the Chinook helicopter that crashed on the Mull of Kintyre. On board were twenty-five senior police, army and MI5 officers, the cream of British intelligence, who were flying to a secret security conference in Scotland. The RAF crew of four also died. All were killed in the crash, which was a pure accident and not IRA sabotage.
9. Ibid., p. 28.
10. *Panorama. A Mountain to Climb*, BBC TV, 21 February 1994.
11. Ibid., p. 29.
12. Speech by the Prime Minister John Major MP at RUC station, Strabane, 7 April 1993, Northern Ireland Information Service.
13. *Northern Ireland. A Chronology of the Troubles*, op. cit., p. 298.
14. *Setting the Record Straight*, op. cit., p. 29.
15. *The Fight for Peace*, op. cit., p. 178.
16. *Setting the Record Straight*, op. cit., p. 30.
17. Ibid., p. 33.
18. Sir Hugh had succeeded Sir John Hermon on 31 May 1989.
19. *The Northern Ireland Peace Process 1993–1996. A Chronology*, Paul Bew and Gordon Gillespie, Serif, 1996.

20. Ibid., p. 25.
21. *British Government Account of Exchanges between HMG's Representative and the Provisional Movement.*
22. *Panorama. A Mountain to Climb*, op. cit.
23. *The Joint Declaration issued by the Prime Minister, the Rt Hon John Major MP and the Taoiseach, Mr Albert Reynolds TD*, 15 December 1993.

Chapter Twenty-four: Breakthrough

1. *The Northern Ireland Peace Process. 1993–1996. A Chronology*, op. cit., pp. 26, 39.
2. *One Spin on the Merry-Go-Round*, Sean Duignan, Blackwater.
3. *The Northern Ireland Peace Process 1993–1996*, op. cit., p. 63.
4. *Behind the Lines. The Story of the IRA and Loyalist Ceasefires*, Brian Rohan, The Blackstaff Press, 1995, p. 127.
5. *Report of the International Body*, Belfast and Dublin, 22 January 1996.
6. *Irish News*, 14 February 1997.
7. *The Times*, 25 February 1997.
8. *Observer*, 20 July 1997.

Chapter Twenty-five: Dissidents

1. *Panorama: Settlement or Sell Out?*, BBC TV, 6 April 1998.
2. Ibid.
3. *The Irish Times*, 8 May 1998.
4. *Irish News*, 11 May 1998.
5. *Newsletter*, 12 August 1996.

Chapter Twenty-six: Agreement

1. The account of the escape of Liam Averill is based on the official investigation *'Report of an inquiry into the escape of a prisoner from HMP Maze on 10 December 1997 and the shooting of a prisoner on 27 December 1997'*, 2 April 1998, HMSO. 658.
2. The killing of Billy Wright is based on *'Report of an inquiry into the shooting of a prisoner on 27 December 1997.'* Op.cit.
3. *The Guardian*, 30 January 1998.
4. *The Irish Times*, 21 February 1998.
5. Ibid.
6. *Panorama: Settlement or Sell Out?*, Op.Cit.
7. Ibid.
8. The Agreement. Agreement reached in the multi-party negotiations, Command paper 3883 HMSO April 1998.
9. Ibid.

Glossary

ADI	Assaults During Interview
ASU	Active Service Unit
CIA	Central Intelligence Agency
CLMC	Combined Loyalist Military Command
CRA	Civil Rights Association
CSM	Company Sergeant Major
DCI	Director and Controller of Intelligence
DUP	Democratic Unionist Party
ECM	Electronic Counter Measures
FBI	Federal Bureau of Investigation
GHQ	IRA's General Headquarters
GOC	General Officer Commanding
GPMG	General Purpose Machine Gun
HMG	Her Majesty's Government
ICJP	Irish Commission of Justice and Peace
INLA	Irish National Liberation Army
IRA	Irish Republican Army
IRB	Irish Republican Brotherhood
MOD	Ministry of Defence
NICRA	Northern Ireland Civil Rights Association
NIO	Northern Ireland Office
NLF	National Liberation Front
Noraid	Irish Northern Aid (Committee)
OC	Officer Commanding
PAC	Provisional Army Council
PIRA	Provisional IRA
PO	Prison Officer
POA	Prison Officers' Association
POTA	Prevention of Terrorism Act
POW	Prisoner of War
PRO	Public Relations' Officer

PUP	Progressive Unionist Party
QMG	Quarter Master General
RIC	Royal Irish Constabulary
RSF	Republican Sinn Fein
RTE	(Irish Television Network)
RUC	Royal Ulster Constabulary
SAM	Surface-to-air missile
SAS	Special Air Service
SBS	Special Boat Service
SDLP	Social and Democratic Labour Party
SLR	Self-loading rifle
SPG	Special Patrol Group
TCG	Tasking and Co-ordinating Group
UDA	Ulster Defence Association
UDP	Ulster Democratic Party
UDR	Ulster Defence Regiment
UFF	Ulster Freedom Fighters
UUUC	United Ulster Unionist Coalition
UVF	Ulster Volunteer Force
UWC	Ulster Workers' Council

Picture Acknowledgements

Battle of the Bogside (Clive Limpkin), Gerry Adams, late 1960s (PA News), Provisionals' press conference, 1971 (Michael O'Sullivan), Gerard Hodgkins, early 1970s (Pacemaker), Gerard Hodgkins, 1997 (David Barker), Provisional IRA leaders (Leif Skoogfors Camera Press), Billy McKee, 1997 (David Barker), Peter Taylor at Lenadoon Avenue, 1972 (Mr Victor Patterson), Cathal Crumley, 1997 (David Barker), Hunger striker Raymond McCartney, 1980 (PA News), Bobby Sands' funeral, 1981 (Pacemaker), Jim Gibney, late 1970s (Pacemaker), Bodies in the street following the IRA's bomb on Remembrance Day in Enniskillen, 1987 (Pacemaker), Loyalist Michael Stone carrying out a grenade and gun attack at Milltown Cemetery, 1988 (Pacemaker), British army corporals being attacked during a funeral at Andersonstown, 1988 (Pacemaker), Father Alec Reid giving last rights to a British army corporal killed at Andersonstown, 1988 (Pacemaker), IRA bomb devastation at the Baltic Exchange, City of London, 1992 (*Mirror* Syndication International), Gerry Adams, Albert Reynolds and John Hume meeting in Dublin, 1994 (Pacemaker), Bill Clinton meeting Gerry Adams in Belfast, 1995 (Sygma), The aftermath of the IRA bomb at Docklands, 1996 (*Mirror* Syndication International), Martin Meehan, 1997 (David Barker), Seán MacStiofáin, 1997 (David Barker), Brendan Hughes, 1997 (David Barker)

Index

ABOUT THE AUTHOR

Peter Taylor has reported Northern Ireland for more than twenty-five years and has made over fifty documentaries on the conflict for ITV's *This Week* through the seventies and for BBC TV's *Panorama* through the eighties and nineties. In addition he has authored several series for BBC television – *Families at War, States of Terror, 25 Bloody Years* and *Defence of the Realm*.

In 1995 he was presented with the Royal Television Society's prestigious Judges' Award for his lifetime's coverage of the conflict. This was added to three other RTS Awards he has received for his BBC documentaries *Stalker, The Volunteer*, and *The Maze*. He has also won several other domestic and international awards for his work.

Provos is his fifth book on the subject. The others include *Beating the Terrorists?* (which won the Cobden Trust Award for the greatest contribution to human rights in 1980), *Stalker – the Search for the Truth, Families at War* and *States of Terror*.

He is married with two teenage sons.